Roland Barthes Writing the Political

Roland Barthes Writing the Political
History, Dialectics, Self

By Andy Stafford

ANTHEM PRESS

Anthem Press
An imprint of Wimbledon Publishing Company
www.anthempress.com

This edition first published in UK and USA 2023
by ANTHEM PRESS
75–76 Blackfriars Road, London SE1 8HA, UK
or PO Box 9779, London SW19 7ZG, UK
and
244 Madison Ave #116, New York, NY 10016, USA

Copyright © Andy Stafford 2023

The author asserts the moral right to be identified as the author of this work.

All rights reserved. Without limiting the rights under copyright reserved above, no part of this publication may be reproduced, stored or introduced into a retrieval system, or transmitted, in any form or by any means (electronic, mechanical, photocopying, recording or otherwise), without the prior written permission of both the copyright owner and the above publisher of this book.

British Library Cataloguing-in-Publication Data
A catalogue record for this book is available from the British Library.

Library of Congress Control Number: 2022910291
A catalog record for this book has been requested.

ISBN-13: 978-1-78527-8-976 (Hbk)
ISBN-10: 1-78527-8-975 (Hbk)

Cover Image: 'The Cry of Mother Courage' (1957), by Roger Pic (copyright ADAGP)

This title is also available as an e-book.

CONTENTS

Acknowledgements		vi
Foreword		ix
Chapter One	'The dialectical logic of Love'	1
Chapter Two	'Amorous dialectic'	21
Chapter Three	'The People chorus'	45
Chapter Four	'Double grasp'	75
Chapter Five	'Stereographic space'	99
Chapter Six	'Non-classifiable'	125
Chapter Seven	'New Dialectic'	145
Chapter Eight	'Opacity'	169
Chapter Nine	'Undialectics'	195
Afterword: Essayism and the Politics of Writing		219
Bibliography		227
Index		247

ACKNOWLEDGEMENTS

I am grateful to the editor and publisher alike for allowing me to draw on the following publications:

'"Préparation du Romanesque" in Roland Barthes's Reading of *Sarrasine*', *Paragraph* 31:1 2008

'Dialectics of Form(s) in Roland Barthes's *Mythologies*', *Nottingham French Studies* 47:2 2008

'Edward Said and Roland Barthes: Criticism versus Essayism. Or, Roads and Meetings Missed', in R. Ghosh ed, *Edward Said and the Literary, Social and Political World*, Routledge 2009

'« Ce que je dois…à Zaghloul Morsy? » Roland Barthes, poésie marocaine et réticence', in R. Boulaâbi, C. Coste, M. Lehdahda eds, *Barthes au Maroc*, L'université Moulay Ismaïl 2013

'Marking a Writer's Centenary … Backwards? The Case of Roland Barthes, 1915-1980', *Forum for Modern Language Studies* 51:4, 2015

'*Classé, surclasser, déclassé*; or, Roland Barthes, Classification without Class', *L'Esprit Créateur* 55:4 2015

'Roland Barthes's *Travels in China*: Writing A Diary of Dissidence within Dissidence?', *Textual Practice* 30:2 2016, and in Neil Badmington ed, *Deliberations: The Journals of Roland Barthes* Routledge 2017

'« L'Histoire ne pourra jamais marcher contre l'Histoire ». Roland Barthes et l'antistalinisme, 1946-1953', *Littérature* 186:2 2017

'Roland Barthes, dialecticien? En dernière instance?', in Jean-Pierre Bertrand ed, *Roland Barthes: continuités*. Christian Bourgois 2017; *Barthes Studies* 3 2017

'Marx and/or Nietzsche? Ancient Greece and Tragedy in Barthesian Theory', *Barthes Studies* 5 2019

'Roland Barthes's Menippean Moment: Creative Criticism, 1966-1970', in Diana Knight ed, *Interdisciplinary Barthes*, Oxford University Press 2020

'The Barthesian "Double Grasp" in Japan: Reading as Undialectical Writing', in Fabien Arribert-Narce, Endo Fuhito, Kamila Pawlikowska eds, *The Pleasure in/of the Text About the Joys and Perversities of Reading*, Peter Lang 2021

'No Wish to "Understand" nor to "Grasp": Opacity in the Work of Roland Barthes and Édouard Glissant', in J. Di Leo ed, *Understanding Barthes/Understanding Modernism*, Bloomsbury 2022.

ACKNOWLEDGEMENTS vii

The following are in press:

'Undialectics: Marx and Hegel thinking through Roland Barthes', *French Forum* 2022
'Pic, Théâtre, Légende: aux origines du photo-textualisme barthésien', *Revue Roland Barthes* 6
'Dialectics of Love in the "Early" and "Late" Writings of Roland Barthes', *Synthesis: An Anglophone Journal of Comparative Literary Studies* 14 2022.

A good number of the letters from Roland Barthes to Philippe Rebeyrol, currently being catalogued at the Bibliothèque Nationale in Paris (under the code 'NAF 28630 – Fond Roland Barthes'), was very kindly shown to me by M. Rebeyrol before his death. Translations of this unpublished correspondence are all my own.

Organizers and participants in the following seminars listened to me present my work:

Simon Hall and Stephan Petzold, 'What are years?', University of Leeds 2016–17.
Centre Prospéro 'Langage, image, connaissance' seminar, Université St.-Louis-Bruxelles, 2019.
Emmanuel Lozerand and the seminar series on *L'Empire de signes* at INALCO (Paris), 2019.

I am especially grateful for financial support to the Institut Français, to the British Academy and to the AHRC; and, in particular, to the université de Paris-Sorbonne-Nord (Villetaneuse) for making me a *professeur invité* in 2018–19.

I have accumulated many other debts, having worked with numerous people, first and foremost my colleagues at the University of Leeds: Di Holmes, Max Silverman, Richard Hibbitt, Margaret Atack, Nigel Saint, Claire Lozier, Nina Wardleworth, Angelos Koutsourakis, Jason Allen-Paisant, Dave Platten, Jim House, Sarah Waters, Martin Goodman, Kamal Salhi, Frank Finlay, Emma Cayley, Thea Piman and Maria Römer, as well as former colleagues: Joe Ford, Jivitesh Vashisht, David Steel, Naaman Kessous and, sorely missed, Françoise Coquet; and colleagues at the université de Limoges, Irène Langlet and Chloé Conant-Ouaked. Others have supported me in ways of which they may not be aware: Laurence Grove, Alex Gefen, Martin Mégevand, Galin Tihanov, Abdellatif Laâbi, Jocelyne Laâbi, Debasish Lahiri, Lydie Moudileno, Etienne Achille, Douglas Smith, Stamatina Dimakopoulou, Aude Haffen, Peter France, Madeleine Renouard, Agnès Calatayud, Frédéric Goldbronn, François Weigel, Jeffrey R. Di Leo, Amanda Rubin, Endo Fuhito, Robin Mackenzie, Susan McManus, Ranjan Ghosh, Vivian Constantinopoulos, Emma Wagstaff, Charlotte Garson, Dominique Combe, Daniel Lançon and Sian Reynolds.

The world of Barthes Studies – if such a grouping exists – involves an ever-growing number of great colleagues and friends: Jonathan Culler, Sam Ferguson, Yue Zhuo, Claude Coste, Ridha Boulaâbi, Claudia Amigo Pino, Diana Knight, Alexandru Matei,

Patrick ffrench, Jean-Pierre Bertrand, Laura Taddei Brandini, Christophe Corbier, Michael Regan, Michael Carter, Eric Marty, Marie Gil, Philippe Roger, Annette Lavers, Mohamed Lehdahda, Márcio Venício Barbosa, Rodrigo Fontanari, Ralph Heyndels, Walter S. Temple, Khalid Lyamlahy, Jane Hiddleston, Lucy O'Meara, Katja Haustein, Tom Baldwin, Kris Pint, Jürgen Pieters, Leslie Hill, Jacqueline Guittard, Marielle Macé, Maarten De Pourcq, Fabien Arribert-Narce, Sémir Badir, Thomas Clerc, Mathieu Messager, Charles Coustille, Ester Pino, Tiphaine Samoyault and Marcelo Villena Alvarado.

As well as Megan Greiving and the team at Anthem Press, I have benefited immensely from discussions with Roxane Jubert, Charles Forsdick, Magali Nachtergael, Neil Badmington and especially Chris May (if only half!).

To, for and with C (toujours!)

FOREWORD

Barthes, Aesthete?

> '[T]he Neutral, for me: a manner
> – a free manner – to be looking for
> my own style of being present to the
> struggles of my time.'
>
> *(Barthes 2005, 8)*

It was once remarked to me that taking the work of Roland Barthes as 'political' was absurd given how much of an aesthete he clearly was. What would it mean therefore to present a 'political' Barthes (Zhuo 2011)? That is the challenge of this book, to affirm and investigate the politicized charge of an essayist, theorist and writer. In doing so, the analysis acknowledges but looks away from the four biographies of Barthes that have been written since his death in 1980. Calvet (1994), Stafford (1998), Gil (2012) and Samoyault (2017) all underline, to lesser or greater extent, the general dislike evident in his life and work of 'official' politics, including left-wing militancy and the associated hysteria it generated. There is no equivalent in Barthes's activities of a Michel Foucault leading the *Groupe d'information sur les prisons* (GIP) in its direct support for prisoners in French gaols.

And yet, writing was a deeply political act, from the start of Barthes's *œuvre* during World War II, right up until the final lectures at the Collège de France four decades later. Forty years then of radical thought, critical theory and innovative essay-writing are to be considered as a form of political activity. In doing so, this book aims to address, if only obliquely, the perceived dichotomy between politics and aesthetics that seems to beset the ways in which critics have read Barthes's writing, to the extent that there would seem to be two very different 'Roland Barthes': a politicized, Marxist intellectual and a disengaged, literary aesthete. In the latter, Susan Sontag (1982, 427, 432) casts Barthes in the Oscar Wilde tradition of the aphorist, interested in the dandy and 'camp', a modern aesthete and excellent commentator on Fashion and fashions more generally, investigating the social and literary mask. Yet we forget Wilde's powerful arguments in favour of socialism at our peril: in *The Soul of Man Under Socialism* (1960 [1890]), Wilde drew on Ruskin, Shaw and Morris, in an essay as utopian as it is essayistic, to expose social alienation, in ways that a Barthes, inspired by Michelet, Fourier and Jaurès, will do too. Unorthodox, Wilde's socialism was profoundly conscious of and troubled by the scourges affecting the popular classes, whilst also anti-populist and anti-individualist in his conception of art and education. Indeed, Bonafous-Murat (2000, 18–19) underlines the similarity between a Wilde trying to define a new aesthetic of the dandy and a Barthes keen to reduce 'the exorbitant privilege' given to the origin of a work and trying to find '*other* ideas, *other* images, *other* significations' (1986, 30–31). Furthermore, Barthes's highly influential reading of Marcel Proust is attuned to the sociology and language of class-mobility, and even Revolutionary history (Hughes 2011, 18, 27).

Other critics whose work that we might place on the 'aesthete' wing of Barthesian studies (Haustein 2009; England 2020; Mavor 2007; Pint 2010; Baldwin 2019) may not recognize at all this designation; just as those who have investigated in Barthes's writing the gay, homosexual and *queer* dimensions (De Villiers 2012; Miller 1992; Greco 2020; Saint-Amand 1996; Stewart 2001) may not accept any 'political' import in their work. These reservations notwithstanding, there is still perhaps a disconnect in Barthes studies. The 'aesthetic' approach tends to ignore the political side of his writing, or (worse) to take it for granted; in the 'aesthetic' Barthes, critics highlight and concentrate on the late, final, Barthes, as if the 'early', Marxian phase was slightly naïve juvenilia. By the same token, the 'political' approach tub-thumps his writing into a militant set of 'positions' and 'opinions' as it glides glibly over the nuances and essayistic skill of the literary theorist, to produce an eternal and unquestioning set of principles. It is clear therefore that Barthes studies is in need of a rebalance.

One way is to insist on the 'interdisciplinary'. In her introduction to a volume marking the British Academy's celebration of Barthes's centenary, Knight (2020, 1–21) does not want to stop short at the mere status of 'writer' (with its connotations of dilettante, if not aesthete), the 'interdisciplinary' being a radical – that is, an unsettling and transforming – approach and that is not simply a 'federating' of all the areas that his work covers. In this academic optic (Knight 18-19), Barthes's fascination with the linguistic is taken as one with society in which the 'secret of parole' and those of 'nature' can be brought together to underscore the ways in which language constructs human societies. The danger here, however, is that Barthes becomes purely academic, his deep suspicion of the Institution hidden beneath a liberating set of research methodologies designed for the reproduction of academic study. Indeed, not only did he famously fail to complete his doctoral research (Coustille, 2018), but also Barthes started his career and made his name in the 1950s away from the Academy, and maintained thereafter a writing career consistently alongside, and frequently outside of, his functions at the Ecole Pratique des Hautes Etudes and the Collège de France.

This also means in terms of intellectual community that there is an acute problem for Barthes's politics of essayism. Hill (2010, 74–75) argues, on the one hand, that Barthes 'should be less eccentric exception than instructive example'; and yet the manner in which he writes, swinging between what Macé calls (2002) the dual, opposing modes of the 'peremptory-provisional', allows perhaps only for a copying of writing practices rather than of political beliefs or actions. And Barthes describes the discomfort and fear in this 'sense of producing a double discourse, whose mode overreached its aim somehow; for the aim of his discourse is not truth, and yet this discourse is assertive' (1994, 48).

This may help explain why his writing has lasted so well into the twenty-first century, how it has been read in so many quarters and disciplines; but 'the double discourse' may well encourage also political ambivalence. The posthumous longevity of Barthes's writing then, his continued success today, is caught in this double bind. It benefits from the 'mastery of non-mastery' (Marty 2006, 331), from 'not holding in order to hold fast' (332n6), of 'finding the ground before the fall' (334–35); but the 'double discourse' that he fears means there is an ambiguity of writing (Samoyault 2017, 281): is it pre- or descriptive? And for all of us, or for himself?

From this double bind emerges, this book will argue, a Barthesian ethics of writing. The comparison in Chapter Eight of his notion of opacity with that of Édouard Glissant will allow us to place his writing in the area of ethics, asking how does writing respond to the Other, to love and to the loved one. Butler (2005, 19) suggests that ethics stems from the relation to the Other revealing to the self its own opacity to itself. Here a number of metaphors will set the tone. On the one hand, Barthes is fascinated in 1959 by the shark in Jules Michelet's utopia in which the man is the 'woman's parasite, [...] the oceanic marriage of sharks which for months drift in the sea coupled to one another: idyllic adventure in which the motionless penetration of bodies is doubled by the external slither of waters' (Barthes 1972, 110); but twenty years later, his chosen metaphor for the human couple moves to Kierkegaard's more pessimistic analogy: 'porcupines suffering from the cold, moving close to each other, spiking one another, moving away from each other and restarting the cyclical process' (2007a, 452).

Barthes 2.0?

What has changed since the first wave of interest in Barthes's work up that went up until the New Millennium? Since 2002, there has been a series of publications of his lectures, seminars, correspondence, diaries, some swiftly translated. Furthermore, alongside the deluge of books, journals and conferences to mark the centenary of his birth in 2015, there has been the five-book series of translations of his scattered, harder-to-find writings (Seagull Press, 2015–16). The startling amount of published research on his work since 2000 suggests that, of all the 'French Theory' writers (Althusser, Badiou, Baudrillard, Blanchot, Bourdieu, Cixous, Deleuze, Derrida, Foucault, Guattari, Irigaray, Kristeva, Lacan and Lyotard, to name the best-known in the English-speaking world), it is Barthes who seems to have persisted (indeed, over 40 years since his death), across most languages, and, by far, in the largest number of disciplines and topics. And this is not just in academic, but also journalistic circles, for example, *The Conversant* special number on 'The Renaissance of Roland Barthes' in 2014; in fiction (Binet 2017; Clerc 2010), and in wider popular culture, such as the new edition of Barthes's *Incidents* with photographs by Bishan Samaddar (2010c). His name even pops up in the stand-up comedy of Stewart Lee, and predictably in the Barthes in Bart Simpson.

The width of his concerns has aided this omnipresence. It is not just Barthes aesthete but also philosopher (De Pourcq 2008; Bittner 2017; Lübecker 2010; O'Meara 2020; Marty 2018); in studies on Rhetoric (Huang 2013); in the art world (Lovatt 2019; Nachtergael 2015); in poetry (Gardner 2018); in cinema (Watts 2016; ffrench 2019) as well as photography (Batchen 2009; Yacavone 2012); in Design (Huppatz 2011) and in legal studies (Guittard/Emeric 2019). And – to move to the furthest extreme from a 'political' Barthes – there is now a Paris street named after him (in the 12th *arrondissement*), a postage stamp, even a Hermès limited-edition silk scarf (Wampole 2015)!

These last examples of a media-friendly, 'aesthete' Barthes merely serve to make more salient the political approaches that some critics, writers and theorists have applied to his work, especially over the last twenty years, in particular in Postcolonial studies. Hargreaves (2005) and Hiddleston (2010) place Barthes within decolonial thought, underlining his critique of the West – of 'Westoxification' as it is called today in Iran (Jameson 2010, 471) – that results from the trips to Morocco, Japan and China. Rejecting Western conceptions of the self, by using, as we shall see, francophone Moroccan poetry to turn-the-tables on the metropolitan French use of the French language, Barthes's work seems to confirm Aamir Mufti's view (2005, 123) that 'contemporary Theory is clearly animated by an anti-imperialist impulse'; though, here, debate is wide and heterogeneous, and even within the views of the same critic. For example, Edward Said (2001, 122–123); having suggested that Barthes is not read properly, Said seems to want to blame Barthes (and Derrida) for making literary criticism break up into ever 'narrower niches'. These 'niches' of Barthesian scholarship have argued, for example, over whether *Camera Lucida* is weak, or not, on the politics of 'race' (Smith 2009, versus Clerc 2017). Indeed, Lydie Moudileno (2019) is surely right to point to the regrettably shorthand nature of Barthes's repeated use of the word 'Negro' in *Mythologies* (2009, 139–40, 142, 145–46); and yet, a point needs to be made about context. Barthes is so often ironically 'voicing' right-wing (here, colonial) ideology – just as Albert Camus does with the word 'Arab' in his story 'The Guest', written the same year as *Mythologies* and set in Algeria during the War of Independence and which, no doubt, helped confirm Said's (misplaced) view of Camus's 'colonial mentality' (1985, 312). In the other direction, Barthes's influence on Japanese Marxism needs to be underlined, such as in the classic study of Marx by Japan's leading critical theorist, Kojin Karatani (1974), which, using semiotics and deconstruction to consider Marx as a literary thinker and *Capital* as a theory of signs, deploys Barthes's view of the literary *preterit* tense to explain the Japanese notion of *ta* (Karatani 1993, 73, 179).

Nevertheless, there is another example of the tendency towards misreading Barthes's ironic, sarcastic voice in *Mythologies* in the perceived misogyny in 'Novels and Children' (2009, 54–55). Indeed, feminist critics are sharply divided over Barthes's writing on women and gender, especially in *Mythologies* and in the work on fashion. Meagher (1996), Weiner (1999), Gallop (in Knight 2000 [1986], 188–201) and Thornhill (2016, 4–6), are, at best, ambivalent about Barthes's 'voicing' of women's experience and the discriminating ideologies that stereotype them – though a consensus does seem to have emerged around Barthes's important role in the development of Critical Discourse Analysis. Others, such as Oboussier (1994), have been more disposed towards the deconstructive import of his work for feminist critique.

It is not just the postcolonial turn of which we must take account but also the so-called 'affective' turn, especially as exemplified in the politicized work of Ahmed (2014). Indeed, much work has emerged recently on both Barthes's own sexuality and the influence of his work on gender and post-gender. In particular, Temple (2020) has traced the gay erotics in the travel-writing, suggesting a 'Barthesian dialectics' in the 'sexual pact' that is always indirectly described (94-95) in what Woods (1998, 195–96) calls, quoting Barthes, 'through the keyhole of language'. Indeed, this oblique approach to the writing of sexuality, of gay eroticism and sex in general seems to place his work alongside that of Eve Kosofsky Sedgwick, who, as Nelson states (2015, 32), 'wanted to make way for "queer" to hold all kinds of resistances and fracturings as well as mismatches that have little or nothing to do with sexual orientation'. For Sedgwick, 'Queer is a continuing moment, movement, motive – recurrent, eddying, *troublant*. […] Keenly, it is relational, and strange' (Kosofsky Sedgwick 1994, viii). This resembles Barthes's 'dialectical' belief that 'the very task of love and of language is to give to one and the same phrase inflections which will be forever new' (Barthes 1994, 114). And yet, in insisting on retaining 'reclaimed terms' – albeit with a 'sense of the fugitive' (Nelson 2015, 32) – Kosofsky Sedgwick seems to go against Barthes's notion of the 'indirect'. It does seem that the strength of Barthes's 'double discourse' is also the source of considerable variations of opinion on the political usefulness of his work.

'Political' Barthes?

> Brecht is so often received with ambiguity: his
> theatre seems too aesthetic to the militant and too
> politically-committed to the aesthete; and this is not
> surprising, since the precise place he is aiming for is
> the narrow zone where the playwright *shows blindness*.
>
> *(Barthes 2002, I, 910)*

The 'double discourse' that Barthes spies in his own work might mean also that he falls between different categories of writer. More so perhaps than in Sartre's *oeuvre*, there are numerous areas in which Barthes could be seen to have 'failed', where his writing gestures towards an activity but one which remains at a purely theoretical level. His fascination with theatre suggests he was a dramaturg *manqué* (contradicted however, as we shall see in Chapter Three, by his startling interventionist work on Roger Pic's photography of Brechtian theatre); novelist *manqué* (though the final lectures on the 'Preparation of the Novel' suggest otherwise); poet *manqué* (though Barthesian *écriture* is often deeply poetic); psychologist *manqué* (despite his close analysis of the self) and philosopher *manqué* (despite being a leading theorist of structuralism and of ideology). Can we add to this list then: militant *manqué*?

Even Barthes's best-known essay, 'The Death of the Author', has its roots, at least in part, in Engels's theories. In his 1956 definition of realism (2015a, 31), Barthes uses Marx and especially Engels's 1885 letter on '*tendentious literature*': '"The more the author's [political] views are concealed, the better for the work of art"'. This idea in turn goes back to an early version of his *Writing Degree Zero* written in 1946 but not published in his lifetime, 'The Future of Rhetoric', which argues firmly against a Lanson-based inquiry into the author, in favour of one on language, and proposes a 'technology of creation' based on Marxian precepts: 'There will be no materialist history of literature', he declares in his trademark peremptory-provisional fashion, 'so long as literature is not restored to the practice of a language' (2018, 107).

Obviously, Barthes's lifelong practice and belief in the writer, sitting in their study and feeling deeply connected with the social and political world, might be very lazily summarized as 'armchair politics'; but, in fact – and the COVID pandemic proves it, as I write – being politically connected in lockdown, on-line, approximates astonishingly well to Barthes's domestic and confined sociality. Nevertheless, against accusations of being 'apolitical', Barthes can insist only upon a hovering over politics, 'to float in a space', as he experiences 'another form of weariness: that of the "position" of the "relation to": "How do you situate yourself with regard to Marxism, Freudianism, to x, to y?"' (2005, 18).

And yet, his 1958 reading of Voltaire is a highly politicized critique of liberalism has, as we shall see, an extraordinary echo in France's very recent reaction to terrorism and twenty-first-century islamophobia, in a political twist on what Badmington (2016) calls Barthes's 'Afterlives'; and Barthes's words on his presence in the world are strangely prescient here: 'In fact, the *present* = notion distinct from the *topical*; the *present* is alive (I am in the process of creating it myself) ≠ the topical can only be a noise' (2011b, 277).

Furthermore, Beckman (2013) makes a strong case for reading *Camera Lucida* – and the rest of Barthes's work on photography – as political and not sentimental. The argument is couched in the belief that the connoted and the denoted of a photographic image need to be held in tight tension, emphasized depending on the context in which the photography is being shown and seen (313–14). Beckmann's astute reading of Barthes's overall work on photography suggests that we over-emphasize at our peril, as many have done (Fried 2005; Wilson 2017), notions such as the *punctum*, and that we should not allow the over-emphasis to lead to mis-readings (Rancière 2019, 9–11). The punctum is after all *only* an operative notion that is abandoned half-way through Barthes's essay, deemed as too subjective, in favour, in the second half of the essay, of the 'palinode' (Oxman 2010, 83). Indeed, Rancière (in Watts 2016, 110) is rather too quick to see Barthes's writings on image (and text) in general as signs of 'withdrawal and retreat from any of the possible political consequences', a narrative of depoliticization in the late Barthes that is regularly repeated especially in affirmations of the 'post-critical' (Felski 2015, 75). What Barthes does however do with the political, as we shall see, is to find other spaces for critique to take place.

'We have to live amid the unlivable' (Barthes 1985a, 87)

On the one hand then, we must resist simplistic generalizations about an apolitical Barthes; on the other, we have to accept that his political militancy, in the traditional sense of an active engagement in 'changing the world' to quote Marx's famous eleventh thesis on Feuerbach (1974, 123), goes further than merely 'interpreting' it, but that relentless critique, in the final instance, has limited effect on challenging or overthrowing Capital. We therefore follow Jameson (2010, 294) who suggests that we can 'think politically' but only outside of traditional notions of politics or political theory. This is therefore not a book about political practice, but politics in theory; however not a politics of 'Theory' (as in Marx-Scouras 1996), more a philosophy of politics carried out through an essayistic, that is, highly stylized, writing. Indeed, the problem with Critical Theory is not that it is too political (Di Leo 2018), but that it is an amalgam that generalizes and thereby often loses sight of writerly and intellectual specificities. Far from 'The Death of the Author' killing off the writer, for example, the essay inscribes a Barthesian performance of political dissidence into the act of reading that must be seen as part of his overall intellectual strategy. 'Theory' glides over such intellectual history too quickly. Wermer-Colan (2016) for example sees a split in Barthes's political approach to writing after May '68 akin to the outcome of the 1848 revolutions that Barthes sees as pivotal for modern writing-forms: whereas, argues Wermer-Colan, the 'early work exposes, critiques, and satirizes', the 'late work baffles, resists, and inspires' (136). However, in this book, we will suggest two continuities in Barthesian thought and writing: intellectual 'responsibility' on the one hand, and the play of dialectics (of the dialectic, of the dialectical) on the other. As Barthes put it in relation to Brecht's revision of Marx and History (2002, I, 910), politics needs to be seen in his writing as will, as voluntarism, and not as passive complaint.

'Sensitive, avid and silent political subject (these adjectives must not be separated)' (Barthes 1994, 53).

While the 'vomiting of the political' is seen by Barthes as part of utopian-socialist Charles Fourier's inventiveness (1989, 88, trans. mod.), Barthes is nevertheless acutely aware of his own political weaknesses. In 'Little politics', he suggests what he thinks would be Brecht's political reproach to him (1994, 52–53). He suggests that Brecht would criticize him for wanting to be both the subject *and* the object of politics, which would be tantamount to being neither. Brecht accepted that he had to 'sacrifice' his life to politics; and Barthes accepts that he too is a political subject, but he does not want to be the '*speaker*' of politics. Barthes offers a solution to this: 'he can at least make the *political* meaning of what he writes', and, like 'the historical witness of a contradiction', he can be the '*sensitive, avid and silent* political subject (these adjectives must not be separated)' (1994, 53). It is this triple, contradictory but concatenated, self-description that will guide this book. Furthermore, maybe the 'little politics' is rather harsh on himself. His 'mythologies' were originally part of French anti-colonial journalism at an acute, decolonial moment between 1952 and 1956 (Stafford 1998, 40–47); the joust with traditional Sorbonne professor Raymond Picard in the mid-1960s was an obvious prelude to May 1968; the rejection of all types of hierarchy and his regular signing of petitions in the 1970s against repressive laws and mores look radical by today's standards, if misguided in some cases (Owen Rowlands 2021).

As suggested with 'Theory', we will investigate not a theory of politics, of the political – as this requires a political, not an intellectual, praxis – but a philosophy of politics. Here, Barthes's Germanistic tendencies emerge, firstly with respect to Marx, Nietzsche and Freud, though they seem less in tune with the Adorno/Kracauer/Horkheimer/ wing of the Frankfurt School, and more so with that of Brecht/Lukács/Benjamin, and to some extent with Marcuse. Wermer-Colan (2016) wants to see a similar mode of critique in the dialectical forestalling operated by both Adorno and Barthes, but this would be to miss the Barthesian spirit, of being with and simultaneously without or alone, in a critical but affective praxis that uses a double position to consider the dialectical, the historical and the self. The different figures and tropes analysed in this book – the 'dialectical logic of love' (Chapter One), the 'amorous dialectic' (Chapter Two), the 'people-chorus' (Chapter Three), the 'double grasp' (Chapter Four), the 'stereographic space' of writing (Chapter Five), the 'non-classifiable' self (Chapter Six), the 'new dialectic' found in Japan (Chapter Seven), opacity (Chapter Eight) and the 'undialectical' (Chapter Nine) – are all concerned, as we shall see, with this double positioning of the writer; and that, furthermore, Barthes is always using the old and out-of-date to think forms of all type into the future is not surprising given that he is a classics scholar!

Liquidate and theorise?

'"Theory"', writes Barthes, is not necessarily 'philosophical dissertation' or abstract system but 'description, multi-scientific production, responsible discourse […] involving dialectically destroying each established discipline in favour of one never seen before' (2002, IV, 171). This echoes not so much the 'liquidate and theorise' in Vladimir's Lenin's critique of the liquidationism evident in Menshevik politics (Lenin, vol 20, 268), rather Barthes's tendency – and here's my obligatory joke – to *liquidise and theorate*. That is, to take politics and, essayistically, enjoy liquidizing the political – similar to what Jacques Rancière (2013) has recently called *dissensus* – but without losing sight of 'responsible' theory and the need to militate.

The popular-theatre militancy of the 1950s seems to illustrate this best. Whereas Stafford (1998) suggests an abrupt move 'from stage to text' in Barthes's sudden abandonment in 1960 of France's militant popular theatre movement in favour of the ivory-tower of the *Ecole Pratique des Hautes Etudes* (EPHE)'s VIth section, Stivale (2002) insists on a radical Barthes right through the 1960s. In a similar vein, Wermer-Colan (2016, 147) describes the 'late' Barthes as developing away from the ideology-critique of the 1950s replacing it with a 'vision of aesthetic modes of resistance in the era of new media'. Yet there seems to be no split between the 'Bureau of mythological information' – in an allusion to the 'Bureau of Surrealist Research' founded in 1924 – that, on the one hand, Barthes advocates in 1959 in opposition to the 'cancer of political activism [that] has stifled the intellectual's perception of the ideological' (2015b, 78–79, trans. mod.); and, on the other, his (slightly ironic) 1973 call for a 'Society of friends of the text' (1975, 14–15), in an allusion to Blanqui's radical but short-lived *Société des amis du peuple* established in 1830. Indeed, as we shall see across this book, Barthesian thought maintains a remarkably consistent engagement with both Marx and Hegel. The risk in the approach taken in this book then is that the Marxological (and Hegelological?) optic will paradoxically seal Barthes off from the political; unless the political is made to work with the 'world'. By contrast, it is faint praise indeed when Edgar Morin suggests that Barthes, typical of many French intellectuals' 'vulgar' Marxism, knew barely more than 'a few pages' of Marx (Calvet 1994, 120).

This is a book then about social relations, of which language is the privileged example. In an interview in 1971, Barthes sets out a plan of research on language that would be 'something like the *Capital* of linguistics' (1985a, 121), a vast project that Lenin, in a note on Hegel's *Logic*, had wondered about: 'History of thought = History of language?', scribbled the Russian revolutionary (cited in Heath 1981, 210). For Barthes, it revolves around the fundamental Marxian category of property.

Describing three types of warning-sign on houses with guard-dogs, Barthes suddenly sees the 'alibis' of language in 'the system of ownership', 'for which no simple science of communication can account: society, with its socio-economic and neurotic structures, intervenes, constructing language like a battleground' (1986, 106), forcing humans to find 'acratic' forms of individual and idiosyncratic communication in a world of increasingly 'encratic' language, power-driven and controlled by society's *doxa* (107–08, 120–21); and it is here that the *para-doxa* – the paradox – finds its political value. The work on what he calls 'translinguistics' (2015a, 123) carried out across the 1970s emphasizes this 'battleground' of property in language, as the analysis moves beyond the sentence towards discourse as both performative and constative. The 'double bind' – or dialectical interaction – that this analysis entails mirrors Marx's schema in *Capital* in which the forces of production and the relations of production are tightly and dynamically entwined, themselves in parallel with the social relations encapsulated by labour-power and value. Theories of 'Meta-Marxism' (Rockmore 1981, Chapter Five) have suggested ways for Marx's historical-materialist method to stand outside of the relations of Capital in order to better analyse their movement: what would this mean for Barthes's 'translinguistics'? How can you be outside of language and yet analyse it *in* language? What, or where, is acratic language if all is encratic? If language and communication represent, and play out, human social relations, how can anyone stand outside and analyse them? This fundamental question for Barthes will become entangled with the human subject who is caught up in the social relations of language.

Indeed, as Barthes does for language, Lucien Sève does for psychology. In order to do away with the contradiction between social and biological dimensions of human personality, psychology too needs its version of Marx's *Capital* (Sève 1978, 39; Roche 2018, 292): For Sève, human personality is made not by individual, but social, relations; and love, in a capitalist economy and as part of the bourgeois family, is 'a scaled-down model of a capitalist society'. Furthermore, Roche (305) suggests, following Malabou's reading of self in Hegel (2005, 156–59), that for the self to signify 'is to alienate'. These brief comments on self and subject will become important coordinates in Barthes's work on the human subject in language.

Barthes 'trotskisant'? Really?

Part of post-war Leftist culture, Barthes works alongside Maurice Nadeau, Edgar Morin and Lucien Goldmann. Not much has been written on Barthes and Goldmann, surprisingly, given that they were friends and colleagues at the VIth section of the EPHE in Paris up until Goldmann's death in 1970. Having translated two pieces by Hungarian Marxist Georg Lukács into French, Goldmann is, in 1966 at least (Said 1984, 324–25), the only Lukácsian in Europe; and, in the 1950s, Goldmann publishes in two journals for which Barthes is an important member of the editorial team (the radical popular theatre journal *Théâtre Populaire* and the New-Left bulletin *Arguments*); and, apart from a spat in the aftermath of May 1968 in the pages of *L'Express*, theirs was, it seems, a mutually-respectful relationship. Thus, in Chapter Three, we discuss the various exchanges and differences between them.

Barthes is also reading the work of Dionys Mascolo, who, alongside Nadeau, Morin, Sartre, Pierre Naville and Henri Lefebvre – whose 1954 play on Kierkegaard, *Le maître et la servante*, Barthes defends (2009, 27–29) – is looking for a political and increasingly aesthetic alternative to Stalinism's disastrous political strictures and cultural diktats. Indeed, Mascolo's 1955 essay on the word 'Left' (2011), and his longer 1953 essay *Le Communisme* are possible political intertexts for Barthes's *Mythologies*. Moreover, the pessimistic comments with which Mascolo berates poets for not being politically responsible (Crowley 2006) have an extraordinary counterpart in Barthes's (posthumously published) 1946 essay 'The Future of Rhetoric', where a sharply worded footnote suggests that 'poetry (and in a sense all of literature) is the opium of the empowered class, suffering not from the evils that it endures but from those that it sees' (2018, 113n). Similarly, Barthes's implicit suggestion that myth is all-encompassing has a contemporary intertext in Mark Fisher's 'Capitalist realism' (2009), especially in the view that Stalinism is the only possible opposite of Capitalism.

Given this dissident, Trotskyist and anti-Stalinist, Marxism, it is surprising that Barthes's writings and interviews from the period 1970–74 should contain a number of asides that suggest his own illusions in the progressive nature of China during the Cultural Revolution (2002, III, 692; 1986, 105; 1985a, 153). Although mildly favourable to Mao's regime, they contain the odd 'perhaps' and 'probably', and are striking for the curiosity that Barthes has for China in the years leading up to his infamous *Tel Quel* visit in 1974.

By the same token, those such as Sarkonak (2009, 18) who have defended the writer Renaud Camus (one time friend of Barthes, and no relation to Albert), despite his white-supremacist idea of the 'great replacement' and repeated endorsements of the gross racism in Le Penism, should know Barthes better than to imply that he never criticized the Gaullist myth of the French Resistance. Not only did Barthes lose his close friend Jacques Veil (Barthes 2018, 26–27) during the Liberation of Paris from the Nazis, he is also highly critical of De Gaulle (2015b, 74–79); the fight against De Gaulle's newly installed regime, opines Barthes in 1959, 'wherever possible […] should substitute action for gesture, and intellectual action for political action' (79).

That said, the only reference to 'Marxism' in the index of *Roland Barthes by Roland Barthes* sends the reader to the curious 'fiction' he imagines of an intellectual having to choose which 'brand' of Marxism to follow (Lenin, Trotsky, Luxemburg, Mao, or Bordiga and so on) as if, in rather decadent fashion, it were an item of clothing to wear (1994, 156), and with 'Trotsky' misspelt ('Trostky') in the original French (2002, IV, 730). It is clear then that, what is needed to determine the political nature of Barthes's writing, is a complex, dialectical mode of reading.

'Dialectise the world' or the Self (Barthes 1972, 146n3)?

'However reluctant Understanding may
be to admit the action of Dialectic, we

must not suppose that the recognition of its existence is peculiarly confined to the philosopher. It would be truer to say that Dialectic gives expression to a law which is felt in all other grades of consciousness and in general experience.'

(Hegel's Logic, cited in James 1980, 33)

In his excellent and near-exhaustive overview of the dialectic, Jameson (2010) misses out etymology. The dialectic's etymology: Dialectic means also 'reading via the act of reading'; being in two places at once; whilst, according to the *Petit Robert* dictionary, it also refers to the 'art of discussing'. These two dimensions – a double act of reading, and a skilful essayism – are the Barthesian style of writing. But this raises the problem alluded to earlier: is this book about Philosophy only; can we not analyse Barthesian trends whilst relating them to the real world of politics? Whereas Marx considered that Feuerbach could not see the world clearly except through the glasses of a philosopher (Tucker 1961, 182), Barthes uses a loose quotation from Gide: 'Master of discourse – The Writer (never a philosopher to be my guide)' (2002, V, 1011), to distance himself from philosophy in favour of writing not militancy. There is also the danger, despite his view that he is trying 'to define things, not words' (Barthes 2009, 131n1), whereby words take over 'things'. Even Barthes's ambivalent use of Freud – a subject that is beyond the scope of this book – displays an acute sensitivity to the 'antithetical meaning of primal words' that Freud found in ancient Egyptian languages (Freud cited in J. Rose 2020, 3): words simultaneously denoting one thing and its opposite have a magic, argues Rose, as they release us into a world of contradiction and mystery. It is Barthes's close reading of Freud, while in Morocco in 1969 and 1970, that sensitizes him to the numerous examples in Arabic of the *add'ad*, or enantioseme (2010a, 155–59), as if the self-contradicting nature of the contranym – 'wicked', or 'sick', in current colloquial examples – requires a 'double grasp'. The word 'grasp' will become an important one in this book. For this reason, there is a modification of various French expressions in which Barthes uses it; in particular, Barthes's startling abbreviation *non-vouloir-saisir* (NVS), in which *saisir* has been translated, variously, as 'possess', 'seize' and 'own'. Here, *saisir* will be translated uniquely, for consistency's sake as 'grasp'; hence, NVS in French becomes no wish to grasp (NWG) in English.

Nietzschean 'Double Grasp'?

Barthes studies ancient Greek theatre for his postgraduate dissertation during World War II. Vaunting the dialectics of Aristotelian theatre alongside Paul Claudel's understanding of human speech as the word 'that acts', he also follows Nietzsche's Dionysian celebration of tragedy (Barthes 1941). In 1954, however, he sees a new form of dialectics taking shape in Brecht's epic theatre that eschews the tragic in favour of the political. Brecht's political impact on the dialectic is such that 'in the dialectic, we want to uncover phenomena and find their ultimate contradictions behind them' (Jameson 2010, 455); though, alongside the Brechtianism and Sartreanism of Barthes's ideological critique in

Mythologies, we will see a deeply Nietzschean strand, albeit based on the earliest writings in Nietzsche's *The Birth of Tragedy*.

Barthes will nevertheless go on to deny that he is a 'Nietzschean' (2007a, 462), despite the regular reference to Gilles Deleuze's Nietzsche in describing the 'Novel' to be written (Han 2020). Indeed, there is a tendency to see Barthes's Nietzschean approaches as fundamentally located in the 1970s (Oxman 2010; Weller 2019); and yet, from the start of his career to the end, Nietzschean influences are in evidence, and not least in the aphoristic, 'abyssal' style of the nineteenth-century philosopher that Barthes uses across his career. Indeed, Macé (2006, 35, 89–95) characterizes key elements of Nietzsche's fragmentary, essayistic style in distinctly Barthesian terms: 'image of thought, conception of existence, refusal of system, discontinuous writing-style', within a strategy of 'fictionalization' that, in the wake of Paul Valéry's essays, dominate French essayism between 1957 and 1980 (249–50). Malcolm Bull (2000) is surely right, alongside Losurdo (2020), to question the radicalism of Nietzschean politics. However, we will see how Barthes finds three radical attitudes in the German philosopher's thought: in the *for me* and its dialectical democracy; in the spirit of *para-doxa* as critique; and in diaphorology as an investigation of the self.

Indeed, it is a Nietzschean suspicion of Socratic dialectics that informs Barthes's unorthodox approach to the dialectic. Writing in 1960, he describes, in a footnote, the strong pressure he feels to 'be dialectical' (1972, 146n3); but being dialectical, he goes on to suggest, is possible only at the level of analysis, and not at all in the way that writing – language, in general – operates: one cannot actually write in a dialectical fashion.

This reticence towards, or suspicion of, the written dialectic dovetails with Barthes's development of semiology and structuralist analyses. Though Saussurean linguistics is based on a differential model of analysis that places the unity of opposites at the base of its method, structuralism develops this unity of opposites – in a manner not dissimilar to the way Mao Tse-Tung (1966) privileged the unity of opposites – towards an unsynthesized dialectic, an open-ended, formalist dialectic that seems at once to eschew the Hegelian and Marxian one and, simultaneously, to posit a hyper-dialectical, equipollent sensibility. Equipollence in Hegel's scepticism is defined as '"setting into opposition equally strong propositions or arguments on both sides of an issue that arises and thereby producing an equal balance of justification on both sides of the issue", producing an equal balance of negativity and the subversion of both alternatives' (Michael Forster cited in Jameson 2010, 56). Whereas Jameson finds this equipollence in the Frankfurt School's 'negative dialectics', here we shall consider it in what Barthes calls the 'two-term dialectic'.

Furthermore, in our reading of Barthes's 1970 essay on Japan, alongside the posthumously published diaries of his 1974 visit to China with the *Tel Quel* group, we investigate how his own writing tries to grapple with the dialectic as a form of writing but which, ultimately (spoiler alert!), seems to elude him. During this period 1970–74, Barthes sees Marx as a 'writer of paradox', since the nineteenth-century revolutionary too was seemingly unable to *write* the dialectic in his research on Capital. The 'writer of paradox' represents then the 'undialectical' that we explore in Chapter Nine.

Barthes's unorthodox use of the dialectic means that he is highly sensitive to what we might call the dialectic 'on the Right', to the petty-bourgeois way of reasoning. Indeed *Mythologies*, as we shall see in Chapter Two, is centrally concerned with the ideological functions of Order, of the *status quo* and of 'common sense', all within an 'ex-nomination' – the 'what goes without saying' – that hides the benefits for Capitalist society. Appropriately enough for an analyst of society, Barthes spots this right-wing dialectic first in petty-bourgeois theatre, exposing its material basis. In a virulent 1953 critique of the performances at the *Folies Bergère* in Paris, he points to a 'fundamental dialectic operating in bourgeois events (including funerals)', whereby '"I destroy Money uniquely so as to show you that I have some"': the sugar-coated performance techniques in petty-bourgeois aesthetics underline how much the spectator is 'violated by Money' (2002, I, 234–35). The 'violation by Money' will become, in *Mythologies*, the obsession with the computational, with value-for-money, that petty-bourgeois frugality distils from the rationality of bourgeois ideology. It relies on a narrow notion of 'balance', itself beholden to an unsynthesized dialectic, the key question (beyond the scope of this book, however) being the extent to which Barthes's 'undialectics' gives (too much) ground to this right-wing, 'fundamental' dialectic. Indeed, before any analysis of Barthesian concessions to petty-bourgeois ideology can be made, we need to characterize his own – highly personal and self-styled – engagement with Marxism.

'I have had just about enough of egotism' (Barthes 1986, 370)

'For me, my soul is cracked'

(Baudelaire 1909 [1859], np)

Barthes's witty 1955 mythology 'Am I a Marxist?' (2015b, 46–48) ironizes Marx's 'I am not a Marxist' (Stafford 2015, 159), in a *paradoxa* for the media age that demands that the writer *answers*. It is one that Marx would have loved; and like Samuel Beckett, Barthes was deeply suspicious about all questions on his work. However, it is not so much that Barthes's writing is a set of literary 'dualistic fictions' (Miller, 2008); but that he sees reality in double(s), including the reality of the self. Marx describes self-recognition in a famous passage of *Capital* thus: 'In a certain sense, a [human] is in the same situation as a commodity. As they neither enter into the world in possession of a mirror, nor as a Fichtean philosopher who can say "I am I", a [human] first sees and recognises [themself] in another [human]' (Marx 1975c, 144n19, trans. mod.). Marx's theory of subjectivity and intersubjectivity shows that it is not just that commodities are realized only in concrete commodity exchange, but also that a human can realize their being only in social relations. Hegelian in form, this dialectic is given its materialist colouring by Marx, to the extent that some, as we saw above, have argued that each human personality derives from social relations (Sève 1978). Baugh (2003, 5) quotes Jean Wahl and his view of Hegel's subject 'that strives vainly for synthesis but instead oscillates between self and non-self'; and, in creating 'RB [Roland-Barthes] I' and 'RB II', we will see how Barthes turns this 'unhappy consciousness' into a virtue of sorts. This is not just for the act of reading – 'a *split* reading [lecture *clivée*]' that involves Freud's view of the '*division* [*clivage*] *of the human subject*' is an 'active reading' (2002, IV, 173) – but also in how Barthes sees the self, his self (as opposed to him-self). It allows this cleaved, split self to read, as 'mediator', all of Photography (1984, 8) as a way to be subjective, but not as *his* subjectivity.

Book structure: Breathe in/Breathe out/Live

In his biography of the self, Barthes uses the metaphor of breathing in and breathing out. This is not surprising for someone so affected by lung illness for the crucial part of his life between 1934 and 1945. In the brief fragment 'Opacity and Transparency' (1994, 138) – a longer version of which we will consider in chapter 8 (2010a, 331–342) – Barthes illustrates his career-long fascination with the Marxian notion of social relations and how this has influenced his intellectual trajectory with the metaphor of the dual act involved in breathing: an acute awareness of social relations has allowed him to breathe in inspiration (and typical of Barthes the etymologist-essayist, the word 'in-spiration' is based on 'taking in air'): thereafter dialectically, 'in-spiration' allows the writer to be able to breath out a critique of these same relations.

This life-giving, double-action, of breathing in and then out suggests a continuity in his life and career: that of the responsible, principled, even consistent, intellectual and writer (2002, III, 77), that stands, (and more importantly) moves, in opposition to the gratuitousness of the aesthete in which the literary is reduced to the hedonist-moralist ethology of 'Literature' (with a capital L). Barthes's 'responsible' ethos is one that is implacably against oppression, discrimination and exploitation: in this book, this ethos will be taken as a given. Hence the dog-leg structure in what is to follow: in order to account for changes and underlying continuities and acts of bracketing, the analysis will, in general, move forwards in time, but will also, sometimes, dart back in time, in a 'backwards' analysis of Barthes's life we discuss in Chapters One and Nine. Hopefully, this will avoid the anachronism that Long and Welch (2009, 13–15) find in Burgin's disappointed attempt to mobilize *Camera Lucida* for his photography theory. Burgin needed instead to place the (apparent) abandonment of a collective critical theory of photography in Barthes's final essay within, as Oxman (2010) has done, the evolving and long-term context of his work on photography and the debates around it in France. By way of a contribution to this continuity, Chapter Three presents the overlooked captioning work in Barthes's 1960 collaboration with the theatre photographer Roger Pic.

This book moves therefore through three types of dialectic: the double; *dédoublement* [splitting]; 'undialectics'. Are we then using a 'double grasp' on Barthes? If so, is this in order to avoid the danger of the book being about Barthes only, and not the world? The ancient Greek chorus is to be taken, across all the nine chapters, as the mode of address in Barthesian essayism, as a collective and interventionist, double-voice, that stands in opposition to the Incantation considered by Lukács (cited by Goldmann 2016, 384) as a 'solitary dialogue'. Indeed, Benoist (1975, 61) hints at the use of the chorus in Barthes's first essay, *Writing Degree Zero*, in which 'the project and the strategy of writing is removed from the full subject of enunciation': in other words, when Barthes writes, it is a theatrical 'voice-off' that speaks.

Finally, therefore, I have my own double-act to fulfil: on the one hand, to convince the Barthes-as-aesthete camp that the political is a key component of his work; and, on the other, to allow those who know his work less to access the 'political Barthes' they may be looking for. There will be then an echo of the double audience for this book in the approach taken, at least to begin with. The main argument of this study is a simple one: Barthes is constantly involved in doubling. This will be our starting point, and it is hoped that by moving through the book to a level of complexity that this simplicity will not be taken as shallow or anti-intellectual, merely as a process through which, artificially, we can appreciate the profound nature of Barthesian political thought.

*

This book – unfortunately – is dedicated to the memory of Callie Gardner who passed away just as it was being finished.

Chapter One

'THE DIALECTICAL LOGIC OF LOVE'

Backwards Barthes?

> It is quite true what philosophy says: that life must be understood backwards. But then one forgets the other principle: that it must be lived forwards.
>
> *(Kierkegaard 1996 [1843], IV A 164)*

> Incoherence seems to me preferable to a distorting order.
>
> *(Barthes 1982a, 3)*

This book operates with the premise that not only should we avoid creating a hierarchy of different moments in Barthes's career (usually the late over the early, often forgetting the middle), but also, by the same token, no text or Barthesian maxim should be taken as the final word: we should not take, for example, *Camera Lucida* 'as Barthes's final or absolute word on the image' (Oxman 2010, 85). Barthes's writings are then a set of texts to be shuffled around, while we remain all the time mindful of their historical and contextual progression, albeit in the fits and starts of a spiral.

Indeed, there are even a number of good reasons to consider a 'backwards' reading of Barthes's work. Even in publishing terms there has been a marked backwards feel to Barthesiana; for example, Hervé Algalarrondo's 'Final Days' was followed, more recently, by the 'First Days' of Barthes (Gury 2012). The former suggests that the last three years of Barthes's life, after his mother's death in 1977, are deeply unhappy ones; the latter that being separated from his Normandy roots in exchange for his Basque/Gascogne upbringing had particular consequences in his work. But more seriously, one major reason for entertaining the idea of 'backwards' biography in relation to Barthes is that there is, in his *œuvre*, a double looking-back.

Since 2002 there has been a raft of posthumous publications of Barthes's lecture and seminar notes and diaries, which have been released (surely for good reason) backwards too – the 1976–77 and 1977–78 lectures in 2002 (2013; 2005), the 1979–80 lectures in 2003 (2011b), the 1974–76 seminars in 2007 (2007a), the China diaries and the Mourning diaries (written in 1974 and 1977–79, respectively) in 2009 (2012 and 2010b), and the 1968-69 seminars in 2011 (2011b). One effect of this 'backwards' policy for the posthumous publications is that the 'late' Barthes (or the second half of his career, 1968 to 1980) has come more into focus, in preference to an earlier Barthes, to the point that the privileging of the post-1968 period could be seen as a teleologically defined reading, inevitably based on, and read through, the last phase – see the 'Roland Barthes Retroactively' conference and publication (*Paragraph* 2008).

Indeed, there is amongst these 'late' (in both senses: late career and posthumously delayed) volumes of teaching materials the extraordinary set of seminar notes (2010a) in which we see Barthes, the seminar tutor, staging himself as a writer in front of his postgraduate students at the EPHE in Paris, and in which they participate, firstly in relation to 'Roland Barthes', and secondly with a view to their own writing (especially of their Self). Barthes writes retroactively, backwards, to account for his own past from the beginning, but from the vantage points, first, of the period 1973–74, and second, of his status as established writer and academic. This literarization of the self raises a key question: can we write our own past, as if it were a journal, but from the distance of much later years? It is a highly Proustian project – and there is no coincidence that the late(r) Barthes turns his attention to the author of *À la recherche du temps perdu* (a backwards-looking novel if ever there was one) – and one which requires extraordinary powers of memory.

It is worth underlining that Barthes was wary of the diary for a writer (1986, 359–73). Indeed, with one short exception, the 1979 'Deliberation' (1986, 359–73), none of his 'journals' (1992b, 2012, 2010b) was published in his lifetime. It implies – quite strongly – that the 1970s seminars at the EPHE, and then the lectures at the Collège de France in the last five years of his life, were all, partly, a form of intimate 'diary'. Indeed, the *Lexique de l'auteur* seminar (2010a) is concerned, in large sections, with 'self' (249–356); and it is also a backwards-looking inscription and contemplation of Self, all in the laboratory of teaching and in the 'play' of writing, and it is then 'essayified', fragmented into the notorious self-biography in the third person (1994). It implies that the backwards look is a quintessentially Barthesian optic.

Even Barthes's illness between 1934 and 1945 – his tuberculosis and consequent sensitivity to the body – displays a backwards feel. Re-reading in Thomas Mann's novel of life in a sanatorium for tuberculosis, *The Magic Mountain*, he underlines, in his inaugural lecture at the Collège de France in 1977, that his body felt 'historical' (1982a, 477–478). The protagonist in Mann's 1924 novel, Hans Castorp, is struck down by tuberculosis, and so Barthes experienced a bodily analogy with Castorp; though his was a 'literary' and fictional identification with Castorp's illness, Barthes nevertheless saw himself as more than 20-years older than he actually was.

Finally, it is Literature itself, if not the Literary, which seems to justify, if only theoretically, an unorthodox direction to an understanding of Barthes's work. The posthumously-published seminar mentioned above, *Le Lexique de l'auteur*, and then the final lectures given by Barthes at the Collège de France before his death, are instructive here; for they show, not so much the semiologist positing 'life as literature' (in the way that Alexander Nehamas (1985) has shown for Nietzsche), nor certainly the intellectual living a life in literature (the main trope of standard literary biography, one might argue), but rather the writer actually living literature as life. What would it mean then to (re-)read the rest of Barthes's life starting in the (final) 1973–80 period of his life (when the 'literature-as-life' phase is in full swing), and 'ending' with his orphaned childhood in interwar France?

Towards spiral, or 'collusion', biography?

> Human knowledge does not follow
> a straight line, but endlessly approximates
> a series of circles, a spiral.
>
> *(Lenin 1981, 357–361)*

'Life as text' suggests a de-hierarchization of time which, though not favouring a backwards trajectory, sets out to equalize succeeding timeframes. In the fragment dated 11 July 1973 (with 'Non' next to it in the margin – that is, not for inclusion in the final published version of *Roland Barthes by Roland Barthes*), Barthes stresses, firstly, that 'life as text' will be (if it is not already) 'banal' unless the following is underlined: it is 'a text to produce, and not to be deciphered' (2010a, 324). He underlines how he has said this already in his career, at very different moments (on Gide in 1942 and on Proust in 1966). Gide's Diary 'produces' the *Journal d'Édouard* (rather than the other way round, whereby we would normally 'read' Gide's Diary from the *Journal d'Édouard*); and in Proust, the *œuvre* 'does not reflect his life; it is his life that is the text of the *œuvre*' (2011b, 209ff). Rather than a walking back up through (his) life, the 'textual charivari' (2010a, 325) that we consider in Chapter Six suggests a different figure for understanding Barthes's life: a circular, parametric, spiral biography, what we might call, following his definition of the 'charivari' of his life (325), 'collusion' biography. This might be a compromise, as it is not backwards as such, but it allows us to approach some earlier texts via late ones. 'Collusion' also allows for the posthumous, in a way that standard biography cannot: if one reinserts the raft of posthumous publications into Barthes's life, one must, by definition, lose the 'flow' of his life (and thereby teleologize the posthumous publications at the same time). If anamnesis deconstructs or modifies this spiral, it does not dispense with the need for a supple, subtle approach to writing Barthes's life and work.

There is a textual counterpart to the historiographical dialectic of walking with/looking back: the recent developments in literary 'genetic criticism', which, concerned with textual genesis, are currently being used to explore Barthes's 'fiches' (card filing system). This approach is, and will continue to be, one that, if used subtly, will avoid the teleology of the published 'final' text. So posthumous texts can also be part of 'collusion' biography, including the posthumous *avant-texte*, such as the seminar on *Sarrasine* which leads to *S/Z* or the *Lexique de l'auteur* seminar which becomes *Roland Barthes by Roland Barthes*. Both the seminar *avant-texte* and the final published texts could be classed as what Barthes calls 'lecturebooks', for which Pierre Bayard's work – on anticipation, on critical intervention, on rewriting endings and even on the detective in literature – has provided a salutary theoretical framework for analysis. Thus an obvious example of collusion, or circularity, in Barthes's *œuvre* is the return, over twenty years later in the 1977–78 lecture course *The Neutral*, of the 1947–53 'Degree zero' thesis and the theory of a blank language, not to mention the return of the critique of 'neither–nor' neutrality in petty-bourgeois ideology set out during the 1950s in 'Neither–Norism' (2009, 93–96).

If, finally, 'backwards' biography raises two key questions that go beyond the scope of this book (can all of our lives be 'textual'? Can we compare 'backwards biography' with another recent trend, that of 'what if', or 'virtual' history?), the acts of inversion of chronology studied here – whether literary or memorial – suggest that any attempt to biography Barthes must perforce entertain the possibility of a hermeneutic in biography. This is not saying simply that we have the biography of a person for our age (which helps explain the extraordinary number of biographies of Winston Churchill – 200 or so), but also that we valorize different parts of a life and a career at different times to suit our own interests. It may be that a circular form of biography, what we have (tentatively) called 'collusion' biography, is the only acceptable compromise (at least in Barthes's case) between a forwards biography that distorts and a backwards one, albeit parametric to its subject, that nevertheless repels and can exist only in theory, making Barthes part of 'queer time' as defined by Judith Halberstam (2005).

Psychoanalytical inversions

'Philosophising consists of inverting the
usual direction in the work of thought.'

(Bergson 1959, 1422)

'"To take me is to mistake me",
That is the motto of Roland Barthes.'

(Miller in Compagnon 1978, 207)

There is a wider context to the case for writing Barthes's life 'backwards': that is, the temptation of using psychoanalysis. The abrupt inversions operated by post-Freudian psychoanalytical theory, especially in its essayistic rather than clinical form, seem to mirror the inversion of history's forward course that is operated by a backwards approach to biography. Psychoanalysis, with its irreverence towards temporal order, reason and continuity, has certainly a role to play in the critique of the standard tropes of teleological biography. In the present day, Pierre Bayard's essayistic work is a good example of this deconstructive approach to life's (seeming) forward movement. His many essays (2005, 2009, 2013) invert the usual historical processes and vantage points, and the first of these essays looks specifically at biography's premises concerning the direction of history. This is precisely what Marie Gil's 2012 biography of Barthes has taken on board. Gil points out, following Bayard's suggestion, that the 'late event' of the death of Barthes's mother (with whom he lived all his life) is, in many senses, the 'centre to come ' in Barthes's life (Gil 2012, 11–12), and that consequently 'life is a text'. Dissatisfied with the rather 'traditional' effort by Calvet (1994), Gil subtitles hers a 'biographical essay' in order to distinguish hers from 'the anecdotal narrative of life' (11). Against the 'smoothness' of standard biography, she proposes the 'parametric' strategy of using one of Barthes's ideas on his own biography. 'Life as text' becomes her strategy for writing Barthes's life, including literary text as she calls her chapter 'the two ways [les deux côtés]' as an allusion to Proust's *Combray*.

Such an approach is also an aid to opening up the possibilities of backwards biography. In *Le Lexique de l'auteur* seminar notes, Barthes hints at a better way to write his (or a) biography:

[W]e do not try to answer philosophically the questions 'What is RB's *œuvre*? Who is RB? What does this *œuvre* mean?', but only 'How does it function?' (2010a, 329).

Gil sees this functional view of life as a move towards 'life as text', for it inverts biography's doxa. The implication of Bayard's point – that a life might be ordered by something that happens much later on, towards the end, and that therefore any biography of that life might be skewed by a simple forwards narrative, from cradle to grave as it were – now poses a clear problem. Given her use of a psychoanalytical strategy, Gil is aware that the final years of Barthes's life, after the death of his mother in 1977, play a crucial role in how we look back over his life. In Gil's analysis, the 'filling of the hole [comblement du vide]' that has been the driving psychoanalytical force of Barthes's writing throughout his life – a reaction to his semi-orphaned life with his mother, then to her new lover in the late 1920s and to the birth of a half-brother – now finishes with her death. Barthes's last years are dominated by his sorrow at this loss and by the compensations offered by a fully literary view of life and of his own life.

Reversibility in memory, literature and writing the self

> That is reading: rewriting the text of a work
> on a level with [à même] the text of our life.
>
> *(Barthes 2002, V, 628)*

Despite the predominance of Barthes's 'The Death of the Author' thesis after 1967 (its original publication date in the United States), a number of critics have tried to find Barthes's interest in biography much earlier. Indeed, the fascination with Jules Michelet, especially in his earlier career, is mirrored by Henri Bergson, whose work, 'rediscovered' by Gilles Deleuze in the 1960s, contains a number of backwards motifs and whose 'vitalist' dimensions have a bearing on life-writing (Bergson 1944 [1907])

From at least 1970 onwards, though there was, according to Gil, no sign of a desire to go back to the 'full' subject of pre-structuralist, liberal-humanist thought, Barthes's writing begins to consider the biographical and is itself generally more biographical. The 'life as text' that Gil sees developing in Barthes's *œuvre* in the 1970s means that (2012, 353) Gil is simply applying Barthesian notions to his own life, and again these are instructive for backwards biography, for the narrative analysis practised by Barthes, especially in his notorious reading of Balzac's story in *S/Z*, has suggested that all narrative (including biography) is a text that is reversible – not to mention easily made into morsels, 'quotes', the 'biographemes' that Barthes identifies (1989, 9). In the seminar notes on *Sarrasine* Barthes sees a blurring transparency in which, 'homologous' to Balzac's corrections on his own story, the seminar group's reading of the story in 1968–69 creates a 'starred text' for which he wonders which is the 'transparency of the other' (2011a, 76). In this way, Barthes's seminar notes begin to see literary history reversed, turned on its head, as part of a critique of literary scientism. As opposed to a 'biography' *tout court*, Gil's 'biographical essay' is doubly parametric to Barthes, because not only was Barthes an essayist, but also the 'essay' contains notions of the provisional, of the playful, of the inventive, and also of the 'unfinished'. Barthes's own writing is full of this type of 'turning-the-tables', not just historical but also writerly, and even historico-writerly. Witness this quote from Michelet that Barthes cites in his 1942 piece on Gide's diaries: '"History, in the march of time, makes the historian much more than it is made by them. My book has created me. I am its work"' (Barthes 1982a, 12). This table-turning is a crucial part of backwards self-biographying. Self-biography needs to be counterposed to autobiography. Having written the literary biography of Michelet (1987a) for the 'by themselves [par lui-même]' series (called thus because each volume contains ample quotes), Barthes famously takes the series' name to heart as he writes his *own* 'par lui-même'– but in the third person; he then wrote a review of it in the press (to complete the illusion of self-biography) called 'Barthes to the Power of Three [puissance trois]' (1985c)! Barthesian theory and writing are replete with these deconstructive inversions of linearity and chronology. Even neological and etymological strategy is prone to inversion; as the poet Michel Deguy puts it (2002, 86), 'Barthes neologises by etymology'; and there are numerous examples of this in his writing, such as doxa/endoxa, atopia, acratic/encratic, proairetic, idiorrythmy, semioclasty and so on (Hanania 2010, Chapter Eight).

But perhaps the most famous Barthesian inversion is 'anamnesis' (1994, 109–110). Anamnesis, the act of unforgetting (as opposed to remembering), has a highly Proustian charge in its search for a lost moment but goes beyond Proust's attempts to recover lost time. Barthes first theorizes anamnesis in his 1973–74 seminar (2010a, 181ff) where he relates it to the spiral, pointing out that 'Michelet's historical *œuvre* is a huge anamnesis' (183–84). He uses the anamnesis to powerful effect in *Camera Lucida* when he contemplates the photograph of his mother as a young girl in the Winter Garden; but it represents a moment (unlike Proust's 'madeleine' episode) which Barthes could not possibly have experienced; and yet (backwards, as it were) the photograph, taken before his birth, affords him a strong memory of his recently deceased mother. Gil argues (14–15), quoting the work of Orlando Beer (1985), that the anamnesis is like the 'biographeme' but which is 'exempt of meaning'; until, that is, until we read a life (Barthes's life) as a text. Similarly, in *The Pleasure of the Text*, written at the same time as the theory of anamnesis, Barthes offers, in a radically off-hand way, a deconstruction – or historical inversion – of the usual 'forwards' chronology of literature and Art. He argues in post-Maoist, terroristic fashion, that Alain Robbe-Grillet is contained in Gustave Flaubert, Sollers in Rabelais and de Staël in Cézanne (1975, 20): 'I savor the sway of formulas, the reversal of origins, the ease which *brings* the anterior text out of the subsequent one' (36). In a manner which (ironically) anticipates Bayard's 'plagiarism by anticipation', Barthes thus up-ends, if not temporarily junks, traditional literary history and its facile chronological progression (interestingly, Bayard's *Le Plagiat par anticipation* does not mention *The Pleasure of the Text*). Thus both anamnesis and reading-literary-history backwards (or 'plagiarism by anticipation') are first theorized at the same time as Barthes starts his *Lexique de l'auteur* seminar. In both of these cases of the de-hierarchization of chronology (the deconstruction of the idea that that which comes first is definitive, or at least influential on what is subsequent), there is an attempt at, or a significant gesture towards, equalizing Time's influence on memories, on writing and on life's direction, in such a way that the impression on the contemporary subject is the source of literary values. Clearly, and as always in Barthes's work, these acts of de-hierarchization are as much tactical as provisional, but they do point to a crucial development in this 1970–73 period in Barthes's work in which the biographical, or what I have called the self-biographical, begins to inflect Barthesian writing. *Le lexique de l'auteur* is an attempt to use the 'laboratory' of the postgraduate seminar to analyse 'the writer', suggesting a social and fascinatingly dispassionate take on the 'self'; we should be wary of deeming Barthes's 1970s seminar practice and final Collège de France lectures as decadent in their romantic presentation of self. On the contrary, the continual placing of his self in the seminar, in the lecture theatre and in the texts of the 1970s, must be seen as a 'scientific' activity, but with literary deconstructions of the premise of 'objectivity' in Science. Barthes is aware of the danger of narcissism and so describes the use of the third person 'Barthes writes…' as both a 'supreme inflation' and a 'supreme deflation', linked, no doubt, to the decision to divide himself for the seminar into 'RB I' and 'RB II'. Indeed, the 'index' and the alphabetical are other ways of presenting the self 'RB' that undermine narcissism (2010a, 102–05, 132–34).

One of the other crucial aspects of these two operations – anamnesis and plagiarism by anticipation – is their highly subjective nature. In both cases, 'the analysis' starts from the subject, the *for me* of Nietzschean philosophy (1975, 13): we remember, recreate, valorize the past (our past) from the present, with all the layers of memory acting in-between; similarly, we should insert literature into the literary institution and its concomitant history, *from where we are*. It is important also that we do not lose sight of the other temporal dimension of a life: the future. In an interview in 1977, 'Of What Use Is an Intellectual?', when asked if he was writing for posterity, Barthes's answer is as peremptory as it is portentous: 'Frankly, no. I can't imagine that my *œuvre*, my texts will be read after my death. I literally do not imagine it' (1985a, 276). Is this further evidence for the justification of backwards biography? Clearly, Barthes is not looking forward, imagining into the future.

In our first chapter therefore, in order to start a consideration of the political in his writing, we use a dog-leg approach to Barthes's life and writing. This will be one by considering one of his final (and most popular) essays, *A Lover's Discourse*, in dialogue with some of the earliest writings that we have, that is his war-time correspondence written to friends whilst having treatment for tuberculosis. We work backwards, in order to highlight the attitude towards love and amorous relationships that emerges in the frank and often moving letters sent first from the sanatorium at Saint-Hilaire du Touvet between 1942 and 1944 and then, at the end of the War, from the clinic in Leysin in Switzerland as Barthes prepares to return to life back in Paris. This correspondence is read retrospectively by way of his penultimate work of 35 years later, *A Lover's Discourse: Fragments*, to illustrate how the 'wave' of ideas on love that return regularly in his work, are also beholden to a striking analysis of dialectics. Thus, even in the tender and passionate world of friendship, love and personal loss, the dialectical plays a crucial role. In so doing, this first chapter modulates the spatial oscillation that Gil's biographical essay sees as part of the 'life as text' that Barthes constructs across the 1970s. Instead, the analysis here instigates a temporal oscillation, book-ending his end of life with the very start of his writing career.

I argue elsewhere (Stafford 2015b) that a backwards biography can be fruitful, both for Barthesian study – showing the circular, spiral nature of his concerns, how they return in different places at different stages of his career – and for a more subjective, communal, even gregarious, relationship with History: a complexity of the past, and of otherness, that never reaches, but could approximate to, a 'totality', though the binary, oscillating antonym – singularity – is, naturally, ever present in its opposite.

If we accept this immanent view of his own life and writing, we have two obvious choices: either we go back in time and read Barthes's texts in their own moment, with no condescension of posterity or teleological approach to its significance (thus ignoring what has happened since, that is, Barthes's fame since his death), which is to take his (very modest) belief quite literally; or we bracket his claim, by having a knowing overview of his life's significance for us today, in which case we cannot then 'go back' to the time of his writings (other than disingenuously). Either way, forwards biography cannot adequately deal with a writer's view of their own posterity, because its constant flitting between immanence (being in the time of the writer) and condescension of posterity (reading the life from the vantage point of the 'after-life' as it were) tends to privilege the latter: the 'late' Barthes controls retroactively (ironically for 'forwards' biography) the early Barthes, teleologically retro-fitting early Barthesian thought with what it later becomes. We must be prepared, then, to plunder the 'early' Barthes to counter the scholarly imbalance that seems to distort, or at least control, our understanding of his work. Indeed, *Writing Degree Zero*, already shows him to be acutely aware of the temporal and 'closed' nature of literary narration, as exemplified by the past historic: because the novel usually uses the preterit tense, it makes life into destiny and duration into oriented and meaningful time, full of anti-teleological motifs (1967a, 38–39, 44). One criticism of Gil's biography is, then, that she privileges in this teleological manner the later writings in Barthes's *œuvre*.

This then raises questions of how we read Barthes's correspondence that is slowly emerging. This material was not subject to the anamnesis work in *Le Lexique de l'auteur*, although the 'RB I' notion of the 'person who will write' is acutely pertinent. Indeed, in a lecture at Harvard in 1932, T.S. Eliot put the problem succinctly:

> The desire to write a letter, to put down what you don't want anybody else to see but the person you are writing to, but which yet you do not want to be destroyed, but perhaps hope may be preserved for complete strangers to read, is ineradicable. We want to confess ourselves in writing to a few friends, and we do not always want to feel that no one but those friends will ever read what we have written. (TS Eliot in Keegan 2020, 7)

We will consider then the letters on love that Barthes wrote between 1942 and 1946. We will not only bear in mind Eliot's striking assertion, but we will encounter the earliest use of the dialectic, which will then be linked to Barthes's work on the discourse of love.

Dialectic of love

> Love first really teaches a man to believe
> in the objective world outside himself. It

not only makes man the object but the object
a man. Love makes the beloved into an external
object, a sensuous object which does not remain
internal, hidden in the brain.

(Marx/Engels 1845, ch 4.3)

To love is to struggle, beyond solitude,
with everything that can animate existence.

(Badiou 2012, 104)

In a recent article on love in the internet age, Alfie Bown (2017) makes a surprising suggestion about Barthes's famous 1977 treatise on the language of love, *A Lover's Discourse: Fragments*. Not only is it Barthes's most psychoanalytical text, argues Bown, but also his 'closest to Marx'. Citing the work of Srećko Horvat, the Croatian philosopher whose *The Radicality of Love* questions (*pace* Badiou 2012) the division of love from politics, Bown goes against much of the 'late Barthes' orthodoxy and its tendency to downplay if not ignore the radical edge to Barthes's best-selling book. Indeed, Bown and Horvat seem to benefit from the so-called 'affective turn' since the turn of the millennium; Ahmed (2014 [2004], 45) has articulated the analogy of 'affect' with Marx's understanding of surplus-value Capital, in which she sees a 'a similar logic' whereby, like money–commodity–money circulation, 'the movement between signs or objects converts into Affect'.

It is true that, when *A Lover's Discourse* is published in 1977, some of the Left in France seem to take a distance on the essay's non-theoretical approach, Louis-Jean Calvet being one of its main detractors; though this shunning by the Left was by no means systematic (Stafford 1998, 208). Despite the large sales, the essay is met, according to Eric Marty (2006, 198–205), with silence from intellectuals, making it an 'orphaned' essay in Barthes's *oeuvre* and suggesting a new intellectual solitude in his life. As Marty points out (202–03), it is not that the topic itself is out of tune with theory of the 1970s; after all, Jacques Lacan is giving seminars on love in 1975 just as Barthes is at the newly-renamed Ecole des Hautes Etudes en Sciences Sociales in Paris (2007a). Marty's main point is that the language of someone in love is the least theoretical subject possible in 1977; the soft sweetness and the ridiculousness of the name 'lover', the references to a 'heavy heart', all make it irrelevant to a radical modernity (Marty 2006, 205). And yet, with its refusal of grand narratives in favour of fragmented micro-stories, critique of abstraction, return of the past over the present, and finally, its generic impurity mixing irony and satire, *A Lover's Discourse* is cast by Marty, rather problematically, as a precursor to post-modernism. Indeed, it is easy to think of love as far from politics as possible; and Barthes himself argues in *A Lover's Discourse* that, alongside Christian doctrine and psychoanalysis, 'Marxist discourse […] has nothing to say' about love or the erotic, because in today's world they have 'no system' (211).

Yet, when Marx writes about love in the 'Economic and Philosophical Manuscripts of 1844' at the end of the section called 'Money' (1975a, 375–379), following the 'misfortune' of unrequited love (379), he goes straight into his famous piece 'Critique of Hegel's Dialectic and General Philosophy' (379–400) where he recognizes Feuerbach's breakthrough with respect to the Hegelian dialectic. In other words – in Marx's mind at least – Money–Love–Dialectic are all tightly connected. For Barthes however, writing in 1977, it is 'today's intellectuals' who 'reluctantly' privilege Love over Need (1990a, 211); it is 'no longer the sexual which is indecent, it is the s*entimental*' (177); this is 'Love's obscenity' (175). As he puts it in his 1975 self-biography:

> [L]et us now imagine reintroducing into the politico-sexual field thus discovered, recognized, traversed, and liberated … *a touch of sentimentality*: would that not be the *ultimate* transgression? The transgression of transgression itself? For, after all, that would be *love*: which would return: *but in another place*. (Barthes 1994, 65–66)

And yet, and as we shall see in support of Bown's view, Barthes's essay on love regularly alludes to Marxism: from the Leninist title 'What is to be done?' (1990a, 62) to the 'revolution' of being in love (151).

We will examine what might in Barthes's essay dissent from any normative or accepted view of love, while exploring much earlier attempts to write about love in the period of his life that Philippe Roger (1996) calls 'the Marx Years'.

A friend of Barthes's in the 1970s, Roger has seen little of his work on Barthes translated into English. In his impressive 1986 essay *Roland Barthes, roman*, he looks closely (232-3) at the political, indeed materialist, import of sections of *A Lover's Discourse*, noting how Barthes rejects the 'not necessarily "depoliticised"' in favour of the 'not being "excited"' (212). Indeed, for Roger, politics is the 'hors-texte' (233) in Barthes's 1977 essay on love: it is there by dint of its conspicuous absence. He points to Barthes's rhetorical question: what can the person in love say, except that they want a 'revolution, in short' and which is 'not so far, perhaps, from the political kind'; and that, in both cases, what Barthes 'hallucinates is the absolute New' (151).

Similarly, Saint-Amand (2017, 638–39) argues that not only is the eroticism in *A Lover's Discourse* a tactile, sensual one, but that it points to the 'materialism' that Barthes always claimed. Indeed, the 'absolute materialism' which Roger sees here as 'very close to mysticism' (233), resembles the quote from Jean Jaurès on using the materialism of Marx and the mysticism of Michelet to interpret history that we cite at the start of chapter 4. It also resembles the oscillation between vulgar determinism to voluntarism in Karl Korsch and Brecht's work (Jameson 2010, 175). This double view of love, both materialist and 'very close to mystical', will inform our reading of the sanatorium correspondence.

Double Hegel

To the 'Marx years' in Roger's account of the early Barthes, we could easily add the 'Hegel years'. The 'early' correspondence (Barthes 2018, 1–63), starting from the tuberculosis sufferer in his mid-twenties locked away in a sanatorium during World War II, shows a young man developing distinctly Hegelian, and then Marxian, perspectives on his heart-felt relationships both in and outside of his constricted sanatorium life. In correspondence written between 1944 and 1946 in particular, we can trace a growing dialectical sensibility, if not a materialist outlook, that will resurface three decades later in Barthes's academic and essayistic work.

Though Marx does not look at the sensuality of sexuality, sensuality is a key element of his early materialism and his deep engagement with Hegel's phenomenology; and Barthes's insistence in *A Lover's Discourse* that he is 'not dialectical' (63), does not then preclude his recognising that 'odd dialectic' whereby 'amorous errantry is a fatality' which even has its 'comical side'; and that, due to this '"perpetual mutability"', the result in love and relationships is the unending search for a lover, a constant and restless move from 'one nuance to the next' (1990a, 101–03).

Indeed, Hegel is present in the 'Discours amoureux' seminar that Barthes gives in Paris between 1974 and 1976. Just as he divides 'RB' into I and II in his 1973–74 seminar *Le Lexique de l'auteur* (324–25), so the 'Discours amoureux' seminar divides Hegel into two: Hegel I is 'love', and Hegel II, 'History':

> The early Hegel could see the reality of human desire and of human action in the microcosm of love. Then Hegel II, the reality of human action in the macrocosm of History. The [human] is this animal species whose essence develops in the dialectic of historical time, the animal that possesses a history. Therefore, the [human] cannot be identified with love. Love is a brief subjective moment in the lives of lovers: it leaves intact the macrocosm of History (which is tantamount to identifying [humans] with death). (2007a, 532)

Citing in a footnote Norman O. Brown's work on psychoanalysis applied to History, Barthes is aware in the 1970s of the importance of love in its nexus with History and death; and yet, in *A Lover's Discourse*, love is deemed to be outside of History:

> Whatever is anachronic is obscene. As a (modern) divinity, History is repressive, History forbids us to be out of time…. The lover's sentiment is old-fashioned, but this antiquation cannot even be recuperated as a spectacle: love falls outside of interesting time; no historical, polemical meaning can be given to it; it is in this that it is obscene. (177-8)

It is this perspective on the seriousness of love that we will now trace in his early career, just as Barthes moves, during the final days of the War, from Gide and Michelet, to Marx and Sartre. We will see in particular that the dialectic plays an important role in his early conceptions of love.

Both *'Tyranny'* and *'A Gold Medal in a Foundation'*

In two letters written to Robert David – his lover from 1944 to 1946 – Barthes refers to Love's extraordinary power over everything. In a letter dated 23 January 1946, from the Leysin clinic in Switzerland where he meets and falls in love with David, he describes to David an evening spent with two friends:

> During the conversation, which was painful as long as Solliers was there because of his growing mythomania (vanity), then more relaxed when I was alone with Mosser, I thought of you intensely many times. I talked to Mosser about passion (in an absolutely general way,

adopting that proverbial tone I love). I surprised myself with the power of the hypothesis on love that I constructed. (2018, 60)

> I reconsidered, reexperienced, and reaffirmed that vocation of passion which is my own and which I understand better and better— without knowing where it is leading me—this is part of it. Some elements that I have often mentioned to you appeared forcefully to me: the dialectical logic of Love, which is one of the most astonishing things I know. (60–1)

Although we now have only a fragment of the letter sent to Robert David from the week before (18 January 1946), he explains the meaning of the 'dialectical logic of Love':

> Love, you see, is a kind of inverse reason, and therein lies its terrible, and terribly beautiful, nature. Love has all the characteristics of reason. It is the most logical action possible, accepting no compromise and basing its progression on a logical line of thought. In reason, logic has the power of royalty; in love, it has the power of tyranny. I cannot do otherwise than accept the panic (before a word, or silence), not through intellectual fidelity to a principle, but through the absolute pressure of an inner dialectic that for me merges with love itself. (314 n.106)

The tyranny of love's dialectic is then described in the 23 January 1946 letter to David, thus:

> One is taken with a surge of emotion at seeing this power of *thought* that makes no act indifferent, that makes a telegram or letter an eternal *sign*, transforming *everything*, absolutely *everything* into the absolute. It's exhausting, but it is undeniably great, this sacredness upon which, in Love, one bases each movement, like a gold medal in a foundation (Michelet). I thought again—but I've already explained this to you—precisely of that discovery of the sacred (I cannot find a better word) that prompts passion. (61, author's original emphases)

We will return to the reference to Michelet in a moment. Citing Maurice Barrès's *Amori et dolori sacrum*, Barthes now makes the crucial link between love and revolutionary politics that, as we saw above, both Roger and Bown identify in *A Lover's Discourse* written three decades after these letters to David:

> I thought again — but I've already explained this to you — precisely of that discovery of the *sacred* (I cannot find a better word) that prompts passion. I sense the degree to which, for example, the vocation of passion and that of revolution are identical. It is an engagement of the same nature. Through that similarity, one can easily understand the chemical formula of the absolute, the eternal. It would be a kind of indissoluble compound — indissoluble for having become a truly living body — of suffering and of loving-suffering, of the horror and the love of love. (61)

The chapter in *A Lover's Discourse* called 'To Love Love' (31) — itself a clear intertext with St Augustine's remark 'I was not yet in love, but I was in love with the idea of love' (cited by one of Fernando Pessoa's many alter egos Alvaro de Campos, in Tóibín 2021, 24) – is clearly prefigured here. However, it would be perhaps too biographical, and even simplistic, to invoke the account by Susan Sontag (1983, 16) of the tuberculosis sufferer as one of wild swinging between utter exhaustion and listlessness on the one side, and then almost superhuman energy in the hunger for life on the other. But her suggestion does point to an oscillation – a dialectic of some sort – in Barthesian thought and writing.

Michelet and Marx

Barthes appears as all too aware of the deep, over-deep even, theorising of love to which he is reduced. In a letter to another friend, Georges Canetti, composed in November 1945, he writes:

> Those who are ill only have speech for expressing themselves. If we were healthy and free, we could experience friendship in silence, as in certain American novels. I truly believe that as long as I'm sick, I will inevitably be saddled with this academicism that weighs on me so heavily that sometimes I go for weeks without writing to avoid assuming the burden of the only habit I have at the moment. (2018, 47)

This highly intellectualised conception of love is soon to become, in the final months of 1945, a much more philosophically complex one, in which Jaurès's joining of Marx's materialism with Michelet's mysticism can be seen implicitly in Barthes's syncretic view of love in his personal life. The comparison of Michelet's expression 'like a gold medal in a foundation' to the 'sacredness' of love is a striking one. However, soon, as we shall see, he will go on to compare the experience of being in love to that of being a revolutionary.

Barthes's fascination with Michelet, as we have seen, is a complex and often contradictory one. Indeed, in matters of love, Michelet, the romantic historian, is surprisingly uninspiring for Barthes. In 1954, he regrets forcefully the historian's division of sentiment from theorisation:

> Michelet greatly contributed to the propagation of a superstition still widespread today: the stupid and harmful distinction between 'idea' and 'feeling'; our anti-intellectuals are still feathering their nests with it. (1987a, 183note)

It is not only in his early letters, but also in the later work on love in the 1970s, that Barthes continually battles this 'superstition' by bringing sentiment and theory together. It is also Michelet's political ideas, his petty-bourgeois ideology that troubles him and this is doubtless a view that is inflected by his initiation into Marxism in Autumn 1945.

Barthes's meeting in the Leysin sanatorium in Switzerland with Georges Fournié in Autumn 1945 and the discussions about Marxism, philosophy and politics take place against the back-drop of the Liberation of Europe, the crisis of Capitalism and the arrival of Sartrean existentialism. Indeed, we can see trace the shift towards dialectical and materialist thought that the discussions with Fournié have in his view of love. On 15 November 1944, while still in Saint-Hilaire, Barthes writes to David, with a very different – but equally important – analogy for love, here between physical love and writing:

> Writing for me would be, I think, like the same sort of pleasure as physical love (I call physical love: sleeping with someone you desire but do not love: in three stages: excitement; release (fulfilment) and disgust.) (unpublished correspondence, Fonds Barthes. Bibliothèque Nationale de France)

The change of both analogy and tone in Barthes's thoughts here is striking. Furthermore, the letter of 8 December 1944, sent from Saint-Hilaire (that is, before Barthes's transfer to Leysin), must be contrasted to the correspondence from Leysin a year later. The use of Hegel here in 1944 precedes a more Marxian account to follow:

> Since all the requirements for a predetermined confession seem empty to me, incomprehensible beside the deep life of my soul, I would even say beside the truth of a certain absence (at least of words) where finally I sense no deception — if I weren't afraid of being misunderstood by your honest heart, your avid intelligence for formulated truths, because your extremely straightforward and delicate soul has something Hegelian about it that tells it the ineffable is nothing but the imaginary, and even if you acknowledged the mystery, you would only do so within the framework of your own confession. (2018, 52–53)

Despite the reference here to Hegel and despite the contradictions in love that Barthes underlines here in 1944, the following lacks the starkly 'dialectical logic of Love' in the January 1946 correspondence we saw earlier:

> Love illuminates for us our imperfection. It is nothing other than the uncanny movement of our consciousness comparing two unequal terms — on the one hand, all the perfection and plenitude of the beloved; on the other hand, all the misery, thirst, and destitution of ourselves — and the fierce desire to unite these two such disparate terms and to fill the void of one with the plenitude of the other. (53)

Even the firm discounting of fiduciary value is less materialist than liberal-humanist:

> The miracle happens, perfection descends upon us when the beloved gives himself, lets his plenitude freely, generously, answer the thirst of the lover. Lovers consider denying one another out of humility, not understanding what is being asked of them. They do not see that it's much more arrogant to bring up questions of value; the value of a being is an extremely fiduciary notion. Without playing on words, it is a market value: your worth is that I love you; that's what must be understood. Only love truly creates; a being who is not loved is worth nothing, has no existence, is an element in the scenery and that scenery is a desert. I believe that a being's moral progress means understanding that and consenting — if only timidly at first — and entering the flaming circle of love in order finally, truly, to be born. And then, how distant grow all the intellectual and moral values of character, etc., how they shrink and shrivel up! How many intelligent beings are nevertheless dead, useless, cold, hard, etc. There is a miracle, there is a life, there is a flame that struggles to emerge between us, a sign that, once raised, would endow us both with our true value, our eternal value, would shower us both with serious things. Having consented to the ultimate weakness of love, we will find ourselves truly strong. (53)

Nevertheless, we find here, already in 1944, a pessimistic sense of self when not in love:

> You were ecstatic over the miracle that there was no more of the intellectual pontiff in me, and yet, at seeing your joy, your joyous surprise, wasn't that when my value was the greatest? And you too, wasn't it in that nocturnal fire that you were worth the most? Did you have a single moment of doubt about your own value? As though we left all of that far behind! But, come day, I could see in the way you would not look at me that you had gone back to those things that, not being part of love, can only be part of pride. Infernal self-pride, and that's why I suffer, even as I am sure of being right, even having already been enriched a thousandfold, just as Pascal suffered and yet…. But neither for you nor for me can I continue this comparison. (53-4)

There is nevertheless a calmness and resignation in this liberal, Hegelian view of love. Indeed, nine months later, in a letter to Robert David dated 28 September 1945, written soon after his arrival in Leysin, Barthes seems to be in control of his feelings of love:

> you know that I take a certain pride in not showing my distress, but the unique mark of our friendship is that I cannot put on an act for you. To bolster my courage, I have adopted a kind of method (you will recognize me there, of course). I begin with this principle: one's intelligence must be in proportion to one's sensitivity; when one is not sure of the first, the second must be decreased. If my intelligence doesn't allow me to overcome a difficult situation, I'm going to try to lessen my sensitivity a bit, reduce the flame. This is all to let the mind retain control; to do that I must avoid certain temptations so they do not destroy me: the image of the Mother and the image of the Lover. I'm trying hard not to be forever thinking of you both. I know that you are always extraordinarily present, but I'm trying not to let myself be monopolized by your images. It's simply because otherwise I lose control[.] (55-6)

However, the political change occurs, it would seem, in the letter to David dated 17 December 1945 (and of which, again, only a fragment seems to remain), in which we can see, following Barthes's reading of Sartre (and doubtless the beginning of discussions with Fournié), a more revolutionary spirit emerging, accompanied by the 'violent thoughts about my life and my character […], anarchistic' (58) that are beginning to undermine his work on Michelet and to raise questions about the bourgeois character of France's 1789 Revolution amidst the rubble of post-war Europe:

> the modern world seems to call for a more 'totalitarian' concept of man. It is very clear that 89, whose death echoes across the continent, will have its last stronghold in the legal mind, in the legal structures, cherished offspring of the Revolution and high priests of the analytical, bourgeois mindset. Thus, within the citadel of the Law, there must be revolutionary minds, applying revolutionary methods to the very subjects of the Law. You will be one of them, I am sure of it. One can be a revolutionary and very gentle. I really hope that, more and more, the new Revolution will be a question of work rather than of blood. (313-14n.101)

Barthes is clearly developing a more politicised view of love in December 1945. We can now return to the letter in which he describes the 'dialectical logic of Love' and which he likens to the 1903 study by Barrès, the 'indissoluble compound – indissoluble for having become a truly living body – of suffering and of loving-suffering, of the horror and the love of love':

> That chemical formula of the absolute, that theoretical body of the eternal, has isomers, so to speak: love itself — as I experience it — the gift of self for an idea, a nation, etc. But in all these acts there are: 1. A *beyond*, efficacy, a kind of practical disinterest, a moral force — and thus, if you will, a despair. To be revolutionary or in love basically entails being in despair — or without hope, which is better. 2. A *sacrificial*, almost ritual element that acts both contradictory and authentic and, thus essential to the true man, that plunges him into what he fears, the fear and love of torture, which pushed generations of men toward the guillotine during the Revolution. And that is why Revolution remains a unique mystery that will eternally set men on fire — certainly not through its political or even ideological content — almost depleted — but through that collective sacrifice that is truly an *example*, the example of a society that, for four years, was perhaps closest to the heart of Nature (men/things/history) in all of History. That is how it is with passion — if it is truly followed to its end — because even as a man who is content with having political *ideas* without being wholly on fire knows nothing of the sacred in revolution, so a man who tries to elude the suffering of love, either by not loving completely, or by abandoning love (the most frequent case), or by sublimating it (perhaps the most contemptible case), will know nothing of the sacred in love, and for him there will be only losses, whereas, for the other, only gains of an essential order. (61-2, Barthes's original emphases)

This is a quite extraordinary marrying of the sacred of love with the sacred of revolution and revolutionary ideas. This analogy seems to be going much further than Tennyson's famous dictum – 'tis better to have loved and lost is better than never to have loved at all': Barthes seems to be saying that being in love, like being a *revolutionary*, requires the utmost personal sacrifice.

It is therefore not surprising that, in his conclusion to this extraordinary treatise on love, he calls this letter 'one of the most intimate letters' he has ever written to David. It is striking also that, in his recent treatise on the radical nature of love, Horvat cites Che Guevara's eldest daughter to a similar effect: 'To be a proper revolutionary, you have to be a romantic' (2016, 110).

It is also the moment for Barthes to underline the gender-sexuality differences he sees in love:

> I was also thinking — in my efforts toward intelligence and wisdom — that one can say all this only when it is a friend whom one loves. I imagine that, with regard to a woman, a whole other metaphysics applies, not at all inferior, that was not my thought. Because the degree of otherness one finds in a woman is entirely different, and that leads to experiencing the issue in an entirely different way. But that, my poor David, is a dangerous direction for the moment. (2018, 62)

This rather essentialising view of woman has its echo in *A Lover's Discourse* when he describes the woman as the person in a heterosexual relationship who 'gives shape to absence' (14). But, before we look at *A Lover's Discourse*, it is worth illustrating the dialectic of love as Barthes begins to conceive it in the mid-1970s, especially in his seminar, as well as antecedents in *Mythologies* and *Michelet*.

One of the keenest dialectics in love for Barthes is that of the 'first time'/repetition. Quoting Heine's neat line: 'It is an old story / Yet it always seems new' (2007a, 55), Barthes is nevertheless aware of the spiral, the eternal return, the dialectic of difference, in the 'first time' of love. This could be contrasted with his belief in the need to 'create an unheard of language in which the form of the sign repeats itself (its voice, the signifier) but never the signified' (94). 'The right to *I-love-you*' is his sharpest example. In its ability to leave behind '*classification*, in order to reach in life itself the s*himmer* [*moire*] of the text', the direct declaration of love to the other is the key to the 'dialectical work (to the success of amorous relations) [...], outside of the Imaginary, because it recognizes the value of a *praxis*, of a transformation'. In *The Neutral*, 'I-love-you' is even described utopianly as a 'transparency of discourse' (2005, 95). However, in his otherwise useful analysis of the seminar versions of the 'I-love-you' section of *A Lover's Discourse* (147-55), Coste (2002) does not mention the fact that Barthes combines, in a perfect counterpoint, the deeply singular personal declaration of love for the loved other, with the most political comments of the whole essay. Not only is 'I-love-you' the longest section of *A Lover's Discourse*, it is also where Barthes sets out in paragraph 7 (1990a, 151) – in a numbered presentational format typical of Hegel and then of the early Marx – the connection between Revolution and the 'absolute New' of love.

As we will see in Chapter Two, the notion of transformation is an important element in the 'woodcutter' metaphor posited by Barthes as a response to – or a continuation of – Marx and Engels's metaphor of the cherry-tree in *The German Ideology*. Similarly here, the lover can *act*. However, that act of saying the immortal words 'I-love-you' risks other dangers and traps. This is the 'will-to-possess' that these words inevitably entail.

In *A Lover's Discourse*, it is the final section '*Sobria ebrietas*' (232-35) that supplies, if not the solution, at least a happy coda. First, Barthes sets out the danger:

> Realizing that the difficulties of the amorous relationship originate in [the] ceaseless desire to appropriate the loved being in one way or another, the subject decides to abandon henceforth all 'will-to-possess' in [their] regard. (232, trans. mod.)

This entails avoiding the 'will-to-possess' (or 'will-to-grasp', in our modified translation), of insisting instead upon the 'non-will-to-possess' (NVS abbreviation translated below as 'N.W.P.' as opposed to our preferred NWG). For Barthes, this means holding the 'I-love-you' on one's lips, in one's mind, in order to avoid the compromises of both speech and affect, tantamount to some kind of solution to the complex dialectics of the play of love between subject and loved one. This seems to be a zero point in his argument, an all-or-nothing:

> And if the N.W.P. were a tactical notion (at last)? If I still (though secretly) wanted to conquer the other by feigning to renounce him? If I withdrew in order to possess him more certainly? The reversi (that game in which the winner takes the fewest tricks) rests on a feint familiar to the sages ("My strength is in my weakness"). This notion is a ruse, because it

takes up a position within the very heart of passion, whose obsessions and anxieties it leaves intact. (233)

This resonates markedly with his words in a letter sent to Georges Canetti 21 November 1945 from the Leysin sanatorium, in which he discusses at length the 'Socratic debate on love':

> Can one play the game halfway? For me that makes no sense. It is and it is not an act. One must risk everything and at the same time one risks nothing. It is an extraordinary sleight of hand and I'm sure the Greeks offered us an example similar to it in their way of believing—and not believing—in the gods. We know very well that through love we enter a universe where the concepts are no longer the same, where truth itself becomes amphibologic, etc., and what troubles us is finding in history, civilizations, literature, religion, etc., reflections of this reversed world that therefore no longer seems to us completely illusory; and that comforts us and confirms our thinking, our surmising that Love is only a myth in a system of fraternal myths pursued for so long by the historical world, and which return very often to tempt it through the impetuousness of their dream, through their truth, if you like. (2018, 46)

The 'internal dialectic' now suddenly resembles the need for the demystifier's 'amorous dialectic' [dialectique d'amour] that will inform the earliest iterations of *Mythologies* (2002, V, 1023). This 'amorous dialectic' is not however exactly the 'logical dialectic of Love'; but, as we shall see in Chapter Two, rather the description of the mythologist confronted with an object's double reality, of its 'phenomenon' on the one hand (Rimbaud the poet), and on the other the myth of Rimbaud (how the poet has been 'consumed'). This 'amorous dialectic', based on a Lukácsian notion of reification and disalienation before the motility of myth, is nonetheless linkable to 'the logical dialectic of Love', of human relationships, via the two areas that he had discovered in the Saint-Hilaire du Touvet sanatorium; namely Michelet, and then the social pressures of living communally.

'Double grasp' versus Strabismus

In the Saint-Hilaire sanatorium between 1942 and Summer 1945, Barthes reads Jules Michelet's huge *oeuvre* doubtless to pass the time, but also because he becomes fascinated with how the historian appears, in various ways and guises, in his works of historiography. There is an important echo of this fascination in his writings on Michelet ten years later. However, this double grasp has its obverse, its negative dimension, in Barthes's experience of social life in the sanatorium.

In his 'Sketch of a Sanatorium Society', written in 1947 but published only posthumously, Barthes is rather candid, if not exceptionally rude, about life and some of the people in the sanatorium (as we saw above, briefly, in the case of Solliers in Leysin). What is striking in the opening paragraph of this proto-*Mythologies* piece is the 'intolerable strabismus':

THE DIALECTICAL LOGIC OF LOVE 19

> In a sanatorium society everything conspires to return one to a situation defined and embellished with the attributes of an authentic society. The costs of this accumulation of artifice hardly matter, but first among them is considering as sufficient a society that is, alas, only parasitic. It is above all a matter of dissociating the consciousness of the ill person from the memory of not having been one; the junction of these two states would result in an intolerable strabismus. (2018, 64)

In the sanatorium, one does not dare, Barthes is suggesting, to have a consciousness that looks in two directions; and we see a similar warning in Frédéric Goldbronn's documentary (*Les fantômes du sanatorium*) that cites the correspondence with Philippe Rebeyrol in which Barthes councils strongly against thinking of one's life elsewhere other than in the sanatorium. The 'intolerable strabismus' is a 'double grasp' *à la* Michelet but of wholly negative use, if not mentally dangerous; and this strabismus has a fascinating return thirty years later in the 1974–76 seminar on the 'discourse of love' and the notes of which became, in very expurgated form, *A Lover's Discourse*.

Here, his attitude is more ambivalent – neither positive in the way he seemed to be with Michelet's 'double grasp', nor negative as in the 'intolerable strabismus' associated with being in the sanatorium – but clearly linked to a 'double' view on love. It involves a pure description of the elision between the seminar tutor, on the one hand, who describes objectively the language of love, but who at the same time is caught up, on the other hand, in the language of love:

> They who speak here is a subject who *has spoken to themselves* the discourse of love, but who at the same time *speaks it to you*. It is within this duplicity, this strabismus, that there is the a*lmost zero* of difference between discourse (D) and amorous discourse (AD), or else the toing-and-froing between the stated [énoncé] and the utterance [énonciation]. (2007a, 352, author's original emphasis)

For Barthes the seminar tutor, 'placed in one of the institutional settings of knowledge', the investigation of the discourse of love is a moment of 'insecurity', of 'discomfort', because the 'stated' is shown to be in its 'infinite return' to the utterance. For personal reasons no doubt, Barthes uses an example which is close to him but not entirely his situation:

> A psychoanalyst in love, or a teacher in love who is writing a thesis on Proust's Albertine or on heroines in Racine's theatre, etc., will have to go through this splitting of language. There will be a play of movement [jeu], a screeching caused by the friction between the two temporalities: between that of the internal text (the amorous text) and that of the external discourse being written: description, analysis, theorisation […]. (352–53)

These two temporalities go directly back to Michelet's 'double grasp', and to what Barthes called the 'dialectic of two temporalities' [dialectique à deux temps] (1953c, 1092–93). It is not just Marxian and Hegelian approaches that persist from his time in the sanatorium, from his radical years of the 1950s; it is also, as we shall now see in

Chapter Two, Michelet's 'truncated' dialectic, the 'amputated' dialectic of *Mythologies* (2009, 187).

The conjunction of the personal consumption in love with that in Revolution does not stop Barthes alluding to their rivalry. In the 1977 *Playboy* interview with Philippe Roger, he seeks to differentiate love and revolution:

> The lover is himself the site of a fierce investment of energy, and he therefore feels himself excluded from other investments of a differing nature. The only human being with whom he could feel complicity would be another lover. After all, it's true that lovers understand each other! But a political militant is, in his fashion, in love with a cause, an idea. And this rivalry is unendurable. On either side. I don't think a political militant could easily put up with someone madly in love. (1985a, 302)

But this, in a way, is Barthes's point. Making the link between being consumed with love and totally devoted to the cause of Revolution in the same person on the one hand needs to be differentiated from passion and revolution *between* persons on the other. It is for this reason that, in the final instance, love and Revolution have moments where they must be divided. Though neither can be done by half, love has implications for immediate social relations including language.

Marty's extreme example (2006, 214) from *A Lover's Discourse* that invokes the 'heavy heart' (52-3) allows him to show what he thinks Barthes is doing. Marty cites the preface to *Critical Essays* where Barthes inverts the usual expected role of literature, that of expressing the inexpressible (though not, states Barthes, through an intentional paradox). To 'unexpress the expressible' (1972, xvii) is, in Marty's words, 'by a conversion of alienated speech into a quotation, to empty it, to erode and neutralise it, allowing language a way out of the already-said [...] to reach possible forms of the zero degree of writing'. And not only does it suggest a strategy of opacity, it points to a new dialectic. Critical of the Marxist vulgate of the time, as he is of the Lacanian one, Marty sees it as Barthes having set up a series of 'reserves, gaps, detours' that avoids the naïve dogmatism of modernity's hardcore theoreticians.

In conclusion, it is not only Marx and Hegel but also Revolution that plays a critical role in a Barthesian understanding of love, to the extent that *A Lover's Discourse* is, potentially, not only Barthes's most psychoanalytical but also his most Marxist essay in that it stretches, contrapuntally, the dialectical and the amorous. So, has he not really shifted between 1946 and 1976? It is difficult – if not sacred – to be a revolutionary, as it is to be in love: but when there is love, Barthes is one. That is certainly a curious, but unmistakeable, dialectic!

The final point is a question: does Barthes's intimate correspondence from 1945–46 represent what *A Lover's Discourse* rejects, namely 'an analysis' of love, a 'psychological portrait' (3)? The replies to his letters from both Robert David and Georges Canetti do not exist (or not, at least, in the public domain), which undermines any 'dialogue' in the ideas discussed. Either way, in both the sanatorium letters and the 1977 essay *A Lover's Discourse*, it is the 'loved object [...] who does not speak'.

Chapter Two

'AMOROUS DIALECTIC'

> [D]emystifying is always enjoyable, except,
> of course, for those who benefit from mystification.
>
> *(Barthes 2002, I, 661).*

In Chapter One, we used a dog-leg structure in the analysis to suggest that Barthes's conception of love is remarkably consistent, from one end of his career to the other, in its use of dialectics. In this chapter, we concentrate on a shorter period of his career, 1954–57, to consider an 'amorous dialectic' that is politicised in a different way.

In an early 'monthly mythology' called 'Phenomenon or myth?' (2002, V, 1022–23), not included in *Mythologies*, Barthes sets out the only strategy that he can see for analysing contemporary myths. Remarkably candid, and neither ironic nor playful, Barthes, here in 1954 at least, describes the political mission of his monthly column. Whenever he sees a new myth (that of Martians or Marlon Brando's wedding) he feels the need to counter the attempts to maintain 'Order' that myth enacts by denouncing and explaining. But here, he concedes, was the dilemma of this political act. Denunciation could only ever be an explanation whose inadequacy and limits he recognizes. Given the nature of human alienation, his explanations of myth must have a dialectical but 'loving' relationship with these myths, the mythologist must be 'engaged with [their] historical moment' in 'a truly amorous dialectic [véritable dialectique d'amour]':

> [T]o the extent that every mythology is the palpable surface of human alienation, it is humanity that is presented to me in any mythology: I hate this alienation, but I understand that, in today's world, it is here only that I can find [retrouver] the humans of my time. (Barthes 2002, V, 1023)

Though there is no mention of the 'amorous dialectic' in *Mythologies* three years later, there is, at the end of 'Myth Today', an echo:

> Any myth with a degree of generality is in fact ambiguous, because it represents the very humanity of those who, having nothing, have borrowed it. To decipher the Tour de France or the 'good French wine' is to cut oneself off from those who are entertained or warmed up by them. (2009, 185)

The difference is that, by 1957, the 'amorous dialectic' has become the 'order of sarcasm', indicative of the mythologist's exclusion from those *'having* nothing', of the intellectual such as Barthes living only a 'theoretical sociality' (2009, 185). Thus, the

1954 formulation – that he can be in touch with his contemporaries *via* the alienation of myth – is forgotten. The word 'palpable' could suggest an aesthetic, feeling, approach, in that *an-aesthetic* represents non-feeling. It would certainly help to confirm the aesthete Barthes we discussed in the Foreword; but this would be to ignore two other dimensions. First, and it is a theme that runs from the ancient Greek chorus through to the lectures on 'How to live together', community is central to the 'amorous dialectic' ('find [retrouver] the humans of my time'); and one to which we return in Chapters Eight and Nine. The second aspect of the 'amorous dialectic' is the political implications, the methodology and 'voice' to be adopted in the analysis of myth, given that myth has the double function of both distorting and revealing the lives of the community at any one time. It is like the *Daily Mirror* newspaper which used to have a strapline: 'If you want to know what is happening in the world, look in the Mirror': the mythologist's connectivity with others in society passes through the alienation of myth; this is the dialectic that is 'amorous'.

At the same time as bringing little-known Marxist theories such as Lukaćs's to bear on contemporary French politics and society, Barthes deliberately couches his analyses in an ancient-Greek optic of myth. In Chapter Three, we will consider the Hellenism in his work on popular theatre, in order to underline the political interest in 1950s tragedy, its definition and its appropriate mode of staging in the modern world. Here the early work of Friedrich Nietzsche links myth and tragedy. Barthes's political interventions in all these areas, we will argue, uses a double voice, in an 'amorous dialectic' in a 'chorus' redolent of ancient-Greek theatre. The 'Commentary par excellence' that is the Greek chorus for Barthes – the 'understood Necessity of [...] deep thought about History' (2002, I, 277) – is part of the 'double voice' in the work of the mythologist.

'Committed sociology'

Mythologies, published in 1957 at the height of France's brutal civil war in Algeria, is doubtless Barthes's most political work, and the one that has had the most political fallout. It would not be unreasonable to place the mythological studies and their final essay on a par with Noam Chomsky's work on media, for the attempt to articulate ideology within political economy. Much has been written on its semiological and protostructuralist premises, but, as Edward Said pointed out with respect to Barthes's literary criticism (1975, 145–47), it is the use of functionalism that dominates. Indeed, there are numerous examples of functionalist expressions in *Mythologies* used to characterize social power. Fundamentally impersonalist, these expressions are what Sartre calls '*praxis* without an author' (1960, 166): 'Order', 'status quo' and 'common sense', all return in *Mythologies* with, as we shall see, astonishing regularity. The aim of this chapter then is to analyse the functionalism deployed in Barthes's study of myth in relation to the 'amorous dialectic', in order to characterize the double voice that the dialectical implies.

The functionalist approach allows Barthes to trace the way in which myth is able to move freely in society, compounded by the intellectual exclusion of the mythologist caused by their using a metalanguage of denunciation and critique of myth – what he calls, following Marx, 'ideologism' (2009, 186): the over-inflated belief that ideas somehow make History. It is Barthes's temporary ('*for the time being*') tactic of using ideologism that we will consider alongside the functionalist methodology in the study of myth.

Functionalism brackets, if not removes, human agency in the creation and circulation of myths, in order to measure a mythical phenomenon by its effects: 'we judge the harm caused by myth, not its inaccuracy' (Barthes 2002, V, 1022). If ideologism informs these acts of judgement, then this approach is linked to political activity for Barthes: 'to introduce explanation into myth is, for the intellectual, the only effective form of political activism [militer]', he wrote in 1953 (2015b, 45). This intellectual voluntarism, part of 'a politically committed current' of sociology described by Barthes in a 1956 radio interview suggests that functionalism and ideologism play a role then in 'the demystification of the whole of social relations' (Barthes interview cited in Stafford 1998, 33). Whilst pointing to the roots of Barthes's method in Marx and Engels's *The Germany Ideology* and even in Nietzsche's *The Birth of Tragedy*, the functionalist sociology deployed in *Mythologies* suggests also the continued influence of phenomenology in radical 1950s thought and writing. However, far from impersonalism and functionalism implying a distance, their use is, paradoxically, a complicity on the part of the mythologist with the people beset by myth, even with myth itself, in a form of analysis that is typical of nineteenth-century French historian of the 'people', Jules Michelet, who 'anticipates the fundamental choice of modern ethnology: to start from functions, not from institutions' (Barthes 1972, 112).

Functionalism and Impersonalism, from Marx to Nietzsche

In 1954 Barthes is reading *The German Ideology*, the rather jumbled and earliest collaboration in 1845 between Marx and Engels – though Barthes regularly refers to this in 'Myth Today' as being by Marx alone (2009, 168n20, 170n22, 178n27). It is extraordinary to think that the place where they had suggested in the 'Eleven theses on Feuerbach' that 'philosophers have only interpreted the world, yet the point is to change it', was widely available in French only from 1952, a full one hundred years after its writing. Quoting regularly from *The German Ideology* in 'Myth Today', the final essay in *Mythologies*, Barthes seems to accept their metaphor of the 'camera obscura' (2009, 168n20), as the metaphorical mechanism to account for the inversion that ideology operates on the human mind's image of the world. The *camera obscura* produces an 'illusion' that hides the material reality of human life, and Marx and Engels famously described this material reality as a practical activity whereby humans in 'developing their material production and their material intercourse, alter, along with this their real existence, their thinking and the products of their thinking' (1974: 47). However this illusionism hiding material reality was not necessarily in Marx's account a sign or imputation of guilt, since the distortion that inverts the true image of the world can be as unconscious as conscious and in no way implied that the person who does so is '*necessarily* a cynical paid servant' of the ruling class that benefits (Tucker 1961, 180–181).

This impersonalism was not just a key element of Marx and Engels's theory of ideology; it went to the heart of the manner in which they wrote. The theatrical voice that Marx in particular uses, especially in the early writings, is no better illustrated than in the opening words of the *Communist Manifesto*. It always perplexes university students when they read, in the opening lines, that 'A spectre is haunting Europe – the spectre of Communism' (1965, 31). They rightly point out that it is strange that a pamphlet trying to win workers to revolutionary communism should begin by making communism into something ghoulish; and Helen Macfarlane, in the first English translation of the *Manifesto* in 1850, makes this all the more stark in her words 'frightful hobgoblin'! (Macfarlane 2015, 261). But this is Marx's highly theatrical language, based on his close reading of ancient Greek tragedy, an 'ironic voice' (Martin 2015, 56) with which he cleverly alludes to the panicked thoughts of the bourgeoisie. In his reading of Maurice Blanchot's 'Three Voices of Marx', Derrida (1994, 17–43) looks in detail at the 'indirect voice' (40-43), but ignores what is called in theatre a 'voice-off'. This voice-off will be a crucial point for our reading of the various mythological analyses, especially 'Novels and Children', in which, as we mentioned in the Foreword, Barthes voices the sexist stereotypes of 1950s France; and the voice-off returns in Chapter Four when we consider 'The Death of the Author' alongside Barthes's reading of Balzac's *Sarrasine*.

This 'ironic voice' is a central essayistic technique in *Mythologies* that, in the manner of Denis Diderot (2002) and Oscar Wilde (1960 [1890]), theatricalizes bourgeois and petty-bourgeois ideology; and, in avoiding an impugning of guilt, it also allows for a more powerful critique of ideology. Thus, Barthes's Marxian commitment to *Mythologies* concentrates instead on acts of explanation.

A good example in *Mythologies* may be 'Poujade and the Intellectuals' in which Barthes excoriates the 1950s xenophobic right-wing leader Pierre Poujade, with his Nigel Farage-style anti-intellectualism and its rejection of 'any form of explicative, committed culture, and what is saved is an "innocent" culture, the culture whose naïveté leaves the tyrant's hands free' (1979, 134). Then again, this commentary on Poujade, appearing in the last paragraph of the final of the 53 mythologies, and coming directly before the theoretical essay 'Myth Today', might not be the best example of impersonalism, because impersonalist critique looks at the how, and not the who, of ideology and its political distortions

It is well-known that semiology and then Structuralism were swiftly denounced by certain sections of the Left, for having evacuated human agency. At the same moment in Spring 1967 as he participates with Barthes in a round-table discussion on tragedy (Simon 1967), Jean-Marie Domenach puts the criticism graphically with respect to 'autonomous activity of consciousness': in structuralism, 'I do not think, *I am thought*; I do not speak, *I am spoken*; I do not act, *I am acted*' (1967, 772). However, Domenach is writing in 1967, a good 10 years after Barthes wrote *Mythologies* during the so-called 'first wave' of Saussurean theory. Indeed, the 'new eleatism' that is Structuralism and which philosopher Henri Lefebvre (1971, 44–110) sees growing in 1966 has barely started in 1957.

At this time in the 1950s, Barthes is in contact with a number of writers who deploy impersonalist approaches. In terms of Marxism, it is the work of Barthes's soon-to-be colleague at the EPHE in Paris, Lucien Goldmann whose *The Hidden God* introduces Barthes to the work of Hungarian Marxist Georg Lukács. Though extant already for over 30 years, even before the start of World War I, Lukács's writings, thanks to Sartre and then to Goldmann, slowly entered intellectual life (Rees 1998, 258n116). Despite

Barthes's denial in 1971 (1998, 254) of any knowledge of Lukács after the Second World War, it is hard to miss the Lukácsian engagement of History in *Writing Degree Zero*, but also in the notion of alienation in the 'amorous dialectic'. Indeed, a key component in Lukács's definition of alienation is the 'impersonal forces, laws of nature which impose themselves on humanity from without' (Stedman Jones 1983 [1971], 13).

Indeed, Said (1984, 131) has suggested that 'Myth Today' follows Lukács in underlining the reification or mythologization of things, that things hide their origins under naturalness, if not also the theory of the very process that created them. Barthes's understanding of Lukács is doubtless filtered through Goldmann's *The Hidden God* as it describes the *Weltanschauung* of the seventeenth-century French ruling class and its reverberations in theatre and theology. Goldmann's ideological critique, or ideologism – an important influence on both Edward Said and Haydn White – locates ideology not so much in individuals, as in the section of the ruling class to whose class outlook their ideas relate. Indeed, Stedman Jones argues (1983, 57) that Lukács's ideologism influenced not just Goldmann, but also Marcuse and, most importantly for Barthes, Sartre.

In a different context of impersonalism, between 1951 and 1954 Barthes is in regular contact with poet and novelist Jean Cayrol whose experience of the Nazi Concentration Camps encouraged a literary aesthetic of human dislocation. Indeed, in a 1954 letter to Cayrol, Barthes wrote: 'The human material of your novels introduces a sociology or a theology, that is to say, an order in which the human entirely absorbs the person' (2018, 135). Furthermore, it is Cayrol who gives his support for Barthes's 1954 book on *Michelet* (1987a), where there is a striking example of historiographical impersonalism.

In 'Michelet The Walker' and 'Michelet The Swimmer', Barthes describes as a 'double grasp' (1987a, 21–22, trans. mod.) the way in which the historian manages, by writing, both to walk with the actors of History (the 'people') – blind (as it were) as they are to the outcome of their actions – whilst narrating this same historical moment from the vantage point of the historian writing in the future. Michelet's 'double grasp' is a dual form of writing, involving, Barthes suggests, 'either the discomfort of progress or else the euphoria of a panorama' (22). It looks then as if Michelet has squared the historian's circle: being able, simultaneously, to be here *and* there, as both historiographer *and* partisan actor *in* History at one and the same time, suggests a dexterity of writerly skill. Might this *double grasp* – 'double apprehension' (1987a, 22) – have an affinity with the 'amorous dialectic'? Are the impersonalism and functionalism deployed in *Mythologies* a form of 'double grasp'?

Before considering the functionalism in Barthes's use of impersonalism, it is worth pausing briefly to nuance Fredric Jameson's view (2010, 326–329) that *Mythologies* belong to an older – (and currently today) out-of-date – form of ideological critique. Jameson prefers Althusser's post-1968 account of Ideological State Apparatuses (ISAs) with which to come to terms with Capitalist ideology in today's twenty-first-century 'late Capitalist' (or 'postmodern') world; precisely because it is related not to the booming economy of 1950s France when Barthes was denouncing myth, but to the neo-liberal era of crisis and illegitimate political elites in today's world of the post-2008 crash. Jameson implies that Althusserianism has much more to say, as a theory of reification and interpellation, about how ideology should be approached in radical thought, in particular in its move away from the 'false-consciousness' model of ideology that predates Marx and which Jameson traces back to the eighteenth-centry philosophers such as Voltaire. Jameson does not suggest that Barthes is using this notion of ideology, rather that it is the Brechtian 'estrangement' of everyday life that appears to define the approach in *Mythologies* (see Sollers's lucid 1971 essay on this, 2017, 46). In fact Jameson considers Barthes's study of myths as a transition to a 'different model of ideology, reification' (328). Barthes's work on myth is nevertheless operating with an out-of-date approach to ideology, and Jameson underlines that we – 'the younger generation' (338) – need not so much an individual critique of instances of ideology, 'to interpret and "demystify" this or that specific literary text' in today's twenty-first-century world; rather, what he calls following Althusser, 'institutional analysis proper' (2010, 338–39), whether this is the 'Institution' of Literature, or any 'general theory of ideology'. His disagreement with what he thinks that Barthes is doing in *Mythologies* stretches to the class determinations assigned by language, though the link between language and class at school (Balibar 1974) that Jameson advocates can work only on a totality of class positions and not in individual circumstances (2010, 355–357).

Jameson seems to be missing a crucial aspect, however, which is Barthes – or the mythologist's – attempts at intervening in myths, not just describing them in particular and/or general political ways; the 'amorous dialectic' could be seen as an interventionist form of denunciation of myth, which, as the conclusion to this chapter will suggest, can be linked to the double voice of the ancient Greek chorus: what Brown (1992, 32) calls 'subversive complicity'.

This can be seen in his famous commentary on the African boy saluting on the front cover of *Paris-Match*. In his writings in Romania, just as the Iron Curtain is falling across the Eastern Bloc in 1948, Barthes makes an important point about how Stalinist language is being used to impose its authoritarian ideology, by way of a quotation from the eighteenth-century renegade Marquis and friend of Voltaire's, Vauvenargues: 'Servitude debases men to the point of making them love it' (2018, 123). It is precisely this 'voluntary servitude' – to cite La Boétie (1574) – that can be seen in the description in 'Myth Today' of the young black soldier on the 1955 cover of *Paris-Match* whom Barthes assumes is saluting the French flag. In order to expose the complex operations of myth, he ironically voices the colonialist pleasure taken in 'the zeal shown […] in serving his so-called oppressors' (139). It is a voicing technique that may not resolve the criticisms made by Moudileno (2019); but its aim to expose colonial ideology precisely as it is used is indebted to an impersonalism (indeed, an impersonation) that reveals how myth functions in creating ideological 'servitude'.

Impersonalist functionalism

If impersonalism and functionalism can be seen working together in tragedy and in historiography in Barthes's analyses of the 1950s, they belong to what Algirdas Greimas calls 'supra-individuality': an anonymous approach that uses 'Durkheimian characters' of language as an 'institution' to consider phenomena in their 'autonomous social dimension' (Greimas 1983, 17). For Durkheim, social language – or myth for Barthes

– reveals 'collective representations' (1995, 436). Other sources for functionalism include the 'functions' described in Louis Hjelmslev's account of language (1968, 53–61), as well as the 'function' of myth in primitive societies as examined by Claude Lévi-Strauss (1963). What distinguishes the use of functionalism in *Mythologies* is that the analyses are socio-politically charged.

Indeed, in the review of *Mythologies* in *Les Lettres Nouvelles* – the monthly journal in which Barthes had published the majority of the book's analyses – Yves Velan praises their 'detergent power': the book was like a 'hand-gun' easily brandished 'at any moment' (Velan cited in Stafford 1998, 73). Part of this weaponry against bourgeois and petty-bourgeois ideology was functionalism.

Mythologies characterizes this ideology using four main figures: common sense, order (more often, Order), status quo and alibi. These four terms appear with remarkable regularity, thereby abruptly nuancing the quotation above as to 'those who benefit from mystification'; for, although the mythologist enjoys exposing myths, rarely do 'those who benefit' actually get named: the ideological enemy in *Mythologies* is largely an impersonal one, an 'impersonal class domination' (Mau 2021, 9–12). Thus, even if Poujade is named by Barthes, it is above all his ideology of 'common sense' that is criticized (1979, 53). Ubiquitous, this 'common sense' can be found in Racinean theatre hidden behind 'the war against intelligence' (1979, 60); in the irrational fear of Martians and the consequent denial of alterity (1979, 29); in the replies in the 'Agony Columns' whose 'knowledge, real and modestly hidden, is always sublimated by the open sesame of contentious bourgeois morality: *good sense*' (1979, 91–92); in the views of the *Figaro* readership for whom strikes 'attack the philosophic basis of bourgeois society, that mixture of morality and logic which is *good sense*' (1979, 99)

Furthermore, bourgeois and petty-bourgeois 'common sense' is supported by an incipient anti-intellectualism, a refusal to explain: 'the morale of the social status quo, in the case of 'Miss Europe 1953', Sylviane Carpentier (1979, 24). The status quo by turn benefits from an absence, an abdication even, in the figure of the 'alibi' which allows ubiquitous myth, at times, to slip away: for example in 'Toys', where Barthes describes 'the alibi of a Nature which has at all times created soldiers, postmen and vespas' (2009, 57). Indeed, it is rare for Barthes to use 'I' in *Mythologies*, and it is, therefore, all the more powerful in the following, betraying at the same time even a certain tiredness on the mythologist's part:

> And I then start to wonder if the fine and touching iconography of the Abbé Pierre is not the alibi which a sizeable part of the nation uses in order, once more, to substitute with impunity the signs of charity for the reality of justice. (2009, 51)

Order

> [O]rder [...] is always a murder in intention.
>
> *(Barthes 1967a, 44–45)*

However, by far the most prevalent of the four impersonal figures of ideology is 'Order' (most often in *Mythologies* with a capital 'O'), a key word for the early Barthes who, in 1953 (1967a, 32), notes how it 'always indicates repression'. 'Order' is the defining feature of the seven types of distortion that myth operates – inoculation; privation of History; identification; tautology; neither-norism; quantification of quality; and statement of fact (2009, 178–83) – and of which inoculation seems to be the most dangerous, and most insidious even with its implication that it requires the participation of the consumer of myth. This is certainly the case in 'Operation Margarine' as it excoriates the French army and its use of torture during the war for Algerian independence: '[t]o instil into the Established Order the complacent portrayal of its drawbacks has nowadays become a paradoxical but incontrovertible means of exalting it' (2009, 39), and in such a way that 'the Established Order is no longer anything but a Manichaean compound and therefore inevitable, one which wins on both counts [...] reliev[ing] you of your progressive prejudices' (40–41).

Barthes repeats the use of direct address to the reader in 'Novels and Children', addressing 'your order' directly and ironically to women, whose freedom depends not on them but on 'his [order]' (2009, 55). This is important when we consider that Weiner (1999) criticizes Barthes for failing to see that women were pleased as mothers to be able to write. This is certainly not an inconsiderable point, but it misses the structural, institutional manner in which sexism operates. 'Order' returns with striking regularity as a Barthesian bugbear in *Mythologies*. In Franco's fascist Spain, 'prosperity' is directly linked in the tourist-orientated *Blue Guide* to the '*application of sound principles of order and hierarchy*' (2009, 88); and in French political posters, the 'photographic convention' of the 'thoughtful gaze' is 'nobly fixed on hidden interests of Order' (2009, 107). In *Astrology* – in contrast to Theodor Adorno's 1953 study of the horoscope (1994, 46–171) which considered the white female middle-class audience of the *LA Times* column to be socially reclusive with obsessive-compulsive tendencies – the stars in Barthes's analysis are silent about any idea of 'total alienation', 'never suggest that the order could be overturned' (2009, 113–14). In contrast to Adorno's Freudian critique, Barthes's Marxian functionalist impersonalism asserts 'order' as a dangerous inoculation with which society 'protects' the population, but whose acts of injection are not attributed, not attributable, to anyone or any specific human agency.

Consequently, the figures of the 'natural' in *Mythologies*, of the 'what goes without saying', are the expression of an impersonalist ideology, devoid of human and individual action in the creation of myths. Neither the readership of the Agony Aunt nor Miss Europe, neither the readership of *Le Figaro* nor even 'a sizeable part of the nation', is involved directly in creating myths of order or common sense; rather *Mythologies* points to an anonymous social 'Order', hidden behind the 'innocent' praxis of everyday life. Thus, to Macdonald (2003, 56) who asks: 'is it the bourgeoisie or ideology which generates myth?', Barthes would probably have two different answers: first, 'order' (or the 'status quo'); in other words, the social system Capitalism, but signified in reverse, in a functionalist–impersonalist way (we should remember that Marx never used the term 'Capitalism', since Capital is above all a relation, not a system); second, and more contentiously, language.

Obviously, in all the examples we have given above, the analysis of 'order' involves 'specific accounts of individual ideologies' both 'concrete and historical' (Jameson, 339–40); but even before moving onto Barthes's systematization of these in the final essay 'Myth Today', we can see above that the use of impersonalism has already begun to 'institutionalize' the critique. It is already a Hegelian technique in Barthes's first essay in 1953, *Writing Degree Zero*, which posits *écriture*, in its dialectical relationship with 'Literature' (with a capital L), as institution (Barthes 1967a; Lübecker 2010), seeing the writing adopted by any writer, following the 1848 European revolutions, as a 'function' of both 'History and the stand we take in it', of 'the relationship between creation and society' (1967a, 7, 20; Greimas 2000, 386). In *Mythologies*, functionalist analysis takes institutional-ideological critique one stage further.

Functionalism – and impersonalism – in acts of exposing myth and ideology has the distinct merit of avoiding conspiracy theories, taking into account also the diffuse nature and mobility of myth. But this form of analysis comes at a cost. Greimas expresses reservations as to the dangers of functionalism and its elision of human agency. Quoting Lévi-Strauss's idea that individuals, as much as human society, are able to create only by using 'certain combinations drawn from an *ideal repertoire*', Greimas wonders whether, in using functionalist analysis, 'the notion of *ideal repertoire* could be reconciled with a conception of history as a creative process' (2000, 382). This reservation raises the question as to the central contradiction in *Mythologies*: on the one hand Barthes insists on History as the counter-weight to myth, whilst, on the other, the analysis posits myth as an ahistorical social function. This apparent contradiction is reinforced by the use of functionalism in the 'amorous dialectic'.

Dialectic of Situation

The 'Phenomenon or myth?' mythology appears in the left-wing monthly *Lettres nouvelles*, soon after the November 1954 uprising in the Aurès mountains which began the Algerian War. Barthes had already bitterly attacked the press fascination with Church, Army and Monarchy, with Martians and the weddings of Miss Europe and Marlon Brando. Now he turns his attention to things more literary, not impressed by the disparaging comments made against René Etiemble who had recently published the first two volumes of his 'Myth of Rimbaud' (1961, 1968).

Rather than a traditional account of Rimbaud's poetry, Etiemble lists the varying modes of reception of Rimbaud in France and elsewhere. 'The value to me of an echo, a book or an article would be inversely proportional to its objective value', he wrote in the introduction (Etiemble 1968, 17); rather than an exhaustive bibliography, he outlines the various mythical images of Rimbaud, glimpsing the reasons for their success. Criticism of Etiemble's 'mythic' interpretation of Rimbaud appeared in a special number of the traditional literary weekly *Les Nouvelles Littéraires*, commemorating the centenary of Rimbaud's birth. Criticizing the reviewer in *Les Nouvelles littéraires* of Etiemble's project, Georges Duhamel, Barthes attacks the way the Rimbaud myth is ignored in favour of Rimbaud the 'phenomenon', 'that is', he writes, 'devoid of causes and finalities, detached from all History':

> At *Les Nouvelles littéraires* the Sun clearly stopped rising years ago, when the Poet was (to quote Georges Duhamel) a 'phenomenon': that is, devoid of causes and finalities, detached

from all History (whether coming before or after the poetry was written), and functioning like a celestial voice reaching the individual ear of a reader who is also devoid of history and society. (Barthes 2002, V, 1022)

The refusal of myth points to an important general attitude towards myth. The political problem in reducing 'obscurantism', Barthes suggests, was not to 'oppose the myth to its truth, like illness to health', but to understand its contemporary significance:

> What matters is the general historical reality in which the myth appears; it is in the name of this History that we must judge this myth, and not in the name of an essence of Rimbaud: we judge the harm caused by the myth, and not at all its error. (1022–23)

The functionalist importance of 'harm' is clear to see here. To gauge a myth by its effects is part of functionalist critique, which joins with the impersonalization of its origins and therefore of those responsible. To discuss Rimbaud as a 'phenomenon' of poetic 'inspiration' – rather than to consider the way his readership since has 'consumed' him as 'myth' – represents the 'least "humanist"' act, because it is the 'one that refuses History' (2002, V, 1022).

The impersonal and functionalist approach that we have characterized, *pace* Jameson, as an incipient 'institutional' critique of Capitalism brings, however, as we saw, the risk of exclusion, of 'ideologism'. However, even here, we need to be alert to Barthes's dialectical manoeuvrings especially those *between* the individual mythological studies.

For example, in 'Racine is Racine' and 'Blind and Dumb criticism', Barthes criticizes those who would deny the explanatory power of the critic; and yet, in 'Adamov and Language', he berates those who do try to 'explain' a work of radical avant-garde theatre by calling up, as he wrote dismissively, 'the enormous cavalry of the symbol' (1979, 57). In Richard Klein's review of *Mythologies* (1973), this contradiction is indicative of a move in Barthes's work from thematic to structuralist forms of criticism; for Andrew Brown (1992, 26–32), it signifies 'drift'. However, there is a dialectical strategy at work here. When the bourgeois critic tries to hide from reality by invoking the ineffable and the inexplicable nature of Racinean theatre, Barthes, the attentive demystifier, is ready to oppose this with explanatory categories; but when the bourgeois critic attempts to 'neutralize' the scandal of Adamov's absurdist–materialist theatre by making it 'mean' something, the mythologist is on hand to stress the play's radical 'alterity', that is, by a refusal to 'explain' Adamov. The supple and attentive dialectical strategy at the heart of Barthes's acts of criticism in *Mythologies* is one in which he positions himself in opposition to bourgeois critics, but one which constantly shifts position as bourgeois criticism and ideology moves its emphasis:

> [Humans] do not have with myth a relationship based on truth but usage: they depoliticize according to their needs. Some mythical objects are left dormant for a time; they are then no more than vague mythical schemata whose political load seems almost neutral [indifférente]. But this indicates only that their situation has brought this about, not that their structure is different. (Barthes 2009, 171)

An 'amorous dialectic' strategy involves treating myths at once as a reflection of human alienation and (as Marx put it in relation to religion) 'a heart in heartless world'. In opposition to Lévi-Strauss's injunction, 'In order to reach the real, one must first bracket the lived [écarter le vécu]' (Lévi-Strauss, in Lefebvre 1971, 63), Barthes is taking myth as the only way to apprehend human consciousness, and yet also as a singular distortion of human values. Rather than the 'modernity-becoming-postmodernity' idea often attributed to *Mythologies*, the mobility of demystification locates *Mythologies* in a modernist, dialectical view of culture. Whereas Marianne De Koven (2004, 115) places Barthes's denunciations of myth in a 'neo-avant-garde' camp – unaware that Barthes is sceptical of the avant-garde both in *Mythologies* and in other 'mythologies' excluded from the volume, not to mention in his popular-theatre writings – Barthes is interested, in ideological terms, in how myth functions, and not in critiquing high and/or popular culture. In this optic, the objects studied in *Mythologies* are taken merely as vehicles (with elements, as Barthes admits, of his savouring them) for myth. Ironically, De Koven thinks she is saving *Mythologies* from the postmodern narrative inherent in cultural studies – 'leftist intellectual contempt for mass culture has been written off in postmodern cultural studies as elitism' (120). Where in *Mythologies* does Barthes show contempt for the objects of mass culture? It is rather petty-bourgeois ideology, dominant in mass culture, that he wants to expose.

The 'amorous dialectic' encapsulates the spirit in which Barthes considers the numerous cultural objects analysed, to be contrasted with the writings of another Frankfurt School essayist, Siegfried Kracauer, whose interwar view of the 'mass ornament' does seem to disdain aspects of mass culture (1995).

Indeed, the narrative of 'modernism/avant-garde' as the form of resistance to bourgeois literary-classical hegemony that Barthes takes is not a real understanding of the rise, and compromise, of the 'critic'. The avant-garde is merely a tactical ally in *Mythologies*. For Barthes it is the 'literary' in general, the 'for nothing', valueless and pointless activity that so offends and repels petty-bourgeois ideology; indeed, Maurice Blanchot, in his 1957 review of *Mythologies* (2000, 48), points to this 'frail, scarcely existing literature, [...] the affirmation most staunchly opposed to myth'. Responsible, critical practice is anti-bourgeois, precisely because it is pointless and gratuitous. *Mythologies* foresees the later Barthes tactic of 'escape forwards' [fuite en avant], of taking 'classical' culture (Racine, Balzac, Proust and Flaubert) and recuperating it, 'stealing' it back: he certainly does not wish to enact 'utopian rage' on 'repressive bourgeois forms' (De Koven 127). The mobility of his dialectical criticism in *Mythologies* – a mobility between, ironically, the immobility of naming on the one hand and the flux of History and explanation on the other – is one in which Barthes aims to be where petty-bourgeois ideology is not; it is, following Sartre, in situation. Moreover, De Koven does not notice the contradictions in *Mythologies*, its dialectical strategy, when she describes Barthes's 'modernist/counter-cultural' ideology in his valorization of nature (over chemistry), poetry and pleasure over use, the essential over the contingent, the timeless over the peripheral (De Koven 125–26). In other words, De Koven is not paying attention to (Barthes's view of) the complexity, the 'mobility', of 'immobile' petty-bourgeois thought: the mythology 'Plastic' is judged to be a sign of Barthes's (future) postmodern sensibility, without consideration for the 'contradiction' it displays with the 'Toys' mythology. In other words, *Mythologies* is 'counter-ideological', not 'counter-cultural' whose 'hyper-dialectics' is a recognition of complexity, as it shows how ideology – myth – attaches itself to forms.

Myth, after all, is, as Barthes insisted, a language and a form, one which transforms a meaning into form; and it is a function (2009, 155), but which is in some sense limited: 'Myth is not defined by the object of its message, but by the way in which it utters this message: there are no formal limits to myth, there are no "substantial" ones' (2009, 131). A myth can attach itself to any object, but cannot say everything, nor cover all angles of it: hence the oppositional critic finding its opposite(s), in situation.

It is here that functionalism becomes a key element. By considering, indeed measuring, myths by the harm they cause, functionalism is concerned with the conditions in which myth operates. Of the seven types of mythical operations, it is inoculation that dominates in Barthes's analyses; it is also the most directly political. The medical metaphor – despite inoculation's positivity in today's COVID world of vaccinations – seems very apt in critiquing bourgeois liberal democracies, and this is true today. For example, a recent online post by the French radical media watch-dog *Médiapart* exposes the silence surrounding colonial massacres during France's war in Algeria between 1954 and 1962 (Le Cour Grandmaison 2020), thereby suggesting – *pace* Langlet (2002) – the continued currency of *Mythologies*.

In Chapter Four, we will return to the origins of the metaphor of 'vaccination' in the writings of Jules Michelet. First, it is important to consider how its functionalist and impersonalist approach connects to the political dimension of *Mythologies*. In 'A Sympathetic Worker', a critique of the film by Elia Kazan, *On The Waterfront*, Barthes does not mince his words:

> [W]e are being given, once again, that truth-vaccine whose latest mechanism I have discussed [...]; we project the exploitive functions of management onto a small group of gangsters, and by this minor confessed evil, posited as a trivial and awkward pustule, we disregard the real evil, we avoid naming it, we exorcise it. (Barthes 1979, 39)

This functionalist reading – exposing the ideological operations of bourgeois ideology in preserving 'Order' using an 'alibi' that confirms 'common sense' – is already a distanced and impersonal, if not anonymized, one due to the fictional status of the film. Other examples of functionalist critique of myth in *Mythologies* are however more real. 'Steak and Chips' begins by locating its analysis of national(ist) myths of food in an 'old film', *Deuxième Bureau contre Kommandantur* (1939, directed by Robert Bibal); but Barthes soon moves directly to a news-item carried by the glossy politically-conservative magazine *Paris-Match* in which the General Castries, having returned from the military rout of France's colonial forces at Dien Bien Phu in Viet-Nam, is reported to have devoured steak and chips in front of the cameras, which, in Barthes's words, 'was certainly not a vulgar materialist reflex, but an episode in the ritual of approving [approbation] regained French community' (2009, 71, trans. mod.). Even if the target is well chosen – 'The general [...] knew that [...] chips are the alimentary sign of Frenchness' – it is the function that links the French readership to the alimentary sign, whilst removing, in the second level of signification, all human agency. It is the sign – without any precise origin – that is speaking here; in other words – and using the words from Paul Claudel that Barthes had cited as the epigraph to his 1941 postgraduate dissertation on ancient Greek theatre – '[i]t is not an author who speaks, but speech which acts' (Barthes 1941; Claudel 1929, 87).

Functionalism is used also in what has been called, guardedly, the 'happy' myth (Knight 1997, 37–43). In 'Paris Not Flooded' for example, Barthes describes with pleasure the 'suspension' of 'functions' (1979, 32). However, functionalism in *Mythologies* aims principally to denounce the ideology that allows injustice. Indeed, Barthes's Marxian, if not materialist, explanation of the ideological abuse of the real – 'in the contemporary bourgeois society, the passage from the real to the ideological is defined as that from an *anti-physis* to a *pseudo-physis*' (2009, 168) – underlines also that 'the essential function of myth' is that of the 'naturalization of the concept' (155).

Some on the Marxist Left may invoke Antonio Gramsci to regret the functionalism used in *Mythologies*. For Gramsci, functionalism reduces all manifestations of culture to the 'social system', thereby reinforcing the status quo (Lears 1985, 572–73). Indeed Gramsci sees 'common sense' as being developed separately by society's different groups (Ligouri 2016, 85–119; Crehan 2016, x); but, even though it is concerned with a group's passions, beliefs and practices, as Barthes's is, Gramsci's 'common sense', albeit often conservative, has 'good sense' in it (1971, 328); whereby, it plays out a 'contradictory consciousness' in its practical transformation of the world (329–33) and it is here that Gramsci's philosophy of praxis (and not necessarily a codeword for Marxism) resists dogmatism (356–57, 178, 407), while disallowing any attempt to link 'contradictory consciousness' to Barthes's 'amorous dialectic'. We will return to Gramsci in a moment.

Class versus Human Nature

One of the advantages of functionalist critique in Barthes's work on bourgeois and petty bourgeois myth is that 'human nature', including all apparent singularity, is integrated into a social human nature, thereby working with Marx' dialectical notion in the sixth of the 'Theses on Feuerbach', in which 'the human essence is no abstraction inherent in each single individual. In its reality it is the ensemble of the social relations' (Marx/Engels 1974, 122). Barthes follows the young Marx of the 1840s for whom there is no 'man' only classes in the historical-materialist account that stresses the '"socialised" or depersonalised' (Tucker 1961, 166).

In his functionalist–impersonalist approach, Barthes applies a class-based analysis. In a 1955 mythology not included finally in the *Mythologies*, 'Enfants-copies', he follows the socialized and depersonalized optic in his account of the petty bourgeoisie:

> [The petty bourgeoisie is] an intermediary class that still knows the cruel realities of wage labour, but which sees its own social promotion only by way of mechanically copying bourgeois freedoms. (Barthes 2002, I, 551)

In 'Myth Today', this Marxian characterization of the petty bourgeoisie, the 'intermediate classes', points to the way in which bourgeois ideology can both 'penetrat[e]' into these classes whilst allowing the bourgeois class 'to lose its name' (2009, 167). The 'residue' of petty-bourgeois 'norms' that it produces makes for a political alliance between bourgeois and petty bourgeois that has dominated French political life since the mid-nineteenth century. The 'symbiosis' has wider ideological implications. Barthes plays on the expression in French 'société anonyme' ('joint-stock company') to describe the bourgeoisie, as it also suggests the ex-nomination that the ruling class performs, forming 'a certain regime of ownership, a certain order, a certain ideology': the bourgeoisie, despite its economic naming as the capitalist class, as ideology and as politics, 'completely disappears' (2009, 164), in words that echo the 'etherealized ideology' that Stedman Jones (1983, 43–44) sees in the early Lukács's conception of class power as one which ignores entirely the bourgeois State. Here then there is an isomorphism between on the one hand the way in which the bourgeoisie as ideology can 'ex-nominate itself without restraint' (165) and the use of impersonalism in Barthes's critique on the other. In one sense, impersonalism is the condition of reality as an 'anonymous ideology' and which is everywhere: 'everything, in everyday life, is dependent on the representation which the bourgeoisie *has and makes us have* of the relations between man and the world' (166). With this in mind, Barthes contrasts the political world to that of myth, the former being the 'whole of human relations in their real social structure, in their power of making the world' (169).

Mepham (1972, 18) sees weaknesses in Marx's metaphor of the *camera obscura*, preferring (as does Jameson) Althusser's theory of Ideological State Apparatuses (1971b); Mepham (14) rejects also the notion of self-delusion, of tricking oneself, imputed to ideology and to myth as a sign of 'self-persuasion', suggesting instead that the origins of our illusions towards reality are, following the Marx of *Capital* rather than of *The German Ideology*, to be found in the 'phenomenal' itself. Barthes seems to make a similar point:

> These 'normalized' forms attract little attention [...], their origin is easily lost. They enjoy an intermediate position: being neither directly political, nor directly ideological, they live peacefully between the action of the militants and the quarrels of the intellectuals; more or less abandoned [...] they gravitate towards the enormous mass of the undifferentiated, of the insignificant, in short, nature. (2009, 166)

And this is all the more true for myth:

> [J]ust as bourgeois ideology is defined by the abandonment of the name 'bourgeois', myth is constituted by the loss of historical quality of things: in it, things lose the memory that they were once made [de leur fabrication]. (169)

Thus, if the distortion of myth originates in the 'phenomenal' realm, it is thanks to the object's 'forgetting' of its origins, an element in its becoming-object that changes the sensuous object into an impersonal commodity, which, in Marx's word, is 'mute' (cited in Mau 2021); and it is from this further impersonalism that Barthes sees depoliticization emerging (170–72), as it too benefits from the ex-nomination, from the loss of its memory, as Marx suggested, of their having been made by humans (170). In order to regain some of this lost memory or forgotten identity of the object, Barthes now constructs a debate with Marx.

For Marx, in *The German Ideology*, this argument is summarized, Barthes reminds us (2009, 170n22), in his metaphor of the cherry-tree which acts as an example of an apparent 'nature' but which is in fact but the product of human cultivation – fabrication – of the world (Marx/Engels 1974, 62). By way of a dialogue, or dialectical argument, with Marx, Barthes replies directly to the arboricultural metaphor by invoking the 'woodcutter' (2009, 172), part of Barthes's 'xyloglossia' (Smith 2014). Xyloglossia designates the human who acts directly, that is, in a non-mediatized way (except, of course for the axe, but which is itself a human-made object), upon the 'counter-nature' that is the cherry-tree. Indeed, for Marx, 'language *is* practical consciousness' – 'Where there exists a relationship, it exists for me: the animal does not enter into "relations" with anything, it does not enter into any relation at all. For the animal, its relation to others does not exist as a relation' (Marx/Engels 1974, 51). This then allows Barthes not only to consider myth as 'stolen' speech, but also, more optimistically, to propose one, but just one, type of language that, truly political, destroys myth:

> [R]evolutionary language proper cannot be mythical. Revolution is defined as a cathartic act meant to reveal the political load of the world: it *makes* the world; and its language, all of it, is functionally absorbed in this making. It is because it generates speech which is *fully*, that is to say initially and finally political, and not like myth, speech which is initially political but finally natural, that Revolution excludes myth. Just as bourgeois ex-nomination characterizes at once bourgeois ideology and myth itself, revolutionary denomination identifies revolution and the absence of myth. [...]. Left-wing myth supervenes precisely at the moment when revolution changes itself into 'the Left', that is, when it accepts to wear a mask, to hide its name, to generate an innocent meta-language and to distort itself into 'Nature'. (2009, 174)

The 'woodcutter', by using an immediate language – both direct and transformative –, cuts down myth, including 'left-wing myth'. It is a perspective emanating from Brecht's theatre – above all in its representation in the theatre photography of Roger Pic, as we will see in Chapter Three – in which, according to Barthes, 'the world can be changed' (1972, 38).

However, the mythologist is unfortunately not able to be the 'woodcutter'. Not only is the mythologist unable to see the 'Promised Land' (2009, 186), they cannot 'speak' the Citroen D.S. car in the way that 'the mechanic, the engineer, even the user' can. Once 'condemned to meta-language' and thereby restricted to ideologism (186), the 'exclusion', once linked to functionalism, itself risks participating in the creation of myths.

This is the critique by Velan of the approach in *Mythologies*, who, as we saw above, praised the book's pocket-weapon format. But for Velan the myth of the 'general strike' in the work of the anarcho-syndicalist Georges Sorel is augmented by the functionalism deployed:

> [A]ll the material is brought together: a 'meta-language' borrowed from workers' traditions, a sign of the taking of power becoming form, into which slides by turn (let's have a bit of

fun) the concept of 'galvanicity', and which then becomes a new signification that through usage has gone through the same transfer as 'quoniam nominor leo': just as the lion in Latin reminds us to make the grammatical agreement, so the strike serves only to maintain the cohesion of the strikers. (Velan 1957, 118)

Thus, unwittingly foreseeing a section of Barthes's 1970 essay on Japan, *Empire of Signs*, which describes what we might call the 'galvanicity' of Japan's revolutionary students the *Zengakuren* generated by their militant slogans in their 'riot, functional as it is' (1982b, 183–86), Velan points to a real danger in this type of functional approach to myth.

Not only was the early Lukács drawn to Sorel (Stedman Jones 1983 [1971], 32), it is interesting to note also that, in his comparison of Barthes and Sorel, Tager (1986) differentiates Barthes by his negative attitude towards myth. This, as we saw with De Koven above, is a misunderstanding. Barthes declares at the end of 'Myth Today' (2009, 187n30) that he 'savoured' the compactness of the objects, in a manner that resembled the sensual of the phenomenal world which for Marx was the 'sensuous activity' and whose absence Marx regretted in Feuerbach's theories. With the 'amorous dialectic', the mythologist seems to accept that they are pulled between two opposing tasks: that of criticizing and denouncing on the one hand, and, on the other, to watch reality evaporate. It is a perspective which, while marrying functionalism and ideologism, hesitates between a historical materialism and phenomenological culturalism. Therefore, the anti-ideological struggle proposed in 'Myth Today' insists more and more on a double understanding of the society ruled by those who, anonymously, hold social power and who must be denounced in two separate dimensions that are described (as so often with important political points in Barthes's writing) in a footnote: '[T]he bourgeoisie should be understood only as synthesis of its determinations and its representations' (2009, 165n17). The bourgeois class, in other words, rules, partly, because the opposition does not attend to *both* of these dimensions.

It suggests that there is a *double* grasp deployed in *Mythologies*, whereby the critical analysis combines both historical-materialist determinisms *and* cultural representations, that is, an analysis inspired by both Marx *and* Nietzsche. Indeed, we will see in Chapter Three, when we consider Barthes's writings on tragedy from the same period of the 1950s, that Marx and Nietzsche vie with each other.

Pace Tager (1986), Barthes seems to like myths, or rather their capacity to put the mythologist in touch with people. Indeed, the 'amorous dialectic' nuances of Henri Lefebvre's 'pleasant' commentary (1971, 19) which suggests that Barthes's 'dialectical thought' was 'a style *cool*' and not '*hot* – tragic, uneven, often passionate'. But Barthes's approach is perhaps closer to Sorel's than either Tager or Lefebvre might concede, in that Sorel saw in 'social myths' no block to humans' ability to 'derive some profit from all the observations made', nor any 'obstacle' to 'normal occupations' (Sorel 1990, 117–18); and Sorel considered the general strike – in a functionalist way, it must be said – as 'the *myth* in which the whole of socialism is encapsulated' (120). However, we must not forget Barthes's critique in "The Man in the Street on Strike' of the way in which petty-bourgeois 'common sense' considers strikes as not the general public's concern (1979, 99–102); nor should we forget that myths are 'the palpable surface of human alienation' for Barthes. Rather than Sorel then, it is perhaps more the early Nietzsche and his positive attitude towards myth, which Sorel discusses only in relation to the general historical Hellenism of the German philosopher (Sorel 1990, 233–35). Nietzsche's infamous rejection of the dialectic – be it Socratic, Hegelian, Marxian or others – seems to have contributed to the unorthodox nature of Barthes's 'amorous dialectic', in that 'Myth does away with all dialectics' (2009, 170).

Ideologism against Myth

Our discussion of functionalism and impersonalism seems to locate *Mythologies* in Jameson's third type of ideological critique (2010, 331–32) in which capitalist ideology is 'in the very process by which daily life is systematically reorganized on all its levels […] so that one might say, metaphorically, that the subject of this process is not an individual or a group but rather capital itself' – though Jameson seems to dismiss in ideological critique 'the analogies and influences between the commodity form and the forms of language' owing to the 'unproblematical affirmation of identity between social and linguistic forms' (354).

For Gramsci, ideologism tends to obscure the fact that Marxism had to fight hard with other ideologies; this is especially evident in the work of Croce, whom Thomas (2010, 261) considers as an early post-Marxist. Gramsci also resists also attempts to liquidate Marxism by ideologism (1971, 399) 'an exaggeration of the voluntarist and individual elements' in history (178), something that has been forgotten in Eurocommunism and post-Marxism's more recent use of Gramsci (Jackson 2020, 143). Barthes's reluctant use of ideologism nevertheless locates his work on myth in the Lukácsian camp.

It is not simply the idea of the 'colonised peoples' as the new proletariat (Barthes 2009, 137n24) that resembles the neo-Hegelian idealism in Lukács of *History and Class Consciousness* roundly criticized by Merleau-Ponty (1955, 283). Barthes explicitly defends the 'early Lukács' (186) against the Zhdanovian view of the transparency of language and Stalin's belief that language can be an aspect of reality that is impervious to ideology. Putting forward the view of language as a tool that is classless and outside of the base-superstructure question, Stalin's view (1973) offered a sphere of unmediated access to human reality which, according to Pierre Daix (1957, 311), showed Stalin's view, rather surprisingly, to be the opposite of a 'mechanical and schematic Marxism'. However, drawing on the work of the lexicologist Georges Matoré (1953, 27–31) – colleague of Greimas and Barthes's PhD supervisor for a short period in 1952 – Barthes uses Marx's example of the cherry tree as a rebuttal. Indeed, even though Stalin (1973, 414) claimed knowledge of at least major parts of *The German Ideology*, he failed to see that Marx (or Paul Lafargue in his pamphlet *Language and Revolution*) considered there to be a 'class character' to language especially in its direct material links to human practice, relations and property (Marx/Engels 1974, 47, 50–51, 100–03, 118). As N. Y. Marr noted, Stalin believed (1973, 415–417) that '"class" languages' and '"class" grammars' were 'fairytales' (418).

Marx had roundly criticized the German 'ideologists' for their petty-bourgeois 'universal love of mankind' (1974, 120) with its fabrication of '"absolutes"'. In a complex move, Barthes defends but also distances himself from Lukács's version of ideologism:

> [T]he mythologist [...] constantly runs the risk of causing reality which they purport to protect, to disappear; [...] the mythologist is condemned to metalanguage. This exclusion [...] is called ideologism. Zhdanovism has roundly condemned it (without proving, incidentally, that it was, *for the time being*, avoidable), in the early Lukács, [...] and Goldmann. (2009, 186, trans. mod.)

Despite his dislike of Stalin and Zhdanov's views on language and ideology, Barthes seems to agree in part with their critique of ideologism. Ideologism, argues Barthes, resolves alienated reality only by an 'amputation', not by a dialectical synthesis, and hence a dilemma for the critical thinker. In an implicit comparison with Lucien Goldmann's work on seventeenth-century thought, *The Hidden God*, Barthes chooses Blaise Pascal, and then wine, as his examples:

> The mythologist gets out of this [ideologistic aporia] the best they can: they deal with the goodness of wine, not with the wine itself, just as the historian deals with Pascal's ideology, not with the *Pensées* in themselves. (187, trans. mod.)

Here is then, implicitly, the 'amorous dialectic' we identified from 1954. In order best to get round the dilemma, Barthes suggests that we are condemned to 'drift' ('voguer'), for which the 'amorous dialectic' has now only the faintest of traces:

> [T]here is as yet only one possible choice, and this choice can bear only on two equally extreme methods: either to posit a reality which is entirely permeable to history, and ideologize; or, conversely, to posit a reality which is *ultimately* impenetrable, irreducible, and, in this case, poetize. In a word, I do not yet see a synthesis between ideology and poetry (by poetry, I understand, in a very general way, the search for the inalienable meaning of things). (187)

At the same time, Barthes is also keen to suggest a Marxian dimension to alienation. He insists that myth hides its own first-order generation of meaning (2009, 199) – replicating how Marx suggested that Capitalism hides its social relations beneath a fetishized set of commodities. For Marx, things take on the appearance of social relations – in the ultimate example of money – just as for Barthes it is 'as if myth shifted the formal system of the first signification sideways' (137). This implicit Marxian parallel in Barthes's semiological work reoccurs in the later work on food, clothing and shelter, not to mention in the much later seminars on the discourse of love.

'Amputated' dialectic

> The study of myth leads us to contradictory findings.
>
> *(Lévi-Strauss 1963, 208, trans. mod.)*

At bottom, it would only be the
degree zero which could resist myth.

(Barthes 2009, 157)

The second dialectical tactic that Barthes adopts in *Mythologies* is the 'amputated' dialectic. In 'Myth Today', he is quite clear about the formalist nature of his semiological enterprise: 'Semiology is a science of forms, since it studies significations apart from their content' (2009, 134): 'one cannot therefore say too often that semiology can have its unity only at the level of forms, not des contents' (137). Agreeing with Stalin's cultural thug, Zhdanov, when the latter berates the philosopher G. F. Alexandrov for suggesting that the planet has a 'spherical structure' when he should have not confused form and structure – at the infamous 1947 philosophy conference in Moscow Zhdanov had rejected Alexandrov's philosophy as 'idealist, bourgeois and decadent' – Barthes in turn accuses Zhdanov of making the same conflation of form and structure in the socialist-realist doctrine: 'The danger, [...] is to consider forms as ambiguous objects, half-form and half-substance, to endow form with a substance of form' (134-5).

At first, 'Myth Today' follows the argument put forward in *Anti-Dühring* (Engels 1954 [1878]), the collection of essays that Engels published defending his and Marx's use of the dialectic with its tripartite definition of quantity-into-quality (an important counter in *Mythologies* to petty-bourgeois ideology's constant quantifying); the unity of opposites; and the negation of the negation. However, to the recognized sciences upon which Engels builds his defence of dialectics, Barthes adds semiology as a new science within this unity:

> The important thing is to see that the unity of an explanation cannot be based on the amputation of one or the other of its approaches, but, as Engels said, on the dialectical coordination of the particular sciences it makes use of. This is the case with mythology: it is part both of semiology inasmuch as it is a formal science, and of ideology inasmuch as it is a historical science: it studies ideas-in-form. (Barthes 2009, 135)

Yet, Barthes seems to justify this same amputation when he defends ideologism against Stalinism at the end of the essay. Having dismantled both bourgeois and petty-bourgeois ideology in the preceding 53 essays, he proceeds at the end of *Mythologies* to a theorization of the semiological method that he has used, but this is done in the political and cultural context of 1956. Demoralized by the marked decline in the fortunes of a truly popular theatre in France, of which he had been an active member between 1953 and 1956, Barthes characterizes the position of the mythologist as one in which the 'Promised Land' cannot be seen; this leads the mythologist to accept that that they are, in some sense, excluded from a truly people's culture and that consequently ideologism, as a form of metalanguage, must be operated from the outside of contemporary culture, in what Stedman Jones (1983, 39) calls the early Lukács's view of the dominant ideology as the 'saturation of the social totality by the ideological essence of a pure class subject'. There is none of the 'catharsis' which Gramsci saw (using Croce's metaphor) in Dante's *Inferno*, whereby the subaltern class is seen to break through, to become a genuine class capable of hegemony (Thomas 2010, 294).

But this ideologism, Barthes insists, is better than Stalinist abdication:

> It is true that ideologism resolves the contradiction of alienated reality by an amputation, not a synthesis (but as for Zhdanovism, it does not even resolve it): wine is objectively good, and *at the same time*, the goodness of wine is a myth: here is the aporia. (2009, 187)

Here Barthes is departing from Engels's 'unity of explanation', and it is surely the third category of the dialectic (the negation of the negation) that ideologism is discarding, or at least radically modifying. The temporary, tactical use of ideologism (despite its idealism) in the denunciation of myth is a forestalling, a truncation, of the dialectic as one which sees the negation, in turn, itself, negated. The aporia seems to be a mutated version of the 'amorous dialectic', shorn of its romanticist notions of community; and it is to become – in dialectical terms, the 'amputated synthesis' – the overall method of Barthesian analysis for the rest of his career.

In contrast to definition given in the *Neutral* twenty years later as a '"logical difficulty with no resolution"' (2005, 68), but one which leaves open, according to Clerc's preface (xxiv), the possibility of a positive 'atopia', the 'aporia' in 'Myth Today' is not ambivalent. It is the acceptance, against the 'palpable surface of human alienation' that Barthes had originally seen in the 'amorous dialectic', that the demystifying intellectual is cut off from the objects of myth, and for which ideologism is the only, albeit 'temporary, solution. Thus ideologism's 'amputation' of the dialectic in 'Myth Today' takes on a strategic, rather than simply tactical, importance:

> Against a certain quixotism of synthesis, quite platonic incidentally [alas], all criticism must consent to the *ascesis*, to the artifice of analysis; and in analysis, it must match method and language. (2009, 134, trans. mod.)

At the level of experience ['vie'] Barthes concedes, that method and language are part of a totality, but on the level of science there needs to be certain self-discipline in scientific analysis. It is here that the formalism of semiology has a crucial role to play in ideological critique (though it is not an ideologism). Part of a 'responsible', politically committed formalism, the 'amputated' dialectic is the most supple and mobile weapon in the battle against what Macdonald has called myth's 'motility' (2003), its ability to move around but to appear logically motivated.

Indeed, though following Marx's idea in the postface to the second edition *Capital* that the dialectic is like 'an abomination for the bourgeoisie', the Barthes of *Mythologies* uses the dialectic as a weapon against the 'immobilism' of bourgeois and petty-bourgeois myth; but his analysis begins to accept that myth too is mobile, agile, dialectical. Impersonalist functionalism allows Barthes to avoid what Slavoj Žižek has called the 'cynical' in ideology – '"they know very well what they are doing, but still, they are doing it"' (Žižek cited in Wermer-Colan 2016, 142) – preferring to be *with* the 'they', to 'refind the people of his time', albeit with sarcasm but not apportioning cynicism. The price to pay for this radical Marxist *popularism* (as opposed to Michelet's petty-bourgeois *populism*) – community-mindedness, even intellectual solidarity? – may be the mobilisation of *form*.

Form = formalism?

Form, then, is but the start for a critical Barthes. Here, however, in 1957 at least, formal critique as pre-critique is dictated by semiological realities. Indeed, myth is, in semiological terms, the beneficiary of two types of signifier: in the first order it is meaning, in the second, 'form' (2009, 140), the former being 'full' (plausible, with a history, reason), only to be emptied by the latter, the parasite, leading to a vacuum to be filled by a new meaning, removing 'memory'. Most important is the 'impoverishing' operation on meaning by the form of myth, and not the 'suppressing': meaning loses its value but stays alive for myth to be fed and then somewhere for it to hide. It is a 'constant game of hide-and-seek between the meaning and the form' (142), a 'moving turnstile' (147) or alternating operation of meaning whose ambiguity the concept can then use; but it is not, insists Barthes, that the myth 'hides' anything, it merely 'deforms' meaning (145); it is an inflexion not a lie, a 'naturalization', read as 'factual' and not as a 'value' (153): myth thus transforms a meaning into form (156). It is then the concept that soaks up all the history that form has tried to hide: grammatical exemplarity, French imperiality, these are then the new motors behind myth, but, unlike form, the concept (or signified of myth) is concrete: having benefited from myth's impoverishing of meaning, the concept can now renew its relation to history, but it is a particular history, open, nebulous, defined by its function and ready to be appropriated. Importantly, in this new mythical realm of communication, form and concept have a particular relation that is important for the mythologist, but which at the same time allows myth to flourish and requires the mythologist to nominate, neologize, in order to arrest the mythical operation (2009, 143).

What Barthes seems to be saying is that there must be a dialectical, supple operation whereby a complex oscillation, between nominalizing and then fluxing, between essentializing and then anti-essentializing, must be deployed in order to meet head-on the subtle work of myth, its 'motility'. We will return to motility and dialectics in a moment. But, first, using the quote on ascetics we can illustrate the second type of dialectic that Barthes seems to favour in *Mythologies*, the 'amputated' dialectic.

As Michael Kelly points out (2004, 197), 'both Barthes and Morin share the notion of a relationship between opposites based on perpetual recursion', in opposition to Henri Lefebvre's classical Marxist *Aufhebung*. This allows us to explain how Stephen Heath's view of Barthesian *déplacement* (1974) can sit with the well-demonstrated *déplacement* of myth in Macdonald's motility argument (2003, 62): not so much 'agonistics' – though, clearly in *Mythologies*, Barthes is wriggling to get away from, or (better) sidle up to, myth – but some sort of 'amputated' dialectics. Macdonald's view of Barthes's *Mythologies* as a book which 'multiplies forms and gestures of intelligence' (65) sits uneasily next to the pessimism of the book's very conclusion – and this may well be explained by the fact that she uses heavily in her argument a mythology, 'At the Music Hall' (1979, 123–26), that is part of the few 'happy myths' in *Mythologies*. What seems to characterize all the 'happy myths' ('At the Music-hall', 'Paris Not Flooded', 'The World of Wrestling', 'The *Nautilus* and the Drunken Boat') are that they are part of movement; they are fleeting, temporary, and not located in objects but part of open space (Knight 1997, 37–39) and this is especially so in Barthes's analysis of the theatrics of the Music-hall. It is the intelligent movement in Barthes's sights that Macdonald prefers to see as the best metaphor for the mythologist confronted with myth's motility. If the 'amorous dialectic' seems to have slipped off the radar in the 'aporia' described above, Macdonald sees a similar double act in the twin approach of 'distraction' and 'dwelling' adopted in *Mythologies*: 'Stance-taking need not be in contradiction with the most delicately complex types of movement: the fullest agility of intelligence only really emerges where a (non-imposing) grip is got on something' (66).

There is however a danger in the 'amputated dialectic' of an incipient formalism within the critique of myth. Formalism, like a myth, attaches itself to everything: form itself has a motility. Where the theory of myth's motility is weak is the overlooking of functionalism; and function helps explain better Barthes's comment that even without motivation-intention (or 'motility', Macdonald, 58), Myth still is able to move; for it is functionalism that allows for this free-floating, subject-less actant that is myth: the 'what-goes-without-saying' goes without saying, if you like! In this functionalist schema, were we to retain Macdonald's tripartite view of 'mobile, intention, parole', then 'langue' would be 'Capitalism' and 'parole' myth. Add this functionalism to what Blanchot calls Barthes's 'formalist study of ideologies' (2000, 45) and we seem to end up with a hyper-dialectic (Merleau-Ponty 1968, 94), a dialectic of forms. But is this a dialectic of formalism? Possibly not, since one cannot, it would seem, be dialectical about formalism: once invoked, formalism (like myth) contaminates all. We might agree with Barthes that when 'form' is taken in opposition to 'system' – when two systems meet – there is history. However, *pace* Barthes, when two *forms* meet, there is, it would seem, only form: form is not modified, for there is no quantity to form. Has Barthes missed Merleau-Ponty's insistence on an *anti*-formalist radical singularity? As Merleau-Ponty puts it: 'It is certainly right to condemn formalism, but it is ordinarily forgotten that its error is not that it esteems form too much but that it esteems it so little that it detaches it from meaning' (Merleau-Ponty 1964, 12). Does the formalism of Barthesian dialectics in *Mythologies* influence his later work, in that hyper-dialectics implies a suspension of determinants, in favour of a formalism of multiple determinants (which risks being no determinants at all)?

It is, perhaps ironically, the much later Lukács who underlines the danger of formalism in theory. Looking back over his earlier career in the 1910s and 1920s, he wrote in 1962:

> It became the fashion to start off from a few characteristic traits of a tendency or a period – traits usually grasped in a purely intuitive fashion – then to synthesize general concepts from them and finally to return deductively to individual phenomena, in the conviction that this amounted to a grandiose view of the totality. (Lukács cited in Stedman Jones 1983 [1971], 38n59)

Interestingly, Greimas's critique of phenomenology (2000) sides with Saussure on the form *versus* substance question as to the nature of language, as Barthes does implicitly in 'Myth Today' (2009, 187n30). Indeed, Greimas's critique of Marcel Cohen's *Pour une sociologie du langage* as Stalin-like simplicity chimes with the end of 'Myth Today' (2009, 186); however Greimas's view (2000, 19) that the language of the popular classes in France had been for 150 years 'the principal motor in the historical development of language in general [ensemble linguistique]' seems to contradict Barthes's assertion in *Writing Degree Zero* that the 'instrumentality' of French came from the classical language of the bourgeoisie (Barthes 1967a, 65).

For Greimas, it is thanks to Saussure's distinction of language as form from language as substance (2000, 372) that allows semiology to move into other human sciences (375). The error in Barthes's (and Greimas's) approach to semiology is, according to Michel Arrivé (preface to Greimas 2000, xix) that they misread Hjelmslev on connotation as metalanguage: 'mythological, religious systems [...], literature' are shown by Barthes and Greimas to be 'building mediated "orders of thought" from *metalanguages*' (377). Indeed, Greimas's conclusion on literatures as metalanguage is applied to Barthes's *Writing Degree Zero* whose 'originality' resides in its 'affirmation of the autonomy of literary language', and whose 'signs are irreducible to simple linguistic signs on the one hand, and involved, at the same, in showing the global signification of the literary forms of any one époque'.

Indeed, alongside Robbe-Grillet's defence of formalism (1965, 42), Barthes is swift in *Mythologies* to accommodate 'form' in his analysis:

> Less terrorized by the spectre of 'formalism', historical criticism might have been less sterile; it would have understood that the specific study of forms does not in any way contradict the necessary principles of totality and History. On the contrary: the more a system is specifically defined in its forms, the more amenable it is to historical criticism. To parody a well-known saying, I shall say that a little formalism turns one away from History, but that a lot brings one back to it. (2009, 134)

Whereas Greimas regrets the narrow formalism of the Prague School, which he sees as a result of a lack of psychology of language (2000, 373), Barthes's formalism wishes to connect with social relations. Is this the formalism that *Mythologies* employs, a Marxian psycho-social account of how, impersonally, myth functions? We will consider in Chapter Three how the impersonal voice of the chorus functions in Barthes's writings on the theatre.

Chapter Three

'THE PEOPLE CHORUS'

> [I]t is because humans come out of a physical milieu that is clearly shapeless [informe] that they are already demystified.
>
> *(Barthes 2002, I, 1067)*

The 'subversive complicity' (Brown 1992, 32) that we have seen in *Mythologies*, using a range of dialectical innovations, will become in this chapter an intervention by Barthes into theatre. If the theatre is a more performative genre than the essay, the 'commentary par excellence' can take on new actions and new possibilities. In this chapter, a consideration of the chorus, the collective commentary, will be the key figure under which Barthes performs a political voice.

In a 1951 article (2015b, 8–11), Barthes likens the 'many dissident' Marxists who reject Muscovite dogmatism to the ancient Greek chorus, trying 'to retain, like the classical chorus, an awareness of misfortune, a sense of hope, and a will to understand' (10); this is, in 1951, in sharp contrast, to his imagining in 1975 a fiction of 'choosing' one's 'brand' of Marxism like a clothing item (1994, 156). Two years later, in 1953, describing ancient Greek tragedy as 'essentially the theatre of a political history that created itself' – the King in Aeschylus's play *The Suppliants* meditating on war and peace is his example – Barthes likens this 'pure human deliberation' to the Greek chorus (2002, I, 266). Between the three levels on the stage – the people, the kings and the Gods – it is the 'people chorus' which holds the ultimate human power: language. However, this chorus is not, as is traditionally thought, a lyrical echo of the actions on stage; rather the chorus is the 'all-powerful speech that explains and resolves the ambiguity of appearances, bringing the actors movements into a causality that can be understood' (266–67). Indeed, as the 'Commentary par excellence', it is the chorus which supplies the tragic dimension of the play, whilst, as Véron notes (2019, 10), it makes sure that the hero is never alone. Barthes regrets that it is precisely this that is missing in modern and contemporary theatre (not to mention sport, daily life) which has promoted human psychology over political commentary, the actor's humanity over that of the spectator who is silent:

> The ancient Greek audience, of which the chorus was nothing but a sort of extension, would dive into the tragic acts on stage, investing them with its commentary and in return feeling each jolt in the depths of its understanding; tragedy thus reached up into all of the steps of the theatre, and in the opposite direction the collective of spectators would add their explanations, as if they were a solemn human gift, following the development of the tragedy on

stage; this is the opposite of our Broadway theatre which, as we know, is not a collective experience rather a collection of voyeurs. (2002, I, 267)

It is precisely this commentary, both radical and collective, connected to the action but simultaneously stepped back from it, that we observed in Barthes's interventions using the functionalism of myth. It is deployed in popular theatre at the same time in the mid-1950s first in arguments around tragedy itself; and then in the 1959–60 captioning for Roger Pic's photo-record of Brechtian theatre. At the same time as writing on Michelet in 1954, Barthes is suddenly, blindingly, inspired by Brechtian theatre following the production of *Mother Courage* by the Berliner Ensemble in Paris in July 1954. Having studied ancient Greek theatre for his postgraduate studies during World War II, vaunting the dialectics of Aristotelian theatre alongside Paul Claudel's understanding of Japanese Noh theatre and Nietzsche's Dionysian celebration of tragedy, he at once sees a new form of dialectics taking shape in Brecht's epic theatre that eschew the tragic in favour of the political. Brechtian theatre has lessons also for political and ideological critique. We will see how Barthes intervenes in what Revermann (2013) calls 'Brechtian chorality', by his captioning of Roger Pic's photographs of the Berliner Ensemble production of Brecht's *Mother Courage*. It stands in contrast to Althusser's 'materialist' designation of *Mother Courage*. Though Althusser's reading (1971a [1962]) alights, as does Barthes's commentary, on Catherine as the hero of the play, it is based upon the spectator: whereas Barthes's materialism, as we shall see, is 'narrated' through the captions he appends to Pic's photographs. Indeed, we might consider his radical captioning as an example of the 'intellectual action' that, in the same year as his work with Pic's photography, Barthes privileges over 'political action' (2015b, 79). Part of this is to bear in mind Hill's suggestion that Brechtian theatre, in Barthes's appreciation, is not one of Marxist tub-thumping but, on the contrary, one of 'indecision' (Hill 2010, 93). Jameson underlines the importance of Ricœur's work in extending Aristotle's notions of tragedy to all narrative (2010, 490); he might also have cited Barthes's much earlier theorizations in the 1950s.

Marxian and Nietzschean Hellenism in Ancient Greek Tragedy

'[T]he Tragic is not a form of pessimism –
nor a Defeatism, nor an Abstentionism – but
on the contrary an intense Form of Optimism:
an Optimism without Progressivism.'

(Barthes 2011b, 298)

Barthes's early passion for Ancient Greek tragedy is informed by two contrasting traditions, Marxism and Nietzsche. As he began his postgraduate studies on ancient Greek theatre with Paul Mazon at the Sorbonne in Spring 1941, the British Marxist Hellenist George Thomson was about to complete the manuscript for *Aeschylus and Athens*, one of the finest examples of Marxist scholarship on Ancient Greece alongside de Ste Croix (1981). Barthes had been using Thomson's 1935 essay on Aeschylean theatre in his postgraduate dissertation which he completed in October 1941, though, for some reason, it was not credited in the bibliography (Corbier 2019). This was to be the beginning of a series of scattered but important references to Thomson's work on ancient Greek theatre that appear across Barthes's career, especially in relation to *Aeschylus and Athens*.

Rarely mentioned in studies of Barthes's work, Thomson's theories on the origins of tragedy and poetry have played an important role in Barthes's materialist aesthetics. The number of references to Thomson's study in Barthes's work, especially in the 1950s and 1960s, suggest more than passing acquaintance with the main thrust of the British Hellenist's arguments; though, as we shall see, Barthes would display contradictory views on Thomson's historicist approach to Greek tragedy.

Nietzsche not Marx?

At the same time as Barthes's use of Thomson's Marxist readings of ancient Greek theatre, the early work on tragedy by Friedrich Nietzsche is a crucial reference point. Much has been written on the Marxian, Sartrean and Brechtian dimensions to Barthes's mythological essays in the 1950s – indeed Jameson (2010, 289) considers that the Brechtian staging of *gestus* played a crucial role in Barthes's 'subject-position' and consequent 'attacks on identity'. But nothing has been forthcoming on the influence of Nietzsche in general and *The Birth of Tragedy* in particular on Barthes's critique of myth; and Drochon (2016) does not mention the critical-theoretical dimensions to *The Birth of Tragedy*.

Despite his later claim that 'I am not Nietzschean' (2007a, 462), the influence of Nietzsche on Barthes's critical theory and ideological deconstructions, alongside Marx, can be briefly traced in *Mythologies*. Barthes's very first publication in 1942, 'Culture et tragédie' (2002, I, 29–32), in the wartime student newspaper *Cahiers de l'étudiant*, was a thinly-veiled but strong endorsement of Nietzsche's own first publication, *The Birth of Tragedy in Music, or Hellenism and Pessimism*, which had appeared exactly 70 years before Barthes's first ever publication.

Indeed, we know exactly when, and to what effect, Barthes had read Nietzsche's essay. In a letter to his lifelong friend Philippe Rebeyrol (1 January 1934) discussing his interest in the 'division between Christian and Pagan', Barthes had underlined how he had been 'all on fire over paganism because of reading Nietzsche on Apollo and Dionysus' (2018, 7), in a clear reference to Nietzsche's 1872 essay *The Birth of Tragedy*. In his only other piece written in 1942, on André Gide and his diary (1982a, 4 and 15) Barthes cites also Nietzsche's *The Dawn* (1881) and *Beyond Good and Evil* (1886).

In 'Culture and Tragedy' in 1942, Barthes praises 'the unity of style' that Nietzsche sought in Hellenic culture, what he calls 'human enigma in its essential meagreness' (2002, I, 29). Barthes's reading follows the early Nietzsche's praise of tragedy, virulently opposed as it is to *drama*, a 'false culture' of the 'corrupted masses' that 'allows them to feel sorry for the petty particularities of their own misfortune, and to embroider with pathos the existence of a higher injustice, thereby removing all responsibility' (Barthes 2002, I, 30); and it is one that is carried over into the 1950s writing on tragedy, as we shall see, but also into *Mythologies*.

For Nietzsche, myth is 'the concentrated image of the world which, as an abbreviation for phenomena, cannot do without miracles' (Nietzsche 1993, 109), and a crucial element in the success of ancient Greek culture and the heights of tragedy. Once myth became challenged by historical perspectives and by Socratism, '[t]he decline of tragedy was also the decline of myth' (111). It is clear that Barthes does not follow Nietzsche's mythical nationalism nor his dismissal of historical critique – without myth 'all culture loses its healthy and natural creative power [...], transforms the most powerful, wholesome nourishment into "history and criticism"' (109–11) – but it is difficult to ignore the double approach to myth taken by Nietzsche: 'our aestheticians [...] have learned nothing of the contrast between the phenomenon and the thing-in-itself'. Nietzsche rejects also the 'entirely false opposition of soul and body' (104); and *tragic myth [...] shares with the sphere of Apolline art an utter delight in appearance and looking, and at the same time it negates that pleasure and draws even higher satisfaction from the destruction of the visible world of appearance*' (113). Furthermore, Nietzsche's use of functionalism is unmistakeable in the double-take on 'the effect of tragedy': 'For we now understand what it means to wish to look, in tragedy, and at the same time to long to go beyond that looking' (115). The influence from Nietzsche continues. As in *Mythologies*, the 'double grasp' in *The Birth of Tragedy* celebrates the '*aesthetic listener*', against the 'half moral and half scholarly 'critic' (107), 'the community of Socratic-critical men' (109), 'the student, the school-boy' (107) whose moral understanding stops them being 'enraptured by the powerful magic of art' (108).

It is the oscillation between, on the one hand, a Marxian Hellenism gleaned through a reading of Thomson, and his inspired reading, on the other, of the early Nietzsche that will inform Barthes's theories and commentaries on Greek tragedy. Mindful that the intersection of Marxism and Nietzscheanism in Barthes's work might encourage us to reconcile these two systems of thought in a crude way that Philippe Roger (1986, 73) has called a 'convenient ruse', we will instead suggest a tension in Barthes's work between the post-romantic and the socio-critical, between the utopianism of Nietzschean critique and the 'necessity' of Marx.

Thomson and the Materialist Reading of Tragedy

Barthes's use of Thomson's theories, though scattered, was not a passing fad. In a round-table discussion 'Towards A Return of the Tragic: From Nietzsche to Beckett' (Simon 1967), broadcast on French radio in May 1967, Barthes staunchly disagrees with the other participants – Yves Bertherat, Jean-Marie Domenach, Jean Duvignaud and Jean Paris – when it was suggested that there had been a return to tragedy between the time of Nietzsche and the theatre of Samuel Beckett (soon to be made Nobel laureate for literature). To Barthes this argument is anathema, especially as it is dehistoricized.

As adjectival noun, he argues, the 'tragic' has been 'essentialized'; whereas the predicate 'tragedy' refers uniquely to Aristotle and 'poetic discourse'. But the real danger in using the word 'tragic', he maintains, is that the word 'tragedy' – just like the Argo ship in Greek myth – changes so much its meaning, yet it remains 'tragedy'. Against this imprecision, he argues then, we should look at the theories of the British 'Marxist exegete', George Thomson, whose arguments about tragedy are highly specific.

In Thomson's definition, Barthes explained, for there to be 'tragedy' there needs to be 'reversal' [revirement]. All three epochs in which tragedy had been at its height – ancient Greek, Elizabethan and the seventeenth-century classical period – exhibited the 'fall' of one or more characters; and Barthes cites the example of 'le comble' [the heights] – and hence the fall – in Jean Racine's seventeenth-century tragedies. Following Thomson's line of argument, he suggests that the 'reversal' is not simply a destiny in tragic theatre in which the central character falls from on high to end up in the diametrically opposite position; it was also highly specific to certain historical and material periods. For Barthes, this means that, in this definition, it is patently not apt to speak of tragedy in the theatre of Beckett or Ionesco, nor indeed in contemporary art. Against the capacious definition of 'tragedy', of the 'tragic', Barthes strives to maintain a strict usage.

He had already made a similar argument in 'Culture et tragédie': 'Outside of these [three] centuries, tragedy – in its constituted forms – falls silent' (2002, I, 29). Here in the 1967 radio discussion, he goes further in his advocacy of Thomson's analysis. Thomson deemed the 'reversal' to be fundamentally linked to the first two of the above periods of tragedy, and above all to the radical changes taking place in their respective epochs. In fifth-century BC Greece and Elizabethan England, Thomson had shown that there was, in Barthes's words:

> the generalised subversion of the values of money; that is, major mercantilist changes [...], the sudden rise in the importance of money and market exchange bring about a sort of sudden change in which, as Plato put it, all things are changed into their opposites. (Barthes, in Simon 1967)

Barthes seems in 1967 to be restating notions on tragedy that he had put forward in his polemical 1963 study, *On Racine* and to which we will return presently. The use of Thomson, as we shall see, develops across the period of the 1950s when Barthes is preoccupied by the popular theatre movement, and into the early 1960s when he is writing on Racinean theatre. Indeed, Barthes's hesitant mobilization of Thomson's theories on the tragedy in 1967 reflects this ambivalence.

He further points out in the 1967 radio-debate on tragedy that Thomson's materialist Hellenism is a 'highly contested opinion', but not without merit in looking exclusively at the three periods of tragedy that we know; and thus, ruling out the existence of tragedy at any other time, including our own, represents a firm restatement of Thomson's materialist explanation of tragedy's origins, what Barthes calls the 'specificity', both economic and social, of tragedy: and, he adds, 'it is this which counts' (Barthes, in Simon 1967).

Barthes's use of Thomson's radical historical-materialist theory started in the 1950s. A first endorsement of Thomson's theory appears in his 1955 review of a Swiss production of Sophocles' *Oedipus King*. Here Barthes warmly commends the choice of play and the adaptation by André Bonnard whose work on the choral parts had managed to bring out 'perfectly the type of lyrical statism' in Sophocles (2002, I, 594–95); however, explains Barthes, he 'profoundly disagrees' with the director's choices, reservations that he repeat two months later when a Dutch theatre company visited Paris with a production of Sophocles' play (2002, I, 608–09). It was not so much the over-articulation of the voices, nor so much the 'excess of virtue' in the materials or the actors' movements, nor even the 'Biblism' of the production that disappoints the most; above all, it was the director's decision to see in Sophocles' play 'nothing but a rhetorical ceremony [...] a bourgeois drama in which psychological suffering [...] can be surrounded only by declaimed entreaties of "spirituality"'. Now Barthes makes the first in a series of firm endorsements of Thomson's work:

> It is the whole of Greece, all its History and its criticism which is covered up in this whole adventure. Sophocles played like a bourgeois tragedy, Aeschylus like a 'fête nègre', it is curious, this mania, this modern obsession with an exoticism going in the wrong direction, with running away at all costs from the *Greek* character of Greek tragedy. [...] Couldn't our directors read some good historians on the question, like Thomson for example? (2002, I, 595)

Strangely, Barthes does not feel the need here to add either Thomson's first name or the title of his work.

A few months after his review of Sophocles production, in the October 1955 number of *Théâtre Populaire*, Barthes writes a (now infamous) review of Jean-Louis Barrault's production of the *Oresteia* (1972, 59–66). Mckeane (2015) articulates Barthes's critique of Barrault's *Oresteia* – and it is one that is repeated in *Mythologies* (1979, 77) – but does not mention that it is Thomson who, alongside Engels and Bachofen, is mobilized by Barthes. In the review, Barthes asks the two key questions that should preoccupy a director of classical theatre: 'what was the *Oresteia* for Aeschylus' contemporaries? What have we [...] to do with the ancient meaning of the work?' (1979, 65). Now Barthes cites – at last, with full name and book title too – '*Aeschylus and Athens* by George Thomson (1941)':

> In the context of its period, and despite the moderate political position of Aeschylus himself, the *Oresteia* was incontestably a 'progressive' work; it testifies to the transition from a matriarchal society, represented by the Erinnyes, to the patriarchal society represented by Apollo and Athena. [T]he *Oresteia* is a profoundly politicized work: it is exemplary of the relation which can unite a precise historical structure and a particular myth. Others may choose to see in it an eternal problematics of Evil and of Judgment; nonetheless, the *Oresteia* is above all the work of a specific period, of a definite social condition and of a contingent moral argument. (65)

This prefigures a key argument to come in *On Racine* in 1963, and to which we will return in a moment as it displays contradictory references to Thomson. But we must underline first how Thomson's work on Aeschylus and ancient Greece, alongside Bachofen's and Engels's, is taken by Barthes as that which, via the play, affords 'courage and hope'. It is with these words – rarely associated with Barthes – that the historical, and not the archaeological, specificity of the *Oresteia* is valorized:

[H]istory is plastic, fluid, at the service of men, if only they try to make themselves its master in all lucidity. To grasp the historical specificity of the *Oresteia*, its exact originality, is for us the only way of making a dynamic use of it, a use endowed with responsibility. (66)

As we noted above, Barthes had indeed mentioned Thomson's work in his 1941 postgraduate thesis, but nowhere in the thesis do we see such a bald and bold statement of militant belief in a radical classical theatre.

Thus, Barthes seemed to be disproving George Steiner's conviction (1961, 342) that 'a Communist can no longer recognize the meaning of tragedy'; for Steiner, tragedy went against Communism's belief 'that the powers of reason can master the natural world and give to human life a complete dignity and purpose'.

It is worth pausing in our discussion of Barthes's use of a distinctly materialist Hellenism, in order to locate the influences on Thomson, not least as they will help us to consider other areas of Hellenism in Barthes's critical theory in the 1950s, especially in relation to myth. Barthes began his undergraduate studies during the heyday of Hellenism of the 1930s, a rich fusion of politics and utopianism (De Pourcq, 2019) which encouraged Thomson to develop his materialist anthropology of ancient Greek civilization. Thomson's analysis of the links between the changes in the economy and the rise of tragedy in ancient Greece emerged especially from the work of Christopher Caudwell in his posthumous *Illusion and Reality* (1977), as well as from that of Jane Harrison, William Ridgeway, Lewis Morgan and Engels, all of whom are credited in the preface to the first edition of *Aeschylus and Athens* in 1940.

Published thanks to Thomson's editing skills immediately after his death while fighting for the Republican side the Spanish Civil War, Caudwell's essay is concerned with the status of poetry today by way of an analysis of the emergence of poetry in ancient societies, especially in fifth-century BC Greece which he describes as a society 'in ferment, in *revolution*' (1977, 54ff). For Caudwell, it was the economic advancement of ancient Greece that favoured poetry; and it is precisely these arguments that Thomson took up in his 1945 essay *Marxism and Poetry* that Barthes also cited, and to which Thomson added tragedy as a further, poetic example of the materialist explanation.

British Marxist scholarship, such as Thomson's, has fared badly in recent times due to its links to a Moscow-dominated form of political and cultural analysis. Indeed, the debates between Hellenists in the 1930s and 1940s, especially on the Marxist left, sought to question the relationship between the economic determinant and the (so-called) superstructure, since the stranglehold of a vulgar materialism emerging with Stalinism risked destroying the true Marxist tradition. The debate revolved also – understandably, given global events in the 1930s – around tragedy; and it was the work in Paris between 1932 and 1938 carried out by the German exile Max Raphael that set the tone. A brief overview of Raphael's theories on ancient Greek culture, via the ideas of Marx, will allow us not only to situate Barthes's theories, but also, by way of a conclusion, to suggest the importance of Nietzsche's Hellenism in Barthes's theatre criticism of the 1950s, and more speculatively for his wider critical theory especially in *Mythologies* and the critique of ideology.

The arguments of Marxist Hellenists during the 1930s around the question of ancient Greece was a complex and intricate one. There is no evidence that Barthes had read Max Raphael's work during the 1930s – though the 1938 work on Marxism and human consciousness might well have been available during the War (Raphael 1938). Han (2021) uses the 1930s Hellenism of Werner Jaeger (2014), and the interest in *paideia*, to engage with the Hellenism of Barthes's late career. However, Raphael's three essays on the sociology of art, published in Paris in 1933 (Raphael 1980), showed an extraordinary similarity with Barthes's writings in his early career. Indeed, the second of the three essays – on Marx, dialectical materialism and Art – contains important discussion of myth and mythology which, 20 years before Barthes's own critique of myth, considered the ideological nature of mythological imagination in Greek art. Coincidentally, Barthes, as we saw above, was inspired by Nietzsche's *Birth of Tragedy* the same year as Raphael's essay was published; but the latter contains no explicit reference to Nietzsche's work; though Raphael implicitly acknowledged the key Nietzschean argument, articulated by Barthes in the discussion above, that Apollonian mythological tendencies in ancient Greek civilization had squeezed out Orphic and Dionysian tendencies (Raphael 1980, 93, 95).

The similarity of concerns in Raphael's work in the 1930s and Barthes's of the late 1940s and 1950s relates to the notions of human consciousness, mythology and ideology. Indeed, Raphael's sophisticated, anti-mechanical application of dialectics to an analysis of art, especially ancient Greek, prefigured much of what Barthes wrote in 1946 in his unpublished article (and early version of the 'degree zero thesis') 'The Future of Rhetoric' (2018, 102–14). Though in a letter in August 1946 to Philippe Rebeyrol where he considered materialism and literature to be incompatible, Barthes informed Rebeyrol six months later (16 May 1947) of his use of materialism: 'I have written [...] a text on literary criticism using materialist postulates'; and it is probably this essay to which he is referring. Though it contained more on modern literature, than anything on ancient Greek, the essay is a testament to a key early moment in Barthes's developing of materialist ideas, especially within the 'degree zero' thesis written and published in the radical-left *Combat* between 1947 and 1953.

Raphael was closely associated with the German sociologist Werner Sombart whose work Barthes regularly cites in the 1950s (2002, I, 512–13, 946); and there are moreover overlaps in Raphael's and Barthes's approach to ancient Greece. First, Raphael's preference for the 'folk theory of poetry' and the theory that 'society itself was the creator of a spiritual product' (Raphael 1980, 100) prefigured Barthes's 'degree zero' promotion of the sociological analysis of art-forms and the subsequent 'death-of-the author' critique of the individualized writer; second, the potential conflict of asserting the time-bound and yet timeless skill of ancient Greek art, which Raphael locates in Marx's writings (1980, 77, 103–04), resurfaces in the historically 'definite form' that we saw above in Barthes's assertion of the *Oresteia*'s historical specificity; third, Barthes's insistence on the 'plastic' nature of History (1972, 66) – as well as part of Hegel's theory of how the individual negotiates the universal (Malabou 2005, 186) – echoed Raphael's notion of how Greek art treated mythology 'plastically' (1980, 92–93, 95); finally, Raphael's theories on mythology and ideology (1980, 88–92) have strong affinities to Barthes's approach in *Mythologies*, in the way ideology is located between mythology, art and culture, but seen as developed by the people's imagination (since there was no priestly caste in ancient Greece). But it is Raphael's anti-mechanical dialectical-materialist method with respect to ancient Greece that displays the most important similarity to Barthes's discussions on the complex relationship between economic development and artistic advancement.

Raphael referred directly to Marx's brief writings in *A Contribution to a Critique of Political Economy* where Marx had set out the problem of the 'unequal development of material production' and that of art; but, against vulgar materialism, Marx had concluded that there was no direct correlation, except that 'it is the intensity of the struggle between man and nature that matters for the purpose of elucidating the interrelationships between art and economy': as Raphael put it, 'Imbalance is the expression of the dialectics of history' (1980, 97, 99). It is precisely this question that begins to develop in Barthes's pronouncements on tragedy, on ancient Greek culture in general, especially in his 1960 essay that becomes, three years later, the final section of *On Racine*, called 'History or Literature?'.

Moreover, it is in his work on Racine that Barthes begins to display an ambiguous view of Thomson's materialist account of the origins of tragedy. The analysis of 'reversal' that we saw in the 1967 radio debate on tragedy first appears in *On Racine* in 1963. In a footnote, Barthes set out how Thomson theorized this, and in doing so he introduced Lucien Goldmann's work into the debate:

> The theory of the tragic reversal dates from Aristotle. A recent historian has attempted to express its sociological significance: the meaning of the reversal ('to change all things into their opposite', in Plato's phrase) is the expression of a society whose values are dislocated and upset by the abrupt transition from feudalism to mercantilism, that is, by a sudden promotion of money (fifth-century Greece, Elizabethan England). But in this form, such an explanation cannot apply to French tragedy; a further ideological treatment is required, as in Lucien Goldmann's *The Hidden God*. (cf. G. Thomson, *Marxism and Poetry*.) (1992a, 41n1, trans. mod.)

The translation of *On Racine* misrepresents Barthes's argument here – Goldmann's work is deemed in Barthes's original French to be an extension of (and not an alternative to) Thomson's work. It is not until the essayistic crescendo at the end of *On Racine* that we encounter the starkest example of reservations concerning Thomson's method. It comes in the context of a further discussion of Goldmann.

On Racine represented a direct, though only implicit, dialogue with, and critique of, *The Hidden God*. This is not to say that Barthes begins to ignore Goldmann's work. Though hinting that Goldmann's method in *The Hidden God* represents a 'disguised determinism' (1972, 153, 270–71), Barthes sees his theories on the novel as dialectical. They make a link between 'the economic structure and the aesthetic structure' and consider the novel form as corresponding with the bourgeoisie's development but not as an expression of its collective consciousness; and Barthes imagines how Goldmann's 'semantic' (or ideological) critique and his own semiological critique (or 'sociologics' of form) might be complementary – hence the 'two sociologies' in the title of Barthes's book review (2002, II, 248–50), implying in his final question that the latter may be more open to the former than the other way round.

Through much of the final essay, and most of *On Racine*, Barthes commends Goldmann's move away in his analysis of Racinean tragedy from a psychology to a sociology of literature. However, in the final pages, he acknowledges that Goldmann too gives in to what he calls the 'postulate of analogy':

> Pascal and Racine belonging to a politically disappointed group, their vision of the world will *reproduce* that disappointment, as if the writer had no other power than to copy himself literally. (1992a, 169)

Barthes makes a similar point in his 1953 piece on Jean Paris' early-structuralist analysis of *Hamlet* and its attendant critique of psychology in tragedy (1953, 63–64), in which he sees Paris' work as 'de-romanticizing' the character in tragedy and thereby opening the play up to mythological critique (2002, I, 281). His point with respect to Racine is that the so-called 'genetic' structuralism used by Goldmann to explain seventeenth-century tragedy is still tied to an individualist psychologism. In his response (1971, 113), though praising aspects of Barthes's reading in *On Racine*, Goldmann regrets that Barthes often 'substitutes his own problems and perspectives for the literal and objective meaning of the text in question' (see also Véron 2019).

However, in a footnote, Barthes qualifies this criticism of Goldmann by way of a comparison with Thomson. Seeming to go to the opposite extreme, he expresses his preference for the 'genetic' to the 'analogical':

> Infinitely less flexible [souple] than Goldmann, another Marxist, George Thomson, has established a brutally analogical relation in Marxism and Poetry between the subversion of values in the fifth century B.C., whose trace he believes he finds in Greek tragedy, and the shift from a rural to a mercantile economy, characterized by an abrupt promotion of money. (1992a, 169)

This (implicit) preference for a more flexible approach – what Raphael calls the 'dialectical interlocking' but 'relative autonomy' in the 'specificity of each domain' (1980, 85) – seems to represent a stark change of idea from what, as we saw above, Barthes had written on Thomson in the mid-1950s. Indeed, could not the same charge of a lack of 'suppleness' be levelled at Barthes in the 1967 radio round-table concerning the definition of the tragic from Nietzsche to Beckett, and at Barthes's views on the material origins of tragedy that we also saw above?

De Pourcq (2008, 85–86) sets out the contradictory approach to Thomson's work that he sees in Barthes's work. On the one hand, suggests De Pourcq, Barthes 'disagrees with Thomson's theory postulating a vast continuity between tribal rituals and tragedy', since, for Barthes, 'ancient tragedy deals with specific social conditions, established by Athenian democracy'; indeed, continues De Pourcq, 'the political import of tragedy determines its cultural value, not its hypothetical genealogy, let alone the forced and dogmatic Marxist analogy between labour, society and literature'. On the other hand, continues De Pourcq, 'Thomson's study of the sacro-social origins of poetry and tragedy [...] does not necessarily disregard the socio-critical function of tragedy'. Indeed, De Pourcq is aware of the influence that Thomson's materialist Hellenism has had since the

1960s, not least in France, and thanks no doubt, in part, to Barthes; this is especially true for a younger generation of classicists such as Barthes's colleague at the EPHE, Jean-Pierre Vernant, who uses Thomson's two-volume *Studies in Ancient Greek Society* for his seminal anthropological approach. However, Vernant, like Barthes, has reservations.

Vernant uses Thomson's work to discuss, with respect to ancient Greece, the following phenomena: the absence of monarchy (296–97); the links between agriculture and the lunar/solar calendar; the development of money and interest (309); and finally, whether there is a direct link, as Thomson had argued, between the new concepts in ancient Greek philosophy emerging on the one hand and the abstract form of exchange which money operated on the diverse objects that begun to appear at the marketplace on the other; yet Vernant questions this final theory of Thomson's as possibly too 'mechanical', as well as anachronistic given Marx's argument that it is only when labour itself is turned into a commodity – in the late eighteenth and early nineteenth centuries – that the commodity form of human products begins to be the dominant social form (Vernant 308–09).

It may also be that, between Goldmann's Lukácsian approach to seventeenth-century tragedy on the one hand, and Thomson's humanist Marxism on the other, Barthes is making tactical choices in 1963. As one of the earliest promoters of the work of Lukács in 1950s France, Goldmann had absorbed the Hungarian's literary history of aesthetic forms and applied them to classical theatre. However, though Lukács was writing in the late twenties and early thirties, in Russian and German, on the question of higher forms of civilization including ancient Greece and the relationship with the level of economic development, and using Nietzsche on ancient Greece and tragedy, *The Historical Novel* was not available in French or English until 1965. Just as Barthes does, Lukács cites Engels and Bachofen's analyses of the *Oresteia* as part of those 'world-historic changes' coterminous with the rise of tragedy in fifth-century BC Greece (1969, 111, 136, 141 and 189).

Goldmann, for his part, largely rejects Barthes's speculative essayism on Racinean theatre. It is, however, Barthes of course, not Goldmann, who is singled out by the conservative Racine-specialist Raymond Picard. Barthes's reaction to the Picard affair is summarized in his famous 1966 comment: 'to be subversive, criticism does not need to judge, all it needs to do is talk about language' (2007b, 33). In *On Racine*, Barthes makes broadsides against academic 'explication de texte' [commentaries], at those readings that merely look for the signified out of a large number of signifiers (1992a, 147n4). The key question for Barthes, by contrast, is: how could his reading avoid a 'naturalization' of Racinean theatre, to become an (early example of a) rewriting, a re-poeticizing, of Racine for the modern era? Indeed, despite a hidden dislike for Racinean theatre, Barthes is noble enough to insist that, if we want to put Racine on the modern stage, we have to 'distance' it from ourselves, perhaps in his essayistic fashion; and Goldmann's Marxist, as well as Mauron's psychoanalytical, approaches are found to be wanting in terms of their view of what an *oeuvre*, creativity, actually *is* (167–72).

It is Goldmann, as we saw, who introduces ideologism – the genetic study of a writer's world-view – to critical theory in 1950s France and which becomes an important horizon at the end of *Mythologies* for Barthes's dialectical strategy. It is alongside this ideologist approach that we need to reconsider the influence of Nietzsche on the young Barthes.

Eternal return of Nietzsche?

Mckeane (2015, 63–64) has pointed out that the early Barthes, in writing his DES postgraduate thesis in 1941, applies a Nietzschean view of tragedy containing a composite of Dionysian and Apollonian motifs; and Corbier (2015) underlines the influence with regard to music. Nevertheless, in the 1953 article on ancient Greek tragedy, the section of which on the chorus we cited at the start of this chapter, shows a Barthes who is sceptical with regards to one key aspect of Nietzsche's enthusiasm for ancient Greek theatre. Despite its 'beauty', the 'Nietzschean opposition of the Dionysian and Apollonian' is to be attributed to Wagner and not Aeschylus (2002, I, 265); whereas both Caudwell (1977, 59) and Thomson (1941, 121) cite the Dionysian/Apollonian dyad in Nietzsche's account uncritically, the former describing it as a 'passage', the latter as 'opposite poles'. For Barthes, by contrast, Nietzsche's dyad suggests 'the very opposite of Tragedy' because it shows the musical elements 'triumphantly' absorbing all the other signs, and this has plagued productions of ancient tragedy ever since:

> [T]here is no greater illusion than believing in a homogenous fusion of the different orders of pathos: in all civilised art (and this is not at all a value judgment), understanding [intelligence] is the original condition of emotion [...]: every tragedy today has its 'stage music'; and yet, our western music, with its powers of pathos rather than those of ethics, is incapable of incorporating itself into the argument of tragedy: either it takes over the tragic, or remains external to it. (2002, I, 265)

Such is the 'fragility' of music's historical dimension to tragedy, it is better, suggests Barthes, to avoid trying to recreate it; rather than destroying the power of tragedy with modern emotional music. But before we can suggest links between Marxian materialism and Nietzschean motifs in Barthes's work, one aspect of De Pourcq's suggestions above – in which Barthes applies the 'chaos' of Nietzschean thought to his understanding of Greece, ancient and modern – needs qualifying.

In 'Culture et tragédie' Barthes cites Nietzsche's view not on the dispersal of human life, but that culture was '"the unity of artistic style in all of its vital manifestations of a people"'; the crucial point – again (implicitly) citing Nietzsche's first ever work – is, writes Barthes, 'to obtain and give the vision of the world that was above all harmonious – but not necessarily serene – [...] to present the human enigma in its essential meagreness': 'In order to merit tragedy, the collective soul of the people must have reached a certain degree of culture, that is, not as knowledge, but as style' (2002, I, 29). Though yet to bring in his materialist argument about the origins of tragedy that he will find in Thomson's work, Barthes already in 1942 is presenting tragedy as dependent on the 'aristocratic' sensibility, either of seventeenth-century France and social rank, or on an original people's culture as found in fifth-century BC Greece.

Following Nietzsche, he distinguishes tragedy from drama. If drama – and then melodrama – moves by an 'ever overwhelming enriching [surenrichissement toujours débordant]' of human ills, tragedy by contrast is but an 'ardent effort' to 'lay bare [dépouiller]' human suffering (2002, I, 30). And though Barthes has not yet alighted on Thomson's view of the fundamental need for a 'reversal' in tragedy, he underlines

Nietzsche's idea, making it thoroughly humanist in relation to the capacity of humans to act:

> [T]he miracle of tragedy […] indicates to us that the deepest questions about ourselves are concerned not with the 'what?' of things but their 'why?'. There is no need to know how the world will finish; more important is to know what it is and what is its true meaning; and not at all within Time – this is a force that is both contestable and contested – but within an immediate universe that has been deprived of the very doors of Time. […] The aim is to find in [suffering] not at all our *raison d'être*, which would be criminal, rather our ultimate essence and with it, full possession of our destiny. (2002, I, 31–32)

It is worth remembering that this is written in 1942, a full 12 years before the discovery of Brecht and the subsequent insistence in Barthes's critical theory for the theatre on a voluntarism of human actions. It would seem to be the case that where Barthes's interest in Thomson is a highly Nietzschean one, by the same token Barthes's Brechtian voluntarism of the 1950s is partly drawn from his early reading of the early Nietzsche.

In good, unorthodox, Barthesian style, we have here a strange *chassé-croisé*. For the discussion of Thomson's orthodox historical-materialist account of ancient Greek theatre, Barthes uses a decidedly contradictory set of approaches; and towards the maverick and unorthodox writings on ancient Greece by Nietzsche, he seems to deploy a classically dialectical strategy. Despite their firm belief, common to both, that ancient Greece was an aristocratic and superior culture, in its use of tragedy in particular, Thomson and Nietzsche are, philosophically and politically, distant from one another. Nevertheless, Barthes's fundamental attachment to tragedy is plain to see in the tortuous trajectory of his engagement with aspects of Marxian and Nietzschean thought (Salazar 1993, 116). However, this has become clear only by way of a triangulation. This triangulation has involved not just people – Barthes *with* Aeschylus *and* Racine, *with* Raphael *and* Goldmann, with Nietzsche *and* Thomson – but also objects (mercantilism with voluntarism; materialism with post-romanticism; analogy with 'reversal'; History with Literature; the *Oresteia* with culture-as-style), both of which help us trace this trajectory. One area emerges especially from this analysis.

Chorus

In Chapter Two, we saw how the 'amorous dialectic' does not simply denounce myth: it intervenes in the descriptions and dialectical-critical acts. However, this attempt to overcome the division between outside and inside – the 'amorous dialectic' that sees in myth both its alienation *and* at the same its human 'warmth' – came, as we saw, at the price of what Barthes calls in 'Myth Today' a 'theoretical sociality', involving concessions to ideologism in the 'amputated' dialectic. Indeed, 'theoretical sociality' has recently been an object of moral and political criticism.

Writing about Barthes's extraordinary reading of film-stills from Eisenstein's revolutionary cinema (1977, 52–68), Georges Didi-Huberman (2016, 121–23) describes it recently as an approach that 'excludes *pathos*', sacrificing solidarity for the *detail*, formalism for affectivity, in a sort of 'theoretical mime' of the Brechtian *distancing effect*

(122). Didi-Huberman appreciates Barthes's mobility, as he 'operates the *displacement* of his eye'. However, Barthes's 'legitimate aim of dividing evidence from the representation' hides a problem: Barthes says nothing of Mother Courage's cry of pain when she breaks down before her son's corpse, describing 'cruelly' her emotion as 'insignificant'; for Didi-Huberman, quoting Barthes's 'theoretical sociality', it is the price to be paid if 'a visuality saturated with understanding [intelligence]' is privileged over 'a surfeit of emotional signification' (123).

It could certainly be said that Didi-Huberman is taking the idea of 'theoretical sociality' out of its context in the critique of myth and placing it in relation to an analysis of radical, revolutionary theatre and cinema; indeed, Didi-Huberman's broadside against Barthes has been roundly rejected by Carluccio (2020). However, the misplaced criticism of Barthes's '*displacement* of his eye' at a moment of high emotion merely serves to underline Barthes's dialectical method. A radical form of criticism can, indeed must, operate on two levels, in what is a far from straight-forward activity. As we saw in Chapter One, not only does the denunciation of myth require a functionalist approach – 'judge the harm caused by the myth, and not at all its error' (2002, V, 1022–23) – but also the mythologist must attack myth first on the level of its philosophical trickery. At the same time, the mythologist who demystifies social distortions cannot be involved in, or is not even capable of, correcting or rectifying them: the 'amorous dialectic' is caught in a double-bind (or 'aporia'), whereby it is not resolved, does not resolve itself, in a synthesis. However, if this 'amorous dialectic' cannot be synthesized theoretically, could it be 'resolved' in practice? By looking at Barthes's intervention in Brechtian theatre through his writing of captions for theatre photography and then, in Chapter Four, by triangulating Barthes's search for a radical, double historiography with that of Walter Benjamin and Jules Michelet, we will see not only a sharp discounting of Didi-Huberman's criticism, but also a further use of the chorus as a form of intervention that is capable of operating on more than one level.

Photo Captions: Brecht, Pic and Epic Theatre

'Anyone can be creative. It's rewriting other
people that's a challenge.'

(Brecht cited in Milling/Ley 2001, 57)

'What I really like, is the link between image
and writing, which is a difficult one, but because
of this brings real creative joys, just as poets in the
past liked working on the difficult problems of
versification. Today, the equivalent is to find the link
between a text and images.'

(Barthes 2002, V, 936)

It is perhaps surprising that, apart from his collaborative work in Canada on film images of Wrestling (Brault et al. 1961), Barthes never intervenes directly in the creation and/or editing of images, neither in the cinema nor above all with photographers with whom he nevertheless works. In the case of the film on wrestling, when asked for his advice by the filmmakers, Barthes is adamant that they should at all cost avoid demystifying the movements in a wrestling match (in other words, not reveal visually its wholly artificial, fabricated nature). It is a striking suggestion for this 28-minute Quebecois documentary, especially when we consider the anti-colonial dimensions of wrestling, whose popularity in the oppressed French-speaking region of Quebec was associated at the time with resistance to the dominant class of English-speaking Canada. The absence of Barthesian intervention in the creation of photographic images is all the more striking. From Pic to Boudinet, Martin to Roche, Bouvier to Bouvard and Faucon to Clergue, there is clearly for Barthes an artistic line with these photographers beyond which he the critic should not go. This is true both of the artists with whom he works and of those, more distant (Avedon and Klein), on whose photography he writes. Indeed, whether it is photography in general, or photography with a specific artist, Barthesian photo-textualism never displays any pretentions to a direct collaboration with the *operator* of the camera. There is, however, one exception in his work with Roger Pic's photography. We will see how captioning can play not just an emotional role, but a radicalizing function at the same time. But first, we will look, briefly, at an example of humour in Barthes's theatre militancy. It also suggests that the non-intervention in the act of photographing (or filming) that we saw above is balanced, even cancelled, out by his skilful written intervention *alongside* the image.

Caption and costume

Our close analysis here of the caption, in its dynamic interaction with the photographic image alongside it, relies on the original versions of Barthes's writings. The first of his books to link text with image is *Michelet* in 1954, which begins with the photographic portrait of the historian that his friend Robert David had sent to him when he was isolated during World War II in the sanatorium for tuberculosis and that fascinated the young Barthes (Calvet 1994, 114–15). The first article to link image and text is 'Pouvoirs de la tragédie antique' (1953a with photographs; 2002, I, 259–67 without photographs), in which, alongside three photographs by 'Viollet' (most likely taken by Hélène Roger-Viollet in 1952) showing the theatre at Delph and two Greek masks, Barthes extolls the 'powers' of ancient Greek theatre. It is a shame then that his *Œuvres Complètes* miss out much of this iconography – above all photographic – that accompanies various articles that he publishes in a wide range of newspapers, journals and magazines; one can but hope that a new version of his Complete Works will one day include this material – though Guittard (2010) has done much to rectify this gap in relation to *Mythologies*. This is a reasonable request for the works of a critical theorist for whom post-war mass culture is defined by the arrival of the image. Indeed, in a 'monthly mythology' in February 1955, he writes:

> I don't know if the *ideological* power of standardised representations has been analysed yet; independent of the myths conveyed, there is by all evidence a rule [morale] of photography that should interest sociologists. [...] As a technical form, it becomes part of History only

when it is taken up by the world of commerce, and is in some sense *alienated* by collective usage. [...] The corresponding historical moment is the birth of the illustrated magazine [in the nineteenth century], whose massive circulation helped to promote the visual as a vehicle for myths – all at a time when the masses had for centuries known nothing other than an oral form for their dreams. (2002, I, 549–550).

Thus, the role of the image in general, and photography in particular, needs to be stressed in Barthes's work of the 1950s. Not only can it help to complete, if not justify, the radical points of view adopted by the young militant of popular theatre who is one of the first theoreticians in France of the Brechtian 'system'; but also to appreciate the conditions in which his career as photo-textualist begins.

Born in 1920, Roger Pic, famous photographer for the Théâtre National Populaire (TNP), had worked in the post-war Communist-Party instigated 'Travail et Culture' movement alongside the *éminence grise* of the *Théâtre Populaire* journal, Robert Voisin. Pic is the first photographer with whom Barthes works closely; or rather (since we have no record of a *direct* collaboration between the two men) with whose photography he works closely. However, before looking in detail at this collaboration, it is worth considering Barthes's first act of captioning, the first example of an interaction of text and image in his career.

The original version in the journal *Théâtre Populaire* (Barthes 1955) of 'The Diseases of Costume', as opposed to the version in *Critical Essays* (1972, 41–50 without photographs), shows a series of photographic images next to which Barthes appends critical captions. The photographic images are presented in order to illustrate his comments on 'bad' – and, to a lesser extent, 'good' – theatre costumes since the beginning of the twentieth century. What is striking, however, is the humour that Barthes applies in the pithy captions.

The photographs consist of a dozen or so reproductions (Figs. 3.1–3.9) of portraits of various actors in their stage costumes. The whole article is an example of what Barthes calls 'Thought out theatre' (1972, 44–45), which stood in direct contrast to the sugary, insipid *Folies Bergère* shows (2002, I, 234–44). In the laconic and often humorous captions, Barthes names either the costume's error, its 'disease' or its 'healthy' counterpart, as found in the photographic illustrations. Though the name of each photographer is not always given, actor and costume-designer (or director) are usually signalled. Alongside of a series of photographic images of actors in costume, Barthes starts his captioning career with a series of laconic, pithy comments.

In the first image [Fig. 3.1], alongside the actor in full owl outfit (for *Chantecler*, in 1910, Le Grand-duke wearing a costume designed by M. Dorival), he begins with a stark and witty caption: 'The absurdity of the factual approach in verism: the actor assassinated by the costume'.

To this example of 'disease' in theatre costume, Barthes opposes the portrait of Gérard Philipe as Lorenzaccio [Fig. 3.2] wearing a costume by Léon Gischia with the following caption: 'The good costume is a global visual fact' (1955, 66). The critique of verism in theatre returns in 1959 and 1960 when Barthes endorses Roger Pic's work whose 'realism' in covering a 'good' production of Brecht stands in sharp contrast to the

FIGURE 3.1 The absurdity of the factual approach in verism: the actor assassinated by the costume

FIGURE 3.2 The good costume is a global visual fact

62 ROLAND BARTHES WRITING THE POLITICAL

'romanticism' of verism. This is the politics of Brechtian theatre applied by Barthes to a critique of costumes.

Thus, there are two costumes that are not beholden to the verist 'disease'; first [Fig. 3.3], the design by Heinrich Kilger for Mother Courage in the Berliner Ensemble's 1954 production: 'costume', writes Barthes below the photograph, 'must convince before pleasing [séduire], in the middle of interminable war'.

Second [Fig. 3.4], by Mario Prassinos for Jean Vilar in *Macbeth* (see also Barthes 2002, I, 566–567), described positively in Barthes's comments as 'The costume-substance: wool and feudality'.

To these two 'healthy' theatre costumes Barthes now contrasts two examples of 'disease'. The costumes for the two main characters by an unnamed designer for the Comédie-Française production of Corneille's *Cinna* [Fig. 3.5] are excoriated in Barthes's caption: 'Aesthetic illness: fashion designer-style [drapé]'.

Likewise in the caption for the outfit worn by the actor in the Château-d'Eau theatre's 1902 production of Wagner's *Crépuscule des Dieux* [Fig. 3.6]: 'The "Frankenstein's lab [Musée Dupuytren]" of theatre costume: the Baroque, 1900' (1955, 70–71).

As he goes through the examples, there seems to be more 'disease' than 'health' in theatre costumes as his captions become exasperated. Thus, for the actor wearing a costume of fruits in the 1901 lyrical tragedy *Les Barbares* [Fig. 3.7, top left], Barthes writes: 'literalness; grapes [means] bacchantes'; and he returns to the *Crépuscule des Dieux* production as he satirizes another costume [Fig. 3.7, top right]: 'poverty: the Wagnerian

FIGURE 3.3 Costume must convince before pleasing, in the middle of interminable war

THE PEOPLE CHORUS 63

FIGURE 3.4 The costume-substance: wool and feudality

FIGURE 3.5 Aesthetic illness: fashion designer-style

FIGURE 3.6 The "Frankenstein's lab" of theatre costume: the Baroque, 1900

night-shirt'. Now it is the turn of the costume worn by Mme Simone in the role of la Faisane in the 1910 production of *Chantecler* [Fig. 3.7, centre right]: 'over-indication: tons of feathers'; followed by Elisabeth I and her consort in the *Folies Bergère* production of *Marie Stuart* [Fig. 3.7, bottom]: 'imbalance: clarity of forms, but affected mannerism of substances'.

He finishes with two 'healthy' examples; 'Le Cid deified and Le Cid disguised' is the caption, respectively, for Gérard Philipe's outfit at the TNP production [Fig. 3.8, left] and André Falcon's for the Comédie-Française production [Fig. 3.8, right].

However, the most striking is the comment on Gérard Philipe's outfit for the TNP production of Alfred de Musset's *Lorenzaccio*; against a large image of the Lothario-like Philipe dressed as Lorenzaccio [Fig. 3.9], there is laconic praise: 'Accord between face and costume' (Barthes 1955, 76). For someone who was studying faces closely (see 1979, 19–22; 2002, I, 268–79; ffrench 2019, 20–40), this photographic portrait (by an anonymous photographer) shows Barthes's interest at this time in face and clothing, not to mention for youth in photography.

Brecht's Political Theatre in Captions

> [T]he content and appeal of the pictures, the
> discourse which justifies them, aims to suppress
> the determining weight of History: we are held
> back at the surface of an identity, prevented precisely

FIGURE 3.7 Top left: 'Literalness; grapes – bacchantes'; top right: 'Poverty: the Wagnerian night-shirt'; bottom: 'Imbalance: clarity of forms, but affected mannerism of substances'

> by sentimentality from penetrating into this ulterior zone of human behaviour, where historical alienation introduces 'differences' which we shall here quite simply call 'injustices'.
>
> *(Barthes 2009, 101)*

The origins of Barthes's interest in, and sensitivity to photography, are doubtless in the theatre. Already in 1953 (2002, I, 273), he had praised the photographic portraits of actors by Thérèse le Prat, and the 'avant-garde' work for the TNP by the young, future film-maker, Agnès Varda; indeed, Varda supplies the theatre photography for the first French edition of Brecht's *Mother Courage*, in the TNP series (Brecht 1952). It is specifically Brechtian theatre that shows this most clearly. The very first link between Brecht

FIGURE 3.8 Left and right 'Le Cid deified and Le Cid disguised'

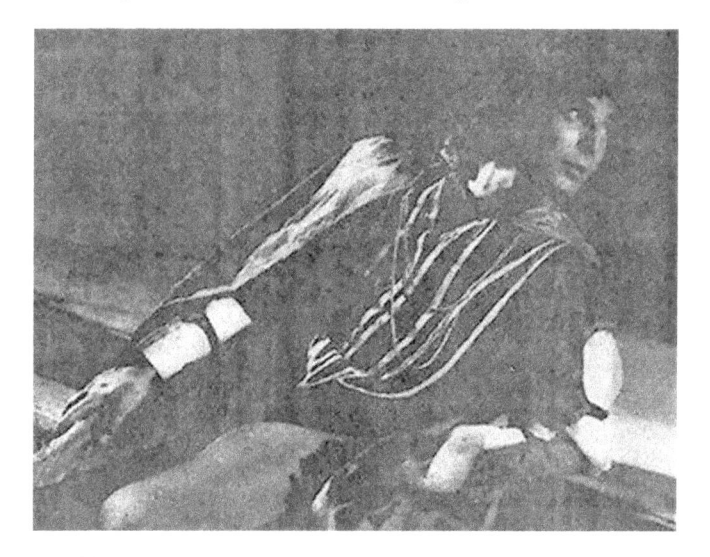

FIGURE 3.9 Accord between face and costume

and photography in Barthes's writing is his short but enthusiastic review in the left-wing weekly *France-Observateur* (2002, I, 654–55) of Roger Planchon's production in Lyon of Brecht's anti-fascist play *Grand'Peur et Misères du IIIe Reich* [Fear and Misery of the Third Reich], also photographed by Roger Pic.

What is striking in Barthes's review-article is, first, the engagement with Brecht's theatre in Planchon's production, as he states how difficult he found watching the play 'without thinking about Algeria, about the France of Poujade'; and second, the manner in which he uses a dialogue from the play with which to caption the photographic illustration of the production that heads the article (though the photograph is unattributed, we might assume that it is by Roger Pic). It shows two prisoners in the striped pyjamas typical of the Nazi concentration camps, former bakers who have been deported and put to hard labour; and the photographic caption drawn from an exchange in Brecht's play between the two victims of the Nazis uses humour as a form of political agitation:

- Why were you deported ?
- I was putting bran in my flour. And you?
- I wasn't putting bran in my flour …

(Barthes 1956, 10)

This quotation from the play is presumably Barthes's condensed version, as it differs from the script in the TNP repertoire (Brecht 1960c, 77). With this caption-quotation, as brief as it is dynamic, as economical as telling, Barthes's article captures the main meaning, including the bleak humour, of Brecht's anti-fascist play. The play represents to Barthes:

> a theatre that takes politics seriously, [...] involving a profoundly political link to a concrete historical situation [...]; at last a critical form of theatre that requires the spectator to turn and look at their own situation [.] (2002, I, 654)

These words are written just nine days before the French government will decide to apply even more brutal military measures in the colonial war in Algeria, the famous 'change of plan' ['tournant'] of 19 May 1956 that saw French troops sent into the Algiers casbah to flush out the FLN insurgents. It is often suggested that French theatre was very slow to react to the bloody colonial war in Algeria; indeed, the plays against the war by Sartre, Jean Genet, and Michel Vinaver all arrive very late in the conflict. However, here, in 1956, a small piece by Barthes at the right moment, using a skilfully laconic photo-textual illustration, shows how theatre can be politically engaged against internecine war. However, it is the collaboration with Pic's theatre photography two years later that best illustrates Barthes's political commitment, through Brechtian theatre, against war, against the war.

Pic had been working for the TNP since its inception in 1951, producing photographic records of each of the productions, for example Brecht's play *Maître Puntila et son valet Matti* (Brecht 1964). When the Berliner Ensemble returns in 1957 for a second production of Brecht's *Mother Courage*, Pic's photographic record of the production is chosen to be included in the new version of the script in the TNP repertoire (Brecht 1960b), replacing Varda's original work in the 1952 edition; and it is this record that involves Barthes. Barthes's two essays on seven or so of Pic's photographs are well-known (1967b; 2002, I, 1064–82); but entirely ignored (and not documented in his bibliography) is the series of captions that Barthes supplies for the whole corpus of 100 images by Pic that emerge from the famous production.

According to Bernard Dort (in Meyer-Plantureux et al. 1995, 17–18), the set-design for the 1957 production of *Mother Courage* is striking for its nudity, for its neutrality and for its stark white light – 'a photographer would say overexposed', suggests Dort (17). Indeed Pic's photography of Brecht's play is 'the instigator of a new theatre photograph that abandons the pose and the flash, preferring to recompose the production in all its facets – the acting style, the props and the décor – in relation to the lighting used', privileging 'the critical eye of the photographer who carefully records the features of the production as it is happening' (Meyer-Plantureux 1995, 19), in a manner that resonates with contemporary, twenty-first-century photographic tendencies (Nachtergael 2015, 52). Furthermore, the two seminal essays that Barthes writes on Pic's images of the 1957 production of Brecht's anti-war play (1967b; 2002, I, 1064–82) indicate to Dort that Barthes was reading them as a '[v]eritable Janus, multiplying their modes of representation […] [looking] at once towards the past (the theatre, Brecht) and also at the future (photography in general)' (19). This is a fascinating comment by Dort, which perceptively inscribes much of Barthes's later writing on photography in the commentary on Pic's record of Brechtian theatre. However, Dort does not mention the other 'Janus' activity in Barthes's work on Pic's photography, an activity that does not stop at a double 'Janus' view of photography, but also involves a direct intervention by Barthes's captions into the story of Mother Courage as 'narrated' by Pic's photographic record of the production.

The two essays by Barthes on Pic's photographs of *Mother Courage* (1967b; 2002, I, 1064–82) comment directly on the images (but only on seven of the 100 or so that were taken), in order to illustrate the Brechtian way of acting and the stage design that epic theatre required. In the first essay (1967b) Barthes's title refers to Brecht's notion of the 'photo-model' – the 'Modelbuch' – which the German dramatist had elaborated using 600–800 photographs for each Berliner-Ensemble production of his plays; and Brecht apparently appreciated Pic's way of creating such a photographic record (Meyer-Plantureux 1995, 31). Barthes's commentary on the 'photo-model' underlines the Brechtian *gestus* using seven images that are all 'based on some of the photographs of *Mother Courage*, from Act 1' (1967b, 44); and it is a profoundly political essay that points to the petty-bourgeois obsession with commerce as a key theme, suggesting, in a Hegelian reading of the master–slave dialectic (1967b, 45–46), that the eponymous heroine is 'doubly alienated: as the exploited and the exploiter' (47). In the second essay on Pic, published in 1960, Barthes comments again on only seven images by Pic, specifically those 'which are not at all edited [apprêtées]' (2002, I, 1064) and which are taken at various stages of the production. However, even though his comments and analyses vary from one essay to the other and the repetition of the images is only slight between the two texts, the approach by Barthes to Pic's photography is basically the same in each. The essayism, using only the occasional caption, analyses the images shown by mobilizing them into a discussion on the Brechtian acting technique of distancing, of the *gestus* and its 'mercantile function', of the 'decisive split' of the audience into both participating in the 'blinding' of Mother Courage and *seeing* 'this same blinding' (1972, 34). In the two essays, Barthes also adopts a certain detachment, if not distance, from Pic's images and from the action represented. The essayist is content to describe the action photographed as part of the Brechtian system of acting and scenic representation; and this approach stands in direct contrast to that taken in a third, completely overlooked, iteration of his work with Pic's photographs of the 1957 production of *Mother Courage*. We will now see how the 'édition illustrée' [*illustrated edition*] (Brecht 1960a), never mentioned by Barthes in his list of publications, shows him intervening directly in the photographic narrative of the production skilfully made by Pic. It is an intervention that will nuance the critique of 'understanding [intelligence]' in which Barthes becomes engaged, and represents, we will argue, the caption's version of the 'people chorus'.

Pic and Barthes on Brechtian Theatre – the Illustrated Edition

As well as publisher of *Théâtre Populaire*, for which Barthes works full-time between 1954 and 1956, Les Editions de l'Arche produces in the 1950s and 1960s affordable editions of Brecht's plays in French translation. Arche also publishes in 1954, alongside Brecht's *Little Organon of Theatre* in 1954, the short essay on Brecht by Geneviève Serreau that Barthes mentions in 'Shock-Photos' (1979, 71). Geneviève Serreau's work on Brecht in general, above all with Benno Besson – a friend and collaborator of the German dramatist – concentrates on the Berliner Ensemble's productions; and their 1951 translation of *Mother Courage* becomes the basis for l'Arche's republication of the play in 1960 that is augmented by seven of Pic's photographs of the 1957 production (Brecht 1960b) and accompanied by Barthes's 'Preface' (2002, I, 1064–82). However, lost in the deluge of Brechtian publications at this time when Epic Theatre is at its most popular in France, is Barthes's third intervention. Different from all the versions that show Pic's photographs of the 1957 production of *Mother Courage* is the 1960 volume in large format, the *illustrated edition*, which, sumptuous even, is the expensive, luxury, counterpart to the small repertoire edition of Brecht's play published by l'Arche the same year. The *illustrated edition* shows not a mere seven of Pic's photographic record, but the full one-hundred photographs which are then followed by the same essay now called 'Postface' (Brecht 1960a, 209–21) – and not 'Preface' as it is called in the standard short small-format edition of the play. If the 'Commentary: Postface' is identical to the 'Commentary: Preface', the first of these follows the full record of one hundred images by Pic and which – and this is the key point – are accompanied by numerous captions. The contention we are making is that Barthes writes these captions. Before we embark on a detailed analysis of these captions, how (if it is not listed by Barthes) can we be sure of this?

First, the advertising for the *illustrated edition* of *Mother Courage* in the journal *Théâtre Populaire* (number 40) in 1960, referring to the volume as a 'whole play in book', describes it thus:

> Two masterpieces: the whole scenario of the play (in the French version by Geneviève Serreau and Benno Besson), and the Berliner Ensemble's production (directed by Erich Engel and Bertolt Brecht): 100 photographs by Roger Pic, presented and commented by Roland Barthes. (*Théâtre Populaire* 1960, back cover)

That the 100 photographs by Pic, numbered 1 to 100 and with captions alongside (Brecht 1960a, 113–208), are followed directly by Barthes's 'Commentary: Postface' (209–21), suggests that Barthes's role, with his knowledge of Brecht's play, is to write the captions too.

Indeed, in the 1959 essay 'Seven Photo models of *Mother Courage*', Barthes mentions this full record of Pic's 100 images of the production: 'we possess a true photographic history of Mother Courage, something quite novel, I believe, in theatre criticism – at least for France', and '[t]his succession of about one hundred photographs' is 'very fine' (1967b, 44). Thus, prefiguring the collaborative work he will carry out with Hubert Aquin in Quebec in 1961 on images of sports in photography and on television (Barthes 2007c), Barthes's 'commentary' on the photographic record of the 1957 Berliner Ensemble production of Brecht in Paris is not restricted to an essay (the 'Commentary Postface'), but includes also Barthes's words *alongside* each of the 100 hundred photographs by Pic. There are other reasons to believe that the captions are Barthes's hand in this attractive volume – with cloth cover and in large format (15cm x 21cm) – that is 'commented' but also 'presented' by Barthes.

Indeed, one of the captions cited in the two essays by Barthes, '*We are in business* [*On est dans le commerce*]' (2002, I, 1004 and 1077), a quotation from Brecht's play (caption for this photograph not included in the English translation in 1967b, 47), also appears alongside a similar photograph in the *illustrated edition*. In the 'Commentary' Barthes even draws attention to the lack of captions for the seven images in the 'Preface', and the potential usefulness of this lack: '[w]ithout caption [...] (and this is what allowed [Pic] to reduce the images to their most discreet size possible), the photographs of *Mother Courage* would not be any more obscure, any more diminished than the legend of Saint Ursula as told by Carpaccio' (2002, I, 1076). In other words, Pic's photographs of the 1957 production are able to say a great deal *without* words. Is this comment, however, partly, a foil for the captions he writes?

What is striking then about the captions, as part of Barthes's work to 'present' Pic's series of 100 photographs, is how direct the captioning is. In his close reading of 'Seven Photo Models' Jim Carmody (1990) underlines the distance that he sees between Barthes's essay and Pic's photographs; not only does the essay consider a mere seven images, argues Carmody, but also Barthes's essay seems to pass Pic's photographs by without really commenting on them. This, as we shall now see, could not be further from the truth with regard to the captions that we attributing to Barthes; and it may be that the large-format *illustrated edition* represents a tight collaboration between Pic and Barthes at the time, but that leads, in the editing that follows, to a detached essayism in Barthes's two well-known pieces on Pic. In the caption-work by contrast, there are at least 100 moments when the images are commented. Indeed, as we will see, Pic's 100-photograph series represents a new way to 'watch' a Brecht play; and Barthes's captions play a crucial, chorus-like, commentating role alongside the visual narration. Moreover, Barthes's captioning resembles Brecht's *modelbuch* for *Mother Courage* (in Kuhn et al. 2017, 183–222).

The 100 or so captions are of two types in the main. On the one hand, quotations of key moments in *Mother Courage*: '*We are in business*' [*On est dans le commerce*]; or else, the exchange between Mother Courage and the soldiers: 'There wouldn't be any war if there weren't any soldiers' (1967b, 49). Only the first of these appears as a caption in Barthes's 1959 essay; and there are no captions in the 1960 essay (2002, I, 1064–82). What is more interesting is the way in which Barthes uses captions as forms of written intervention in the play's plot as it moves forward in the unfurling of Pic's images. The caption-quotations – the diegetic voices of the characters – selected by Barthes are augmented by extradiegetic captions that are used to briefly describe the action. In other words, these two types of caption work together as a way of critically commentating on the narration of Brecht's play operated by the photographs. This is strikingly similar to the way in which Barthes characterizes the ancient Greek chorus, that is, a means of encouraging the critical reading of (here) the readership of the illustrated edition of Pic's photographic record, thereby imitating in book-form what the audience at the production in the theatre would have experienced. For example, next to image 9 – which is image 5 in the 1960 'Preface' (2002, I, 1070) and described in the commentary in relation to Catherine's ponytail but not captioned (1074) – we read Barthes's first extradiegetic caption:

> And in order to keep the recruiters away, Mother Courage sets about predicting the future to the Corporal: a piece of paper is folded in two … (Brecht 1960a, image 9)

The captions are not only next to each image by Pic, but also complete the storyline. Whereas 'Seven Photo Models' gives the scantest of context – 'A covered wagon approaches, drawn by two young men' (caption not included in English version, 1967b, 48) – the captions in the *illustrated edition* help the reader see the tragedy of the play:

> The cart which doubles up as her shop is pulled along by Mother Courage's two sons, the timorous Eilif and the honest Swiss Cheese. Sitting on the cart, Mother Courage is happy, the journey is a moment of rest for her: she sings accompanied on the harmonica by her daughter Catherine who is mute. (Brecht 1960a, image 7)

The readership of this 'true photographic history of *Mother Courage*' (1967b, 44) is thus well served by Barthes's captions alongside the powerful images by Pic. It raises the question, however, as to why Barthes suppresses the vast majority of this captioning material when he comes to write the 1960 'Commentary-Preface'. It is not simply due to the reduction of the 100 images to seven: the captions aid the reader in following the plot, whilst commenting on these same images in a chorus-like, even dialectical, way. Indeed, at key moments in the action, for example when Catherine begins to turn against her mother, Barthes's caption supplies crucial, extra information not available in the photographs. This is especially true of the action-image (no. 91) in which we see Catherine on the roof refusing to come down whilst the soldiers wait below hoping to dislodge her. Here is Barthes's crucial, if not agitational, caption for this image [Fig. 3.10]

> Alerted by the noise of the drum, the soldiers and the young peasant have returned. Catherine drums harder and harder. What is to be done [Que faire]? (Brecht 1960a, image 91)

[Photograph with upper caption: "Alertés par le bruit du tambour, les soldats et le jeune paysan sont revenus. Catherine bat de plus en plus fort. Que faire ?" and lower caption: "— Descends, suis-nous jusqu'à la ville, tu nous désigneras ta mère, et elle aura la vie sauve."]

FIGURE 3.10 Alerted by the noise of the drum, the soldiers and the young peasant have returned. Catherine drums harder and harder. What is to be done?

What is striking in Barthes's caption is the interventionist nature of the commentary. The 'what is to be done?'– even if we do not take it as an allusion to the title of Lenin's famous 1905 essay – represents for the readership of Pic's photograph a radical orientation of its significance. This is the crowning moment for Barthes's captioning. The captions up until now have used Pic's photographic record in order to communicate the three human values that pertain to each of Mother Courage's three children (Eilif's courage; Swiss Cheese's honesty; Catherine's solidarity). These values are nonetheless, as the irony of Brecht's play underlines, but the cause of the decline for each character. This pessimism has encouraged some critics to see the chorus that Mother Courage and her three children represent in singing their telling songs as an 'anti-chorus' (Revermann 2013, 162–63); first, because only one of this chorus survives who is Mother Courage, thereby heralding its demise; second, not only did the ancient Greek chorus survive the catastrophe in each tragedy, it also represented collective wisdom and not the collective ignorance of Brecht's play (168). But this pessimism is entirely absent from Barthes's chorus-like captions. The caption above the image by Pic allows Barthes to attribute to Catherine the status of 'true' heroine of the play, made all the more poignant by her inability to speak. Indeed, the trap that the soldiers have laid for Catherine indicates the depth to which her fortunes have declined, even if she uses the drum to alert the village and thereby save its inhabitants.

Barthes is acutely aware of Pic the photographer's powerful images which, unlike the usual photographs of theatre productions that highlight choice moments, allow us to experience and understand a situation as a 'duration' that is full of meanings (2002, I, 1064). The images are 'faithful' but not 'servile', Barthes argues as a premonition for the brief preface to his 1970 essay *Empire of Signs*: 'The text does not "gloss" the images, which do not "illustrate" the text' (1982b, xi): Pic's images 'do not illustrate, they help us to discover the profound intention of the play: for this reason they are truly critical' (2002, I, 1064). Indeed, Catherine's mutism and refusal to stop drumming seems to illustrate well the '*sensitive, avid and silent*' in Barthes the political subject who, alongside Brecht, is looking for 'little politics' (1994, 53).

Despite the concatenation of these three qualities, it is the 'discontinuous' that Barthes most praises in Brechtian theatre, mirroring the 'rupture' underlined by Walter Benjamin in 'What is Epic Theatre?', his only article published in *Théâtre Populaire* and signalled by Barthes in a footnote (2002, I, 1075). It is as if the contradictions between 'sensitive', 'avid' and 'silent' are augmented by their concatenation. How do Barthes's captions for Pic's photographs respect, amplify and engage this same discontinuity? Even if he considers Brecht's Epic Theatre as one that abandons Aristotelian theatre, both the quotations from the play and the commentary that he appends to Pic's photographs are chorus-like interventions.

Michaud (1989, 109) notices with respect to the fragmentary photo-textualism in *Roland Barthes by Roland Barthes* that 'the commentary [alongside] works at a distance' without 'coincidence nor correspondence'. This seems to be true too of Barthes's chorus-like investment in his captioning, be it alongside Pic's images of Brechtian theatre or the ironic, humorous comments on theatre costumes we saw above. However, whether 'commentary par excellence' on a play (as in Pic's photographic record of *Mother Courage*) or assessing costume designs, the captions always have a serious, political aim. Indeed, in both cases, the photographer matters less than the photograph, which, in series, is fragmented, but directed by the written caption from without.

In the second of his essays on Pic's photographic record, Barthes recognizes what is revolutionary in *Mother Courage* (2002, I, 1081–82): the figure of Catherine 'whose work of consciousness is to understand the real' despite her inability to speak. This 'highest form of intelligence' that he sees in the figure of Catherine can be glimpsed not just in his two essays on Pic but also in the captions that Barthes appends. The *distancing* in both caption and essay are not at all a sign of a mere 'theoretical sociality' as Didi-Huberman contends; to 'mimic' Brechtian *Verfremdung* in his approach to captioning Pic's photo-record is not at all 'cruelly' to ignore the pathos in *Mother Courage*. Moreover, Barthes does not forget Mother Courage's pain; instead, he compares it to Catherine's 'sensitivity [sensibilité]', a pathos that is implicit in Barthes's captions precisely because it is explicit in Pic's images. As well as a sign of 'another', future, politics of the image (Watts 2016, 57–58), the analysis of Eisenstein stills is a further example of the 'double grasp', applied by Barthes to his caption work on Brechtian drama: after all, '[t]he originality in the Brechtian sign', as he will suggest in 1975, 'is that it is *to be read twice*' (2002, IV, 789).

It is not simply Brecht's (and Eisenstein's) 'pregnant instants' (2002, IV, 341) that he wishes to capture. With the full set of Pic's photography of Brechtian theatre in the *illustrated edition*, Barthes's interventionist captions manage already in 1960 what he intends to do in *Camera Lucida* in 1980, that is, neither critique nor expressive (or both), to present 'the uneasiness' of being 'a subject torn between languages, one expressive, the other critical' (1984, 8). Such an experience of directly working alongside photography of Brechtian theatre clearly influences the work on connotation in the photograph (1977, 19). Indeed, the 'double grasp' here appears to be much less an oscillating act, as a doing-two-things-at-once.

The 'double grasp' captioning of Pic's images will influence the 'stereographical' approach that he begins to initiate across the 1960s: after all, as *S/Z* insists, writing (be it essay, commentary, caption, or whatever) is a 'citation'; all writing is the *already written* (1974, 21). This 'duplicity' will extend to how he writes the essay alongside André Martin's images of the Eiffel Tower (1979, 3–18) as part of a double act of vision of the 'seeing' and the 'being seen' in structuralism and existentialism respectively; to the advocating, in 'The Death of the Author', of Vernant's view that ancient Greek theatre, as a 'duplicity' of words, is 'exactly the tragic' (1977, 148). 'Neither pure subjectivity, nor pure exteriority, pathos, like conscience, is located in the articulation of the look with the object, of the spectacle with the spectator' (Coste 2016b, 8).

Before we consider the 'dramatized' commentary in the late 1960s with respect to Balzac's story *Sarrasine* and then to the poetry of the Moroccan writer Zaghloul Morsy, we will first look at Barthes's appreciation of Michelet in tandem with Walter Benjamin's. All involve commentary, but all also represent interventions *into* the objects around which the commentary is built, precisely the way in which Barthes describes the Greek chorus.

Chapter Four

'DOUBLE GRASP'

My interpretation of history will […] be marked by the materialism of Marx and the mysticism of Michelet.

(Jaurès 1956, 167)

The specificity of History is to organise the progressive unveiling of what happened by way of an epicentre that is external to the crisis itself; it is to substitute the idea of time by that of structure.

(Barthes 2002, I, 541)

Radical [Hi]story

With these words, we mark in this chapter the extraordinary and life-long fascination that Barthes has with the nineteenth century (Sun 2014), even imagining Marx, Mallarmé, Nietzsche and Freud meeting in 1876 (2013, 6). Indeed the quotation above from Jean Jaurès – from the introduction to his huge 'socialist history' of the Great French Revolution – seems to go to the heart of Barthes's political ideas at least at the start of his career, up to and including what Stedman Jones (1983, 48) calls the early Lukács's 'marriage between romantic anti-scientific *lebensphilosophie* and historical materialism'. First, because Jaurès was assassinated in 1914, whilst trying to argue against a war that was going to turn into a blood-bath, and in which Barthes lost his father he never knew (Stafford 2015a, 15–17). Second, the strong influence of Jaurès's socialism, well attested in Barthes's early correspondence in 1932 with his life-long friend Philippe Rebeyrol (Barthes 2018, 2, 4–5) points to the consistency of Barthes's left-wing beliefs. But, perhaps the most important for the purposes of this chapter, is that Jaurès was a historian (and not the first) that we now call 'from below', who used a historiographical writing that went directly against official History. This 'History from below', typified by the works of its recent practitioner, Raphael Samuel – younger member of the group of mainly British Communists who, by turn, were influenced by the French historians Georges Lefebvre, Lucien Febvre and Albert Mathiez – is what characterized the interest that Barthes had developed in the historiography of Jules Michelet.

    The play on words 'history/story' in the title of this section above refers, at the same time, to Barthes's extensive work of 1968–69 on the curious story by the nineteenth-century writer (and contemporary of Michelet) Honoré de Balzac called *Sarrasine*, the 're-writing' of which by Barthes and his postgraduate students in Paris became his 1970 essay *S/Z*. The aim is to show that the 'stereographic space' in Barthes's radical

1968 reading of Balzac's story (1974, 21) suggests a parallel if not a remarkable similarity between *S/Z* on the one hand and his earlier *Michelet* on the other. As befits the quote from Jaurès above, we will first discuss Marx's materialism in tandem with Michelet's 'mysticism', which we will then compare to that of another near contemporary and fan of both Marx and Michelet, the German philosopher Walter Benjamin, in order to propose a much wider notion of stereography, of 'double' writing.

The 'Suppleness' of the Dialectic

Indeed both Benjamin and Barthes are close readers of Marx's *18th Brumaire*, possibly because Marx showed History putting 'its worst foot forward' (Jameson 2010, 287). In a letter to Philippe Rebeyrol dated July 1946, Barthes sets out his hesitations with Historical Materialism, especially after reading, with disappointment, Marx's *Holy Family*. Such is the simplistic nature of materialist analysis that he would never be able to 'overcome [his] repulsion for materialism as a philosophy', involving 'confusion, weakness and puerility, in the extreme': '[n]ever' would he be able to believe that 'the *nec plus ultra* of psychology is behaviourism'. 'What's more, continues Barthes, 'all these Marxist commentators are ludicrous in their severity'. There is, he concedes, 'one sole exception'; he finds it 'very telling to have been so persuaded by a mere commentator of Marx (Sidney Hook) and so disappointed (so far) by Marx himself'. Yet, 'politically', he can barely think in any way other than 'Marxistly [marxistement]'. The 'description of the world' by Marxists 'alone' is 'correct'; and the 'suppleness' and the 'intelligence' of Marxist theory is sorely lacking in Marxian practice. Barthes then describes his two reservations about his own political commitment; feeling 'reticent for the moment', he questions, first, 'the link between a materialist philosophy, notoriously insufficient, and the Marxist revolution', which seems to him to be true', second, 'the place, the *nature* of the intellectual in this revolution'.

Sidney Hook was an American theoretician, and, in the 1930s, a Communist activist, whose 1933 book *Towards the Understanding of Karl Marx* exerted a major influence on American Marxism. Translated into French in 1936, *Pour comprendre Marx* is, for the Barthes of 1946, the only book by Hook available in French. Hook's analysis contains important considerations on myth and ideology in an alienated society which doubtless influence the mythologies Barthes wrote ten years later. It considers Philosophy and Marxist practice, using voluntarist conceptions of the actor in History drawn, on the one hand, from Karl Korsch for practice, and on the other, from Georg Lukács for the Marxian dialectic. As a non-orthodox Marxist in the 1930s, Hook was helping to reinvent Marxism, in the aftermath of its 'castration' by the Second and then the Third International, both of which, he suggested, had marginalized the 'philosophy of action' in Marxism. As a precursor to what Perry Anderson (1979) calls 'Western Marxism', Hook mixed the instrumentalist pragmatism of a John Dewey with the method of historical materialism; for Hook (1936, 14–34, 59ff), it was the 'suppleness' of the dialectic in Marx that mattered in the marrying of the theoretical and the practical. For example, Hook (1936, 14) declares that 'the philosophy of Marx is a dialectical synthesis of those objective and subjective moments'. Then, in his study of historical praxis (1943), Hook tries to describe the Marxian notions of 'base' and 'superstructure' in terms of pragmatism. On this subject, Barthes writes the following in the newspaper version of 'Triumph and Rupture of Bourgeois Writing' (1950, 4), in a discussion about the 'deep rapport' between 'Form' and 'History' not included in *Writing Degree Zero*: '(It may be [...] that the problem of the determinism of superstructures will one day be resolved by looking more at forms and structures rather than at the traditional history of ideas where the intermediaries [relais] are more numerous and more complex)'.

If there is a clear trace of Barthes's interest in the 'suppleness' of the dialectic in the ideas of Sidney Hook, there is, as we saw in Chapter Two, equal influence of Lukácsian ideas in 'Myth Today'. His investment in Marxism is highly ambivalent. In a letter dated 16 August 1946, he expresses to Rebeyrol admiration for Marx's 1851 essay on the *coup d'état* by Napoleon III: 'I have risen above Marxism; I think that I have got it out of my system [exorcisé]; I have just been reading, with greatest pleasure, *The 18th Brumaire of Louis Bonaparte*, a beautiful work, powerful in its cohesion, its air of truth'; 'but', he adds, 'our Marxists today, so pretentious, so proud of their materialist philosophy, are miles away from the *active* intelligence of this book, from its suppleness even. Indeed, someone who believes, to whatever extent, in literature cannot be absolutely Marxist. It requires such partisanship'.

We saw in Chapter Three the influence of suppleness in the critique of 'brutal' historical analogy in Thomson's, and to a lesser extent Goldmann's, work on tragedy. But the most important part of Barthes's work where we find the 'suppleness' of the dialectic is in his writings on the nineteenth-century (post-)romantic historian, Jules Michelet. For Barthes, the 'dance of the dialectic' (to borrow Bertell Ollman's expression) is unmistakeable in Michelet's voluminous writings, which Barthes 'devoured' during his war-time years spent in a sanatorium recovering from tuberculosis.

History From Below: Michelet's 'Double Grasp'

In his study of modern forms of observation, Jonathan Crary (1992) sees the nineteenth century – and not at all the *camera obscura* in the seventeenth and eighteenth centuries – as the key to modern tropes of seeing. In parallel with Crary's bold assertion, we trace the 'double grasp' to Barthes's 1954 presentation of Michelet's writings. It is useful first to underline the influence of Michelet even on concepts we have considered in *Mythologies*. In a letter to Georges Canetti dated 20 December 1945 Barthes excoriates Jesuit thinking thus:

> There's a way of thinking, of reasoning, that even without being sectarian is Christian (Socratic) and is nauseating because of its emasculation of passion, its slack objectivity (Jesuit perfidy, what Michelet calls—brilliantly, admit it—the vaccine of truth, that way of constructing all human fact on the 'undoubtedly.... but nevertheless.' (2018, 49)

This interest in Michelet's double understanding of Jesuit discourse is a crucial element, first, in Barthes's critique of myth, the 'amorous dialectic' that we considered in

Chapter Two, but second, as we saw in Chapter Three in the caption-interventions that he applied to Pic's photography of Brechtian theatre. However, between the amorous dialectic and the visual representation of revolution there lies a huge gulf, that of seeing two things at once. Before we consider the perceived solution to this in Michelet's writing of history, we need first to return, briefly, to the theoretical essay that ends *Mythologies*, 'Myth Today', in order to consider the obstacles that 'stereography' encounters.

Visual multi-tasking

In 'Myth Today' Barthes is acutely aware of the difficulty of doing two things at once, to the extent that the essay which ends *Mythologies*, whilst offering a systematic, semiological critique of mass communications, hesitates to paint a world that is 'upside down' as it is in (the early) Marx. Barthes seems to be insisting rather on the complex difficulty of stereoscopy. The problem for the ideological analysis of myth is that myth is a 'double system', in which the signifier is already a structure of signification in itself, which is made of the 'constantly moving turnstile that presents alternately the meaning of the signifier and its form'; at once 'a language-object *and* a metalanguage, a purely signifying *and* a purely imagining consciousness', myth relies on an 'ambiguous signifier, at once intellective *and* imaginary, arbitrary *and* natural (2009, 147, emphasis added). Myth then is essentially a 'double function', pointing out *and* notifying, making us understand something whilst imposing it upon us (140).

Much is made of the notion (and acts) of multi-tasking, and its practical application in twenty-first-century life. Yet, in visual terms, Barthes seemed persuaded – at least in 'Myth Today' in 1957 – that humans were not actually able necessarily to see two things at once:

> If I am in a car and I look at the scenery through the window, I can at will focus on the scenery or on the windowpane. At one moment I grasp the presence of the glass and the distance of the landscape; at another, on the contrary, the transparence of the glass and the depth of the landscape; but the result of this alternation is constant: the glass is at once present and empty to me, and the landscape unreal and full. (2009, 147)

However, it is not a form of multi-tasking that is required to battle myth, but the contrary: a crucial element in the mythologist's armoury is that of artificially ignoring, or bracketing temporarily, one of the two dimensions:

> To wonder at this contradiction, I must voluntarily interrupt the turnstile of form and meaning, I must focus on each separately, and apply to myth a static method of deciphering, in short, I must go against its own dynamics[.] (148)

This 'pass[ing]' from reader of myth to mythologist, ironically a 'static' one, involves not only a refusal of a visual multi-tasking, but it also has to ignore the mediation. One 'static' glance out of my window as I write, by way of a test of Barthes's phenomenological theory, 'brackets' *either* the tree at the end of the garden *or* the pane of glass next to me (and if we add the movement outside the window-pane during a car journey, then the mediation, by turn, of countryside and then pane goes – if one pardons the pun – out of the window).

Barthes's – and our - difficulty with the 'grasp' of two things at once may seem pessimistic in the domain of myth. However, as we shall see, in Micheletist historiography, at least one type of 'double grasp' can be glimpsed. Zenetti (2011) has begun a study of optical metaphors in Barthes's writing, especially that of opacity and its replacement of mediation in Barthes's work, to which we will return over the following two chapters.

In 1955, Barthes saw a 'double grasp' at work in the research of André Ombredane (1898–1958) involving comparative psychological tests on Belgian and Congolese students, using films by Jean Painlevé and Jacques Cousteau (1972, 52–53). Following Edgar Morin's work, Barthes considered this 'ethnological experiment' by Ombredane to be indicative of the conditioning taking place in the European mind (on Ombredane, see Barthes 1972, 52–53; 2007b, 16–17; 1984, 49–50; Morin 1956, 115). The experiment also suggested that '[t]here is, then, a conflict between the purely optical world of objects and the world of human interiority' (1972, 53). However, it is in Michelet's writing that Barthes spied something of a solution, at least in historiographical terms.

Indeed, in his very first publication on Michelet in 1951, Barthes presented the historian as a god of the future, acting as a magistrate of History, all this by dint of his position of ulteriority; however – and this is crucial – in Barthes's eyes (2002, I, 110–12), Michelet is also an 'eater of History', that is, the person who walks *with* the actants of History – the 'people' – who are blind, so to speak, as to where their actions will end up. This gymnastic dialectic (at once, here *and* there) – what the British Communist historian Edward Thompson calls 'the enormous condescension of posterity' – makes Michelet, to use Edmund Wilson's expression, the 'historian from below' *par excellence*. As Barthes maintains, the 'foundation of History' for Michelet was 'in the final instance' – echoing Friedrich Engels's words when affirming Marx's materialism –, 'the bodily death of millions of humans'; and Michelet, the 'body Historian', had found a way of '[r]emaking the life of the dead' (122). 'In the final instance' is a materialist-inspired expression that can be found regularly in Barthes's writing; it is redolent of Althusser for an older Barthes, but here, in 1951, it is to Engels that Barthes seems to be alluding (preface to Engels, 1884). Indeed, Petitier (2000, 113) sees Barthes's Marxist 'signature' as an allusion to *The German Ideology*.

Barthes is suggesting then that Michelet could, in a utopian manner, be simultaneously here and there, able to put himself both outside and inside History. It is a technique that uses a double form of writing which, suggests Barthes, involves 'either the discomfort of progress or else the euphoria of a panorama' (1987a, 22). Above all, it seems that the 'historian's squaring of the circle, [...] the *summum* of historical research' as Barthes calls it (2015b, 44) has been achieved by Michelet: being able, simultaneously, to be here and there, as both historiographer and partisan actor in History, at one and the same time, suggests a dexterity of writerly skill:

> Michelet's presence in *La Sorcière* is anything but a simple romantic expansion of subjectivity. What Michelet must do, in fact, is to participate magically in the myth without ceasing to describe it: his text is both narration and experience[.] (1972, 111)

This is Michelet's *double grasp* [double saisie] or 'double apprehension' (1987a, 22). As well as 'resurrecting' (if only in writing) the forgotten masses of History, Michelet gained intellectual and historiographical sustenance from this 'double grasp' of the people's past:

> [...] History can be the object of an appropriation only if it is constituted as an authentic object, supplied with two ends or poles. History can be an aliment only when it is full as an egg; hence Michelet has filled his, has endowed it with two goals and one direction: his History has actually become a philosophy of History. History is to be consummated, i.e., on the one hand, concluded, fulfilled, and, on the other, consumed, devoured, ingested, so as to resuscitate the historian. (Barthes 1987a, 25)

Michelet, writes Barthes, enjoyed both the position of 'supervisibility which allows him to order History as a spectacle and not a movement', and that of 'suffering, struggling, hoping' in the past 'alongside the total mass of History' (2002, I, 110).

Edmund Wilson's writing on Michelet, published in 1940, precedes Barthes's study of Michelet by a decade. As a colleague and comrade of Sidney Hook, Wilson also puts forward a voluntarist view of history. Though there is no evidence to suggest that Barthes had read Wilson's chapters on Michelet, the similarities are striking.

According to Wilson, Michelet's historiography was inspired by Vico, Bacon and Grotius, and underlined the 'organic' nature of human progress; similarly, Barthes points to the *Scienza Nuova* by Vico – a form of sociology conceived long before the birth of the discipline of the same name according to Wilson – as a major influence on Michelet. And, just as Barthes will do, Wilson underlines the contradictory aims in Michelet's historiography. First, Wilson suggests, Michelet had tried to find a fusion of distinct materials, in his keenness to establish the interrelations between diverse forms of human activities (similar to the notions of 'structure' and 'tableau' in Barthes's Michelet). Second, Michelet wanted to capture the colour and feel of a period, that is, by returning to the past while being (or, pretending to be) ignorant of the outcome (this is the 'narrative [récit]' in Michelet for Barthes), maintaining the illusion of having no historian's distance. Finally, in terms that prefigure those of Barthes, Wilson emphasizes the capacity of Michelet's prose to supply a general tableau whilst, at the same time, focusing attention on a single historical object, only then to break off in order to draw the large historical tableau (see also Carrard 2017, 33). Quoting, just as Barthes does (1987a, 208–10), Proust's pastiche of Michelet, Wilson insists on how much Michelet had tried to live the history that he was narrating. For Wilson, the enormous contradiction in Michelet's life and in the writing strategy deployed in his historiography, was that Michelet loved the people, saw them as the agents of History, but that, Wilson notes, it was Michelet alone who spoke, acted and resurrected the past. As we shall see, this secular 'resurrection' is part also of Walter Benjamin's approach to history, in which 'the present can rescue the past from oblivion, while the dead can be summoned to the aid of the living' (Eagleton 2021, 27).

It is not surprising then – though the wording might startle a little those such as Coste (2009; 2016b, 29–54) who see Barthes as always escaping 'totality'– that in his favourable 1954 review of *Michelet* Bernard Dort (1954) congratulates Barthes for the 'totalitarian' approach (totalitarian in the good sense of attempting to reach totality). Indeed, *totality* is one of the three key categories of the dialectic according to Engels and Lukács, and we saw how the dialectic fares in the hands of Barthes the mythologist. How does this 'totalitarian' spirit of Michelet appear then in the very final thoughts of a near contemporary of Wilson's, Walter Benjamin? There are some interesting similarities, parallels and dissonances in the Michelet presented by Barthes in relation to Benjamin's fragments partly inspired by Michelet and written just before his suicide in 1940.

(Late) Walter Benjamin in 'Dialogue' with (Early) Roland Barthes

Though we have no record of Barthes's having read Benjamin's 'theses on the philosophy of history', as an avid reader in the post-war period of Sartre's radical journal *Les Temps modernes*, he may well have read Benjamin's fragments on History when they appeared in Sartre's journal after the War (Benjamin 1947). Surprisingly little, with the exception of an important book on photography (Yacavone 2012), has been written on a possible meeting of minds between Benjamin, on the one hand, and Barthes, on the other. Both are inspired by Brechtian theatre; and, like Barthes, Benjamin is fascinated by the writing of the fragment and, as with Barthes's work on the citation (in *S/Z* and on Japan especially), famously planned to use the quotation to write about Paris (2002).

This gap in studies of Barthes with Benjamin is especially evident in relation to history and history-writing, up till now possibly explicable by the lack of translation into English of Barthes's first journalistic writings. Indeed, as John Berger points out (2001, 186), Benjaminian thought brought together – in an uncannily similar fashion to the quote from Jaurès at the start of this chapter – the theological and the Talmudic with the materialist and the dialectical in what Berger sees as Benjamin's combining of the 'antiquarian' with the 'revolutionary'; for Berger (187), Benjamin's engagement with history is trying at once to consider a 'fixed object […] in historic time, in order thereby to measure time' whilst also (simultaneously, we might say in relation to Barthes's view of Michelet's 'double grasp') aiming 'to grasp the import of the specific passage of time'. In an uncanny intertext with Barthes's 1970 essay *S/Z* and its 'stereographic', double grasp, Berger, also writing in 1970, sees Benjamin's approach as rejecting the 'disinterested' approach to works of art that 'explain the appearance of a work', preferring to 'discover the place that its existence needed to occupy in our knowledge': as Berger puts it for Benjamin, 'Works of art await use' (189). We will return to this 'functional' view of a 'work' when we consider Barthes's *S/Z* in more detail. Furthermore, Berger underlines in Benjamin's concept of history a scepticism as to the 'so-called historical laws […] implied by the notion of overall Progress or Civilization' (Berger 190), an anti-teleological and anti-formalist view of history that we will consider in Barthes's writings in the next chapter.

Only a decade separates the young Barthes reading and annotating Michelet, critiquing analogy and laws in history, and the pessimistic Benjamin exploding the notion of a continuum of history. Though much seems to separate the two thinkers, a comparison of four articles by the French theorist – on André Joussain, on Roger Caillois (twice) and on Jules Michelet, all journalistic pieces written between 1950 and 1952 (Barthes 2015b, 1–6, 7–11 and 21–26) – with Benjamin's seminal, albeit complex, critique of antiquarian notions of history-writing seems to point to a striking coincidence of thought.

The following comparison of Benjamin and Barthes emerges from informal seminar discussions around the question of 'What are "years"?'. This might seem to be an issue on which (late) Benjamin and (early) Barthes largely differ. Whereas Benjamin's 'Theses on the Philosophy of History' highlight the moments during Revolutions in which insurgents take aim at time itself – 'tilting at clocks', overthrowing the calendar, establishing a new way of recording and marking years – Barthes's early pieces on history and historiography, by contrast, are keen to underline the specificity of History, usually written, following Hegel and also Michelet, with a capital H. If Benjamin sees revolutionaries' tilts at clocks as their bid to explode the continuum of history and thereby snatch history back from the ruling classes, Barthes for his part wants to underline the singularity of the historical event in order to prevent comparative histories from finding a law in historical change which denies human agency. Clearly, both theorists are operating within a Marxian, historical-materialist, optic in their critique of bourgeois history; but the former wishes to found historical account anew, the latter to affirm its inalienability. And yet, as we shall see, both Benjamin's romantic conception of history and Barthes's literal, if not literary, conception seem to turn on those three key terms mentioned above.

I *was* going to proceed with my comparison of Barthes first in the 1950s and then Benjamin in 1940, by looking at the later of these writings and then to see how Benjamin's theses fit with Barthes's – backwards as it were. With Barthes there are good reasons for this. First, Barthes's deconstructive reading of the past, especially in later life, is hard to miss; as we shall see in Chapter Nine. Furthermore, and closer to our discussion of history and historiography, Barthes's spending World War II recovering from tuberculosis in a sanatorium reading closely the complete works of a nineteenth-century romantic historian, represents a looking backwards for an understanding of the twentieth-century world at war. Benjamin too is often characterized as a thinker obsessed with the nineteenth century, whose 'task [is] to brush history against the grain' (2001, VII); though one critic has described this idea as an indictment of 'historicist notions of culture' suggesting 'the extreme anti-evolutionary notion of "history"' marking Benjamin's 'unusual (and selective) reading of Marxism' (Lunn 1982, 225). Above all, the Angelus of history in Klee's painting that informs Benjamin's outlook on history looks backwards. However, it is better to run the comparison of Barthesian and Benjaminian historiographies as if it were a real dialogue between the two.

Interestingly, if Barthes's Michelet has the 'two sexes of the spirit', the work of Klee and Benjamin has been read by feminists as 'bisexual' in outlook (Niethammer 1992, 114). And, as far as a comparative study of Barthes and Benjamin goes, at least in relation to photography, Yacavone argues (13-27) that Barthes's theories and approaches to photography between 1950 and 1980 were always already there in Benjamin's work on photography in the 1920s and 1930s.

Benjamin – despondent about Nazi Germany's seeming unstoppability and dismayed by Stalin's pact with Hitler – wants to leave behind, marginalize, arrest even, the flow of history. This is a crucial challenge to a 'years'-based, 'King's history'; for, as we shall see, not only does the positivism of history's antiquarianism serve the victors (the ruling classes), but also the only solution – short of a Revolution taking place – is, radically, terroristically even, to refound history.

Walking with _and_ looking back from ahead: dialectical historiography

In a manner that replicates, in uncanny fashion, the key dictum of Antonio Gramsci – 'we must have an optimism of the will but a pessimism of the intellect' – Benjamin's (so-called) 'Theses on the Philosophy of History' or the version called 'On the Concept of history' we use here (Benjamin 2001) do not lead, unfinished as they were, to a simple, singular interpretation: they are 'to be read as signposts rather than a coherent system' (Niethammer 1992, 104). The fragments do, however, put forward, using Paul Klee's painting of the Angelus Novus, an overview of history and approaches to it, albeit looking backwards:

> The Angel of History must look just so. His face is turned towards the past. Where we see the appearance of a chain of events, he sees one single catastrophe, which unceasingly piles rubble on top of rubble and hurls it before his feet. (Benjamin 2001, IX)

Benjamin is categorical about why we need to adopt this approach to history. As fascism – and capitalist modernity – risks plunging the world into a second global war in 1940 – what is needed is a powerful critique of complacency in progress ('*this* storm'), of the position of fiddling-while-Rome-burns that mainstream politicians have adopted in their 'servile subordination' (2001, X) in their strategy that had seemed capable of opposing Fascism but has in fact failed. The 'accustomed concept of history' is undoubtedly the slow and inexorable accumulation of 'years', of the slow and simplistic continuity of the past meeting the future that Benjamin has in his sights; and it is a certain type of Historical Materialism that is to blame, a fatalism redolent of the Third International that has 'corrupted' the German working-class into believing 'that they were swimming with the tide' (XI).

It is striking that at exactly the moment when Benjamin's last philosophical testament is finally published in France (Benjamin 1947), Barthes is about to leave Paris for Romania to become a French Lecturer in Bucharest, and we will consider in Chapters Eight and Nine the young intellectual's attitude towards Stalinism during this pivotal period in world Communism. It is whilst the Iron Curtain is falling across Europe and in Romania, that Barthes makes a startling intervention. In a lecture he gives about the forced closure of the French Institute in April 1948, he ends with the words 'History will never be able to march against History' (cited in Calvet 1994, 88, trans. mod.). We do not yet have a full version of Barthes's speech, but Roger (1986, 314) suggests that such a belief in a type of historical determinism is typical of post-war Trotskyism.

Indeed, in his 1948 reading of Hegel, the Trinidadian Trotskyist C. L. R. James describes Stalinism as a 'cruel obstacle' but as 'part of the process' (James 1980, 65,

182); and for James, according to Daniel Bensaïd (2002, 67–68), it is the petty-bourgeoisie that represents the 'social base' of State Capitalism under Stalinism, and, in a manner not dissimilar to Barthes's *Mythologies*, considered that on both sides of the Iron Curtain this universal tendency was indicative of the new organization of production East and West.

Similarly, Benjamin denounces the way in which technological progress is perceived as 'political achievement' for the working classes; and in it, he sees dark, ideological outcomes:

> This vulgar-Marxist concept of what labour is, does not bother to ask the question of how its products affect workers, so long as these are no longer at their disposal. It wishes to perceive only the progression of the exploitation of nature, not the regression of society. It already bears the technocratic traces which would later be found in Fascism. (2001, XI)

Clearly, we are on the terrain now of what the Frankfurt School theorists Theodor Adorno and Max Horkheimer called 'negative dialectics', in which the reason, rationality and 'progress' of the Enlightenment have merely led to the Nazi's extermination camps. In the critique of technocratic conceptions of human labour, Benjamin introduces a utopian element that prefigures Barthes's post-war interest in Fourier. Barthes even considers, in his later career, that Fourier is a historically more important writer than Flaubert (1994, 92), and Knight (1997, 68) comments on Barthes's mobilization of Fourier in his post-1968 work in relation to Marx and Engels's contradictory views on his utopian socialism. However, the early Barthes's interest in Fourier is such that, in 1952, he was due to include in his PhD thesis on social language between 1827–34 (on which more below) a critical edition of Fourier's *De l'éducation militaire* (2018, xxiii); and in both areas of Barthes's work on Fourier, the utopian element has much in common with Benjamin's.

Indeed, in his 1940 theses on history, Benjamin uses Fourier in a manner that dialogues with the view on human labour that, as we saw in Chapter Two, Barthes puts forward in 'Myth Today', as one of acting upon, but in harmony with, Nature:

> Labor, as it is henceforth conceived, is tantamount to the exploitation of nature, which is contrasted to the exploitation of the proletariat with naïve self-satisfaction. Compared to this positivistic conception, the fantasies which provided so much ammunition for the ridicule of Fourier exhibit a surprisingly healthy sensibility. According to Fourier, a beneficent division of social labor would have the following consequences: four moons would illuminate the night sky; ice would be removed from the polar cap; saltwater from the sea would no longer taste salty; and wild beasts would enter into the service of human beings. All this illustrates a labor which, far from exploiting nature, is instead capable of delivering creations whose possibility slumbers in her womb. To the corrupted concept of labor belongs, as its logical complement, that nature which, as Dietzgen put it, 'is there gratis [for free]'. (Benjamin, XI)

The utopian fantasies of a Fourier suggest, however, a less negative dialectic in Benjamin's conception: we must constantly *earn* our links to Nature, creatively, and not blithely affirm year-on-year progress. It is a Hegelian conception of humanity's interaction with Nature that, nascent in 'Myth Today', becomes, as we will see in Chapter Nine, a key element in Barthes's move towards structuralism.

Benjamin is looking for a politicization through looking backwards at history, and one which is partisan as it is in Michelet's conception. However, this is a battle. Social democracy in Germany since Marx had 'in the course of three decades' only 'succeeded in almost completely erasing the name of Blanqui, whose distant thunder [Erzklang] had made the preceding century tremble'. For Benjamin, the historiography of a partisan Michelet in Barthes and Wilson's account in which history was made by and written for the people, is all but forgotten:

> It contented itself with assigning the working-class the role of the saviour of future generations. It thereby severed the sinews of its greatest power. Through this schooling the class forgot its hate as much as its spirit of sacrifice. For both nourish themselves on the picture of enslaved forebears, not on the ideal of the emancipated heirs. (XII)

Barthes too is suspicious of Michelet's 'post-history' which began as soon as the French Revolution had happened (2002, I, 113). Against the 'homogenous and empty time' that progress in history imagines and implies, Benjamin posits the 'open-sky of history', dialectical, revolutionary, in what Alex Callinicos calls (1995, 152) the 'most serious attempt, in the Marxist tradition, to undertake "a critique of progress itself"'; though, as Callinicos points out, Benjamin did accept Blanqui's theory of 'eternal occurrence', as his critique of progress rejects the 'conclusion that the modern is no progress'. Callinicos argues furthermore that classical Marxism inherits from Hegel a dialectical conception of history as a spiral movement, in which each advance contains within itself an element of regress, for example in the *Communist Manifesto*.

In words that echo Barthes's *Writing Degree Zero*, Benjamin's critique of progress posits that '[t]he consciousness of exploding the continuum of history is peculiar to the revolutionary classes in the moment of their action'; his example is the July days of the 1830 revolution in Paris – whereas for Barthes's it is the 'June days' of the 1848 revolution (1967a, 66) – when 'an incident took place which did justice to this consciousness. During the evening of the first skirmishes, it turned out that the clock towers were shot at independently and simultaneously in several places in Paris' (XV). Benjamin is suggesting, in Lunn's analysis (1982, 227–29), that 'true revolutionary classes seek to perpetuate the moment in which the ordinary sequence of ticking seconds is ruptured', spelling out 'the need to arrest […] the very flow of clock-time, a 'redemptive action' rescuing 'the hopes of earlier generations for the present juncture'; rather than the additive, smooth transmission of tradition, Lunn sees Benjamin searching through the debris of a smashed history just like the Baudelairean 'rag-picker' in nineteenth-century Paris. Lunn sees this as more Nietzschean and Blanquist than Marxian, quoting Benjamin's view in the 1930s that revolutions should be seen not so much as Marx's 'locomotives of world history' but as 'a grasp for the emergency brake' (Benjamin cited in Lunn, 228).

There is an important parallel here with Barthes's writings in the early 1950s, whereby a questioning of the 'laws of history' leads to a suggestion of the specificity of history. Abstracting events from their individual context not only denies the specificity of each event, it also helps to disallow actants any effect in and on history. In the voluntarist mode of social explanation typical of post-war Trotskyism in France — whereby the 'masses' ('the people' in Micheletist language) are unconstrained by determining structures — Barthes deems that History (with a capital H) is made, not by the structural, systemic changes that he will later invoke, but by the people. Thus, in his 1950 review, Barthes rejects the 'laws' that Joussain (1950) believes underpin history's social upheavals, criticizing the formulaic understanding of the way change has taken place, for the way in which it alienates history from human agency. By trying to deduce a law of revolutions from a comparison of ten very different historical incidents — Barthes is outraged that Mussolini's or Hitler's or Pétain's 'national revolution' are equated with the Russian Revolution — Joussain was simply doing what historians had done 'from Herder to Hegel and from Montesquieu to Michelet' (2015b, 4). Joussain's downplay[ing] of revolutions' (5) by his erroneous comparisons were possible only because he considered revolutions 'from the greatest possible height, [...] from the most formal standpoint' (3); but his attempt to understand the laws of revolutions was thwarted by revolution itself. Rather than the comparative history that Joussain invoked, typical of history-writing since the romantic period, what is needed, according to Barthes, is an explanation of revolutions (indeed, of history) that covered a number of concrete dimensions – 'economic, social, intellectual etc.' – after which the problem for historians is to achieve a synthesis of the crucial factors in human society. For Joussain, by contrast, history was nothing more than a 'sum' of causes, accidents and individualities which, when simply mixed together, could not account for history's diversity of events. Barthes's central point seems to be that the denial of humanity's ability to make history, the alienation of history from the masses, is integral to the formalistic and mechanical way in which Joussain classified revolutions and then analogically equated radically different historical moments. Just as Linnæus's classifications of animals always left out an animal that they could not fit in, so Joussain's attempt to classify social upheavals using historical analogies failed to account for the specificity of each revolution.

Barthes's critique of historical formalism appears again a year later in two reviews of a short sociological study of Marxism by Roger Caillois (1950). In the second of these reviews of Caillois's book (2015b, 21–26), Barthes carries on the critique of analogy and metaphor. Here, he attacks the analogical manner in which Caillois equates Marxism with the Church, as a faith not a science:

> This [method] consists in teasing out similar general characteristics from two different historical facts, setting up a sort of historical constant, and bringing Marxism and Christianity within the bounds of a purely institutional History, [...] a sociology of Forms. (2015b, 22)

Caillois too was using, suggests Barthes, the nineteenth-century technique of explanation, the analogy. We have seen how his critique of Joussain's account of the laws of revolution points to the manner in which the 'content' – or specificity – of history had been evacuated; now Caillois's 'analogical history' offered, in a very similar way, a shallow view of history, in the form of a philosophy of history:

Analogy was the scientific method par excellence, because nineteenth-century science, dominated as it was by the requirement for a Nature that was composed like a picture, could not be satisfied with a pure description of historical phenomena. It had, at all costs, to find their secret order and their engine - the reason, law, spirit, or organisation that underlay them – and it was at that time that this latter term first gained the prominence ever since. (2015b, 23)

This has important parallels with Benjamin's concept of history. Just as Benjamin wants to 'explode the continuum of history', so Barthes exposes the analogical degradation of historical specificity and agency:

[W]e don't have the right to relate what determines the actions of a peasant in Luther's time to what drives a lawyer in the Constituent Assembly of 1789 or a worker in the Paris Commune. We don't have the right to substitute a general human mechanism for these specific figures, a mechanism whose revolutions would fall, more or less ripe, like fruits from a single tree. (Barthes 2015b, 5)

Barthes makes a similar point about historical specificity in relation to Albert Camus's novel *The Plague* (2002, I, 573). Benjamin too wishes to defend the specificity of the event in history:

The historical materialist cannot do without the concept of a present which is not a transition, in which time originates and has come to a standstill. For this concept defines precisely the present in which he writes history for his person. Historicism depicts the 'eternal' picture of the past; the historical materialist, an experience with it, which stands alone. He leaves it to others to give themselves to the whore called 'Once upon a time' in the bordello of historicism. He remains master of his powers: man enough, to explode the continuum of history. (Benjamin, XVI)

Or is there slippage here? Is Benjamin talking about acting in history, or how we write it down? Indeed, Dahmer (2021, 494–96) points to the historiographical use that both Benjamin and Trotsky make of analogy, and of which Barthes seems unaware. There is possibly then the danger of this type of slippage in a dialectical view of history, between agency *in* history and subsequent historiographical representation *as* History.

In the first addendum to his 'On the Concept of History', Benjamin seems to agree with Barthes's Micheletist idea that historical phenomena have changing and multilinear meanings across history:

Historicism contents itself with establishing a causal nexus of various moments of history. But no state of affairs is, as a cause, already a historical one. It becomes this, posthumously, through eventualities which may be separated from it by millennia. The historian who starts from this, ceases to permit the consequences of eventualities to run through the fingers like the beads of a rosary. He records [erfasst] the constellation in which his own epoch comes into contact with that of an earlier one. He thereby establishes a concept of the present as that of the here-and-now, in which splinters of messianic time are shot through. (Benjamin 2001, A)

Benjamin's 'now-time' seems to liberate all those forgotten by traditional history, 'for the freedom of further effectivity' (Niethammer 116). This is very close to Barthes's Micheletist idea of 'resurrection' of the masses, except that the resurrection in Michelet's writing of history is linked by Barthes to a redemption, albeit in history-writing only: that is, a 'resurrection' in which Michelet 're-establishes a bridge [palier] between two timescapes [états du Temps]', thereby creating the 'Dream of a life and a death that are reconciled' (2002, I, 123). In effect, for Barthes, Michelet dissolved himself, his own death and life, into the lives and deaths of the past.

Benjamin even comes close to a structuralist view of history, with an uncanny anticipation of the Barthesian notion of the 'degree zero', here of time:

> Historicism justifiably culminates in universal history. Nowhere does the materialist writing of history distance itself from it more clearly than in terms of method. The former has no theoretical armature. Its method is additive: it offers a mass of facts, in order to fill up a homogenous and empty time. The materialist writing of history for its part is based on a constructive principle. Thinking involves not only the movement of thoughts but also their zero-hour [Stillstellung]. Where thinking suddenly halts in a constellation overflowing with tensions, there it yields a shock to the same, through which it crystallizes as a monad. The historical materialist approaches a historical object solely and alone where he encounters it as a monad. In this structure he cognizes the sign of a messianic zero-hour of events, or put differently, a revolutionary chance in the struggle for the suppressed past. He perceives it, in order to explode a specific epoch out of the homogenous course of history; thus exploding a specific life out of the epoch, or a specific work out of the life-work. The net gain of this procedure consists of this: that the life-work is preserved and sublated in the work, the epoch in the life-work, and the entire course of history in the epoch. The nourishing fruit of what is historically conceptualized has time as its core, its precious but flavorless seed. (2001, XVII)

For Benjamin – just as it is for Barthes's 'specificity' of the past – there is an urgency of the present moment, which, far from opening onto the future, needs to concentrate on the past effects on the here and now:

> It is well-known that the Jews were forbidden to look into the future. The Torah and the prayers instructed them, by contrast, in remembrance. This disenchanted those who fell prey to the future, who sought advice from the soothsayers. For that reason the future did not, however, turn into a homogenous and empty time for the Jews. For in it every second was the narrow gate, through which the Messiah could enter. (2001, B)

Callinicos (1995, 160) sees this messianism as distant from Marx's concept of history; for Benjamin, 'avenging "enslaved ancestors" provides both psychological motivation and ethical justification for revolutionary violence'; whereas, for Marx, the only hope is that 'the victims develop the strength to take power for themselves'. We have moved a long way from the 'theology' which sits behind Historical Materialism that opens Benjamin's piece. Or have we? Is Benjamin's writing 'against the grain', following Hegel, what Callinicos calls a 'secularized theodicy' (163), and which is deemed by Barthes as a 'Christomorphic revolution' in Michelet (Barthes 1987a, 62, 74)? Here perhaps then is the nub of the debate. Does he take Michelet's morale of history, that is, of being blind as to the outcome of the actions of the People? For Benjamin, this artificial blindness is to be jettisoned as a relation with the past:

> Fustel de Coulanges recommended to the historian, that if he wished to reexperience an epoch, he should remove everything he knows about the later course of history from his head. There is no better way of characterizing the method with which historical materialism has broken. It is a procedure of empathy. Its origin is the heaviness at heart, the acedia, which despairs of mastering the genuine historical picture, which so fleetingly flashes by. (2001, VII)

Niethammer (120) puts it thus: 'Through his tiger leaps, the historian must stand at their [the masses'] side and blast the repressed hopes out of the progress-levelled past'. This seems to be Benjamin departing swiftly from Michelet's 'double grasp' in the way that Barthes has defined it; however, we need to see this suggestion within the fullness of the argument.

Similar to Barthes's Michelet, Benjamin's aim is not some antiquarian knowledge of the past, as this merely confirms from the present the view of the victors – so far – of history. He seems nevertheless to be criticizing the notion of 'resurrection' that Barthes finds powerful in Michelet's historiography of the forgotten millions and minions of history:

> The theologians of the Middle Ages considered it the primary cause of melancholy. [...] The nature of this melancholy becomes clearer, once one asks the question, with whom does the historical writer of historicism actually empathize. The answer is irrefutably with the victor. Those who currently rule are however the heirs of all those who have ever been victorious. Empathy with the victors thus comes to benefit the current rulers every time. This says quite enough to the historical materialist. Whoever until this day emerges victorious, marches in the triumphal procession in which today's rulers tread over those who are sprawled underfoot. The spoils are, as was ever the case, carried along in the triumphal procession. They are known as the cultural heritage. In the historical materialist they have to reckon with a distanced observer. For what he surveys as the cultural heritage is part and parcel of a lineage [Abkunft] which he cannot contemplate without horror. It owes its existence not only to the toil of the great geniuses, who created it, but also to the nameless drudgery of its contemporaries. (Benjamin 2001, VII)

This also seems to be departing from Barthes's chorus-like, active interventions that we have seen in Myth, in Tragedy, in captions for Pic's Brechtian theatre photography. Indeed, the word 'distance' here is at odds with how G.A. Cohen sees a Marxist theory of History operating, not as in Hegel 'a reflective construal, from a distance, but a contribution to understanding [History's] inner dynamic' (Cohen cited in Callinicos 1995, 420). However, it is now that Benjamin makes his strong case for stepping outside of history, or at least bending the (dialectical) stick towards this 'distance', away from the antiquarian resuscitation of the past. And, just as Barthes points to the double grasp in Michelet's 'tableau' / 'overview [survol]' (in which Michelet is seemingly able to be *both* with and then historically 'ahead' of the People), so Benjamin underscores how we *really* can get hold of the past:

> The true picture of the past whizzes by. Only as a picture, which flashes its final farewell in the moment of its recognizability, is the past to be held fast. 'The truth will not run away from us' – this remark by Gottfried Keller denotes the exact place where historical materialism breaks through historicism's picture of history. For it is an irretrievable picture of the past, which threatens to disappear with every present, which does not recognize itself as meant in it. (2001, V)

Obviously Benjamin is writing at a very different historical juncture in 1940 from Barthes's in 1950–51; but for both it is crucial that the grasp of history be one of a dialectical inside and outside. For Benjamin what underpins our attitude to history as future is the all-important important moral that is encapsulated by the expression of our own times in 2021, that of *shocked-but-not-surprised*:

> To articulate what is past does not mean to recognize 'how it really was'. It means to take control of a memory, as it flashes in a moment of danger. For historical materialism it is a question of holding fast to a picture of the past, just as if it had unexpectedly thrust itself, in a moment of danger, on the historical subject. The danger threatens the stock of tradition as much as its recipients. [...] The tradition of the oppressed teaches us that the 'emergency situation' in which we live is the rule. We must arrive at a concept of history which corresponds to this. Then it will become clear that the task before us is the introduction of a real state of emergency; and our position in the struggle against Fascism will thereby improve. Not the least reason that the latter has a chance is that its opponents, in the name of progress, greet it as a historical norm. – The astonishment that the things we are experiencing in the 20th century are 'still' possible is by no means philosophical. It is not the beginning of knowledge, unless it would be the knowledge that the conception of history on which it rests is untenable. (2001, VIII)

Clearly, Benjamin's notion of the catastrophe could be seen to relate to a much later Barthes, that of *Camera Lucida*, in which the catastrophe of the written is compared to that of the photographic image (Prosser 2004, 211). Nevertheless, this comparison between Benjaminian and Barthesian critiques of history, separated by a mere ten years but a world apart in terms of historical moment, points to Barthes's interest in a dialectical historiography. Best exemplified by Michelet's attempt to write the people's experience of history *both* alongside the masses at the time *and* from ahead as the historian looking back in time, both inside and outside history, in what Barthes calls Michelet's 'double grasp', it is part of what he calls Michelet's 'two-term dialectic'.

'Two-term dialectic'

In his second publication on Michelet, in *Les Lettres nouvelles* in 1953, Barthes proposes that in Michelet's writing 'History knew only a linear dialectic, two-stroke [à deux temps]'; whereas, in 1951, he describes Michelet's dialectic as 'two-term':

> The alterity of historical objects [in Michelet's writing] is never total, History is always familiar, as Time is there only to support an identity between them; its movement is equational, its dialectic is of two terms. (2002, I, 111)

This is repeated in 'Féminaire de Michelet' (1953c, 1092–1093, not included in Barthes 1987a). It deliberately, and strategically, forestalls what Lefebvre calls 'the Third Term' (2003, 16, 20, 58). Is the 'two-term dialectic' linked to the 'amorous dialectic'? Indeed, not only does this 'two-term' dialectic resemble the truncated, 'amputated' dialectic of the mythologist's approach to myth (2009, 187) that we considered in Chapter Two, and which Barthes hesitates over (135); it also becomes an approach that will return at various moments in the later work, for example on fashion, whereby the 'Fashion system' is 'the result of a series of choices, of amputations' (1990b, 15). Indeed, the resemblance between this dialectic of Michelet using two terms only, on the one hand, and the 'stereographic space' applied to Balzac's 1830 tale *Sarrasine* on the other, is striking.

A crucial aspect of the levels of analysis in the resultant essay of 1970, *S/Z*, is precisely the mobility of the reader (aware and critical), on one side, and that of the 'blind' protagonist, Sarrasine, on the other. To be able to be both a critic of the strange story that Balzac delegates to a narrator to tell, and, at the same time, to trace the castrating trap of the anecdote (which is itself narrated by an old man to a young woman at a party) could be described as a dialectical form of reading, as it is able to be both external and internal to the plot. What Barthes calls 'paragrammatic' literary criticism deploys a particular type of analysis which, to use his words about Michelet in the 1950s, consists of 'overview [survol]' of the story – or history in Michelet (Barthes 1987a, 20–22) – of the tricked sculptor Sarrasine, *as well as* the 'tableau' of the same story, in what Barthes calls a 'stereographic space' of reading (1974, 15). It is certainly not new for a novelist to put themselves inside the head of a fictional character; but a literary critic using a dialectical, toing-and-froing between the outside and the inside of the story certainly is!

In the final section of this chapter, we bring *S/Z* together with Barthes's writings on Michelet. We will then consider in Chapter Five the creative criticism that Barthes develops across his 1966–67 seminar called 'La linguistique du discours' and which will be enacted in *S/Z*. However, it is important to underline that the other half of his seminar is on the 'discourse of history': we have then the first potential link between *S/Z* and Michelet. Could the stereographic space claimed in *S/Z* therefore be applied to *Michelet*? As we saw in Chapter Two, in *On Racine* Barthes signals his search for a 'flexible [souple]' mode of research in his criticism of Thomson (1992a, 169) and in his wish for a less analogical approach. It is precisely this ambivalence that we find in 'stereography', this double, dialectical writing, beholden to the mobile eye of the writer-critic.

Historiality

The manner in which Barthes sees Michelet's writing of history as an intervention *in* history, in both its actantial and its historiographical dimensions – the 'double grasp' – will become a guiding element in his literary criticism of the second half of the 1960s. In a comparison then between the character Sarrasine in Balzac's story and the 'people' in Michelet, there is a level of subjectivity in which the Barthesian reader (and writer) must experience the blindness of the actants. The 'all possible readers' level that Barthes assigns to the notion of general reader (2002, III, 645) operates in tandem with the approach of the literary critic who must recognize what he calls in 1960 an 'intransitive' form of writing (1972, 149). This resembles precisely the 'two-term' dialectic that Barthes finds in Michelet, in which the historian – a populist scribe of the people – sees and, as people, does not see, what happens in the end.

One of the few potentially useful concepts in the critique of *S/Z* by Bremond and Pavel (1998) – in an otherwise disingenuous reading of Barthes's radical re-writing of Balzac's story that we will discuss presently – is the notion of 'historiality'. Unfortunately, though named and briefly referred to by Bremond and Pavel (1998, 50–51), the historiality in *S/Z* is (for unknown reasons) discounted from their analysis of Barthes's essay. Without a strict definition, we will use the notion, first, to play on History and story, and then in Chapter Five to see it as part of Barthes's intervention, his creative criticism.

Barthes had already looked at the historiality of Balzac's third-person in *Writing Degree Zero* (1967a, 42). Historiality is often associated with Martin Heidegger's thought where it is understood as the historical character of a phenomenon, especially of humans in society, as opposed to temporality. *Geschichtlichkeit* – historiality – in *Being and Time* is a sort of 'historicity immanent to life itself' (Greisch 1997, 6) in which, within Heidegger's notion of 'hermeneutic intuition', there is this definition: 'Life is historical; no slicing it up into its constituent elements, but cohesion' (Greisch 6n4 citing Heidegger). It is important in our working definition of historiality that Barthes refuses all notion of a hermeneutics in *S/Z*, and the essay is rather a stereography, a writing of a double reading, that is properly dialectical. And even if fifteen years earlier, he describes in his book on *Michelet* how it is 'not excessive to speak of a veritable hermeneutics of the Micheletist text' (Barthes 1987a, 206), the 'unveiling of meaning' in *Michelet* leads, according to Petitier (2000, 113), in the opposite direction to hermeneutics, 'towards a re-veiling, [...] to a new enigma, [...] the body'. Just as the analysis of enigma in *Sarrasine* leads Barthes to consider the production of meaning that starts with bodies – that is, the body of the eponymous protagonist Sarrasine, that of the narrator and narratee *and* that of the reader of the short story – so Michelet is, as we saw above, the 'carnal historian', a comment repeated in his 1977 inaugural lecture (1982a, 477).

Indeed, Barthes appears acutely aware of the historical and historicizing (as opposed to historicist) nature of his work on Balzac between 1968 and 1969, in the seminar and in the subsequent essay *S/Z*. The period in which Balzac wrote *Sarrasine* had formed the basis of Barthes's earliest research career in 1951 and 1952. Guittard (2014) suggests a direct influence of Barthes's abandoned thesis project with the lexicologists Charles Bruneau and Georges Matoré on his later work. Guittard relates Barthes's research on the language used by bosses, workers and the French state, between 1827–34, to the drafting of the 'Writing Degree Zero' thesis, published a year later, though she does not mention the work on Fourier that Barthes had aimed to add. In choosing Balzac's 1830 story *Sarrasine* nearly twenty years later, Barthes seems to be renewing this early, unfinished research. His historical knowledge of the lexicon of the period around 1830, when Balzac is writing *Sarrasine*, is certainly important in *S/Z* (see also Barthes's 'The Man in the Street on Strike', in *Mythologies* 1979, 99). Furthermore, in the 1960s, he is highly aware of the weight of classical literature, not just in the joust with Picard over Racine, but in relation to other great classics; and anachronism becomes a central question for the critic.

In the final essay of *On Racine*, 'History or Literature?', Barthes argues against the philological methods of a Picard which restrict the explanation of Racine's *œuvre* to its own time and do not allow it to escape from the seventeenth century. Here, for Barthes, is the value of the 'nouvelle critique'. It shows that, through Racine – but outside of the Institution –, the values of literature could be reassessed. Barthes's 'historiality' is such that, in a 1970 interview, he locates Balzac as a writer coming *prior* to the 'epistemological shift' of the second half of the nineteenth century heralded by Mallarmé and Marx; and he is quick to underline, following Bataille, that Balzac's story, although made up of 'readable writing [écriture lisible]', is also a 'limit-text', typical of those that, 'in the *œuvre* of a great writer, represent very strange enticements that make them, in some way, sometimes anticipate modernity [...]' (2002, III, 643). Mikhail Bakhtin also sees elements of polyphony in Balzac, 'but only elements': 'Balzac did not transcend the object-ness of his characters, nor the monologic finalization of his world'; 'Shakespeare and Cervantes, Voltaire and Diderot, Balzac and Hugo' prepared for polyphony in a '*fundamental* way' (1984, 34, 178); though Bakhtin cites a letter from Dostoevsky to his brother in 1838, in which he states that 'Balzac is great', his characters 'the work of a cosmic mind': 'Not the spirit of the time, but thousands of years have prepared with their struggle for such a denouement in the human soul' (302 n11).

The 'stereographic' is concerned then not only with reading and rewriting as a double act, but also (and consequent on reading and writing) with the undecidability between the 'lisible' (readable) and the 'scriptible' (writable), themselves based on a historiality of text and writing. We will see in the next chapter why the dilemma for Barthes is 'Menippean': Balzac's writing is both classically 'lisible' and also, at the same time, acutely able to show premonitions of modernity, in the following sense:

> [W]hat can we nevertheless do with these old texts which we are able to read using an extremely rich symbolic investment, but which, due to their historical language, are no longer part of a modern theory of the signifier nor of writing [écriture]? [...] My question is no longer: 'Do we have the right to discuss Racine in a new way?', but simply: 'Can we discuss Balzac or Racine?' (2002, III, 644).

What is extraordinary then is that, in a letter to Georges Canetti in 1945, following a long explanation about his fascination with the nineteenth-century historian, Barthes asks almost exactly the same question concerning Michelet as he would later do with Racine and then Balzac:

> The big question that's worrying me right now is this: Is he (that is to say, is studying him) modern? Can one work on Michelet and remain in our world of 1945? That is essential. It's no good leaving our epoch out, it's the only one we have to live in. For two days I have been a bit deflated. If reconciliation is not possible—or too artificial—I will mercilessly drop the old goat. But that would make me sad, especially since, despite everything, it is not light-heartedly that all alone one enters the hard flame of 'today'. (2018, 48–49)

It is not surprising, given this historial sensitivity, that, in the 1968 seminar notes on *Sarrasine*, Barthes shows himself acutely aware of the way in which writing's use of codes marks it historically: 'The codes in Balzac are class codes, in that the bourgeoisie recuperates a sort of ancient-classical vulgate and uses it as alibis (the codes of social classes are schoolboy ones)' (2011a, 517). The seminar notes emphasize this historialist dimension, as Barthes explains to the EPHE seminar group the importance of the 'Code of common knowledge [sapientiel mondain]'; because, 'despite the fastidious repetition', it is one of the codes that 'point, probably very precisely, to the *outdatedness* of Balzac, to what shows him to be outside of literary writing [écriture]' (2011a, 238). In this way, both in the seminar notes on *Sarrasine* and *S/Z*, Barthes's ambivalence as to whether Balzac is 'lisible' *or* 'scriptible', classical *or* modern, becomes a form of hesitation, or double grasp of the contradiction.

This historiality is also an important element of creative criticism; as Benson and Connors put it (2015, 48): '[a]s with so much creative criticism, the writing acknowledges its own prior entanglement in the subject about which it proposes to speak'. Barthes's criticism seems to be able to look backwards at tradition (to Balzac's 'lisible' classicism, but also to the oral, performative tradition of story-telling), at the same time as creating a new intergeneric, or post-generic form, that uses a new stylized type of writing. Writing about writing is certainly not new, but to make the essay part of the 'battle to break up [fissurer] the symbolic order of the West', as Barthes put it in 1970 (2002, III, 696), certainly is; and such an enterprise needs to have a tone of 'assurance', albeit tactical and provisional. Indeed, Compagnon (2004, 79, 81, 107) seems to insist on an overly one-sided view of the 'referential failure' of language set out in *S/Z*, regretting the 'restricted dialogism' of intertextuality and the lack of freedom afforded to the reader by textualism. But, surely, the essay *S/Z* is more an attempt at reconciling criticism of literature with society; if anything, Barthes's essayism could be accused of voluntarism, as he plays out the dialectical approach of being *at once* the 'general' reader, 'all the possible readers' (2002, III, 645), *and* the creative critic. In this way, we can see that the active (writing-/re-) reading in *S/Z* is provocative, provisional and performative, and, as we shall see in the next chapter, able to undermine the codism and the literalism typified in the account given by Bremond and Pavel (1998). In other words, could the notion of 'scriptible' – as defined ambivalently by Barthes in relation to Balzac – be extended to *Michelet*? Petitier (2000) seems to hint at this.

Barthes uses the text by Marx that he had enjoyed reading in 1946, *The 18th Brumaire of Louis Bonaparte*, to summarize briefly Michelet's 'classic credo of liberal petit bourgeois around 1840' (1987a, 11). He does not sense the need to gloss this long quotation from Marx (1978, 46–47); but it illustrates an analysis of the petty-bourgeois mind-set that we saw in Chapter Two that is two-fold. First, its being – its position in social relations – determines its consciousness; and second (though Barthes elides this section of the quote from Marx), the petit-bourgeois mind is fixed on a 'transformation of society in a democratic way, but a transformation within the bounds of the petty bourgeoisie' (Marx and Engels 1978, 46). In other words – and perhaps *Mythologies* does not stress this enough – the petty bourgeoisie is, in Marx's account (but perhaps only in his time and not in Barthes's time one hundred years later), *actively* participating in establishing social-democratic 'harmony' (indeed, Marx then goes on to describe how the petit bourgeoisie's political representatives in the French parliament at the time of Louis Bonaparte's *coup*, the 'Montagne' led by Ledru-Rollin, fell into the parliamentary trap of trying to impeach Bonaparte, leading to their defeat and to Bonaparte's chance to seize power). Barthes's analysis of the petty-bourgeois class in *Mythologies*, by contrast, insists on its cultural-ideological role in the new mass culture of post-war Europe, but possibly implies that these events in 1849 cowed the social-democratic impulses and thereafter tied the petit-bourgeois outlook to that of the 'Big Bourgeoisie' of Capital right up until Barthes's time of writing, and hence Barthes's hinting that its fascist tendencies, in the darker moments of recent history, are dependent on this (1979, 54).

Once the disclaimer that his work will be but a 'pre-criticism' of Michelet's ideology is established early in Barthes's text (1987a, 3), he can then examine closely 'how style becomes writing' (Petitier 2000, 119). In a similar way, by comparing Barthes's notes for his 1968–69 seminars on *Sarrasine* with the book version in *S/Z*, we can see that he has 'essaified' the original seminar-based research. Indeed, even the typographic layouts in *Michelet* and *S/Z* resemble each other, cut, as both texts are, between original text (by Michelet and Balzac, the 'tutor-text') on the one hand and interspersed commentary on the other. What is more, both *Michelet* and *S/Z* use digression heavily, what Barthes calls in the latter, in a neat oxymoron, 'the systematic use of digression' (1974, 13). This lays the basis for Barthes's extensive research in the 1970s on writing and how to write, encapsulated in a question 'What is the meaning of a pure series of interruptions?' (Barthes 1994, 94).

This dialectical historiality suggests that 'History' (in Michelet) and 'story' (in Balzac, as rewritten by Barthes) are linked, in French (*Histoire* and *histoire*), by more than a simple phoneme of identity (Noghrehchi 2017). Therefore, by selecting the tale written in 1830, *Sarrasine*, fifteen years after his abandoned research project on social language, Barthes seems to be unearthing elements of this unfinished research. Thus anachronism becomes an important question in 'stereographic' criticism, and one which relies on a certain theatricality of writing.

Dramatization

S/Z represents a new writing style for Barthes. Samoyault (2017, 419) quotes an unpublished note written in 1973–74 in which he is looking back over his work: 'It seems that, right from the start of *S/Z*, the style changed into its current form: something more finely honed, more continuously successful'. One aspect of this new 'style' is the use of drama in his reading and rewriting. This, however, is not as new in his writing as the note above suggests.

Long before the work on Racine, before he discovered Brechtian theatre in the heady days of the popular theatre movement in the mid-1950s, Barthes had, in his very first formal piece of writing, tentatively explored 'dramatized' reading. It may not turn out to be a significant addition to Classics scholarship, but the (hopefully imminent) publication of *Evocations et Incantations dans la tragédie grecque*, his postgraduate thesis at the Sorbonne in 1941 supervised by influential Hellenist philologist Paul Mazon, will be, to Barthes scholars, both revealing and confirming in equal measure.

Using an approach which prefigures that later deployed in *S/Z*, Barthes spends the early years of the Second World War reading and commenting closely on the 'power of the word' in Ancient Greek – mainly Aeschylean – tragedy and culture. The appropriateness of this to the situation of France in 1940–41 is not suggested by Coste (2016a), the editor of this work by Barthes, nor do we have the space here to do so. But it hardly needs underlining that both 1941 – when he writes his postgraduate thesis – and 1968 – when *S/Z* is starting to be written – are both especially acute moments in French politics and society. To ignore the 'theatrical' manner in which Barthesian literary criticism responds to these moments would be, precisely, an example of the 'asymbolic' approach regretted by Barthes in 1966.

Already in *Criticism and Truth* Barthes refers to the 'dramatized discourse' that Georges Bataille had noticed in Ignatius Loyola's 'spiritual exercises' (2007b, 24; Macé 2006, 222). Now, in *S/Z*, he puts this into his critical practice. In *S/Z* Barthes gives many hints on the dramatization in his reading, at one point, for example, wondering whether Marianina's '*addio*' could be performed (1974, 80). More importantly, at key moments in the story, he cuts the Balzacian prose with a digression using a 'voice-off'. A good example is the digression XXVIII–XXXI, where the drama is visible in Barthes's own style; it is even more evident at the moment when Balzac's story starts proper, immediately after the prologue ('I will obey'), and following the digression XXXIX (88–89). It is particularly here that the dramatic, performative and theatrical feel of the text *S/Z* encourages us to qualify heavily Bannet's view (1989, 61) that the 'Summary of Contents' in Annex 3 (260–65) indicates 'something approaching a coherent and connected meditation'. The 'drama' in the reading (and rewriting) directly interrupts and deliberately reorders the literary scientism associated with the content of the digressions, in an undermining manner that explicitly – 'This is not an "Explication de texte"' (90–92) – and in practice, echoes Denis Diderot's curious eighteenth-century tale 'Ceci n'est pas un conte' (2002, 51–75), in which the narrator of a love story is in constant, and dramatized, dialogue with a listener; not to mention Oscar Wilde's treatise on creative criticism, *The Critic As Artist* (1960 [1891]), which is written in the manner of a Diderot dialogue. Indeed, Barthes dedicates *S/Z* to the 'listening' of his postgraduate students, an active form of listening which 'wrote' the reading during the 1968 seminar at the EPHE in Paris, and of which the digressions in *S/Z* are a trace, somewhere between essayistic recounting and narrative enacting of a collective reading. This oral, dialogic aspect to *S/Z* is what Macé (2006, 297) calls, following Barthes's comment on the status of the essay-form as 'easily dramatisable', 'the epidictic genre, a "prose spectacle"'. This 'prose spectacle' has affinities to the oral tradition of French literature not just in Diderot, but also in Marguerite de Navarre's *Heptaméron*, and is epitomized in the Medieval period in its ways of pluralizing writing into four activities, what Paul Zumthor (1990, 11–18) calls 'the creative gloss', and on which Balzac's narrative style also relied (Balzac 1964).

We have seen how the theatrical, stylized dimension that the fragmentary, double typography lends to *S/Z*, the 'pure series' opening out onto the drama of Barthes's text. The 'drama' of the commentary in *Michelet* by contrast is much less developed and of a different order; it is evident in the many neologisms that Barthes attaches to Micheletist discourse, often short phrases whose elements are linked by a hyphen – 'water-as-fish', 'Goethe-as-dog', 'History-as-plant', 'History-as-equation', 'Pebble-men, Fish-men', 'Women-fish-dove', 'The world-as-women', 'Death-as-sleep and Death as Sun', 'Wheat-as-flint' (twice), 'Robespierre-as-cat, Marat-as-toad', 'Blood-as-corpse', 'anti-bloods', 'Blood-as-philter', 'Woman-as-wild-strawberry' (twice), 'Man-as-chambermaid' (twice), 'Language-as-nurse' etc. The neologisms attempt to summarize each figure or theme in Micheletist historiography; but, as they start each fragment, they appear as even more peremptory and dramatic in their startling abruptness. Only then, occasionally, for Barthes then to split the hyphenated phenomenon, such as 'Water or fish?', in what Calvet calls (1994, 114) a writing of 'duality' In both cases (*S/Z* and *Michelet*), the drama is brought about by digression and interruption. But there is one final, and we might say, crucial element in the digressive nature of both texts; that is, a certain cult of error in Barthes's acts of reading.

It is as if, in *S/Z*, Barthes too is experiencing Balzac's tale as a naive reader, while playing the role, simultaneously of alert semiotician who wants to account for their symbolic, parametric and narratological approach. Indeed – to pick up on the notion of 'asymbolia' which Barthes sees as a crucial error in literary criticism (2007b, 37) and which we will discuss in more detail in the next chapter – Knight (2007, 23–25) suggests that there is an important isomorphism between Barthes and Balzac. In *S/Z* there is a gap – a failure even – between the symbolic analysis of the statue of Zambinella in Barthes's reading of *Sarrasine* and the consequences for the eponymous hero (as well as for the character the prince Chigi who, also, is a loser in the end) on the one hand, and on the other that of the keen reader-consumer of literary realism. Barthes has in some sense – unbeknownst to him? – played out the knowing/not-knowing dialectic, the 'double grasp' of reading Balzac's story as both semiotician *and* 'general reader'.

What then would be the equivalent 'error' for the historian Michelet? Pretending to not know the outcome of history events? This is precisely what we have seen in Barthes and Wilson's writings on Michelet historiography, in its double, supple, dialectical dimensions. Indeed, this knowing/not-knowing dialectic returns at various stages of Barthes's career. In *A Lover's Discourse*, for example, in a remark about Balzac's character Captain Paz who must not let his friend's wife know his passion for her and therefore invents a lover, Barthes makes a similar point about the 'active paradox': '*at one and the same time*, it must be known and not known' (1990a, 42); the 'double vision' extends to how he sees the loved one, 'sometimes as object, sometimes as subject' hesitating between 'tyranny and oblation'. The 'evaluation' that Oxman (2010, 81–82) senses in Barthes's 1970 reading of Eisenstein is a similar 'double' approach that, very much (*pace* Didi-Huberman 2016), empathizes with the emotion on the film-stills; and we saw, in Chapter Three, the double function of the critical-expressive in the caption-as-chorus for the 1960 work on Pic's theatre photography.

The dramatization of reading in *S/Z* is a dialectical recognition of the blindness and insight involved in reading and critical engagement with literature; and it is a complexity upon which Barthes bases his mobile essayistic position. The dramatized essayism furthermore seems to corroborate Bannet's point (1989, 61–63) that *S/Z* 'subverts language as nature by subverting and inverting [the] hierarchy' of connotation as 'literary' and the denotative as 'scientific'; this subversion relies on an isomorphism (and not an anamorphosis) between Barthes's critical essay and Balzac's story, as both are, in Bannet's words, 'graphic inversions and mirror images of each other', in the way both reveal 'a hollow centre., a playful verbal artifice [...] castrated by its inability to penetrate the real'. Another critic (Detweiler 1978, 144–145) suggests that *S/Z* 'dramatizes' Roman Jakobson's famous claim that language itself is, ultimately, a consideration *on* language.

In terms of the stereographical, the 'alterity of historical objects' in *Michelet*, and the forestalling of totality in the Michelet's 'two-term' dialectic, have links to *S/Z*. If *S/Z* and *Michelet* are isomorphic in the relationship to their objects – History and story – and if, in *S/Z*, Barthes re-writes Balzac's *Sarrasine*, where is the re-writing of Michelet in Barthes's œuvre? Following the comments on 'The ethnological temptation' (Barthes 1994, 84–85), I want to put forward, in a provisional fashion, the hypothesis that this is *Mythologies*. We will see in subsequent chapters how the ethnographic 'appropriation' of France, in diminishing form, allows the 'Self's certitude' to 'grow [] lighter' (85): the ethnography of France via Michelet's writings uses a methodology that 'does not adulterate the Other by reducing it to the Same'. This 'double grasp' has a dialectical outcome in *Mythologies*, as we saw in the 'amorous dialectic'. Indeed, the point of view that Barthes has on Michelet, as we saw above in the December 1945 letter to Canetti (2018, 48–49), is highly ambivalent to such an extent that he seems to dismiss, alongside Hegel, the 'History-as-equation' (1987a, 36n2) as a central example of Micheletist tautology (the typical figure of petty-bourgeois ideology in *Mythologies*, we will remember); and yet, at the same time, he seems to be considering positively, in 1955 at least (2002, I, 548–49), the myths created by Michelet as progressive in the battle against bourgeois ideology: '[T]his dreamer, purified by the innocence of his dream can have the good conscience of escaping from bourgeois mystifications; he has not yet arrived at denouncing them, but at least he avoids them' (549).

In conclusion, Barthes's *Michelet*, in the *par lui-même* series in which he will publish his own 'par lui-même' in 1975, is a paradox, a sarcasm that will characterize *Mythologies*, not so much in its political, rather in its moral, influences. *Mythologies*, in summary, is a 'double grasp', both a critique and an account of myth's functions: a sociology or a social *psychology, from below*.

Chapter Five

'STEREOGRAPHIC SPACE'

> [I]n a world condemned to signs [...], what we call
> mass culture can only be judged very ambiguously,
> very dialectically [...]. [I]t is a culture that conceals the sign,
> that works on values that are always presented as natural and
> conceal the arbitrary character of the sign systems.
>
> *(Barthes 2015a, 119)*

So far we have considered the dialectical interventionist, and especially earlier, Barthes, by looking at the twin inheritance from Michelet and Marx, whilst asserting the competing epistemologies of early Nietzsche. Across theatre (both ancient Greek and modern Brechtian epic), contemporary myth and the historiality of criticism, Barthes's use of a 'double grasp' has signalled the political nature of his writing as it confronts a responsibility of forms within a determined defence of left-wing critique. Now the analysis moves onto a more creative and mobile form of critical praxis.

Macé (2006, 232) locates both *Empire of Signs* and *S/Z* on the cusp 'between a metalinguistic and a fictional moment'. The 'double grasp', as we shall see, involves the pleasure of reading, but also then writing. However, the pleasure of the 'double grasp' is also in its very deconstruction. In what Barthes calls a 'new dialectic', the very notion and practice of the 'double grasp' will be shown to undergo a 'mutation'; and it is in his 1970 essay *Empire of Signs* that we will trace its trajectory in Chapter Seven, before showing the limits of this 'new dialectic' in the diaries Barthes kept during his 1974 visit to China. Before this, we need to consider two major elements in the 'mutation' that takes place in Barthesian thought and critical praxis across the 1960s. In Chapter Six we will consider the critique of systems and classifications, but first we need, for the philosophy of politics we are aiming to define, to track what it means to start 'losing ground' (Brown 1992, 13–63). However, the metaphor of 'drifter' that Brown attributes to Barthes will be replaced by a much more active, even voluntarist, metaphor, that of *perte*.

Turning the Tables: Creative Criticism and the Loss of Self: From Historiality to Apersonalism

Weakly (and pessimistically) translated as 'loss' in English, Barthesian *perte* – as distinct from the version in Georges Bataille's thought – is the politicized corroding of the notion of self, a relentless but not aggressive critique of personal identity, of national, linguistic and cultural tropisms that underpin selfhood. Linked to the impersonalism we saw in the functionalist account of myth, this is now an apersonalism. In this second section we will see then a Barthes not so much intervening, chorus-like, in ideological debates and politicized representation; rather, a dispersing self, turning the tables, upending the assumptions, but, as ever, *pace* Hiddleston (2010), involving a principled advocacy of radical change.

Barthesian critical theory represented for Edward Said the shift from 'objectivized historicism', with English or French studies at its centre, to a kind of international critical apparatus important for its activity (1984, 142–43). Eric Marty (2002, III, 15) notes that *Empire of Signs*, published the same year as *S/Z*, is Barthes's first *proper* book, that is, not containing texts published before nor emanating from seminar or lecture notes – up till then, all of Barthes's books had started either as lectures, seminars or journalism.

Within the complexity of humans trying to grasp two things at once, Barthes begins to relativize all notions of 'grasp'. Mitchell Cohen points out (1994, 74) that Goldmann's Kantian Hegelianism is premised upon refusing the 'fact / value dichotomy', a crucial element for Barthes, especially in *S/Z*, though he traced this fact / value 'collapse' back to Nietzsche not Kant. Gérard Fabre (2001) uses Goldmannian sociology to shoehorn Barthesian essayism into a technology of reading; but in so doing he ignores the obverse of reading, that of a rewriting of text. The aim in this chapter then is to analyse Barthes's essayism and creative criticism.

Barthes's Menippean Moment: Creative Criticism, 1966–70: S/Z *and the Double*

One solution for Barthes of finding a way between ideologism and realism is to consider a literary text both historically and structurally, to fill in with an analysis of literary language which Marxist literary criticism found 'mysterious'. This then allows for a critical essayism that is not 'discovering' the work but 'covering' (1972, 259) the text with the critic's language, and, following Bakhtin, treats literary criticism as 'dialogic', 'parametric', with text.

It is Gérard Genette who, in a response to a 1963 questionnaire on literary criticism in *Tel Quel* (1963, 69–70), sets out the creative criticism debate. Noting how literary critics are 'readily accused […] of lacking creative power', he predicts that there will soon be a 'moment when criticism will no longer have literature as its object, because literature will have taken criticism as its object'. Similarly, Barthes sees a Renaissance-like shift taking place in which 'certain frontiers are opening, if not between the artist and the scientist, at least between the artist and the intellectual' (1972, 277).

Thus, across the 1960s, Barthes begins to reject the 'distinction between works and theory' (2002, III, 648, 691). Instead, 'ideological' parametrism as a method of critical practice in relation to a text's content (in which the critic changes the approach as a function of the content) becomes, in Barthes's creative criticism, a formal (or formalist) parametrism, in which the critic-writer now places themselves at the same level as the form of the text, at the textual level.

In the schema of the *écrivain* versus the *écrivant*, or better in the 'bastard type' middle-term that is found between the two (1972, 149), Barthes emphasizes the former, bending the stick in a writerly, creative direction. This is creative criticism as tactical form, in a dialectic with Barthes's own time: not repeatable (except in a spiral), singular, what we might define in the essay (in Raymond Queneau's neat expression) as 'definitively provisional' (cited in Samoyault 2017, 296). '[T]he difference between literature and criticism consists perhaps only in the fact that criticism is more likely to be blind to the way in which its own critical difference from itself makes it, in the final analysis, literary' (Johnson 2000 [1978], 174). As Richard Howard puts it in his preface to the English version of *S/Z* (1974, xi): 'This criticism is literature'. Indeed, the move to creative criticism after *Criticism and Truth* is possibly a more positive move than Hill (2010, 102–05) concedes.

Following his reading of *Criticism and Truth*, Claude Lévi-Strauss suggests to Barthes in an unpublished letter that it is too beholden to *la nouvelle critique* (Samoyault 2017, 253), thereby running the risk of using 'a hermeneutics à la Ricoeur' (254); and hence, as Samoyault points out, Barthes's 1967 essay 'From Science to Literature' (1986, 3–10) in which literary scientism is replaced by critical 'écriture'. It is not only Lévi-Strauss misreading Barthes's essay. Tzvetan Todorov's (1968) definition of poetics divides the current literary criticism into only two camps: one whose 'final aim' is the work itself, and the other looking for 'something else'; however, the latter consists largely, via the social sciences, in a search for what he calls 'literariness' (99–107).

Both Todorov and Lévi-Strauss, in their reading of *Criticism and Truth*, are thus missing a crucial development across Barthes's work in this mid-1960s period. His 1966–67 seminar, 'La linguistique du discours', followed by that in 1968-1969 on Balzac's *Sarrasine* that becomes the essay *S/Z* (1974), represent an important development in Barthesian literary critical practice, as it clearly and squarely leaves behind *la nouvelle critique*. We will see how both seminars represent a missing link between *Criticism and Truth* and *S/Z*, what Barthes calls, in his seminar notes on *Sarrasine* in February 1968, 'the new and urgent task [...] of rethinking the writing [écriture] that has in its sights writing [écriture], that is, criticism – forms of criticism' (2011a, 61). We will also address what might be a considerable irony in literary criticism, namely that the notorious reading of *S/Z* we mentioned above by Bremond and Pavel (1998) is *itself* a re-reading if not a re-writing of Barthes's own re-writing of Balzac, were it not for the 'traditional' scholarship to which these detractors finally advocate a return. The aim then is to begin an analysis, an explanation even, of why the editors of a recent anthology on 'creative criticism' suggest that Barthes 'has some claim' on being 'the patron saint of creative criticism' (Benson and Connors 2015, 48); and since Benson and Connors cite *A Lover's Discourse*, *Camera Lucida* and *Roland Barthes by Roland Barthes* as examples, the aim here then is to locate stirrings of this creativity in Barthes's earlier literary-critical writing. Indeed, as we have seen – especially in the captioning for Roger Pic's photographic record of the Berliner Ensemble in Chapter Three – Barthes's chorus-like interventions involve a creativity on the critic's part that accentuates the historiality of critical practice.

Parametrism, Symbolism and Anamorphosis

Both *Criticism and Truth* and Barthes's first essay *Writing Degree Zero* are renowned for their critique of 'French clarity' (2007b, 9–13; 1967a, 64). However, in the intervening

13 years between the two essays and following the attacks on Barthes and *la nouvelle critique* by Sorbonne professor Raymond Picard in 1964 and 1965, Barthes is forced to state his positions. As well as the obsession with clarity, verisimilitude and good taste, Barthes's *Criticism and Truth* has another category of literary criticism in his sights.

Though there are two extremes in the existing forms of literary criticism – traditional criticism mainly in universities, and *la nouvelle critique* for a more radical literary intelligentsia – these two differing approaches, for Barthes in 1966, actually come together in one important way. In failing to 'symbolize' literary meaning university-style criticism's literary-historical approach is far too literal; but importantly, Barthes suggested that *la nouvelle critique* also suffers from this '*a-symbolia*', albeit in a different form; that is, it is far too reductionist in its various attempts to apply modern critical theories to literary texts:

> In both cases it is the absolute disparity between the languages, that of the work and that of the critic, which causes the symbol to be missed: to wish to diminish the symbol is just as excessive as obstinately to refuse to see anything other than the strict letter. *The symbol must go and seek the symbol*, a language must fully speak another language: it is in this way finally that the letter of the work is respected. (2007b, 37)

This concern with symbolism and asymbolism will return in *S/Z* four years later, and to which we will return. In *Criticism and Truth*, Barthes is suggesting that the symbolic level on which criticism should be conducted is itself already a transformation of the text under scrutiny; the critic 'separates [dédouble]' meanings in an 'anamorphosis' of the text with four requirements: criticism must not allow a text to be pure reflection, on the one hand; and, on the other, anamorphosis must transform everything in the text, parametrically (or, according to certain laws) and always to the same effect (2007b, 32). As has been pointed out (Bannet 1989, 60), it is within this assertion of the anamorphosis of the critical act in *Criticism and Truth* that Barthes will set out the plan of attack on *Sarrasine* two years later. But, before embarking on this symbolic and anamorphic reading of *Sarrasine*, there is one other major hurdle to clear.

In *Criticism and Truth* there is the realisation that asymbolia might leave criticism – 'ancienne' or 'nouvelle' – in a difficult situation. Unable to stand outside of the material that makes up the literary work – because literary criticism itself has to use that same material, that is, language – the critic is disarmed in any attempt to engage scientifically:

> Faced with the science of literature, even if they glimpse it, the critic remains infinitely powerless, for they cannot use language as a possession or an instrument: *they are a person who does not know where they stand in relation to the science of literature*. (2007b, 37, trans. mod.).

This is not to say that Barthes is in any way unsympathetic to *la nouvelle critique*, as a 1965 interview in *Le Figaro littéraire* in response to Picard's attack attests: 'modern criticism [la nouvelle critique] has the merit of using the same language as the literature [creations] of our time. A modern novel has, more or less clearly, a Marxist or psychoanalytical background. That language is familiar to modern criticism' (1985a, 40). This 1965 interview is an early example of a growing *iso*morphism between essay and novel in Barthes's conception; and he is acutely aware of this conundrum in *Criticism and Truth*, underlining 'a *general crisis of [the literary] Commentary*', analogous, once more, with the 'passage from the Middle Ages to the Renaissance [humanisme]' (2007b, 24–25, author's original emphasis; Macé 2006, 233). Citing Mallarmé's Preface to 'Un coup de dés jamais n'abolira le hasard' [A Throw of The Dice Will Never Abolish Chance], Barthes defines, using a vivid, musical metaphor, what he understood by the 'parametrism' required of the critic, of the parameters that literary criticism should respect:

> The measure of critical discourse is its *exactness* [*justesse*]. Just as in music, although a note which is exactly in tune [juste] is not a 'truthful' note, nevertheless the truth of the singing depends, when all's said and done, upon its exactness, because exactness is made up of a certain unison and harmony, so the critic, in order to be true, must be exact and try to reproduce in their own language, according to '*a precise spiritual mise en scene*', the symbolic conditions of the work, failing which, precisely, they cannot 'respect' it. (2007b, 36–37, author's original emphasis; trans. mod.).

Thus, an attention to a text's literary symbolism is tightly related by Barthes to a parametric approach to any text, yet with a wide-ranging requirement of anamorphosis. In her preface Katrine Pilcher Keuneman (xvii) maintains that Barthes's 1966 essay is arguing for a rigour in literary criticism, one not based on the choice of code, but in the consistency with which the code is applied. If rigour there is in *Criticism and Truth*, it is doubtless the requirement of anamorphosis that helps Barthes to move away from consistency in the use of the codes, towards a critical practice that institutes a new conception of the link between symbolism and parametrism.

Between 1966 and 1970, Barthes makes a key move, crossing, as it were, the *Rubicon*, a 'mutation' rather than an evolution, from semiology to 'semioclastics' (Ungar 2004, 168). In this 'mutation' he develops a new way of 'respecting' the work to be criticized. Critics of *S/Z* – such as Bremond and Pavel (1998) – suggest that the approach '*dis*respects' Balzac's story. But in the seminar notes (2011a, 65), Barthes uses a play on words to underline the act of 'covering': to re-write Balzac's story stereographically is to 'cover' it with a new writing, to 're-cover' the narrative's double aspect. It is the 1966–67 seminar, '*La linguistique du discours*', that seems to operate this 'mutation' in literary praxis.

The seminar notes show (O'Sullivan 2014) clearly how, from the second half of 1966 onwards, Barthes becomes influenced by Jacques Derrida's critique of 'voice', by Julia Kristeva and Todorov's importation of the work of the Russian literary critic Mikhail Bakhtin and then by Jean Starobinski's 'second wave' of Saussure concerned with the anagramme. But, above all, we can see how Barthes moved towards what he called a 'Menippean' definition of reading and then of literary-critical practice.

In the first part of the 'La linguistique du discours' seminar – the second half, somewhat is his study of historiographical language, 'The Discourse of History' (1986, 127–140) – Barthes looks closely at the problem of parametrism for the literary critic. He proposes, following the recent, bruising quarrel with Raymond Picard over his reading of Racine, that there is a sharp divide between two types of criticism. On the one hand, there is, broadly-speaking, his own:

> dialogic, stereophonic, polygrammatic (or paragrammatic), double (or multiple), bi-vocal, tabular, menippean, carnavalesque, whose espace is 2. (O'Sullivan 2014, fig. 7)

This dialogism stands in marked and radical opposition to the approach of a critic such as Picard:

> monologic, monophonic, monogrammatic, single [simple], univocal, linear, logical, epic, scientific, descriptive, theologic, whose space is 1 (the undivided). (fig. 8)

Thus, during this seminar across late 1966 and 1967, Barthes sets out, in the seminar that directly precedes his famous reading of Balzac's *Sarrasine* in 1968, the wide divergence in literary criticism:

> 2 large territories, 2 graphic poles, that of Science, or Theology, of the Single Voice, and that of the Menippea, of the multiple Voice. (fig. 8)

Yet, Barthes's application of this in his reading of *Sarrasine* two years later is compromised by the very title *S/Z*, which, according to Bannet (1989, 59–60), symbolizes Barthes's 'single totalising meta-meaning' to which all the codes lead, to that of castration's contagion for the character's in Balzac's tale whose names begin with S and Z, his essay being then his 'weaving [of] a cast-iron dress' for this single reading. Indeed, this might well be the consequence of 'respecting' (in particular) the 'symbolia' of the text at the same as obeying the four rules of anamorphosis in criticism, especially the first – the understanding that the work under scrutiny never lends itself to pure reflection. In this optic, *S/Z*, as we will now see, is concerned with a provisional and tentative resolution of these contradictory tendencies in criticism, a writerly, essayistic 'solution' in which the monologic – Bannet's insistence upon the 'inescapable singular' in *S/Z* – is used, temporarily, then discarded and replaced. It is important to stress that the tactical use of the 'monologic' in the seminar is not ruled out, as Barthes considers it as the first of three 'liberties' to be used in the reading of Balzac; and his way of defining it looks remarkably similar to *la nouvelle critique* (2011a, 65–66); furthermore, his tactical use of the 'monologic' here, and that he will later employ in *S/Z*, resembles the tactical use of 'old concepts' advocated by Derrida, in his 1967 essay 'Structure, Sign and Play' (2001, 359). This essayism benefits from the spirit of Menippus, augmented by an attention, inspired by Saussure, to the deep ambiguity of a text, the 'paragramme'.

The Menippea and the Paragramme

Despite his own specialism in Classics, Barthes seems to have taken the word *Menippea* directly from the work of Bakhtin and his *Problems of Dostoevsky's Poetics*. Menippus lived in the third-century BC, and, originating in Gadara (now in Jordan), was a follower of Diogenes Laertius and Cynic philosophy; and, as a Satirist, Menippus, according to Plato, defended poetry against philosophy. Menippus was a crucial element in Bakhtin's poetics, and in particular for his theory of fiction as carnival, in that Bakhtin saw it as both 'serio-comic' and auto-parodic. Similarly, in a letter to Barthes on *Criticism and Truth* from Louis-René des Forêts (Barthes 2018, 197), the poet mentions the serio-comic, to underline how rightly 'serious' Barthes's argument was in opposition to the 'frivolous' nature of the Picard position. There are clearly Barthesian sympathies for a Menippean form of literary criticism.

R. Bracht Banham (2005) suggests that, for Bakhtin, the carnivalesque – or serio-comic – benefited from three transforming elements: first, a relationship with temporality, with the now; next, a new attitude towards classical genres, based on myth; finally, a new relationship to the word based on heteroglossia (and then intertextuality). Without mentioning Barthes's stipulations on anamorphosis, Bracht Banham (13–17) lists the fourteen ways in which Bakhtin sees the serio-comic in the development of the motley form of the novel, amongst which the seventh – 'experimental perspectives that produce a "radical change in the scale of the observed phenomena of life"' (e.g., Lucian's play *Icaromenippus*, in which Menippus is sitting on the Moon and looking down on humans who look like ants) – and the fourteenth, topicality (overt or hidden polemics), seem pertinent to Barthes's concerns. Furthermore, the Menippean carnivalesque for Bakhtin mediates between the classical and non-classical, with one foot in the old and one in the contemporary. According to Bracht Branham (6), Bakhtin saw the novelistic as made up of three key roots: epic, rhetorical and carnivalesque. For a structuralist such as Barthes oscillating between binary oppositions, the carnivalesque is an appropriate figure; as Bakhtin put it (1984, 159): 'The carnivalization of passion is evidenced first and foremost in its ambivalence: love is combined with hatred, avarice with selfishness, ambition with self-abasement, and so forth'.

Relihan (1993, 28) sees Menippean satire as an anti-genre, a 'satire on literature itself and all its pretensions to meaning', in which the serio-comic is anything but 'comic'; what it refers to is the performative side of 'comic'. Barthes makes this point in the 'Linguistique du discours' seminar (O'Sullivan 2014, fig. 9), and, as O'Sullivan points out (note 23), both irony and parody are considered 'monologic' in *S/Z* (1974, 44–45, 139).

In order to see in more detail the relevance of this definition of Bakhtinian Menippeanism to Barthes's creative criticism, we must first consider Kristeva's influence. It is Kristeva who points out in 1966 that, amongst the polyphonic, carnivalesque and Menippean writers for Bakhtin – Rabelais, Cervantes, Swift, Sade, Lautréamont, Dostoevsky, Joyce, Kafka – there was also Balzac. Written in 1966 and given as a paper in Barthes's seminar in late 1966 or early 1967, but not published until 1969, Kristeva's 'Word, Dialogue and Novel' (1986a) argues that the Menippean satire, with a long and influential history in post-Hellenist literature, is 'capable of insinuating itself into other genres […] politically and socially disturbing' (1986a, 52). Using a language tending towards 'the scandalous and the excentric', it destroys humanity's 'epic and tragic unity' as well as the 'belief in identity and causality' (53). The *Menippea*'s fascination with the 'double' of the self and that of language is part of its 'logic of opposition replacing that of identity' and of its 'graphic *trace*' which is an 'all-inclusive genre, put together as a pavement of citations […] whose structural signification is to denote the writer's distance from [their] own and other texts'; crucially, Kristeva concludes:

> The multi-stylism and et multi-tonality of this discourse and the dialogical status of its word explain why it has been impossible for classicism, or for any other authoritarian society, to express itself in a novel descended from Menippean discourse. (1986a, 53)

Menippean satire is even 'a sort of political journalism of its time', its dialogism, a 'practical philosophy' which 'constitutes the social and political thought of an era fighting against theology, against law' (1986a, 54). Furthermore, for Kristeva, the 'ambivalence' of the *Menippea* is both literary and linguistic, it constructs itself as '*hieroglyph*, all the while remaining a *spectacle*':

> Menippean ambivalence consists of communication between two spaces: that of the scene and that of the hieroglyph, that of representation *by* language and that of experience *in* language [...]. (1986a, 55)

Finally for Kristeva, Menippean experience is not cathartic, but a 'festival of cruelty', 'a political act' but which does not transmit any 'fixed message', for it knows nothing of a theological principle's 'monologism': its dialogism 'stands against Aristotelian logic' (1986a, 54–55).

It would be somewhat extreme to try to apply *all* of this to Barthes's *S/Z*. Kristeva's account of Bakhtin's theory of the *Menippea* is beholden to the polyphonic and irreverent nature of the novel, not of the essay that Barthes is writing in 1968 and 1969; and, although in this period he is vaunting the 'baroque' in the novels of a Severo Sarduy or Edoardo Sanguineti (2016a, 76–85), the latter described as 'carnivalesque', 'Menippean' – 'the revolutionary literature of a non-revolutionary world' (85) – Barthes's *own* writing now needs to shift, parametrically, to mutate, 'paragrammatically', in this direction. In a key move towards creative criticism, Barthesian writing begins then to import Bakhtinian Menippeanism; and this is precisely the same period in which the 'romanesque' – the novelistic – becomes an important horizon, a 'value' in his work; and, as we saw above, despite his moves away from *la nouvelle critique*, it is this latter that had indicated to Barthes, in 1965, that there was indeed an *iso*morphism between literary theory and the novel. By 1968 then, Barthes is slowly shifting his writing towards a 'novelistic', indeed novel, essay-form, in which the symbolic and the parametric normally applied to the text begin to extend to the critic's 'text'. This 'contagion' between essayism and the novelistic – to redeploy a key metaphor in *S/Z* – is one of radical ambiguity and indeterminacy, were it not for the highly theorized problematic that we know now Barthes explored in the seminar that occupies him between *Criticism and Truth* and the work on *Sarrasine*.

It is during the 1966-1967 seminar on 'La Linguistique du discours' then, that Barthes sets out why and how literary criticism needs to take into account the paragrammatic nature, or ambiguity, of the text. Crucially for creative criticism, it must do so without betraying this same ambiguity by using a critical discourse that is assertive or 'dissertative', both of which imposed the Institution (literary, political, academic, etc.), and against which Barthes's *écriture* will aim, itself assertively, to operate, by deploying a curious mix of the peremptory and the provisional (Macé 2002).

This is what happens in 'The Death of the Author' (1977, 142–48), in which the reader-writer-critic is firmly pushed into the central place once occupied by the author, whose authority is subsequently decentred and displaced, if not destroyed. Indeed, Carlier (2000, 388–89) argues in his study of 'The Death of the Author' that this essay is more like a Menippean satire than an essay, both pedantic and anti-pedantic, but also performative (in the Brechtian) sense, as Barthes institutes a distancing of the voice of the writer, the 'voice-off' of a literary critic. If, as Samoyault argues (2017, 281), this distancing of 'self' from 'writer' is evident as early as Barthes's 1964 preface to his *Critical Essays* (1972, xi–xxi), then 'The Death of the Author' becomes a brilliant attempt to prove itself. Following the 1960 distinction Barthes had made between 'authors' on the one hand and 'writers' on the other (1972, 143–150), the author [écrivain] (or Barthes) distances themself, via a range of technical voicings, from the writer [écrivant] with an aim or cause. This *écrivain/écrivant* distinction had also posited a 'bastard type' in-between these two poles of the 'oblique' author on the one hand, and the committed on the 'other' (1972, 149). If Barthes sees himself as occupying this 'bastard' position, obliqueness added to commitment must presumably lead to a parodic status of some sort, close to the image of the voice that emerges from the Menippean satire. In our final section, we will now consider how Barthes's Menippeanism plays out across *S/Z*.

S/Z, or Creatively Re-Writing

In the 1968 notes on *Sarrasine* written for the seminar with his postgraduate students, Barthes seems acutely aware of the enormity of what he is – they are – doing:

> This reading, *which is passionate about what it knows*, is one of the forms of the *work* [travail] of modernity on the Text, as the destruction of linearity and the constitution of a volume-space of the text, that is first epitomised by Mallarmé's *Throw of the Dice*. I say that we should not let up in any way in this work, *common to all forms of writing [écritures]*, be it by writer, critic, film-maker, or musician (tonal music is linear; painting has been so for a long time); because it is a revolution that is perhaps more important (as it transgresses the institutional compartmentalisation of substances) than the previous one in painting that, with cubism, brought about the space of perspective or the destruction of the flat canvas. (2011a, 83)

However, it is one thing to vaunt the seismic shifts taking place in critical acts of reading; it is another to put these into some kind of writerly practice. Indeed, the move from seminar notes to *S/Z* – the 'essaification' of the teaching materials used across the tumultuous period of 1968 – is striking in Barthes's *œuvre*. Yet, *S/Z* is often his least popular book (Compagnon 1990, 62). Even Eric Marty, in the preface to the second edition of the *Œuvres complètes*, calls *S/Z* a 'strange book', highly ambivalent if not downright contradictory; the five codes which Barthes finds are, as Marty puts it, at once an encoding and 'the opposite of an encoding', in an approach that is both 'totalizing (*à la* Jakobson)' and 'a game of snakes and ladders in which the idea is to lose oneself'; indeed, continues Marty, the 'ambiguity of the enterprise' is evident in the use of Lacanian psychoanalysis in *S/Z* – for example, the 'purloined letter', ought to produce, according to Marty, 'the reading of a text that is an allegory of its method', but instead this is eschewed in favour of 'an astounding form of reading' (Marty in Barthes 2002, III, 13–14).

Other critics, whilst not strongly advocating *S/Z*, have pointed to a radical stance. Its 'bizarre montage' – to quote Roger (1986, 141) – is an attempt not only to smash the very genres of literature, to overcome the divisions between essay, criticism, and literary theory, but also to 'undo the institutional limits put on literature', which raises the question of whether Barthes's *own* writing is itself 'paragrammatic', deploying the 'scriptible' of radical ambiguity. *S/Z* and Barthes's two essays, 'Writing the Event' (1986, 149–154) and 'Linguistics and Literature' (2015a, 71–84), both published in Winter 1968, might at least qualify some categorical view, such as Hanania's that Barthes never claims to have written any 'scriptible texts', such is his imposition of an 'rational architecture' on his criticism (2010, 132).

Our analysis here of the codes in *S/Z* will concentrate instead on Barthes's writing as a way of breaking out of a seemingly tight, even unopenable, strait-jacket of codes. According to Bannet (1989, 59–60), *S/Z* sems to 'lock [the text under scrutiny] into an inescapable singular'; instead however, *S/Z* can be seen as Barthes's 'Houdini' act, in which the passage from the seminar notes on *Sarrasine* to *S/Z* itself, *is*, partly, a 'locking' of Balzac's short story (and the reading of it) into a relatively small number of codes (and then into the mere 'Three entries' of the conclusion); only then for a liberation of reading and its pluralness (or, polysemia), of its re-writing and of the Text, to emerge. Indeed, one of the main aims in *S/Z* – the 'wager' of the essayist, we might call it – is to show that, even with a highly restricted number of codes, parsimoniously chosen, it is still possible to show their 'dispatching', that is both multiple and complex.

Bremond and Pavel (1998) are rather unoriginal in deciding to concentrate on the codes, in that most of the scholarship on *S/Z* tends to concentrate on the five codes. Belsey (2002, 44) even sees the codes as a parody of structuralism This 'codism' then ignores what one critic has called a 'poetic of digression' (Chambers 1999, Chapter One). By contrast, in the seminar notes on *Sarrasine* (2011a, 64, 70), Barthes appears more relaxed about the number of codes than in *S/Z*. The infinite number of codes in Balzac's *Sarrasine* means that the reading has both to respect their role, whilst also, at the same time, arresting their continual generation in order to track their multiple functions. Hence the typographical division in *S/Z* between lexies and digressions that structures the essay. Bannet's division of denotative and connotative levels of writing in *S/Z* – the first approximating to the commentary on each lexical item, the second to the digressions aggregated into the 'single-totalising meaning'– points to this double activity in *S/Z*; and she even hints at a ludic re-reading of *S/Z* (Bannet, 61) One could read *S/Z* tactically therefore, without reference to the codes and analysis of the Balzac story via these codes; and, in which case, we would end up with 93 essayistic digressions. Indeed, it is the digression – the systematic undermining of a continuous analysis of a narrative – that is the first example of Barthes's Menippean form of creative criticism.

S/Z and Digression

Given that, as one Balzac critic has argued, Balzac used digression as his narrative motor, one could infer that, in *S/Z*, the use of digression is being merely 'parametric' with Balzac; and, as we saw, in Menippean terms, Balzac is listed by Kristeva and Bakhtin as, potentially, a polyphonic novelist. Indeed, according to one critic (van Rossum-Guyon 2006, 109), Balzac makes the series of digressions into the very motor of suspense. Hence the challenge for Barthes, for the critic-essayist that he has now become in the aftermath of his response to Picard in *Criticism and Truth*: how to be Menippean with respect to a literature that is already Menippean?

As we saw, the Menippean approach is also concerned with stepping outside of the normal lines of debate, and Balzac in 1968 – as today – is a heavily analysed, if not policed, literary heritage in France, and, also, an extraordinary publishing bonanza. Indeed, this is part of the wager in *S/Z*: how to win back Balzac's Menippeanism from the institutionalized and tightly-controlled manner in which *la Balzacie* operates? The first way might be to marginalize, if not undermine, any pretensions to scientificity:

> [T]o study this [single] text down to the last detail [...] is, finally, in the very writing of the commentary, a systematic use of digression (a form ill accommodated by the discourse of knowledge) [.] (Barthes 1974, 12–13)

Bremond and Pavel (1998) ignore this and turn Barthes's radical approach on its head. The title of their study of *S/Z* seems to have a neat 'deconstructive' twist of going backwards in literary history (from Barthes to Balzac), syllogistically and ambiguously critiquing Barthes's 'fiction'; yet, at the same time, they recommend (in Part Three) a return to a more traditional, literary-historical reading of Balzac. Nevertheless, their title seems deconstructively in tune with the reading. Indeed, in the seminar notes on *Sarrasine*, Barthes questions the order of literary history as we experience it, at one point declaring that, as Proust once said, *in* order to pastiche a writer, you needed the '*air*' of an author: 'as if Balzac *was pastiching* Proust' (2011a, 163). We will consider in Chapter Eight how this 'backwards', radically deconstructive reading of literary history, resurfaces five years later in *Pleasure of the Text*, (1975, 20).

However, Bremond/Pavel's title sounding deconstructive in the manner of *S/Z* is deceptive. Their co-authored analysis is, as we will see, wilfully dismissive of Barthes's overall strategy (dismissive in the sense that they never mention it) and even ultimately – given the proximity of semiotician Bremond to Barthes's evolution across the 1960s as a colleague at the EPHE – disingenuous in their account of *S/Z*. Published just before the death of the famous semiotician, *De Barthes à Balzac* is an unabashed attack on *S/Z* from two distinctly orthodox directions. Pavel lumps Barthes's in with the type of criticism that 'defends primacy of linguistic expression over its referent'; Bremond for his part operates a close analysis of the codes – as if they were some analysable structure, be they in Balzac's story or Barthes's essay (Bremond/Pavel 34). Pavel underlines that, as a 'hard to overestimate manifesto of a new philosophical and artistic era', *S/Z* 'summarizes a whole epoch', with its 'new vision of an inherent multiplicity in literary works'; but for Pavel, though the five 'big' codes (hermeneutic, proairetic, cultural, semic and symbolic) are shown by *S/Z* to be sounded out by the reader and writer alike without 'priority given to any one of them', they are nevertheless 'heavily used [imposés]' by Barthes (1998, 50, 76). Indeed, he is not alone in thinking this.

More recently, Jean-Louis Dufays (2010) has pointed to a double-sided imprecision in *S/Z*, in which Barthes's use of the word code is criticized either – at one extreme – as 'a catch-all concept devoid of rigour' involving very restricted sign systems (such as the hermeneutic code), or – at the other extreme – as 'vast constructions [ensembles]' (such as the proairetic code) (58). This perceived imprecision is precisely what Bremond underlines, as he stresses the gaps in Barthes's analysis. Bremond complains, for example, that the 'Annex 2' section at the end of *S/Z*, offers only one of the five codes, the proairetic (1974, 255–59). Bremond is surprised (101) that the 'science of the text' which is promised on the cover of *S/Z* is nowhere evident in the book's annexes, where Bremond wants to see (at all cost, it would seem), a complete list of the codes so as to decipher the mode of operation of all five, and not simply the code covering 'the Sequence of Actions'.

In Pavel's view furthermore (1998, 9), *S/Z*, as a classic of postmodernism, displays three 'stances', which, together, have an 'obvious contradictory nature'. First, Barthes confuses poetic conventions and literary messages; then the reduction of Balzac's text 'to the arbitrary playing out of the purely semantic codes' ignores both the plot and the 'discursive procedures of the narrative', in favour of a 'vague generality that does not even master the codes'; finally, argues Pavel, 'the historiality of the Sign' in *S/Z* satisfies neither the historicism of Hegelianism and Marxism, nor the 'concrete scholarship university-critic' (50-1, 58). Indeed, Pavel thinks (61n) that he can see 'the demand for non-contradiction' disappearing between *Criticism and Truth* in 1966 and *S/Z* four years later.

What is crucial then in the hostile reading of *S/Z* by Bremond and Pavel is the search, via the five codes, for a positivist science, with all the neo-technocracy implied in this. It is very revealing when Bremond refers to Barthes's 93 digressions as 'developments' (99). In other words, by concentrating on the codes and on their pertinence (or not), their concerted attack on *S/Z* overlooks the provisional status of the 'divagations' and the role of the contradictory nature of the essayism in *S/Z*: in short, the *literary* nature of digression.

The concept of digression suggests 'an interesting affinity with the concept of error' (Hibbitt 2011, 27). Indeed, Knight (2007) explores the 'error' in Barthes's repeated assertion that the statue of Zambinella is smashed by Sarrasine, attributing this to Barthes's empathy with Sarrasine and contaminated by the latter's blindness; Knight analyses this 'error' as *S/Z*'s attempt to 'stage' how both Sarrasine and the consumer of literary realism – including Barthes himself, Knight implies (28–29) – fetishize the *plenitude* of representation; it is as if Barthes too is going through as both a 'naïve' reader *and* a semiotician keen to enact a symbolic and parametric approach.

As well as a meditation on reading, *S/Z* is also (and above all, we might say) a rewriting, a literary writing which itself deploys a textual and analytical wandering, in a series of digressions (if this paradox is allowed) attached to a Balzac text which has been broken up by the 'lexies' and the codes in Barthes's reading; in short, a literary essay, both experiment and record, that mobilizes digression in order also to break up that same reading. In other words, we could ask: what would happen if we read the 93 'divagations' in *S/Z*, not as 'developments', but as essays somehow going *against* the commentaries that Barthes makes for each of the 'lexies' and from which the digressions are supposed to emanate? This 'digressive' reading of *S/Z* will help us to appreciate the second aspect of his creative criticism; that is, to dramatize the reading, or rather re-writing, that Barthes affords to Balzac's story, a dramatization that will require a stylization of writing.

In a considerably ironic moment for literary theorists, the 'reading' of *S/Z* by Bremond and Pavel – their 'rewriting' or 're-covering', we might be tempted to say – completely disfigures Barthes's own text, his own re-writing of Balzac's tale. Instead of taking *S/Z* for what it is – in his preface to the English edition Richard Howard underlines that Barthes originally added the subtitle 'essai', and this appears on the cover of the English translation (1974, xi) but then disappears completely in later French editions (and later English translations too) – those following in the footsteps of a Barthes in full post-68 and post-structuralist flow have tended to consider *S/Z* as a 'model' of reading, as if the 'pulverization' of reading was actually deploying, especially in the five codes, a 'science' of the literary text for all time, for any text. Let us note then the refusal by Barthes in an interview in 1970 of *S/Z* as 'as a scientific model applicable to other texts', except perhaps if the method undergoes 'deformations' (1985a, 81).

Instead, *S/Z* the essay might be better considered as a 'performance' of a reading-rewriting, but not at all THE reading–rewriting of the scientific and scientist type that Bremond and Pavel find wanting. It would seem that the Menippean ambivalence in Barthes's *S/Z* is precisely what Bremond and Pavel have missed in their attempt to show that the science of the text in *S/Z* is faulty, contradictory; to the extent that their own version of the science of Balzac's text, as one critic of their work has suggested (Reid 2001, 449–450), looks uncannily like that of a Raymond Picard! In order to complete our study of the Menippean in Barthes's creative criticism we now consider, the dialectics of the loss of self in his appreciation of the poetry of Zaghloul Morsy.

'What I owe … Zaghloul Morsy'

> It thus itself appears in another, and allows this other to appear in it, and consequently that, speaking generally, what is, only seems.
>
> *(Hegel 1805–1806; cited by Barthes in the French original, but omitted from Barthes 2005, 222n46)*

The title of this section is a deliberate parody of the title of Barthes's 1978 preface 'What I owe Abdelkébir Khatibi' (2002, V, 666–67). This is for the simple reason that Barthes's close friendship with the Moroccan sociologist across the 1970s comes about, initially, thanks to the Moroccan poet Zaghloul Morsy, who, in the 1960s, invites Barthes to lecture at Mohammed V university in Rabat (Samoyault 2017, 321). It is here that Barthes writes some of his controversial (but only posthumously-published) set of literary notes *Incidents* (1992b). Written in 1969 during his stay in Morocco, these frank and sexually-charged brief fragments have been recently republished alongside striking photographs by Bishan Samaddar, taken mainly in India but also in Morocco, to create a photo-text that goes a considerable way to attenuating the perceived 'orientalism' of Barthes's narrations of interactions with Moroccan boys (Knight 1997, 115–40).

There is also certainly much work to be done on the friendship and intellectual exchange with Khatibi. Though the references to each other in their respective published writings are rather limited – Khatibi merits but a footnote, albeit a fascinating and tantalising one, in Barthes's *Sade, Fourier, Loyola* (1989, 78–79n2, 'Khatibi' missing in the English trans.) – Barthes generously prefaces Khatibi's seminal decolonial autobiography, whilst Khatibi's move in the late 1960s from Marxism to post-structuralism has important dialogues with Barthes's work (Stafford 2020). And, in the other direction, Khatibi's innovative 'street' poetry drawing on the Casablanca uprising in 1965, published in the radical journal *Souffles* (Harrison/Villa-Ignacio 2016, 37–38), is a possible influence on Barthes's fragmentary style in *Incidents*. Indeed, the *addendum* of *Incidents* describes – in a manner which goes back to the 'wood-cutter' that Barthes invoked in 'Myth Today' in response to Marx's cherry-tree (see Chapter Two) – how his writing of *Incidents* is his acting directly on reality, 'in a position of someone who is doing something, and not talking about something; not studying a product, but producing; abolishing discourse on discourse; the world not as object, but as writing, a practice' (*addendum* not included in collected and translated versions; cited by Chiquer, in Boulaâbi et al. 2013, 115n4).

In the essay describing his debt to Khatibi, Barthes makes a striking suggestion: Khatibi's writing manages to 'find [retrouver], at the same time identity and difference', 'that which allows us to grasp [saisir] *the other* starting from our *self* [notre *même*]' (2002, V, 667). It is a hugely essayistic – that is, thought-provoking – idea. What is also striking in it is the similarity of this idea to those in his 1969 review of Zaghloul Morsy's epic, decolonial (that is, anti-colonial as opposed to post-colonial) poem. *D'un soleil réticent* (1969) is welcomed by Barthes in the left-wing *Nouvel-Observateur* magazine in June 1969 (2002, III, 102–03).

According to the poet Noureddine Bousfiha (1992, 127), Morsy's *D'un soleil réticent* is 'one of the greatest works in francophone Moroccan literature'. The 'reticent' in the title is ironic for Barthes's writings, as there is precious little on poetry in his published oeuvre. A number of commentators have discussed this (Coste 2016a; Gardner 2018, 2–4); but one could easily suggest – in good structuralist fashion – that, given their rarity in Barthes's writing, writings on poetry thereby become, or need to become, weightier in our minds. Not that poetry is always far from Barthes's other work such as teaching and lecturing; for instance *Le Discours amoureux* (2007a), his seminar in Paris in 1974-1976, contains extensive commentary on, mainly, German-romantic and Arabic poetry (both in French translation), of which very small amounts end up in *A Lover's Discourse* – Baudelaire, Heine, Verlaine, Hugo, Sappho, Goethe, Ronsard, Rilke but also haiku, Djedidi; compared to music, philosophy, psychoanalysis, or prose literature, strikingly little, also when compared to the seminars on 'amorous discourse' (1990a, 26, 77, 91, 97, 106, 155, 157, 174, 186, 188, 219, 226 and 233).

Not dissimilar to Barthes's 1970 essay on 'the outsider' Julia Kristeva (1986, 168–171), his warm reception of Morsy's epic decolonial poem is a fine example of Macé's view of the peremptory-provisional in Barthes's writing. We will consider this essay, with an eye on a striking article written at the same time, 'Ten Reasons to Write' (2015a, 85–87), with which to explore aspects of Moroccan poetry famous at this time for the 'violence of the text' (Gontard 1981). Furthermore, it is a mark of the importance of Barthes for Moroccan writers and intellectuals during the so-called *leaden years* – of repression, state terror, and imprisonment – that the first ever book on Barthes's 'erotics of language' was by the young Moroccan Mohammed Boughali (1986; see in general Boulaâbi et al. 2013).

Amongst Morsy's students at Mohammed V university in the early 1960s are the young radicals (Abdellatif Laâbi and Tahar Ben Jelloun most prominently), the graduates who launch the radical journal *Souffles* which ran for only seven tempestuous years before being closed down and its activists jailed by the regime of a deeply paranoid Moroccan King Hassan II. It is not surprising then alongside the *Souffles* writers' 'violence of the text' that Morsy's poetry should be guided by his injunction: 'Apprenons à écrire périlleusement' [Let's learn how to take risks in our writing] (in Ben Jelloun 1976, 144).

The journal *Souffles* contains only one reference to Barthes. In Abdellatif Laâbi's broadside against certain Arab journals (1970), he criticizes avant-garde journals in France for the way they sow confusion on literary writing in French, including one 'Roland Barthes' with an implicit reference to *Tel Quel* as the quintessentially Parisian intellectual journal of the time. Morsy is not mentioned in *Souffles* for his part; but he pays homage in 1970 to the journal's 'decolonisation of culture', though he is suspicious of its *prise de position* in favour of oral literature, with all the attendant dangers of folklorism' (Stafford in Boulaâbi et al. 2013).

The poetic writing that Barthes welcomes in Morsy's 1969 collection certainly has none of the violent or militant tenor of the 1960s writings by a Laâbi (2012) or a Mohammed Khaïr-Eddine (2020). Indeed Khatibi (1971), about to leave *Souffles* to set up a new Moroccan journal, *Intégral*, considers the originality of Morsy's poetry to be not only in his knowledge of Arabic but of a refined French poetry (Mallarmé, Saint-John Perse), a 'polyphonic chant [...] that jumps ahead and bangs on the door of the future' (Laâbi 2005, 195; Ben Jelloun 1976, 8). Although he regrets the 'academic' nature of Morsy's poetics and wishes to see a more 'radicalized' syntax, Khatibi underlines its originality in a way which echoes Barthes's praise, as Morsy 'manages to transgress the traps laid for him by the culture of the Other' (Khatibi 1971, 17). It is precisely this interest in the Other – a code-word for 'French' in this late 1960s period of neo-colonialism in francophone Africa – that characterizes Barthes's favourable reading of Morsy.

Like Morsy's poetry, Barthes's classes at Mohammed V university in 1969 are largely ignored by Moroccans (Coste in Boulaâbi et al. 2013). As Barthes tries to teach the 'bourgeois' writers Marcel Proust and Jules Verne, *Souffles* is promoting the *guérilla linguistique*. In this context, Morsy's refined avant-garde poetics is more subtle; and his 1974 injunction to 'learn to take risks in writing' (1976, 128), resembles the spirit of Barthes's 1973 essay *The Pleasure of the Text* whose epigraph from Hobbes – 'La seule passion de ma vie a été la peur' (in Latin, in Barthes 1975) [The only passion in my life has been fear] – seems to echo Morsy's desire to write 'perilously'.

Whilst writing his review of Morsy's poetry in June 1969, Barthes is completing his two important projects, *Empire of Signs* and *S/Z*, heralding a relatively militant period that runs from 1969–72. One glance at Barthes's response to a 1969 questionnaire launched by an Italian newspaper, 'Ten Reasons to Write' (2015a, 85–87), confirms his intellectual and writerly 'mutation', not just towards a creative criticism but also to his assistance with what he calls the 'fissuring of Western society's symbolic system' (86, trans. mod.). This 'fissuring' of meaning's system will play an important role in the 1970s, but it is a 'secondary political activity' (Barthes 2002, V, 903) that is 'never an end in itself' but one part of a 'dual valence' (Oxman 2010, 86, 87).

Indeed, what is striking in this 'Ten Reasons to Write' is the mixture of militancy with a pathos, even a tenderness, in which writing's aim is to 'to gratify friends and irritate enemies' (2015a, 86). Barthes's essay on Morsy also betrays, not surprisingly, his concerns of the moment contained in *S/Z*. Thus, in Morsy's poetry, he finds, first, an emphasis on 'citational space', but which does not need to use inverted commas; and second, prefiguring his later praise of Khatibi's writing, Barthes welcomes the way in which Morsy, this non-French poet writing in French, '*hijacks* [*détourne*]' (Barthes's emphasis, 2002, III, 102) the language of the ex-colonizer, and 'all the better to question its ownership'. It is an extraordinary moment in Barthes's writing in and after which he begins to turn the tables on a neo-colonial France and its 'marginalisation–recuperation' of francophone literature (Jack 1995), thereby prefiguring a 'world literature decentered' (Almond 2021).

Morsy's *D'un soleil réticent*, he suggests, typifies the unending circulation of languages, and the effect of this 'plurality' of different types of non-metropolitan French reaches to the heart of metropolitan France:

> [*D'un soleil réticent*] shows us how the *other* language (ours) is heard, how it operates on the other side: but this time, it is we [French people] who are placed opposite: *we are placed opposite in our own language*. (103, author's original emphasis)

This notion and act of 'hijacking' [détournement] that Barthes finds in Morsy's poetry, can be found, according to Ralph Heyndels (in Boulaâbi et al. 2013), also in *Incidents*. Heyndels shows how the writer's subjectivity itself becomes 'incidental [incidentaire]', thereby suggesting that Barthes's review of Morsy's poetry represents a counterpart to *Incidents*, in the sense that the very epigraph '*In Morocco, not long ago …*' (Barthes 1992b, 13) implies a French language viewed 'from the other side', 'excentered' or 'decentered'. Thus Barthes finds his own writing strategies in his acts of literary criticism, in a mode of essayistic creativity that we could call 'Menippean'. Furthermore, Morsy's erudite avant-garde poetry, mixing Mallarmean thematics with the great tradition of Sufi Arabic poetry, will go on to inspire Barthes's engagement with Arab poetry in the 'Discours Amoureux' seminars which use the academic work of Tahar Labib Djedidi (2007a, 67 and ff). But here, in 1969, it is the effect of Morsy's use of French language well before his friendship with Khatibi that is important. Indeed, Barthes begins his review with an analogy between clothing and language. Quoting the painter Eugène Delacroix's belief that the best place to find the ancient Greek style of clothing was

Morocco, Barthes argues likewise for a 'lyrical [...] superlative form of French, obliging French people to consider 'our French language as if stamped with an exteriority in its very essence' (III, 102). 'Articulated by a double civilisation, by a double language, Islamic and Western, Maghrebi and French', Morsy does not choose to dramatize the division between cultures, preferring to 'continually inscribe [the division] in his language' (102). Long before the Khatibi of the 1970s and 1980s who, alongside Derrida and Glissant, will vaunt the 'bilingualism' and multilingualism of the Other, Morsy in 1969, in Barthes's reading at least, sees value in playing out the dialectics of linguistic peril in the conflict between cultures (1976, 128); and, aware of the dangers of recuperation by the literary institution, Morsy aims to avoid 'all pathos', and advises 'any third-world revolutionary writer' to be the 'gravedigger' of the 'game' that forces the writer to choose one culture or another.

Moreover, Morsy (1976, 130n5) uses the essay form to 'diswrite' [désécrire] his own poetry in a manner not dissimilar to Barthes's 're-writing' of Balzac and even to his later thoughts about his own work in the retroactive view that Barthes begins to adopt, and which we consider in the final section of this chapter. The four key themes that Morsy finds in his own poetry in *D'un soleil réticent*, as he looks back and 'diswrites' this poetry (1976, 130n5) – temporality/practice of history, the dual space/ecology of Arab being, the love/primacy of the political in relations to the Other, and considerations of the linguistic medium (forms, aesthetics) – are precisely Barthes's in his 1969 review and, as Fatima Ahnouch argues (2004), those of Khatibi across the 1970s and 1980s.

Whereas Tahar Ben Jelloun (1976, 11) rejects all utilitarian, 'political' poetry, praising those new Moroccan poets who refuse to be 'the voice of a political project', Morsy, like Barthes, adopts an intermediary position. For Morsy, poetry has a role to play in achieving total decolonization, but following Barthes in *Writing Degree Zero*, Morsy considers that the 'rupture' or 'break' [cassure] of the 'colonial moment' needs to be figured directly, dialectically, in the very language (French) of the colonizer: anything else, in the light of the historic defeat of Arab nations in the 1967 war with Israel, would be a 'simulacrum of liberation, indeed an agreed and resigned reification' of all decolonized Arab culture (1976, 133). This would entail a 'counter-idea of the West in which its own values are turned on it', a long game of total decolonization involving a 'double "disenunciation" and a methodical destruction of all the entwined configurations'. Though Morsy – like Barthes – has none of the cultural terrorism of *Tel Quel*'s Maoism, he cites Mao's China as an example but not the 'model' (136–37). However, the key decolonial act concerns, as it does for Barthes writing 'from the other side', a critical consciousness 'but which is *internal* to our language and culture': 'Colonialism now dead, decolonisation is our exclusive responsibility [...] and it will be in vain if it is not based on a reappropriation of language and culture' (140).

The exchange between Morsy and Barthes, crystallized here in 1969, is an important one, not simply because it happens just as Barthes is passing through his post-1968 'mutation' and visiting both Morocco and Japan. Within the creative criticism that is typified by *S/Z* and the start of a creative practice in Morocco in *Incidents*, there is also now a political critique of culture that, as we saw in Morsy's writing, opens out onto a critique of French and France, and of the West in general; and it is counter-culture that is becoming increasingly suspicious. Barthes is in Rabat in 1969 when he writes an excoriating essay on the hippy culture he sees in Morocco; and interestingly, Barthes's politics of culture in 1969 resembles the manner in which Abdellatif Laâbi characterizes the work of the journal *Souffles* as involving a 'rebalancing of politics and culture, ideological discourse and artistic creation' (Tenkoul 1983, 9); Barthes writes:

> So here is the dead end for a critique of culture that is cut off from its political argument. But what's the alternative? Could we conceive of a political critique of culture which is an active form of criticism and no longer a simply analytical or intellectual one, which would operate beyond the ideological conditioning by mass communications, in the very places, both subtle and diffuse, where the consumer is conditioned, precisely the places where the hippies play out their (incomplete) clairvoyance? (Barthes 2006a, 113)

His conclusion is concerned with new and radical ways of living, in a manner that sets out the radical domestic and personal themes of the 1970s, especially in his 1977 lectures on *How to Live Together* (2013) and his work on Fourier (1989, 76–120):

> Could we imagine a way of living that was, if not revolutionary, at least unobstructed? No one since Fourier has produced this image; no figure has yet been able to surmount and go beyond the militant and the hippy: the militant continues to live like a petty bourgeois, and the hippy like an *inverted* bourgeois; between these two, nothing. The political critique and the cultural critique don't seem to be able to coincide. (2006a, 113)

It is not clear, here in 1969 at least, how and where Barthes will manage to avoid ways of living that are petty bourgeois on the one hand and 'inverted' bourgeois on the other. Perhaps this explains why 'novelistic simulations' is the subtitle of his lectures on *How to Live Together*: it points to the utopianism of his Fourier-based critique of modern ways of living. However, one possible way to move towards this is to begin to chip away, to perform what the 1970 preface to *Mythologies* calls '*semioclasm*' (2009, xviii), which, in the wake of May 1968, is needed 'in our country and the West' (xvii). We will now consider one key element in this critique, that of the person, the self. Here then Barthes's work will dovetail with the Khatibi wing of radical Moroccan writing and his seminal decolonial 1971 autobiography (2016).

Loss of Self and Preparation of the 'Novelistic'

> For a hundred years, (literary) madness has been [...]
> an experience of depersonalization. For me as an amorous
> subject, it is quite the contrary: it is becoming a *subject* [...].
> *I am not someone else*, that is what I realize with horror. [...]
> I am indefectibly myself. [...] I am mad because *I consist*.
>
> *(Barthes 1990a, 121)*

Part of the creative criticism that the period 1966-1970 inaugurates is not only 'The Death of the Author' – itself a radical text whose publication in France is delayed by the student uprising of May '68 after the English version was published in 1967 – but also the notion of the loss of self. It is evident in two aspects of the seminar notes on *Sarrasine* (2011a): first, in the 'drugged reading' that Barthes proposes, and then through his ambivalence to the literary character.

Barthes alludes to May 1968 in his final lectures, when suggesting that some writers' lives have a historical break in them with a concomitant '*mutation in sensibility*', his being May '68 (2011b, 285). He hints at his admiration for Balzac's comment that 'hope is a memory which desires': 'Every beautiful work, or even impressive work, functions as a desired work, albeit one that's incomplete and as it were lost *because I did not write it myself*; in order to recover that work, I have to rewrite it' (2011b, 132). This idea, and what he calls 'a third term: either the relation itself, or a new work, *inspired* by the old' (2011b, 135), could easily be applied to Barthes's own *œuvre S/Z*, and its relation to Balzac's 'tutor-text'. However, it is the 'mutation' that May 1968 inspires that we will now consider, first, in the 'drugged reading' proposed in the seminar notes on *Sarrasine*; and second, in the deconstruction of the notion of a literary 'character'. The aim is to links Barthes's Menippean reading and re-writing of *Sarrasine*, in both the seminar notes and *S/Z*, to the final lectures on *The Preparation of the Novel*. The example of 'life-writing' dovetailing with an academic interest in literary texts is the lecture 'book-course' described in *The Preparation of the Novel*.

This meeting of text and life in an institutional setting is best summarized as one of loss, or effacement of self. Both his writing on the literary character in relation to literature in general and to *Sarrasine* in particular, and the idea of 'drugged reading' seem to prepare us for the notion of a loss of self, or desire for the loss of self. It is a notion that seems to characterize the period between *S/Z* and *The Preparation of the Novel* and that is a distinct strategy in the writing of *Roland Barthes by Roland Barthes* (1994) and *A Lover's Discourse* (1990a) in particular; it is also detectable in *Empire of Signs* (1982b), in *The Pleasure of the Text* (1975) and even in *Camera Lucida* (1984). Unlike the perverse notion of *loss* such as in the work of Georges Bataille and especially in relation to the writing of poetry (1970, 307), and more active than the 'happy' fading that both *S/Z* and *A Lover's Discourse* find in textual aphanisis, Barthesian *loss* is deeply human, if not 'humanist', for it seeks to counter the human alienation caused by the desire to 'possess' the Other (by pigeon-holing them), by the self finding itself 'solidifying' under the weight of a whole and centred 'character', by that 'image' of the writer 'earned' by a critic working in the (highly orthodox) field of literary criticism in France.

Loss I: Drugged Reading

'Step by step', is, we will remember, the slowed-down method of reading a text advocated in *S/Z* (see digression VI), and which is germane to the cinematographic action of slowing a film to analyse the stills (1977, 52–68). Excised from the final version — though Barthes does talk about re-reading the text 'as though under the effect of a drug' (digression IX) — is any specific reference in *S/Z* to a 'drugged reading', and to its role in 'slowing-down' the text. Yet in the seminar notes on *Sarrasine* the 'drugged reading' has equal place alongside, is even linked intricately to, the 'step-by-step' of the slowed-down reading, as the following section of the notes shows:

> Step by step: the ideal movement for reading (there is a prejudice that reading is jumping, omitting). The ideal is a reading without residue, without omission, pure: a reading made up of acuity, precision, division and perspective: cf. a state that is not dream-like but an hallucination: to read is not to dream (and even less to daydream), it is to hallucinate, to take a drug (with the idea of hyper-precision that this word has in Baudelaire): Step-by-step: a mode of hyper-aesthetics: drugged reading: erethism in reading (= drugged reading), impatience to deflower: the Don Juan approach to reading: do not start again that which has been read once (...): what I have called a drugged reading obviously cannot be explained by any phenomenology of reading, as this type of reading assumes that we do not know where the subject is: in any case, they are no longer in an armchair. (2011a, 79, 81, 83)

Clearly, an important intertext for the reading of *Sarrasine* and pretext for *S/Z* is Charles Baudelaire's *Artificial Paradise* (2000 [1860]). However, in citing the 'hyper-aesthetics' that Baudelaire experiences with hashish and opium, Barthes also takes up a position with regard to drugs that is diametrically opposed to Baudelaire's (and, as we shall see, to Balzac's). The 'greenish-yellow pomade' (2000, 27) that Baudelaire himself takes and the perceived effects on a range of people whose experiences he narrates leave him decidedly unimpressed. Despite the sharpening of the senses occurring under both drugs, it is especially hashish that alters nothing, Baudelaire suggested: drugs heighten acutely our feelings and thoughts (Barthes's word 'hyper-aesthetics' is his own, it would seem) but no more than that. Hashish is not simply 'impure'; more importantly for Baudelaire, it 'is much more devastating than opium' and 'altogether more disturbing' (2000, 69–70). Baudelaire describes seeing Balzac refusing to partake in drugs and criticizing them for their encouragement of 'abdication' (88–89); as a good Balzacian, Baudelaire is acutely aware that hashish tends to disarm the will — and here we begin to see the opposing position that Barthes is taking in his proposed method of reading Balzac.

However, by alluding to the hyper-aesthetic of a 'drugged reading', Barthes seems to be placing himself, the reader (if only metaphorically), precisely where Baudelaire does not want to be. The 'decentering' of self (author, text and reader in particular) that is so characteristic of *S/Z*, as poststructuralist as it is Zen-Buddhist, seems well summarized in Baudelaire's (negative) analysis of what happens with hashish: 'Sometimes a loss of ego occurs (...), the contemplation of the outside makes you forget your own existence. (...) You feel yourself evaporating and you attribute to your pipe the strange power of smoking you' (2000, 52–53).

Another intertext, from the early 1960s, is Henri Michaux's 'Readings on hashish'. Michaux writes: 'Reading whilst on hashish opens up the interior space of the sentences and the hidden preoccupations emerge from it, it pierces them in one go' (1967, 175). However, the metaphorical 'drugged reading' that Barthes is invoking in 1968 is prized not so much for the perspicacity to which Michaux alludes, but for its positioning of the self as reader. If it is a loss of self that Baudelaire regrets, then this is exactly what Barthes's 'drugged reading' is looking for in his reading of *Sarrasine*.

Despite the acceleration Baudelaire sees in the effects of hashish, he is aware also of its slowing-down, rhythmic aspect that destroys reasoning, its 'rhapsodic' train of thought also being 'storm-tossed (...), infinitely more accelerated and more chaotic' (2000, 69). This accelerated, but rhapsodied, 'abdication' seems to characterize Barthes's 'drugged reading', as the musical sensitivity becomes crucial for the destruction of reasoning in the *S/Z* approach to *Sarrasine*. Not only does the 'stereographic space' (1974, 21) underline the competing meanings that mark the act of reading in *S/Z*, but also Barthes's reading is deeply idiosyncratic. The division of the units of meaning in *S/Z* treats some of the sentences in *Sarrasine* so quickly so as to ignore a hermeneutic and experiential (or closed), centred reading of the Balzac story; the 'reading' itself is contradictory enough to enrage the *belle-lettriste*, scientistic sensibilities of Bremond and Pavel, to the extent that, as we saw above, they completely overlook the profoundly essayistic, even literary nature of *S/Z*. We will return to the question of essayism in the conclusion; first, we must establish a link between the 'drugged reading' and the second manner of dissolving the self.

In his lectures on the *Neutral* of 1977–78, Barthes returns to Baudelaire's treatise on 'artificial paradises' when he discusses the 'excessively natural' of consciousness that Baudelaire sees drugs producing. As an example of the 'neutral', the 'total sensibility' brought about by drug-taking is then specifically related to a loss of persona: 'one becomes everything, one is no longer anything' (2005, 99). Thus, with this good example of *loss* under discussion here, we have a stepping-stone between the *Sarrasine* notes and *The Preparation of the Novel*. But before we look at the importance of 'disarming' in *The Preparation of the Novel*, we must consider our second *loss* in more detail.

Loss II: Depersonalization

It could be suggested that the 'drugged reading' invoked by Barthes in the seminar notes on *Sarrasine* is merely 'parametric' with the reverie in the Balzac story (just as the pensive marquise at the end of *Sarrasine* reflects the 'suspension' of judgement operated by the reader/rewriter in *S/Z*). But this would be to ignore the distinction that Barthes makes in the notes between dreaming and hallucinating. It would also be to take away the force of 'deconditioning' — an idea used first by Barthes in relation to Alain Robbe-Grillet in the 1950s — that the 'drugged reading' operates. If Barthes's idea of a 'deconditioning' of reading (here via a hypothetical late-60s drug-taking) goes back to his 1950s writings on the *nouveau roman*, this establishes Barthes's notion of the *Romanesque* as part of a wider loss of self and thereby links the late 1960s to the late 1970s; that is, the central question of characterization and nomination within literary discourse. Depersonalization, even anonymity, is a key feature of the post-war French novel, especially of the *nouveau roman*, and an important theme in Alain Robbe-Grillet's famous dismissal of the Balzacian literary character (1965, 27–29). We will have good reason to come back to the generic question around the literary-theoretical essay, such as Robbe-Grillet's, in the conclusion. Thus, and so typical of the way Barthesian literary theory often runs parallel to (and occasionally dovetails with) a certain literature of the moment, *S/Z* seems fundamentally concerned with literary 'character'.

As Bremond and Pavel insist, the literary character is a central feature of *S/Z*, even to the point that Barthes, they say, distorts its role in the semic code (1998, 137, 142–143). However, this (so-called) distortion seems to me to be central to Barthes's 'novelistic' strategy. Rather than generalize the literary character ('generality' is Nathalie Sarraute's Sartrean solution in her novels for example, 1956, 10), Barthes's strategy in his reading of *Sarrasine* — and we will see how this relates to *The Preparation of the Novel* in a moment — is to accept the contradictory status of the literary character and then to exploit this contradiction.

Rice and Schofer point to the seeming contradiction in relation to the analysis of name and literary character in *S/Z*, the 'double synecdochal role' (1982, 33n5): indeed, as suggested in *S/Z*, 'what is obsolescent in today's novel is not the novelistic, it is the character' (1974, 95). Yet Barthes still recognizes, or accepts, even laments, the predominance of literary character. In 'Introduction to Structural Analysis of Narratives', Barthes points to the way in which Russian formalists such as Tomachevski and Propp had either considered character as irrelevant or had reduced it to a mere typology, not based on a psychology, but a function of the actions imparted by the story (1977, 79–124). But there is no story in the world without some kind of character or 'actant': 'If one section of contemporary literature has attacked the "character", it is not in order to destroy it (which is impossible), but to depersonalize it, which is quite different' (257n45). Furthermore, even Philippe Sollers's radical, seemingly characterless, 1965 novel *Drame* must accept that the subject of the novel, language, is itself a kind of actant or character. However, by the time of *S/Z* four years later, Barthes seems to reconvert this stricture into a more nuanced view of the literary character: 'From a critical point of view, (...) it is as wrong to suppress the character as it is to take them off the page in order to turn them into a psychological character (...): characters are types of discourse and, conversely, the discourse is a character like the others' (1974, 178–79, trans. mod.). Chatman (1979, 115) sees this as evidence of Barthes 'changing his tune' between 1966 and *S/Z* in 1970; but perhaps we can see this as less a shift than a dialectical formulation. For it seems, in *S/Z* at least, that character is viewed in a 'double grasp': at once inevitable, and yet also fatally flawed in relation to the real and contaminating all aspects of discourse. This markedly Barthesian ambivalence towards the literary character, especially across the turbulent 1968 period, is further compounded by the tempered criticism of the literary proper-name in his 1967 piece 'Proust and Names', at the end of which the suggestion is that, in the wake of Proust, it may be impossible to be a writer without believing in a 'natural', motivated link between names and essences (1990c). Therefore, rather than naively celebrate, or glibly regret, the homo-nominalizing potential of literature, *S/Z* represents, in poststructuralist fashion, Barthes's 'novelistic' strategy of wedging in between (or outside) of these two poles; and it is then precisely this tension in his thought, between the apparently 'obsolescent' textual character and its literary inevitability, that (as so often in Barthes) is revisited ten years later in *The Preparation of the Novel*. This answers, in part perhaps, Scheiber's (1991) implicit question as to where the structuralist critique of literary character disappears following *S/Z*. However, by the time of *The Preparation of the Novel*, the critique of character has become a virtue, an aim, even a utopia: if the fictional person is lost in a double bind, then it is precisely this 'lost' persona that, in a good Barthesian spiral, seems to return in *The Preparation of the Novel*. The implication of the self (reader, critic, writer), the inscription, or rather the description, of self (as writer about to write, but also as professor at the Collège de France), are the subject of important sections in *The Preparation of the Novel*, even before we reach the séance called 'Life as Work' (2011b, 207–08) and before Philippe Hamon's treatment (1977, 118–19) of the subject: 'There is a dialectic inherent to literature (with, I think, future potential) that makes it possible for the subject [them]self to be presented as a work of art; art can be involved in the very making of the individual; there's less of a conflict between the human and the work if they make themself into a work' (2011b, 167). If what stops Barthes writing his 'novel' in these 1979 lectures is the literary character, then indeed we could call *The Preparation of the Novel* a performance of depersonalization (there is no novel, but there is an acting of *a* novelist about to write); and this is tantamount to a stage in the move towards 'life as literature' as Nietzsche would have wanted, the dissolution of his – Barthes's – life into literature.

Dissolving the self (especially in the fascination for Michelet, Haikus and Zen Buddhism) is equally important in both *The Preparation of the Novel* and in *S/Z*, in the play on the loss of self that both the *koan* and the 17-syllable Japanese poems reflect. But Barthes's Zen is not so much existential (as in Albert Camus's for example) as intellectual and writerly: to be a non-novelist in both senses, non-person and to produce no novel. As Barthes puts it in note-form, so succinctly, in *The Preparation of the Novel*: 'talking like a book ≠ living as a book, as a Text' (2011b, 98). Thus *The Preparation of the Novel* is trying to achieve the utopian position whereby not only is character eschewed (there is no novel, only the 'novelistic'); but also whereby the writer/critic/academic is also effaced: 'In fact, narration strictly speaking (the code of the narrator), *like language*, knows only two systems of signs: personal and apersonal' (1977, 112, my emphasis).

We have seen how depersonalization was conveyed in the late 1960s by an 'impersonalist' 'drugged reading', in which 'text' was set in opposition by Barthes to a 'scientism' of literature towards which structuralist literary analysis had been edging ever closer; however, this was a generalized reading, albeit slowed to a 'step by step'. It is the addition of the deep ambivalence towards naming and characterization, in a life-into-literature strategy seemingly required by an academic context, which allows Barthes to glimpse a utopian novel, though this is still defined negatively in *The Preparation of the Novel*. This negativity is conveyed by Barthes's aim of stopping the '*daily grind [ronron]*' of the writer's oeuvre (2011b, 6). It is an apersonalism (not simply impersonalism) that has an important bearing upon how Barthes writes across the 1970s — what we might call his 'novelistic' period — in that it constantly tugs at the 'solid', even solidified, figure of the self that the mid-1970s Barthes tries to 'neutralize'. Just as the narrator is seen in *S/Z* as a character, so too, one could argue, is the writer in its Barthesian version; except that, and this is the importance of the 'novelistic' for the essayist-professor, it is a depersonalized version that Barthes's writing is instrumentalizing: to avoid being the Proper Name which he describes in *S/Z* as 'an adjective, an attribute, a predicate' (1974, 190). The Proper Name, the character, may be unavoidable in narrative, but it is precisely this that Barthes, the French intellectual figure, strives to avoid in himself, in his imaginary and in his 'image', and which, in a manner not dissimilar to the North African superstition towards Photography, wishes to escape the box into which the Other tries to place him, to escape a kind of death. Interestingly then, in *The Preparation of the Novel*, Barthes characterizes the dialectical outcome of his lectures in Sartrean terms of 'death', which we could apply easily to his reading (and then rewriting) of *Sarrasine*: 'when I write, once my writing is finished, my subjectivity is objectively determined by the Other; [they] deny my freedom: [they] put me in the position of one who is Dead' (2011b, 166). To counteract this 'death', it is a form of loss [*perte*] that Barthes actively seeks; hence in *S/Z*, and in *The Preparation of the Novel*, he must accept the to-ing-and-fro-ing between being radically singular (*S/Z* and *The Preparation of the Novel* are literally uncopiable performances), and yet producing an image which then could (potentially, though Barthes is careful not to let this happen) ossify him into certain positions. The sensitivity to naming in *S/Z* — 'to read is to struggle to name' (1974, 92) — is undermined, by the late 1970s, by an essayism that refuses to say his name, in an essayistic enactment of a famous question of Jacques Lacan: 'Is the subject I speak of when I speak the same as the subject who speaks?', asks Barthes citing Lacan (1977, 112n1).

Barthes's 1968 reworked version of his 1965 review of Sollers's novel *Drame* (coll. 1968, 27–42) is useful in tracking his critique of 'character', especially the 'notes' I–III that Barthes adds to his original review. Indeed, it is the contradictory nature of the character — a contradiction that Bremond and Pavel either do not see (profoundly), or judge harshly by way of a science of the text — that is important in *S/Z*, and then in *The Preparation of the Novel* (Gane/Gane 2004, I, xiv, and Wilson 2000). In other words, the essayistic *perte* of *S/Z* — its provisionality, its contradictory ideas, its 'failure' as method (according to Bremond and Pavel) — is its 'novelistic' strength. *Perte* signifies the refusal to control, to own, or to finish. The gap between the 'true-to-life' and the 'intelligible' that Scheiber (1991, 302–03, 309–10) sees as a fundamental tension in Barthes's literary analysis of the referential illusion (in both character and textual 'insignificance') is the same gap that Barthes will open up in trying to undermine his own 'image' (or 'character') that 1970s media-dominated culture in France is trying to impose. If removing (Balzacian) 'will' from reading is equal to the refusal to write a novel in *The Preparation of the Novel*, then these final lectures are a writing that is now 'step by step', 'drugged': in abdicating and disarming the novelistic sensibility required to start writing a novel, Barthes is also the ex-nominated novelist of *perte*, and ready for the *vita nova*. We are now in a position then to suggest the generic links between the 1968 reading of *Sarrasine* and the thoughts on preparing an act of novel-writing of ten years later.

To conclude, we may wish to consider the generic nature of the *Sarrasine* seminar notes, genetically as it were: what are they? They are perhaps the first example of what Thomas Clerc has hinted at in his preface to *The Neutral*, when he describes these lectures as being given by a 'unique' image in French literature, that of the 'artist-professor' (2005, xxv). Indeed, Barthes call his notes and seminars on *Sarrasine*, before their publication in book form in *S/Z* in 1970, an example of 'lecture-books [livre-cours]' and even imagines writing the one on *Sarrasine* collectively with his postgraduate students (2011a, 335, 488). Similarly, ten years later in *The Preparation of the Novel*, he describes the lectures as a 'Book-Course', even a theatrical 'Play-Course' (2011b, 167) and talks about, one day, even lecturing on the 'Preparation of the Course'! (171). This essayism forms the basis of both his seminar and lecture notes, in 1968 seminar-writing and in 1979 lecture-writing: digressive; provisional in their use of effacement; a challenge to 're-write' Balzac and a discussion of how to write a novel; 'semelfactive' performances (or theatricalization) as forensic experiments, but also generically experimental (seminar or lecture theatre as laboratory): not just 'lecture-book', but somewhere between essay, fiction and experiment, what he calls in *The Preparation of the Novel*, following the German Romantics, a 'motleying' of genres (2011b, 143), an inter-generic (or extra-generic) form for which *perte* becomes seemingly indispensable. What then is the difference between *The Preparation of the Novel* and what we might call 'the 'preparation of the novelistic', and above all when one is a preparation for the other? One could use the deconstructive, intertextual 'turn' of *The Pleasure of the Text* and suggest that *The Preparation of the Novel* anticipates the 'preparation of the novelistic' in *S/Z*. We could also apply an approach that is thoroughly romanticist instead, whereby *The Preparation of the Novel* and the 'preparation of the novelsitic' are in parallel (or dialogue): equal, identical in their institutional Foucauldian 'play'. Either way, Barthes's essayism — a fictionalized, provisional and highly digressive form (or 'divagatory', to quote Mallarmé) — informs and launches, in both seminar notes on *Sarrasine* and in *S/Z*, the *romanesque* that is crowned by *The Preparation of the Novel*. This essayism, or 'novelistic' writing, is not (or is less) compromised in language than that deployed by a novelist such as Sarraute or Robbe-Grillet, in their switching to use the prose essay to discuss the novel and the new literary sensibility of the post-war period, in the most standard and unproblematic fashion. In this sense, Barthes's 'lecture-books' are far more honest: language is, after all, faulty or deeply ambivalent especially in non-fictional prose concerning fiction; and Barthes's essayism, institutionalized but fully aware of its potentiality as 'text', is also far more productive, in that the relationship between tutor-text and critical-text is not beholden to any scientism, is also parametric to its intertexts, a creative form of criticism. We can now perhaps suggest a rule-of-thumb for the 'artist professor' or 'critic-novelist': the essayistic wager that marks Barthes's *écriture* is such that the more 'institutional' or more constrained the context, the more corrosive and provisional the writing that emerges; the more an essayism is beholden to complicity with participants in an academic situation, the more a notion of *perte* is required. As he puts it in *The Preparation of the Novel*, 'to my mind, a lecture is a specific production: not entirely writing nor entirely oration, it's marked by an implicit interlocution (a silent complicity)' (2011b, 7).

If essayism (at least in Barthes's version of it) and *perte* are crucial components for the 'artist-professor', then the 'novelistic' now becomes the risk for Barthes of not writing a novel: just as the reading of a Balzac story is easy compared to its rhapsodic, drugged slowing-down in a university seminar room, so writing a novel is 'easy' when compared to discussing its 'preparation' in a Collège de France lecture series.

However, *The Preparation of the Novel* lectures do have one fundamental difference from the *Sarrasine* seminar notes: what is crucial, with respect to *S/Z*, is to determine whether these seminar notes that precede it are a simple avant-texte crowned by their publication in the essay and 'romanesque' form that is *S/Z*; or whether the 'lecturebook'

— that is, the institutional status of the rewriting of Balzac — has increased the essayistic nature of the enterprise, to which *S/Z* then becomes a (poorer?) testimony? In other words (and this question does now apply equally to *The Preparation of the Novel*), what is the relationship between teaching, lecturing, seminaring, and the essay, the essayistic, the 'novelistic'? The only answer to this is alas, for the moment, in the form of another question: 'So what do you do?', laments Barthes at the end of *The Preparation of the Novel*: 'I am not fully a writer and am not worldly[.]' (2011b, 204).

Chapter Six

'NON-CLASSIFIABLE'

'History Cannot March Against History'

Barthes's speech in Bucharest in September 1949 finishes with these words. Not only does the tone resemble the 'messianism' in Walter Benjamin's theories on history we considered in Chapter Three, it suggests a voluntarist take on historical change. Furthermore, given that his initiation into the Marxism of his sanatorium friend Georges Fournié in 1946 occurs only one year before he becomes a French Lecturer in Bucharest, it is important to consider the young intellectual's attitude towards Stalinism during this pivotal period in world Communism which we will do in Chapter Seven. Before this we need to lay the basis for an analysis of the dialectical form of thinking that Barthes develops following this extraordinary injunction on history in Bucharest. To do this we will consider in Chapter Six his writings on Japan and China. But first, in this chapter we will consider, in the light of the 'loss' of self that we saw in Chapter Four, how Barthes deals with these two forms of determinism, the systematic and the classifying.

The System that is suppleness is not entirely original in *Mythologies*. Baudelaire's *naiveté* in his 1855 view that art criticism should be 'free of a system' (cited in Shawcross 1997, 51–52) is mirrored in Barthes's critique of the systematic that, as we shall see, is not at all systematic. Nevertheless, Barthes is certainly tempted by some form of system, especially in relation to History. For Michelet, Voltaire 'dissipated history like dust in the wind, by consigning it to blind chance' (1962, 244), and – despite his two-part history of the reign of Louis XIV – failed to understand history. As we shall see, the Barthes of the 1950s takes this blind chance view of Voltaire's and subjects it to a penetrating critique in 1958 precisely for its lack of system.

However, in his 1971 essay on Fourier (1989, 109), Barthes uses a quotation from Marx/Engels's *The German Ideology* (1974) to underline the paradoxes of systems whereby orthodox followers of system end up as the 'exact antipodes' of that system (hence Marx's famous dictum: 'I am not a Marxist'); and makes an important distinction:

> system, in the terminology of Marx and Engels, is the 'systematic form', i.e., pure ideology, ideological reflection; systematics is the play of the system; it is language that is open, infinite, free from any referential illusion (pretension); its mode of appearance, its constituency, is not 'development' but pulverization, dissemination (the gold dust of the signifier); it is a discourse without 'object' (it only speaks of a thing obliquely, by approaching it indirectly […]) and without 'subject'. (1989, 110)

In a continuation of the 'voice-off' of the essayist that we saw in Chapter Four with respect to 'The Death of the Author', he now argues that the writer does not allow themself 'to be involved in the imaginary subject', as the writer '"performs"' their 'enunciatory role in such a manner that we cannot decide whether it is serious or parody' (1989, 110). Indeed, in his definition of *Kairos*, the 'asystematic character of the Neutral' (2005, 169) has become 'enunciatory': 'I don't construct the concept of Neutral, I display Neutrals' (2005, 11). That there is no non-system (or zero degree of system) is merely a prelude to finding a way out of this aporia; and which he then applies to method (*Paideia*): '"a premeditated decision", a direct means, deliberately chosen to obtain the desired result' (2013, 133; De Pourcq 2008); except that this method involves a journey:

> How does the text advance? Once it's begun, how does it develop, proliferate? How does the mutation of situations, of the sites (*situs*) of discourse operate (we're already making progress if we are talking about sites rather than units)? What's the key to its development, to its unfolding, to how the discourse 'comes together', 'takes' (cf. Being held by discourse), the translation of its units (its sites)? Such questions would pertain to a kinetic science of speech: a mechanics (what are the motors of discourse of the *cursus* in *dis-cursus*?). And also to an art of travel. How does the text travel? (Here we'd recover the *hodos* [path] in *hodoiporia* [voyage], in travel and in method). (2013, 156)

Indeed, method is a 'path' in Tao: 'Tao: what matters is the path, following the path, not what you find at the end' (2011b, 20). System too has aspects of 'path'.

In Chapter Nine's discussion of Voltaire and Barthes's critique of power, we will consider the dialectics and 'undialectics' of the Neutral. First, we must underscore not simply the sharp critique of Voltaire, but also underscore it as an example of an 'extreme-contemporary' Barthes whose views dovetail, in an extraordinary fashion in 2015, with the critique of the 'Je suis Charlie' movement in France that rose following the appalling bombings in Paris.

Voltaire and System

> It is precisely in affirming the series of your
> judgments is finite that you deny it, for in so
> doing you add a new judgment to this series.
>
> *(Lyotard 1994, 128)*

Already, in Bucharest, Romania, in 1948, Barthes had given a lecture on Voltaire underlining that, although a historian, Voltaire came before the century of history, the nineteenth century (Calvet 1994, 84). His 1958 preface on Voltaire, written ten years later just as General de Gaulle was about to perform his 'coup' at the height of the Algerian War, is republished in edited form in *Critical Essays* six years later. It is an essayistically hostile account of Voltaire's relevance – or not – to the 1958 debacle. It stands in marked contrast to the 'praise' Adorno and Horkheimer offered to the eighteenth-century philosopher 15 years previously (1979 [1944], 218–219); but it prefigures the 'Happy Consciousness' that Marcuse saw in the new conformism of the early 1960s (Marcuse 1991 [1964], 87–88).

Indeed, 'Voltaire, The Last Happy Writer?' is the title Barthes gives to his preface to the 1958 edition of Voltaire's *Romans et contes* and which appears first in the in-house magazine *Actualité littéraire* in March 1958, and then finally in the Gallimard Folio version of 1979. The difference between Barthes's original essay and the much better-known *Critical Essays* version (1972, 83–89) goes beyond the fact that the later version's title, 'The Last Happy Writer', removes 'Voltaire' as well as the question mark.

One critic – in a notoriously conservative assessment (Thody 1977, 121) – calls the essay on Voltaire 'condescending'; though this same critic deems Barthes's essay on Japan, *Empire of Signs*, to be reminiscent not only of Montesquieu's *Lettres persanes* but also of Voltaire's Eldorado in *Candide*. Indeed, in 1947, Barthes sees Voltaire's writing as a rare example of one coming close to a 'degree zero' style (1947); but this is to mistake a minor but not inconsiderable aversion to Voltaire's view of history.

Barthes lists in the recent publications on Voltaire in 1958 the special number of the centre-right journal *La Table Ronde* 'Voltaire au présent' (122, February 1958), and against which he is doubtless reacting. He begins by saying, using a mixture of philosophical analysis and humour, that we seem to have so little in common with Voltaire:

> From a modern point of view, his philosophy is outdated. These days we believe a lot less in disorderly History and in the fixedness of essences; atheists no longer throw themselves at the feet of deists and who no longer exist. The dialectic has killed off Manicheanism, and no-one discusses Providence any more. As for the enemies of Voltaire, they have disappeared or transformed themselves: there aren't any Jansenists, or Socinians, Leibnizians, Aloges nor Carpocratians; Jesuits are no longer called Nonotte or Patouillet. (Barthes 1958, 13)

The Abbé Claude-Adrien Nonotte, in *Les Erreurs de Voltaire* in 1770, had regretted Voltaire's powers of seduction; and the Abbé Patouillet wrote a pamphlet against Voltaire. Having humorously ended his list of eighteenth-century religious phenomena against which Voltaire steadfastly stood, Barthes nevertheless hesitates:

> I was going to say: the Inquisition no longer exists. This is false of course. What has disappeared is the theatrical nature of persecution, not persecution itself: the *auto-da-fé* has subtly found a place in police operations, as the butcher in a concentration camps, discretely ignored by the neighbours. (13)

Barthes writes this 1958 preface at the height of the Algerian War, and in the aftermath of the horror of the Holocaust; and the stark differences between the middle of the twentieth century and the middle of the eighteenth century are underscored by the figures:

> [I]n 1721, nine men and eleven women were burned in Granada [...] and, in 1723, nine people in Madrid for the arrival of the French princess: they had probably married their cousins or eaten meat on Friday. This was a horrible form of repression, the absurdity of which runs through Voltaire's *œuvre*. However, from 1939 to 1945, six million men, amongst others, perished in the tortures of deportation, because either they themselves were Jewish, or their father or grand-father were.
>
> And we did not get a single pamphlet against this. (13)

There are similarities with Barthes's 1955 criticism of Albert Camus's novel *The Plague*, in which he suggests that '[E]vil sometimes has a human face and about this *The Plague* says nothing' (2002, I, 543).

He is not suggesting that Voltaire had been wrong, of course; but rather that Voltaire in 1958 is completely irrelevant; whereas Steiner (1961, 194) considers Voltaire to be modern in terms of his 'melodrama' approach to tragedy. Barthes's attitude is that it is easy in hindsight to suggest it, but something good had indeed come out of Voltaire's attempts at imposing Enlightenment notions of religious tolerance – at least in law –, and his campaign of 'Ecrasez l'infâme' [Destroy Intolerance] could be seen, ultimately, as a prelude to the Great French Revolution of 1789 that followed soon after Voltaire's death. By contrast, and as Jean-François Lyotard later argued in relation to the *singularity* of the Holocaust (cited in Shapiro 2004, 77n17) – and Barthes was prefiguring the idea here in 1958 – the Holocaust not only did not produce any pamphlets against it: it produced *more* than nothing, that is, nothingness itself.

Suggesting that, 'simplistic as it might seem', the figures involved are proportional to the critical weapons deployed, Barthes now arrives at his main point about Voltaire:

> There is a proportional relation between the lightness of the Voltairean weapon […] and the sporadic nature of religious crimes in the eighteenth century: quantitatively limited, religious persecution was becoming one of principle, that is a target; this is something of an enormous advantage for those who fight against it: it makes for a triumphant writer. (Barthes 1958, 13)

Voltaire had it easy, whereas, in today's world, things are much more complex, in proportion to the size of the crimes committed:

> The very enormity of the political and racist crimes committed, their organisation by the State, and the ideological justifications afforded to them, this all requires from today's writer something well beyond the pamphlet, requires them to have a philosophy much more than irony, an explanation rather than astonishment. (13)

And within this modern and contemporary philosophy, there are subtleties of which Voltaire knew nothing:

> [I]n the time since Voltaire, History has locked itself into a difficulty which is the very negation of Voltairism: no freedom for the enemies of freedom. No-one can give lessons on tolerance to anyone. (15)

Following this stark, even peremptory diagnosis of modern political morality, and in a section of Barthes's essay which is not included in the 1964 version, the paradox of liberalism is underscored:

> There is a fact of major significance in the history of our ideas: theories of violence (Bonald, Maistre, Engels, Sorel) came after those on liberalism. But the paradox in this order of succession is clear to see. Voltaire's attacks were aimed at a theocratism which was already in

ruins, they were not about finishing something off; but they would have been a crowning moment only if History had stopped at the rehabilitation of Calas. (15)

We will return to the Calas case in a moment. Though seemingly contradicting his own argument that Voltaire 'was' the last happy writer – he would never experience the crowning moment when writing his best-known pamphlet of 1763, *Treatise on Tolerance* – Barthes implies that Voltaire had the luxury of not knowing what followed the rise of liberalism. Anticipating much of the work on the 'concentrationate' (from David Rousset and Jean Cayrol to Max Silverman), Barthes sets out an acute problem for writers and intellectuals in the modern, post-Holocaust world. The new world of twentieth-century mass horror requires a new socio-political dialectic which can overcome the immobilization of History in Voltaire's obliviousness to what follows the founding of Liberalism:

> So History did then continue, there was a new departure again, a new type of split, no longer between church and bourgeoisie, but bourgeoisie and proletariat. (15)

This is not the 'post-history' found in Michelet's historiography that follows the Revolution and which is slowly destroyed by events (2002, I, 113–14), so much as Voltaire's belief in progressive liberalism.

For Barthes, the clarity of this division, in today's modern world, is not replicated in questions of democracy, freedom of expression nor religious tolerance. The alleged 'progressiveness' of Voltaire's battle against intolerance is dismissed in an acerbic and ironic aside about the economic 'benefits' of religious tolerance; and, in contrast to the 'nothingness' of the Holocaust and its utterly *non*-dialectical nature, Barthes pushes Voltaire back beyond the historical line that divides the old world from the modern world:

> Voltaire is certainly on the far side of the major change in History: essentially, and we are well aware of how vigorously he did it, he knew how to sort out a situation; tolerance is the ultimate demand (partly an economic one, we must not forget), following which the world will be reasonable, that is, as far as it is possible, perfect; take Holland: the diversity of its sects makes for Stock-Market prosperity: fifty-three religions living side-by-side mean fifty-three million business deals in a day (*Pot-Pourri*). (15)

In the introduction to Voltaire's *Traité sur la tolérance* (2000, 70–73) Renwick details the 'economic' argument put forward by Voltaire and to which Barthes is referring. Though destined to be the preface to Voltaire's *Romans et contes*, Barthes's essay spends more time on Voltaire's essays, journalism and pamphlets than on his fiction. In a shrill Marxian mode, Barthes exposes Liberalism and religious tolerance as perfect for bourgeois accumulation and ownership:

> Voltaire can feel that he is close to his aim; there is no need to build the future, all he needs to do is to clear out the past a little bit more; there is no contradiction between Voltaire's (conservative) taste and his metaphysics or his politics: they are all behaviours consistent with an owner of property who is happy. (15)

This whole section is removed from the 1964 edition of Barthes's essay; and the candid and forthright critique of Voltaire in March 1958 – just as De Gaulle is readying himself to retake political power in France, in May 1958 – is a staunch refusal to mobilize Voltaire, and a wider critique of Liberalism in general, of what Roberto Schwarz would later the 'misplaced ideas' of liberal ideology in a world of forced labour (Schwarz 1992, Chapter One):

> In as much as there has been a posthumous destiny for Voltaire, that is, in as much as Voltaire is a great writer, this is essentially a conservative idea. The fundamentals of Voltairism, that is, this mix of passion and system which defines a writer at heart, is what we call today anti-intellectualism. [...] He has only one system and that is the hatred of system (and we know that there is nothing as fierce as the former system); his enemies today would be the doctrinaires of History, of Science [...], of Existence: Marxists, progressives, Existentialists, left-wing intellectuals. [...] Voltaire founded liberalism but he also revealed its contradiction; because liberalism is a dogmatism which dare not admit it, and which abandons the risk and the concerns attached to the choice it makes. (15)

Here, Barthes's critique of Voltaire partially departs from Marcuse's exposure of the 'Happy Consciousness' in which 'the real is rational and [...] the system delivers the goods' (1991 [1964], 87); for Voltaire's rationalism eschews, in some sense, system (albeit, paradoxically, systematically). Through never having earned the real crowning glory of History's victory, Voltaire was oblivious to what was to follow, 'happy' in his 'simplicity'. Rather than scold Voltaire for not being alive in the twentieth century, Barthes points to the obvious inheritors, conservative-minded, who are quick to quote Voltaire in the troubled times of late 1950s France.

Barthes identifies few of Voltaire's works which might have helped create this conservative inheritance, except for Voltaire's 1765 story *Pot-Pourri* (explicitly) and the *Traité sur la tolérance* (implicitly, by citing the infamous case of Jean Calas). It would be difficult to deny that the *Traité sur la tolerance*, published for a restricted audience in 1763, is considered, at least within Voltaire studies, as the epitome of his writing and action against the cruelty and injustice of religious persecution in mid-eighteenth-century France. Shocked and disgusted by the case of the protestant Jean Calas – broken on the wheel in 1761 for seemingly having murdered his own son who, Calas allegedly feared, might convert to Catholicism – Voltaire turned the *affaire* into a *cause célèbre*, writing his treatise in order to exonerate Calas and his family, but also to change the law and, perhaps most crucially, to argue for religious tolerance. That said, the *Traité* was not written for general consumption but for a restricted audience of enlightened and persuadable members of the aristocracy and political ruling class in France at the time. Furthermore, it is important to stress that Voltaire pointedly did not blame the judges nor the judicial system guaranteed by the King (Louis XV), but rather the baying crowd who manufactured and spread the accusation that Jean Calas had murdered his son for fear of his converting to Catholicism.

There is something historically ironic that Voltaire should then return to modern French life through extraordinary numbers of sales of his works in the aftermath of the horrendous attacks on the offices of the satirical magazine *Charlie-Hebdo* in January

2015. Over half of the editorial board were gunned down by two brothers angered by the Islamophobic 'humour' of the magazine, though Cole (2015) puts the casualties in a global perspective. The bloody attack spawned an enormous movement in France, 'Je suis Charlie', with badges and a book defending, in some cases, the magazine's right to be 'secular' and even to mock symbols of religious belief such as Mohammed (coll. 2015). On the front page of 12 January 2015 edition of *Le Monde,* Plantu's cartoon of the solidarity march on the boulevard Voltaire in Paris showed the two Muslim gunmen in the devil's cauldron asking themselves 'Who is Voltaire?'.

The vogue for Voltaire's *Traité sur la tolérance* in France between January and March 2015 was well attested and welcomed by the Voltaire Society which noted how his essay had been selling in France 'like hotcakes' since the *Charlie-Hebdo* attack, citing the extraordinary figure of 120,000 sales of the pamphlet (Bulletin de la Société Voltaire 2015). In his introduction to the *Magazine littéraire* (March 2015) special dossier on Voltaire, including extracts from the *Traité sur la tolerance,* André Versaille (38) suggested that we should 'read Voltaire "innocently"', proposing that there are indeed Muslim versions of tolerance today such as in the work of Abdennour Bidar. However, rare were the voices in France, as Tariq Ali has pointed out (2015), that actually rebuked *Charlie-Hebdo* for having incited religious offence against Muslims in the first place, with its gross caricatures of Mohammed the prophet; the rare principled exception was Henri Roussel, the founder of *Hara-Kiri* and forerunner to *Charlie-Hebdo,* whose article in the *Nouvel-Observateur* decried the Islamophobic turn taken by *Charlie-Hebdo.* Islamophobia has afflicted even the far-Left in France, as in the case of an election candidate for the *Nouveau Parti Anticapitaliste,* Ilham Moussaid, who in 2010 was required to remove her veil. So, what about Voltaire in the twenty-first century? Did he suddenly in 2015 overcome the 'outmoded' label that Barthes gives him back in 1958? Can he really still speak to us over two centuries later?

Provisionality, Openness and Radicality

In conclusion, we might want to say that Barthes's 1958 essay is being classically dialectical – critiquing the Voltaire myth not the Voltaire phenomenon, aiming at a specific debate and 'adversary' in the French press, affirming the dialectical over the Manichean. However, it is by way of a triangulation that we can best understand the argument.

Barthes's conclusion to his 1964 version of the essay adds a small but telling section on Voltaire's philosophical adversary Jean-Jacques Rousseau, in which Barthes suggests that Rousseau countered the immobilization of History characterized by Voltaire's fundamentalist cry for 'tolerance' and anti-dogmatism. Rousseau allowed History to restart again, he argues, by positing the 'principle of a permanent transcendence of history'; but the price of this was to bequeath to literature what Barthes calls a 'poisoned legacy':

> Henceforth, ceaselessly athirst and wounded by a responsibility he can never again completely honour or completely elude, the intellectual will be defined by his bad conscience: Voltaire was a happy writer, but doubtless the last. (1972, 89)

Barthes may be using a dialectical version of History in his views on Voltaire; but for literature and the intellectual – politics, in short – the 'poisoned legacy' analysis is decidedly *un*dialectical. It means approaching what Neil Badmington (2016) has recently called the 'afterlives' of Roland Barthes in a different way, converting the 'undialectical' death that Barthes predicts for himself in his last book, *Camera Lucida*, into a *new* Barthes for the twenty-first century. And this might mean being fully dialectical about Voltaire: 'Ecrasez l'islamophobie' [Smash islamophobia] would be the slogan: if, that is, there is anything of Voltaire left…

The relevance of Barthes's 1958 essay on Voltaire to 2015 France is striking and it vindicates a comment that he makes at the end of his life: 'Obviously, in the case of the consumer – of the reader – Necessity comes after the fact' (2011b, 194):

> Whence the fantasmatic privilege accorded to the Last Work, a last Testament: another work! This will be the last, the one in which I'll say everything, and then be silent, etc. Fantasy of the Testament, Reality of the Testament that's constantly being reworked. (2011b, 149)

Barthes's staunch criticism of Voltaire's refusal of system – if not method – will return in a different form in the 1970s, which we will consider in relation to the Neutral in Chapters Seven and Eight. Part of the later critique of system will depend on Barthes's growing suspicion of all acts of classification.

Classification without Class

> Nothing is more essential to a society than
> the *classification* of its languages.
> To change this classification, to relocate
> discourse, is to bring about a revolution.
>
> *(Barthes 2007b, 23)*

Classification — and associated activities of *de*classifying, or unclassifying — is a key, if not the key, theme in Barthes's work. Classification is an activity in which we, as researchers in literary and cultural studies, are constantly involved; and yet the ordered, scientific pigeonholing inevitably entailed by classifying seems antithetical to the creative, 'free' nature of the literary and cultural objects that we analyse. It is almost as if humanities study — as a structured method of taxonomy and variation — is not, or should not be, part of academia; for the aims, methods and objects of humanities analysis are seemingly traduced by the need for a university-measurable output (not to mention 'impact'), which is constantly 'boxed' into tweetable sound-bites fit for the auditor and paymaster and no longer for the academic community. One of the enduring skills of Barthes's radical approach to this conundrum is his ability to navigate between, on the one hand, the desire for understanding and explaining (including classifying) aspects of the contemporary world and, on the other, the refusal to cover them with catch-all, simplistic and ideologically controlled generalizations.

Barthes's suspicion of classification extends to the very way in which we interact with others, with the Other, in society. Classification in Barthes's research is clearly a useful tool – for the study of fashion forms, for the codes of literary meaning, for understanding language and communication; but it also locks humans, their creative capacities and the ways of negotiating their personal identities and freedoms into a straitjacket of stereotypes, solitude and social alienation. However, trying to understand the function of classifying in Barthes's work is possibly not a good idea for two reasons. First, as the entry by Peter France in the *Oxford Companion to French Literature* (1995) suggests, Barthes is 'a writer who evades classification'. Second, Gil (2012) presents this classification-evader, very persuasively, as an 'oscillator'. She shows Barthes flitting constantly between opposing positions, holding dialectical tensions in non-synthesized open-endedness; and (in the latter stages of his career) Barthes is seen in this optic valorizing the 'suspension of judgement', the *Wou-wei* of Taoism, as a radical intellectual strategy in the face of society's cloying 'doxa' that acts against the figures of '[o]ur whole West: moral ideology of the will, of willing (to possess, to dominate, to live, to impose one's truth, etc' (2005, 177). Second, an authoritative bibliographical source – the key words in the *Bibliographie Barthes* (Philippe 1996) – contains no reference to Barthesian ideas on classification. Not only does this omission obliquely justify Peter France's bold suggestion, but it also allows us to make a singular reading of singularity in Barthes's work: the notion of exception, of the scandalously unclassifiable. How does Barthesian thought move from classification to declassification, from social-class determinism to the unclassifiable intellectual?

Déclassé

In a short fragment from 1929, Georges Bataille links the *déclassé* to the 'formless [informe]' (1970, 217); indeed, though normally in French referring to a class demotion, 'déclassé' can also have the rare, more positive meaning of 'unclassified', removed from classification or from any social-class attribution. Can deeming Barthes to be an 'oscillator', as Marie Gil has done, fully account for this trajectory?

In her biography Gil presents her subject as dualistically constructed. It is a fascinating biography which reads Barthes's life — appropriately enough — as a 'text'. Gil's metaphor of oscillator is the basis of her psychoanalytical approach, and, as an *essai biographique*, her 'fictional' reading of Barthes's life as literary text seems to be parametric to the writer's own concerns. And yet, the main point of her biography — that the fundamental trauma of Barthes's life (the death of his beloved mother, towards the end of his own life) structures our view of his life (backwards, as it were) — seems at odds with its subject and overly teleological in its presentation of this sad moment of grief in 1977 as the defining event of Barthes's life (2012, 20–25). This is especially true in the way Gil describes the 'empty matrix' as the prelude to the 'photographic metaphor', to the gradual 'revelation' in which Barthes's life was always leading up to the death of his mother. Samoyault (2017) is less inclined to use a psychoanalytical framework to account for the trajectory in Barthes's life. Indeed, the 'closure' that this highlighted event of his mother's death invites — according to which Barthes, once again, is viewed overwhelmingly via his 'late' career — seems to reinstate, in Gil's teleological approach, that very spirit of 'wish-to-grasp' [vouloir-saisir] against which Barthes's lectures at the Collège de France (and *A Lover's Discourse*) try to suggest radical alternatives. Instead, it is an 'oscillating' attitude to classification (applied to himself, to society, to research), from the earliest stages of his career up until his final writings. In her hurry to see how the oscillator stops oscillating, following the death of the person who, psychoanalytically, had helped generate his oscillation, Gil seems to deny to Barthes any years, but the last three of his life, outside of the 'hole' to which his semi-orphaned status had consigned him. Did Barthes *really* spend all of his life, up until 1977, flitting purposelessly around in a hole formed by the absence of the father and the determining presence of his mother? We could therefore invoke a different psychoanalytical metaphor, such as that of the Houdini-escapologist recently investigated by the British psychoanalyst, Adam Phillips (2001) who shows that though some people try to escape from the hole they find themselves in, others find freedom in a self-imposed confinement. It could therefore be argued that though able to avoid cultural impoverishment -

'Poverty made him a *desocialised child*, but not *déclassé*' (Barthes 1994, 45) – his work is constantly moving towards not just a de-systemization but a non-classification (*déclassé* in the rarer, positive sense of avoiding being classified).

However, the competing metaphor that we will use here, for reasons to follow, is drawn not from Freud, Lacan nor Winnicott, but from Marx. Our survey of Barthes's attitude to classification begins, appropriately enough then, with his own social, personal and class position, a topic that went even as far as the act of reading. To the four levels of reading, Barthes advises adding the two 'permanent [...] integrators', one of class and one of the person's response to that class-relation: 'social code (levels of culture, class position, ideological pressures)' on the one hand, and 'desire, fantasm (levels and types neuroses)' on the other (2002, IV, 172).

'Classed - War Orphan'

> [O]ne quarter landed bourgeoisie,
> one quarter old nobility, two quarters
> liberal bourgeoisie, the whole mixed together
> and unified by a general state of impoverishment.
>
> *(Barthes 1998, 250)*

The very first form of classification then is the one dealt to us all by society. Not only a war orphan, socially defined, Barthes is also locked away in a sanatorium during early adulthood, his tuberculosis requiring a distinct classification of his body, and removing him from the experiences of the War in a social isolation that rested on the fear of contagion, in an interruption to his studies that will stymie his academic and professional career. To his war-orphan, tuberculosis-sufferer and professionally excluded status must be added his (largely hidden) homosexuality and even his left-handedness. The marginalized and marginal social and class position that classifies Barthes — marked by impecuniousness for over half of his life (until the inheritance from his maternal grandmother, Noémie Révelin, in 1954) — will go on, however, to be a key route of escape from the social 'hole' in which he finds himself in 1945; his highly singular social position is to became the space within which his writing is to play out.

Barthes's acute sensitivity to singularity and to exceptionality is illustrated by the most curious of animals used as a metaphor. Thus, early in Barthes's writing career, the eighteenth-century Swedish naturalist Carl Linnæus appears as an important reference. Linnæus' acts of scientific and zoological classification (distinction, division and designation) famously stumbled over how to classify the amphibious but mammalian animal native to Tasmania, the duck-billed platypus. In a strikingly regular use of the 'ornithorynx' as a metaphor for the unclassifiable, for the exception, the 'paradoxical platypus' (Hall 1999) becomes linked in Barthes's work to singularity, including specificity, and then to a critique of analogy that betrays an acute awareness of the *semelfactive* (of that which happens, irreversibly, only once), and thereby challenging classification's claims to comprehensiveness.

Umberto Eco (1999, 62) suggests that this 'strange animal [...] seems to have been conceived in order to defy all classification' and provides a useful overview of the prolonged struggle to classify it (246–53). On a regular occasions in his writings between 1950 and 1964, Barthes refers to Linnæus's seminal *Systema Naturæ* (first published in 1735, continually updated until the thirteenth edition in 1770), and in particular to the *paradoxa*, the collection of 'cryptids', the odd, inexplicable, unclassifiable, creatures — the Yeti, Loch Ness Monster, the Sasquatch — around which there was no scientific consensus on classification. But it is in the early Marxian phase of his career that the metaphor's use is the most sustained.

Rather than taking Jorge Luis Borges's route of imagining *paradoxa* — mythical animals — Barthes uses the *paradoxa* as part of a critique of analogy. It is the period 1947–56, the most Marxist of his career — be it in the popular theatre movement or in the numerous critiques of bourgeois and petty-bourgeois ideological distortions — in which he displays an acute sensitivity to social classification.

Indeed, Linnæus appears at an important moment of Barthes's 1953 essay 'The World as Object', in which, analysing seventeenth-century Dutch painting, he notes how 'it is not a coincidence' that the word 'class' serves two notions that are 'as distinctly separated as Linnæus's zoological classes': the patrician class and the peasant class first, and then their morphological classification within their class (1972, 7–8). Just as in Linnæus's division of animals, suggests Barthes (possibly gesturing towards the racist discourse of the nineteenth-century to which Linnean classifications of humans were subsequently mobilized), so classical Dutch painting physically divides its social classes: 'each [class] encompasses human beings not only of the same social condition but also of the same morphology' (8).

But the first major reference to the platypus in his writings is part of his Marxian defence of history against the work of Joussain and Caillois that we considered briefly in Chapter Three. Here, as we saw, Barthes makes an important connection between nineteenth-century analogy and the epistemological problem posed by the specificity of the unique historical event. He equates this failure to account for specificity in his own analogy, that of Linnæus confronted with the taxonomically anomalous duck-billed platypus. The failure of science to account for and classify satisfactorily the *ornithori anainus* resembles Joussain's and Caillois's use of analogy as it masquerades as scientific sociology (of revolution in the former and of Marxism in the latter). Furthermore, Joussain's scientific formalism annoys Barthes, with its exhaustive (Linnæus-style) catalogue of factors (such as psychological, social, permanent, periodical, intellectual and historical); as with the undermining of Linnæus's scholastic attempts to classify all animals by the existence of the unclassifiable, so Joussain's 'tables always contain, in the end, some solitary, inalienable, paradoxical event that defies all classification – namely the revolution itself' (2015b, 3). In a manner that prefigures the later critique that we considered above of Voltaire's conception of history and its liberal myth of asystemic immobility, Barthes implies that the radical specificity of historical events, their 'inalienability', is what allows History to operate. Barthes never mentions that Linnæus abandoned the *paradoxa* in the sixth edition of 1748, but it is clear that the 'scandal' that Caillois saw in Marxism's popularity in 1950, and the consequent analogy with religious irrational and fanatical belief, is precisely the type of exception presented by the duck-billed platypus: if you cannot explain it, analogize it. Of course, and as we saw in Chapter One, the dialectics of flux invoked in *Mythologies* is an antidote to this analogizing of romanticism: Barthes's radical acts of explanation invoke the specificity of History against the 'alibi' of analogy and, what we might call the superficiality of historical formalism. And yet, in *Mythologies*, as we saw also, Barthes revalorizes formalism (2009, 134).

With the definition of semiology as a 'science of forms', Barthes's work from 1957 into the mid-1960s will not only use semiology to study 'ideas-in-form' but also deploy classification in its methodology; and the ideological criticism of classification in his earlier Marxism becomes, as we shall see, a radically formalist critique of the distortions of ideology that, itself, uses classification.

We have an example of this strategy in his 1954 book on Michelet when he suggests that his account of the nineteenth-century historian's writing of history is but a 'precriticism' to a full-blown ideological critique (1987a, 3); in other words, the classification of forms is but a prelude to historical critique. This is a thorny methodological problem: do we need to systematize forms – analogize – in order to be able then to affirm radical specificity? This question is made all the more complex by the fact that the late Barthes is trenchant in his critique of classification:

> Language is its legislation, speech is its code. We do not see the power which is in speech, because we forget that all speech is a classification, and that all classifications are oppressive[.] (1982a, 460)

And yet, despite a suspicion of classification, his research in the 1960s relies heavily, if only methodologically, on the act of classifying.

From Platypus to Fashion

Taxonomy – classification – is a crucial first step in all of Barthes's structuralist work on clothing and fashion, where the item, in order for its function to be understood, first needs to be subject to an extensive taxonomy. Having abandoned, by 1959, any attempt to understand how clothing forms change and are modified over history, Barthes makes three important decisions in his work on clothing. First, following the advice of Claude Lévi-Strauss, he sets out to consider clothing uniquely via the written discourse attached to it; second, he relinquishes the historical, or diachronic, dimension in order to concentrate on contemporary, or synchronic, manifestations of clothing; which leads to the third innovation, that of studying fashion, women's fashion, as a nexus of novelty, innovation and social function. In this research in the early 1960s in particular — but also in his 1966 collaborative work on the structuralist analysis of narrative — Barthes relies heavily, if only tactically and provisionally, on the act of classifying; and it is in this over-classification that the platypus's singularity is given a new outlet in the 1960s.

Before starting his doctoral thesis on fashion, Barthes is aware of the two elements of his analysis: written clothing as part of a social system and then, in the wonderful 1961 essay on gemstones and jewels, 'From Gemstones to Jewellery' (2006a, 59–64), the fundamental, if not determining, role of the detail. This latter article is important because, on the one hand, it shows the growing awareness of arbitrariness in fashion: as long as the / a detail fundamentally alters the outfit, then fashion can be shown to work, and can move forward; at the same time, the essay on gemstones shows the architectonic, chthonian links that certain 'natural' but rare objects have for humans, and underlines the function that their materiality fulfils in our unconscious and primal desires. So, in the midst of the systematic and scientific attempt to account for (women's) fashion and its language of persuasion and seduction — which is semiologically classified, first in his 1960 article '"Blue is in Fashion This Year"' (2006a, 41–58) and then, in 1967, in *The Fashion System* (1990b) — Barthes comes to an important structural discovery.

First, a fashion ensemble can be radically altered by the addition of the smallest of details (a brooch, button, or other accessory); second, the significance of a phenomenon within a totality (such as a literary text, or a fashion ensemble) is not dependent on its size or its regular occurrence, but on its structural function within the totality. In other words, it is the combination, the *combinatoire* (2002, II, 1309), and not the frequency nor the relative 'weight' of each phenomenon, that determines meaning and explains functions; and, crucially for our argument here, the *combinatoire*, though initially reliant on classification, actually points to classification's *in*ability to perform explanation, and it does so by going beyond its phenomenal, objective act of listing. However, it is only during acts of classification — an artificial, analytical act of taxonomy that Barthes borrows from linguistics — that this operation of combining can be seen to be working. Thus, it is on the level of their relative functions that fashion items are classified within a fashion whole, or narrative functions within a particular story (1977, 79–124). However, this procedure requires a preliminary, and provisional, act of taxonomy in order to establish structural significance. This is at once a tightening of the contextual argument that Barthes uses to criticize Joussain's and Caillois's formalism, and, at the same time, an attempt to overcome the exceptionality posited by the platypus, by showing how the detail, a form of exception, functions within a structure. In a sense then, the 'detail' of history and of political sociology whose absence he angrily regrets in, respectively, Joussain's and Caillois's books, is now, in this 1960s structuralist phase, being used to analyse fashion forms and literary functions. The exception illustrated by the platypus has been, we might say, tamed, by showing how the detail functions within the whole. In evolutionary terms, this would be equivalent to showing how the platypus functions as a historic — and very rare — link between mammals and their amphibian (and even aquatic) past (Eco 1999, 249).

Classifications thus allow for the operation of any system in a slowed-down version, artificially stopping it but which are subsequently bracketed, if not abandoned, so that the *combinatoire* can then be seen to operate: the tighter the classification, the clearer the combining functions. The operative advantages of classification are crucial but temporary. However, this model comes full circle once the detail is introduced to the fashion ensemble. The detail both conjures away and reaffirms at the same time the classification, by moving the overall meaning of the *combinatoire* onto a new level. The detail ('scandalous' as the platypus was for Linnæus) is an operative feature of the fashion ensemble precisely because it stands out(side) from (of) it: the detail seems to have no structural or classificatory importance, and yet functions as a fashion game-changer.

It is precisely within this newly adopted structuralist paradigm of the combination that Barthes's Linnæus reappears in relation to the platypus in 1962, in his article on the 'Structure of the *fait divers*':

> the *fait-divers* would [...] derive from a classification of the unclassifiable, it would be the unorganized discard of news; its essence would be privative, it would begin to exist only where the world stops being named, subject to a known catalogue (politics, economics, war, amusement, science, etc.); in a word, it would be a monstrous item, analogous to all the exceptional or insignificant, i.e., anomie phenomena classified under the modest rubric Varia, like the platypus which gave poor Linnaeus so much trouble. (1972, 185)

Given that the content of the *fait divers* depends on where it is published, it would be better to look at it structurally: 'a difference in structure and no longer a difference in classification' (186). In other words, like the duck-billed platypus, the *fait divers* needs to be considered not for its classificatory identity (which is fruitless because it is entirely singular, irreducibly semelfactive), but for its function within other news reports. Thus, Barthes has hoisted the platypus example out of his 1950s critique of historical formalism and brought it to bear on the function of phenomena within a totality. His metaphor (analogy?) remains the same — the platypus escapes classification — but he now seems to be suggesting that structure trumps classification; that functionality within a totality undermines, or (finally) does away with the need for, taxonomy. For example, in *Elements of Semiology* (1968), Barthes submits the social phenomena of signs and communication, temporarily, to a rigorous classification, by dismantling the workings of various objects such as fashion and filmic and literary texts, but only in order to show how meanings are generated in relation to each other. Using four classifications — language and speech, signifier and signified, syntagm and system, denotation and connotation — he reads the fourth chapter of Saussure's *Course on General Linguistics*, in order to show that meaning is nothing but an order of 'divisions', an 'arthrology' or 'science of apportionment' (57). But these divisions—as the platypus example above suggests—are again (as with revolutions and Marxism) dependent upon the specific context in which they appear, and, crucially now in this structuralist period, upon the structure in which they function.

At the very same time, Barthes seems highly critical of the separation — or 'arthrology'— that he was, tentatively, advocating. In the 1964 article on 'The Plates of the *Encyclopedia*' he makes a link back to his view of social class in seventeenth-century Dutch painting (cited above). Quoting Bernard Groethuysen's description of the Renaissance as an 'adventurous knowledge' as opposed to the 'learning of appropriation' of the *Encyclopaedia* published over two centuries later (and based on the fragmenting of objects), Barthes now appears deeply wary of acts of classifying:

> [W]e cannot separate without finally naming and classifying, and at that moment, property is born. [...] Encyclopedic nomenclature [...] actually establishes a familiar possession. (1982a, 222)

All attempts at classification — be they of animals in Linnæus, the machinery described in the *Encyclopaedia*, revolutionary moments in history, or the sociological forms of political systems such as Marxism — run the risk of denying specificity; all attempts at classification tame and domesticate ideologically that which challenges classification and that which could subvert the naturalization of ownership and of social control. Classification is a tricky act, that, though formalizing in order for critique to take place, systematizing phenomena by form, risks re-affirming the proprietorial of Capitalist social relations. Suddenly, the asystematics roundly criticized in Voltaire is now in need of re-evaluation in the face of classification's unreliability.

One major option now seems open to the semiologist confronted with the dilemmas of classification. However, before moving onto the non-classifiable, we must consider the period 1967-1969, in which Barthes's complex attitude towards classification is further manifest.

Detail versus classification = Self versus Institution?

Reducing narrative to its functions and indices (1977, 79–124), analysing ancient Rhetoric for its structural significance (1987b, 11–94), results, as we saw in Chapter Three, in what has been considered by some as the most classificatory work of Barthes's career, namely *S/Z*. In his 1968 piece on Flaubert's short stories (1986, 141–48), he shows that even the '"useless detail" signifies'. So, if everything signifies, if all details of a story mean, how do we classify these details now as functions and indices? Barthes's response to this classificatory conundrum is the use of codes in *S/Z*.

Though critics such as Thody (1977, 116) regret the manner in which the essay reduces the codes in Balzac's story to just five, have they not missed the point of *S/Z*? That is, how to build up the structure of a text only to destroy the classification through the text's plural voices and its (infinite) structuration through the combination of the codes? 'And so, one must take on codes [Il faut se coder]; in order to outplay them, it is necessary to enter into them' (1985a, 145). *S/Z* illustrates then, not so much Marie Gil's oscillator theme, but rather Barthes as Houdini: the tighter the classification, the better the subsequent *un*classification. In this escapologist optic, *S/Z* becomes the decentred record of the seminar across 1968. The *Sarrasine* seminar – in its deployment of the critical analogy of proportion (what we might call 'parametrism') – gives way, in *S/Z*, to a new essayistic form, a form that is unclassifiable then and perhaps still is today. The notion of the *paradoxa* that we saw in the platypus now becomes attached to Balzac's story *Sarrasine*; but, crucially for our argument here, *S/Z* becomes the singular essay on the plural, and, at the same time, a semelfactive rewriting of Balzac: a set of paradoxa from which only the essay can help Houdini-Barthes to escape and emerge into another period.

Indeed, in the post-68 world, Barthes recognizes the lack of room for manoeuvre and he now turns to the question of the 'institution'. Dovetailing with the work on the 'instituted' by René Lourau (1969, 1971), Barthes begins, in 1970, to see a link between institution and classification:

> [I]nstitutions or *the* Institution, the social institution always takes on the surveillance work on meaning, keeping a watchful eye on the proliferation of meanings; […] with the interpretation of literary texts there is also a sort of institutional surveillance taking place, by the University in fact, as to the freedom of textual interpretation. (2015a, 96)

Philology, suggests Barthes, is the science whose role is to 'spy on polysemic excesses': 'Nearly all of humanity's ideological battles, in the West in any case, have, for centuries, have always been battles over meaning' (510). Typical of Barthes's contradictory attitude to classification – or rather, the perceived need to classify *before* historical critique – he proposes a 'vast scanning of the horizon (thus, with little rigour), a sort of classification of […] *the different anthropological regimes of meaning*', with three components: the 'monosemic', the 'polysemic', the 'asemic' (511).

Little doubt that the last of these will return as the 'exemption of meaning' tactic. Indeed, the period 1967-1971 seems to be a key Houdini moment for Barthes that goes via what we might call a *de-institution*. The *Sarrasine* seminar of 1968–69 (2011a) and the 'Author's Lexis' seminar of 1973–74 (2010a) could be considered, paradoxically, as precisely a form of *de-institution*, in that the objectivity of social-science research is dissolved across an objectified writing self that is radically subjective in its literary approach: 'we have to accept that we have to play with the Institution, […] subvert not contest it' (2010a, 52–53). In *The Neutral* he announces: 'Institution, [academic] course […] they prepare a site of mastery. Now, always my problem: to outsmart mastery (ceremonial showing-off [la 'parade'])' (2005, 10, trans. mod.).

In contradistinction to the seminars that Barthes leads in the 1960s involving the sustained attempt to classify (if only temporarily) functions and indices, the period that follows May 1968 is marked by a much more micro-structural attention to the detail. It is the singularity of the literary text — and structuralism's tendency to homogenize all texts into a relatively small number of narrative functions — that begins to turn Barthes away from the super-classifications of the 1960s; the opening page of *S/Z*, in 1970, which signals the move away from 'an in-different science' (1974, 3), leads to the opening page of *The Pleasure of the Text* in 1973, in which he suggests we '[i]magine someone

[...] who abolishes within themself all barriers, all classes, all exclusions' by using '*logical contradiction*' (1975, 3, trans. mod.).

One of the key elements in this 'late' suspicion towards classification is in the work and writing on Barthes's own 'image' in 1970s French society, involving a series of classifications which he begins to interrogate in *Le Lexique de l'auteur* (2010a). One strategy of undermining the classifications to which he feels exposed — the 'language (of others) transforms me into an image, as the raw slice of potato is transformed into a *pomme frite*' (1986, 353) — is to use the third person in *Roland Barthes by Roland Barthes* (1994). Here, it is as if by externalising the voice of the self, when writing about his self, that the writer can crack open the classificatory straitjacket that society continually places upon that self. Here Barthes seems at his closest to the 1960s critical theory of Herbert Marcuse on uni-dimensionality and the possibilities for liberation (Marcuse 1991 [1964], 2000 [1969]); though Barthes's strategy is at once physical and bodily, more than intellectual and culturalist. His strategy of the 'atopic', of taking the self out of the place to which it is assigned, has links to classifications of the self, and specifically to those of social classification.

'Déclassé' or not classified?

> *Pigeon-holed*: I am pigeon-holed, assigned
> to an intellectual site, to a residence in a caste
> (if not in a class). [...] [W]ho does not feel how
> *natural* it is, in France, to be Catholic, married and
> properly accredited with the right degrees?
>
> (Barthes 1994, 49, 131)

In the later stages of Barthes's career, his ambivalent attitude towards classification seems to harden: not just in personal, but also in epistemological and linguistic terms, including a heightened awareness of the negative role of the adjective, and of adjectivization that we will consider in Chapter Eight. At the same time, following his attribution of the title of 'classifiers' of new languages to the unlikely combination of Sade, Fourier and Loyola in his 1971 essay (1989), all classifications — including the oscillatory *non*-classification — are now impulses for writing. For example, Barthes uses an alphabetical order of his fragments as a false classification, that is, arbitrary (or in-between, falsely 'motivated'). Indeed, according to Hanania (2010), Barthes's use of etymology is just this: an arbitrary oscillation between 'classification and dividing up' on the one hand, and an application of the key structuralist denial of an origin which potentially undermines all etymology, on the other. The dialectical outcome of this oscillation in his work is a constant translation, inexorable circulation, of the *etymon*. It is, as Hanania hints (16), the mature, later Barthes who begins to play with etymology in order to declassify meaning. A similar point could be made in relation to his use of neologism.

Also – as suggested by the innovative form of his 1970 essay *S/Z* – 'genre' questions begin to undermine classification in the later Barthes: the 'essay', the academic lecture, the seminar, journalism, the 'collection', all become formally interchangeable. From *S/Z* onwards, it is the 'lecture book' (texts emerging from teaching), travel-writing (in Japan and China), that come to the fore, built overwhelmingly on the writing of the fragment – to the point that we might wonder, following Ginette Michaud's linking of the detail and the fragment in their 'detotality' whether the fragment itself unclassifies (1989, 50–53); though Bensmaïa astutely distinguishes detail and fragment in Barthes's work by suggesting that the detail is the '"inside"' of the fragment (Bensmaïa 1987, 41–46, especially 43–44). Indeed, all oscillatory attitudes towards classification now lead to writing, but not in any fixed form, and involve what Patrizia Lombardo has called 'the existential search for a form' (1982, 79). For example, in the diaries written during his 1974 visit to China with *Tel Quel* (2012) Barthes is famously short on commentary, deploying a 'silence' that is played out in the *Le Monde* article (2015b, 94–104), where, unlike his visits to Japan in the late 1960s, he struggles to find anything 'to classify' (2012, 57); and yet, he begins to transform this into writing. In *Roland Barthes par Roland Barthes*, the three pleasures related to the spatial arrangements for 'jouissance' are listed as painting, writing and classifying. Similarly, the 'pharmakon' view of French vocabulary in *A Lover's Discourse* —in which language is presented as both illness and remedy — is but the premise, a starting point, for writing. Indeed, the 'escape forwards' [fuite en avant], the image that is 'down-graded' [déclassée], the use of onomastics, the notions of 'loss' [perte] and dissolution of self that we saw above, all seem aimed at undoing the classification of self. It is the 1977–78 lectures on *The Neutral* that provide the theoretical basis for these ideas.

Here Barthes defines this undoing of classification as the Neutral as it 'denies uniqueness but recognizes the incomparable' (2005, 83). But crucially he realizes also that he (we) cannot get away from the Other, be it in love, in his lectures about his fantasy of living together (2013) or in his family and home-life, especially with his mother. All of these relations with the other come into conflict with notions of classification. It is now that the 'late' Barthes begins to glimpse what the Marquis de Sade referred to as 'fineness' [délicatesse], the 'tact' required in maintaining the singularity of the self, the uniqueness of person, what he terms the 'aristocratic' notion of distinction in relation to the social *combinatoire*. The aristocratic, it must be stressed, needs to be understood not in the social or class sense, but as exception, as distinction, similar to the way in which Barthes, in 1962, considered the Dandy (2006a, 65–69). The aristocratic self is linked to the 'délicatesse' of Japanese culture (especially in its food and in the 'lightness' of the Haïku). Specificity now begins to rub up against acts of classification; and 'délicatesse' plays a clear part in this singularization. Dependent on the ethics of non-vouloir-saisir (NVS), or, no-wish-to-grasp (NWG) described in *A Lover's Discourse* and in the *How To Live Together* lectures, this critique of possession and ownership is subsequently theorized in *The Neutral*, where NWG and 'délicatesse' are 'kinds of active protests or unexpected parrying against reduction, not of the individual (it is not a matter of a philosophy of individualism) but of individuation' (2005, 36). The risk is that 'the other's discourse (often well meaning, innocent) reduces me to a case that fits an all-purpose explanation or classification in the most normal way' (36). Against this Barthes proposes the 'social obscene (the unclassifiable)' (35).

Indeed, the 1970s see Barthes looking for singularity of the self, this 'délicatesse' is often found in literarization, in attempts to turn life into literature. For example, in *Le lexique de l'autueur* seminar (1973–74), having referred to his own work on Gide's *Journal* (in 1942) and to his assertion (in 1966) that Proust's life is not reflected in *À la recherche du temps perdu*, but the opposite – 'it is his life that is the text of his work' (2010a, 324) – Barthes moves into the third person to exemplify how this has happened in his own life and work:

> For example, this year (1972–1973), he produces a particular text by operating a number of collusions [sic] between different rendez-vous; he sees time after time subjects emerging from contexts that are heteroclite, incompatible (going to a 'nightclub' straight from a meeting with a Communist activist); this smashes the discourse of life's monotonous law, producing a sort of textual charivari. (2010a, 324–325)

This moment points, perhaps obliquely, to a fundamental final theme in his career, 'life as text', or 'biographématique' in which the author, dialectically in a spiral, returns (2010a, 349–54). Barthes uses his own life to illustrate this 'vie comme texte'.

Introduced by the exceptionalism of the (literary-inspired notion) of 'délicatesse' the 'charivari'– or clash – of different worlds in Barthes's life (in which a visit to a night-club clashes with a discussion about Communism) suggests not simply that he is a 'subtle mover [passeur]' sliding imperceptibly, subtly, between different worlds, but also that the 'passeur' can achieve some form of non-classification. This non-classified self, atopic if not utopian in socio-political terms, is part of *délicatesse*. It is prefigured in *S/Z* in what Barthes calls the 'inorigin' of wealth, whereby his reading of Balzac's *Sarrasine* categorizes the origin of the Lanty family's wealth as a textual mystery (1974, 21, 41–42) – though we suspect, as readers, that their fortune comes from the price of La Zambinella's castrato status. But, by the 1970s, Barthes seems to be considering the 'inorigin' of self – the non-classified or lacking a social-class determinism – as a utopian state which allows the self to escape classification in any social class. This appreciation of the 'inorigin' of wealth, of social determinisms, now becomes, in the late Barthes, the search for what he calls the 'aristocratic' self. Not so much the 'sovereign' self as theorized by Georges Bataille, Barthes's aristocratic self is defined in relation to the other, in relations with others. For Bataille, the sovereign self is one which violently asserts its refusal of power in an excessive, crazed manner, in *La Méthode de méditation* (1973, 221). In his paper at the Cerisy conference in 1977, Barthes (implicitly) links *délicatesse* and the unclassifiable to democracy. Quoting a commentator of Spinoza, he suggests that the democratic is not at all defined as 'stifling gregariousness' but as something which emerges from 'aristocratic souls' (1986, 354). By the time of *Camera Lucida* this 'aristocratic' self becomes the '*impossible science of the unique being*' (1984, 71), the unclassifiable radical singularity of the individual, here, that of his recently deceased and much mourned mother.

The *combinatoire* understanding of self – radical in its detail and specificity – now allows us a perspective on oscillation. Marie Gil's use of oscillation in her biography of Barthes seems to deploy a two-term dialectic, without closure or synthesis. But her psychoanalytical schema does inevitably lead to a classification of Barthes as 'oscillator'. We may be persuaded by her suggestion that Barthes oscillates between figures throughout his career (his critique of 'Neither-Norism' in *Mythologies* in the 1950s becomes the positive *Neutral* of the 1970s, for example). However it hides not only an essence but also teleology. The teleological aspect of Gil's 'biographical essay'– that Barthes's life and writing were always leading up to the tragedy of his mother's demise – resembles, in particular, the 'law of revolutions' that Joussain posited in a mechanical and analogical fashion, if not the 'sociology' of forms in Caillois's description of Marxism.

Not so much 'contradictory' as 'dispersed' (1994, 143), Barthes can begin to undo classification, but can nature accept a classificatory vacuum? In her study of Barthesian etymology, Hanania quotes Barthes's view in *Roland Barthes by Roland Barthes* that 'binarism was for him a veritable amorous object' (1994, 51, trans. mod.). To Hanania, this comment suggests that the 'dichotomy working in his classifications' was an 'externalised and rhetorical reflection of a more general personal division, of a doctrinal disarray "translated" by a fundamental ambivalence towards writing' (2010, 139). This 'disarray' explains the 'both the need to touch on and the desire to affirm' that she sees as so typical of Barthes's writing, tantamount to 'a great paradox between the demand for theoretical "fragility" and rhetorical *tours de force*' (40).

It would seem then, despite its claims otherwise, that a psychoanalytical reading of Barthes's life (at least in Gil's version), leads to an essentialized, classified closure (albeit an oscillating one). Is Gil's 'dualism' in relation to Barthes *really* a 'dialectic of two terms'; or does it synthesize him – teleologically – into a 'totality' that she seems to want to ignore in her own classification? Our reading of the 'early' Barthes's use of Marxism helped to open up questions around analogy, exception, explanation and metaphor. So do we not need a critique of the totalizing nature of the metaphors of psychoanalysis? We will return to this question in Chapter Nine. Before that, we will consider the wide question of dialectics in Barthesian theory, first in his attempts to write dialectically, on Japan and then in China.

Chapter Seven

'NEW DIALECTIC'

It was C. L. R. James who famously claimed, in a letter to John O'Neill, that he had managed to understand the dialectic in action: 'I take the liberty of sending you a work of my own ... a study of the dialectic of Hegel, not explanations of the dialectic but directly the dialectic itself ... I regret to say that it is the only direct study of the dialectic that I know' (cited in Dunayevskaya 1972, n1). It is precisely the writing of the dialectic that we trace in Barthes's accounts of his trips to Japan and then China.

Throughout the 1960s and into the early 1970s, Barthes is looking for a dialectical way of writing. In three separate essays – 'Authors and Writers' in 1960, in a 1965 article on Edgar Morin's 'dialectical writing', and 'Writers, Teachers, Intellectuals' in 1971 – he comes to the same conclusion. It is worth quoting in full the footnote in 'Authors and Writers', to show the view of the *non*-dialectical nature of language:

> Structure of reality and structure of language: no better indication of the difficulty of a coincidence between the two than the constant failure of the dialectic, once it becomes discourse: for language is not dialectic, it can only say: 'we *must* be dialectical [*il faut* être dialectique]', but it cannot be so itself: language is a representation without perspective, except precisely for the author's; but the author dialecticizes themself, they do not dialecticize the world. (1972, 146n3, trans. mod.)

Despite the injunction for the responsible intellectual 'we *must* be dialectical', language itself is incapable of being dialectical because, he argued, it is 'monodic and linear': it can speak of more than one phenomenon not at once but only in series. 'La dialectique *parlée*' – in a sentence which is, inexplicably, left out of the English translation – 'est un vœu pieux' [the *spoken* dialectic is wishful thinking] (2002, II, 405n2).

The danger is that we consider this turning away from the world to the self as one of antipathy to politics. Indeed, the 'new dialectic' that Barthes finds in Japan should not be seen, however, as a harbinger of so-called 'postmodernity'. The reception of *Empire of Signs* in Japan itself has involved a tendency to consider the essay as part of a proto-'postmodernism' (Karatani 1995, 43); rather than showing that the 'ideal model of Japan is nothing but a representation of the Western mind', the essay is 'taken out of its original French context and read by Japanese postmodernists as a new version of overcoming modernity' (Karatani 2012, 188). By the same token, *Travels in China* is deemed indicative mainly of Barthes's fundamental boredom with politics (Badmington 2017, 305–25). The examination of 'the new dialectic' will now nuance the postmodern and non-political tags attached to Barthes's travel writing.

Empire of Signs seems to enjoy a freedom from political pressures. Whereas China, as we shall see later in this chapter, gives energy to French Maoism at the beginning of the 1970s – and *Mythologies*, as an ethnography of France in the 1950s, shows a political engagement – Japan for Barthes does not require any external dialectic: there is no 'So, How was Japan?' to write on his return, as there is for China (2015b, 94–104). We will also see, following the discussion of loss of self in Chapter Six, that Japan represents, not a place that is '*ultimately* positive' where 'decentering is the only way for the subject to recover his or her balance' (Lucken 2021, 47), but one where 'double grasp' gives way to 'no grasp'.

The 'Double Grasp' in Japan

Good prose is like a windowpane.

(Orwell 1946)

[B]ecome, in writing, *someone*.

(Barthes 2012, 6)

We saw in Chapters Four and Five that *S/Z* represents a new form of writing for the Barthes of the late 1960s; but he takes most pleasure in writing the essay of the same year, *Empire of Signs*, as it suspends the constraints of self: '[W]hen I wrote that book I felt a pleasure unmixed with anxiety, untainted by the *imago*' (1985, 229). This deceptively simple account of Japan involves, however, an analysis with a level of complexity that is, at times, dizzying. As Abdelkébir Khatibi suggest: 'Barthes locates himself, as he has often said, between the person who writes that they are writing, and who writes that they are analysing' (Khatibi 1987, 63). It is this double seeing, this in-between two activities, that we will investigate here as a potential source of pleasure. Written in Morocco in 1969, after his second visit, the same year, to Japan, *Empire of Signs* is published in a collection called *Les sentiers de la création* (Coste 2016b, 88). Furthermore, it may be surprising to underline, as Eric Marty has done, that the essay on Japan is actually Barthes's very first 'freely' written piece of his career (Marty, in Barthes 2002, III, 15). As journalist, critic, researcher, and teacher Barthes never published anything in book-form, before *Empire of Signs*, that did not exist already in one form or another - though 'Lesson in Writing' (1977, 170–78), published in *Tel Quel* in Summer 1968, is a prelude to 'The Three Writings' section in *Empire of Signs* (1982b, 48–49, 54–55), albeit a relatively small part of the section. *S/Z* emerges from the seminar notes that he wrote for his students at the EPHE in 1968 and 1969; *On Racine* is a collection of reviews and articles published in a variety of journals between 1959 and 1962 – *Mythologies*, *Michelet* and *Writing Degree Zero*, likewise. The only exception is *Criticism and Truth* (1966) – however, if this essay seems to come from nowhere in terms of previous texts and writings, the essay is written as a direct response to the shrill criticisms of *On Racine* by Picard, thereby suggesting, strongly, a jousting – rather than a creative – type of essay. Thus, we could indeed say that *Empire of Signs* is Barthes's first real, proper creation; and its pure creativity relates to the creative criticism developing, as we saw in Chapter Four, between *Criticism and Truth* in 1966 and *S/Z* in 1970. However, why look in *Empire of Signs* for examples of the 'double grasp'?

There are many candidates in Barthes's work that display a 'double grasp'. In *Writing Degree Zero* in 1953, we can already see a 'double grasp' at work in the way he argues for both a literary 'responsibility' and, at the same time, a political form of *engagement*. Otherwise, we could look to *Mythologies* – despite the denial of (visual) multi-tasking that we saw in Chapter Four – in which a 'double grasp' is at work in the hyper-focussed analysis that Barthes applies to both meaning and the real of an object, written using a dialectical suppleness. In the first half of the 1960s, we could have consulted *Elements of Semiology* (1964), where semiology is taken as a classic example of 'double grasp', with the division between signifier and signified. Likewise, Barthes's very precise work on fashion across the sixties, in *The Fashion System* (1967) and in other texts, takes women's clothing and fashion styles both as 'written' clothing (already a type of 'double grasp'), only then also for Barthes to insert his own analysis within a methodological relativity that underlines the power of the 'detail' (brooch, bracelet, button, etc.), a complexity that pertains in any type of *combinatoire*; and this is all presented as if it were a *prosopopeia* of Woman in the middle of persuading herself about her next fashion purchase (Burgelin 1974, 12). *S/Z* too displays a 'double grasp' as it reads and rewrites Balzac's disturbing and disruptive story using the 'stereographic'. Then in *On Racine*, the analysis of theatrical narration style displays a structural attentiveness to the story as, simultaneously, both an anthropological and an unconscious category; and Racine's theatre is deemed one which is both intransitive and excluding of mediation: 'the Racinian world is a world of two terms; its status is paradoxical, not dialectical: the third term is missing' (1992a, 49). As well as reminiscent of Michelet's 'two-term dialectic', this critique of Racinian theatre gestures towards an influential treatise on the dialectic that emerges in French around the same time (Kosik 1970). Indeed, just as Kosik underlines the transformational and transitive dimension of the dialectic, so the analysis in *Empire of Signs* is concerned, as we shall see, with agency, with the day-to-day transforming of the everyday world.

The transitivity of the world in Barthes's Japan is part of the 'new dialectic'; and this relates to his 1968 piece on Bunraku puppet theatre, 'Lesson on Writing', which suggests that the dialectical principle of contradiction is a Western one, absent in Japanese culture:

> Antithesis is a privileged figure of our culture. Bunraku cares nothing for these contraries, for this antonymy that regulates our whole morality of discourse. (Barthes 1977, 147)

This brief disqualification of the antithetical will become, by the time of writing *Empire of Signs*, a wider consideration of the dialectic in both Japanese and Western culture. It is accompanied by a Barthesian creative criticism, a dialectical formalism which recognizes that the 'double grasp', in its act of apprehending the world, needs to be confronted with writerly creativity. The idea suggests then a further level of complexity to our discussion of Barthes's essay 'on' Japan; partly because, not only is the essay not a scientific presentation of Japanese culture (so it is not 'on' Japan), nor is it 'about' France or Europe (the 'West'). Instead, *Empire of Signs* is all these things, except that it is (also, via) a 'stereographic' writing, but 'on' writing.

If the levels of vision now seem dizzying in their number, interaction and complexity, then this is appropriate to the philosophical and theoretical level at which the creative criticism of essayism is operating. Barthes's stark proposal that 'the author dialecticizes [them]self, [they] do not dialecticize the world' (1972, 146n3) suggests that the grasp of the real is not able to accommodate window and countryside simultaneously; and, at the same time, this very non-accommodation must become part of the writing. The challenge in *Empire of Signs* is then to write dialectically, but using a 'double grasp' that shows Japan in relation to the West what Khatibi sees in *Empire of Signs* as its 'non-logocentric ethnography' (1974, 64). Indeed, Khatibi's 'splitting [dédoublement]' of the self in his 1971 autobiography *Tattooed Memory* (2016) – especially in the last chapter, 'Double against double' – is a form of 'double grasp' and which sees the tattoo as releasing script from the antagonism of the dialectic (Flores Khalil 2003).

Essayism versus the impressionistic?

This written 'double grasp' is historically situated. 1969 and 1970 are the post-1968, but not quite the moment in which Maoism would, briefly, tempt Barthes between 1971 and 1973, a brief moment that had all but ended by the time of the famous visit with *Tel Quel* to China in 1974. Given this context, it is difficult not to be frustrated by any reading of Barthes's essay that is falsely simple, simplistic, disingenuous. Recent, supple readings of *Empire of Signs* do exist – for example the 'double gay reading' neatly explored by Nachtergael (2017, 425–26). But hostile readings have begun to surface. To put it in more pessimistic, negative terms, if the double dimension of the 'double grasp' – complexified – is ignored, if we look only at the 'countryside' of *Empire of Signs*, without looking also at the window, we risk a 'mono' (as opposed to a double) 'grasp'.

In a deeply antagonistic book on Barthes, René Pommier (2017) maintains, for example, that Barthes's disdain in 1970 for 'the sign that has, sadly, been weighed down by its meaning [signifié]' had overlooked something simple: the fact that a sign without a signified 'is no longer anything' (2017, 53, 56n80; see also Bremond/Pavel 1998, 71–72). Only for Pommier then to concentrate on what he calls Barthes's 'language tics', especially the use of 'precisely', which, we are told, Barthes deployed in 'an incongruous manner' (153, 183n15). Pommier cites the following important suggestion in *Empire of Signs* by way of support for his argument:

> Writing is precisely that act which unites in the same labour what could not be apprehended together in the mere flat space of representation. (1982b, 14)

Two critics (Genova 2016; Forsdick 2005, 137–40) have pointed to the wide variation in the reception of Barthes essay on Japan; but the disingenuous nature of Pommier's critique is astounding. Pommier reminds us that Barthes makes this comment about writing while he is writing about the 'clear soup' eaten daily in Japan. What detains Pommier is utter dismay at not understanding how Barthes arrives at writing via soup! Suggesting an extraordinary gap in his understanding of the French essayistic tradition (running from Montaigne to Gide), Pommier wholly traduces *Empire of Signs*, ignoring the idea that Barthes's Japan might be the 'utopian opposite' of *Mythologies* (Ehrmann 1973, 52). Pommier's aim by contrast is to insist that Barthes's critique of petty-bourgeois ideology's attachment to 'not seeing' – calmly excoriated in the mythology 'Blind and Dumb Criticism' (2009, 27–30) – now come back to bite the posthumous Barthes. And if it is essayism that Pommier overlooks, it is also at the expense of a subtlety in Barthes's writing. For the 'double grasp' here, a 'stereography' even, is a practice that will be deconstructed across the essay *Empire of Signs* as the strategy becomes one of finding how to undermine the traditional dialectic, specifically in his writing of food.

A more serious critique of Barthes's work points to the supposed ignorance and simplistic impressionism of Japan of the essayist. The danger of mistaking literary essayism for ethnography notwithstanding, there is also an argument for bending the stick towards what the Caribbean writer Edouard Glissant calls, as we shall see in Chapter Eight, an 'opacity' with respect to Japan (Glissant 1994, 126–28). This essayistic licence, does not, of course, give Barthes the right to say just what he likes about Japan (as Pommier has implied). Indeed, the window/countryside dialectic must respect 'parametrism', in which critique, following the 'pertinence' that Barthes found in André Martinet's linguistics, must aim for an exactness with regard to the object observed. It is a 'parametrism' that he praises in Morin's 'dialectical writing' (2015a, 57–60) in 1965, just as he is about to leave for Japan for the first time. In his praise of Morin's 'dialectical writing', Barthes suggests it is concerned not so much with being dialectical rather how to write in a dialectical fashion. Though Barthes does not name any of Morin's texts, one glance at the methodology section at the end of Morin's influential account of his group's ethnographical work in the Breton village Plozevet, and especially the notion of multi-dimensionality (1967, 403–04), suggests a possibly important intertext for *Empire of Signs*. How then to respect parametrism in (on) Japan? Barthes's reply is clear: 'What can be addressed, is the possibility of a difference, of a mutation of a revolution in the propriety of symbolic systems' (1982b, 3–4).

Writing as 'Dialecticising the self'

'My book has created me. I am its work'.

(Michelet cited by Barthes 1982a, 12)

'[F]or the romantics, travel had an entirely
different effect from its modern counterpart;
nowadays we participate in a journey by "eyes
only"'.

(Barthes 1987a, 20)

Carrard (2017, 185) underlines how Michelet's historiography was obsessed with personification, and Barthes how much the historian's self also became one with nature (1987a, 50–51). It would seem to be a short step then for Barthes to reverse this notion. Within the 'undialectical' form of writing that Barthes develops in his creative criticism is the unhinging of the self in the writing process itself. As mentioned earlier, in his postgraduate dissertation on ancient Greek theatre (1941), he had used as his epigraph Paul Claudel's idea that 'It is not a writer who speaks, but speech which acts', and Claudel has a presence in *Empire of Signs* that has been explored in part (Apel-Muller 1971; Corbier 2015). However, if Barthes alludes to Claudel's essays on Japan (1929), the essayistic writing deployed in *Empire of Signs* does not repeat the heavy style of Claudel's prose, nor, as we shall see, does Barthes endorse Claudel's notion of the Japanese soul – though Genova (2016, 157) cites Claudel's much earlier set of essays (1973 [1900]) as an intertext for *Empire of Signs*. If the Bunraku has multiple authors (1982b, 54–55), the decentering of self can be seen most keenly in Barthes's early writing on Michelet. The 'two-term dialectic' in Racine's world is unmediated and intransitive; but in the Micheletist 'double grasp', although it is 'equational', the historian's ability simultaneously to be both in the now of writing *and* in the then of history, is a 'dialecticising of self' that Barthes uses in his writing on Japan to begin to unhinge the Western self:

> This situation of writing is the very one in which a certain disturbance of the person occurs, a subversion of earlier readings, a shock of meaning, lacerated, extenuated. (1982b, 4)

This does not preclude a political reading of *Empire of Signs*, but it may involve asking different questions from those we might apply to his diaries on China. If Western, Hegelian dialectics is too methodical for Japan, then in the double grasp of semiology, will the signifier simply be privileged over the signified? Does an ascetic sumptuousness allow the hand to move the pen – to the extent that Diana Knight has suggested (1997, 164) a sexual analogy of masturbation with pachinko? It is in the deployment and then the eventual discarding of the 'double grasp' that this political reading will emerge.

Language as Critique

In order to trace the dialectical – or rather undialectical – strategies in *Empire of Signs* we must start with Barthes's view on Japanese grammar that he gives in 1968:

> Japanese makes the subject not into the all-powerful agent of discourse but rather into a great, stubborn space enveloping the statement and moving about with it. (1987c, 45, trans. mod.)

Is this similar to the writer 'dialecticising themself' rather than 'dialecticising the world' that we saw above? It does indeed suggest that, first, Barthes is looking for a parametric form of writing and, second, this discourse uses a 'double grasp', even a 'two-term' dialectic. In this way, the 'double grasp' starts to mutate. Moreover, in his 1941 postgraduate thesis, he had brought together ancient Greek theatre, armed with its spoken and performed dialectic, with the Japan described in Claudel's work. Here in 1970 by contrast, there is nothing of the sort. In *Empire of Signs*, Barthes goes beyond many aspects of dialectics that are implicit in notions of intersubjectivity – be it of a Sartre or of a Merleau-Ponty.

Thus, the human subject speaking in Japanese, 'a great envelope empty of speech', is decentred. Indeed, this implicit discussion with Sartre's and phenomenology in

Being and Nothingness, and its phenomenological insistence that consciousness is consciousness of something, is precisely that which the Japanese verb seems, to Barthes, to undermine:

> how can we *imagine* a verb which is simultaneously without subject, without attribute, and yet transitive, such as for instance an act of knowledge without knowing subject and without known object? (1982b, 7)

What Barthes calls (with a glance towards Japanese martial arts) 'such exercises of an aberrant grammar' is then able to open out onto a political discourse in *Empire of Signs*, by deploying a truncated dialectic: Japanese grammar – Japan – as an empty critique of the West, of 'the very ideology of our speech' (8). This politicized essayism that alights on Japanese food as a meal that is 'decentered' is, *pace* Pommier (2017), a deliberate ploy. It allows Barthes to forestall, truncate (rather than refuse) the dialectical. Rather than an orientalist tract or a penetrating view of Japan, his essay declines to comment, except to construct Japan as the *paradoxa* to the West, like a Japanese present he brings back to Europe but which is an empty box.

Thus, the 'double grasp' found in Michelet's writing of History seems to move, in Barthes's writing of the Japanese meal, towards a critique of the very notion of 'grasp'. First, the danger of a positivism is refused. This refusal uses an appropriately 'abyssal' style, replicating the writing 'from abyss to abyss' used by Nietzsche (1985a, 72). It is evident in the following list:

> an emptiness of language constitutes writing; Zen, in the exemption from all meaning, writes gardens, gestures, houses, flower arrangements, faces, violence. / The dream: to know a foreign (alien) language and yet not to understand it. (1982b, 4–6)

The jolt that generates this 'abyssal' way of writing is provided by the word 'violence', following as it does a list of distinctly pastoral themes. The jolt is repeated in another abrupt ending in the section called 'No Address', in which Barthes moves seamlessly from the level of culture to that of writing: 'to visit a place for the first time is thereby to begin to write it: the address not being written, it must establish its own writing' (36). If there is a 'double grasp' in these early examples, as we go through the essay the very notion of grasp begins, especially in the second half of *Empire of Signs*, to melt away.

'No wish-to-grasp' versus the 'double grasp'

Barthes begins his description flattering our perception, based on our reading of the *tableau* – and let us not forget that, for Barthes, it is the combination of the 'discomfort of progress' through history and the 'euphoria of the panorama in the 'tableau' (or 'overview') that is the basis of Michelet's 'double grasp'. Citing Piero della Francesca, Barthes designates our 'double grasp' reading method as alternating between surfaces and bodies; but it is an essayistic trap: we must, he insinuates, read the tray of Japanese dishes in a radically different way:

such an order, delicious when it appears, is destined to be undone, recomposed according to the very rhythm of eating; what was motionless tableau at the start becomes a work-bench or chessboard, the space not of seeing but of doing – of *praxis* or play. (11)

This game – or 'work' – marks the way food is eaten in Japan:

> this kind of work or play bears less on the transformation of the primary substance (Japanese food is rarely cooked) than on the shifting and somehow inspired assemblage of elements whose order of selection is fixed by no protocol: you yourself make what it is you eat; the dish is no longer a reified product, whose preparation is, among us, modestly distanced in time and space. (12)

In opposition to the passivity of the person eating a Western dish, Barthes is struck by the activity before the Japanese dish; and this activity seems to replace the Western gaze (both penetrating and surface) – and maybe already the 'double grasp' – which is our only activity: whereas *over there* he notices, on the part of the person eating, a direct agency (i.e., unmediated) *on* what they are eating.

There is undoubtedly a very classical, dialectical formation lurking here; however, Barthes, ever the drifter, is very quick to undo the dialectic by truncating it. In the same way as he begins to consider the clothing item from 1967 onwards, the writing on Japan undermines the power of determination by inverting it. The two examples he uses are the smallness of food in Japan and then the function of chopsticks:

> There is a convergence of the tiny and the esculent: things are not only small in order to be eaten, but are also comestible in order to fulfil their essence, which is smallness. The harmony between Oriental food and chopsticks cannot be merely functional, instrumental; the foodstuffs are cut up so they can be grasped by the sticks, but also the chopsticks exist because the foodstuffs are cut into small pieces; one and the same movement, one and the same form transcends the substance and its utensil: division. (15-16)

If there is a sort of 'double grasp' here, it is operated as an equalization, or levelling, of former hierarchies; Hegel has not so much seen his dialectic turned on its head rather denied its dialectical synthesis: it has been reversed and turned inside out. What is especially skilful is that by writing about food in an analytical and philosophical way the reader is invited to analogize socially and politically: the decentred; the inverted determinant; the exemption from meaning, are all examples of challenges to Western ideology. In analogizing this way we nevertheless maintain a taste, an air, of the food as it is from where the analogy first sprung. In sum, then, unstated analogy invites mixing of original topic (here, food) with its suggested significance (here, politics and society). The same could have been said about language in the Japanese grammar example above.

This levelling of determinants – a partial overturning of Hegel, we might say – returns in the chopstick – which is the 'two chopsticks together [la double baguette]' as Barthes calls it (16), 'double' just as 'the gesture is double' in Bunraku (49, 54). The material act of eating by bringing food to the mouth using chopsticks belongs also to another function, namely the 'deictic' movement of pointing to the food; this fine, almost delicate, act is thus compared to that involved in the West of eating using a knife and fork. Deploying a wide functionalism, Barthes equalizes – if not overthrows – the determining order in the act of eating: the chopsticks show, point to, what they are going to put in the mouth. There is a sort of finesse which complements the suppleness of the dialectic with which Barthes represents the Japanese act of eating in a sort of multi-tasking. And it is what leads him – in an essayistic fashion – to distinguish two types of agency: the 'bird food' (in a reference to Claudel) of the chopsticks – which pinches the food – versus the Western 'predation' of the fork which pierces it (18).

The expert writer of the provisional/peremptory (in the neat, double expression proposed by Macé 2002), the Nietzschean writer who writes 'from abyss to abyss', has other strategies for undermining continuous prose: that is, by using essayistic writing in one long sentence. One example suffices. The section 'Rawness [*Crudité*]' is, in the original French version (2002, III, 367–68) made up entirely of two sentences only; the first is 10 lines long, the second, 32 (compare to the English version which introduces full-stops, 1982b, 20–21): Proust – even Philippe Sollers – would have been proud of this 'uninterrupted text' indeed. The essayistic flow – working in an opposing fashion to the 'abyssal' style discussed above – is clear to see here; but it is the last line of this section that the analysis moves to another level. From this section of *Empire of Signs* onwards, writing and object begin to become conflated in the 'pinching of writing [la pincée d'écriture]' (55; 'sliver of writing' in the English translation misses the allusion in 'pincée' to the chopsticks' way of picking up food). Furthermore, what Barthes calls 'illusion of totality' (59) – linked to his critique of the Western self, especially in Claudel's conception of it in his essay on the 'Japanese soul' (1929, 9–38) – is radically contrasted, by the work of communication in Japan in which there lurks an agency which is not interiorized:

> In *Bunraku*, since the puppet no longer apes the creature, man is no longer a puppet in the divinity's hands, the inside no longer commands the outside. (62)

Not only does the exteriority represent a refusal of depth, of the hidden and of the intimate, Barthes hints that the Bunraku puppet involves a human activity that is non-passive and which undermines the Western 'person'; and the critique of Western personalism is continued in the critique of intersubjectivity implied in the 'who is saluting whom?' caption (64–65, 68). Indeed, in Japan, communication itself is thwarted by a spiritual emptying of self:

> All of Zen thus appears as an enormous praxis destined to halt language, to jam that kind of internal radiophony continually sending in us. (74)

The Haiku is deemed to be one that has an 'accuracy [justesse]' that is parametric, as Barthes puts it in a parenthesis:

> which is not at all an exact depiction of reality, but an adequation of signifier and signified, a suppression of margins, smudges, and interstices which usually exceed or perforate the semantic relation. (75–76)

Barthes proposes a Japanese route towards a true liberation of the self, undermining the coded version in the West and moving towards a free form of personality in which we quote but never incarnate: hence the surprising clothing combinations he notices in Japan (97). In an ironic, dialectical way, this new person derives from quantity (the millions of bodies in Japan); and it is delivered in a deeply Hegelian voice:

> One might say Japan imposes the same dialectic on its bodies as on its objects: look at the handkerchief shelf in a department store: countless, all different, yet no intolerance in the series, no subversion of order. Or again, the haiku: how many haiku in the history of Japan? The result – or the stake – of this dialectic is the following: the Japanese body achieves the limit of its individuality: it is pure of all hysteria, does not aim at making the individual into an original body, distinguished from other bodies. Individuality is simply difference, refracted, without privilege, from body to body. (97–98)

'Without privilege': the equalization – the 'dialectic of two terms', we might say – is in full flow, going towards the void, by deploying the abyss, *both* in the 'countryside' *and* in the 'window'.

Another example is the jump between pages 102 and 103. Following a fine excursus on the eye-lid, Barthes moves abruptly to the *Zengakuren*, in 'The Writing of Violence', albeit cleverly prepared by the vigorous playing of Pachinko in a much earlier section (28). Here we have the functionalism of *Mythologies* that we analysed in Chapter Two in relation to Sorel and Yves Velan's humorous notion of 'galvanicity', in the description of the militant political action overturning the expected determinants: as a way of mobilizing, the *Zengakuren* shout slogans that are 'empty', phatic even: '*The Zengakuren are going to fight*' (106). Is this politicized form of phatic language what Barthes means by the 'woodcutter' in *Mythologies*? If we remember from Chapter Two, this is his response to Marx's (pessimistic) cherry-tree metaphor that regrets ideology's tendency to mediate human reality: is the *Zengakuren* slogan then an example of a *direct* political language act that chops at Marx's image of mediation? In designating 'only this action itself' as 'pure', and not 'what one is fighting for or against', Barthes's argument contrasts sharply with John Berger's Sorelian 'symbolism' in his 1968 essay 'The Nature of Mass Demonstrations' (2001, 246–49).

Mongin (1989) sets out the main effects of May '68 on social sciences, most prominently a democratization involving a 'refusal to hierarchize forms of knowledge' in which the 'degree of scientificity' in any discipline or method of work no longer has any weight (24), in an 'equivalence of objects' that not only splits the literary from the scientific (25), but also favouring, paradoxically perhaps, the return of religion, albeit religions that are 'marginalised [contrabande]'.

Indeed, the reversibility of determinants, the equalization of differences, the tactical *de*-hierarchization in *Empire of Signs*, opens out onto, works towards, the void of Zen: 'No wish-to-grasp and yet no offering up [Aucun vouloir-saisir et cependant aucune oblation]' (2002, III, 436) is the penultimate caption next to an anodyne photograph of a domestic room (1982b, 149, though the caption and photograph are both, inexplicably, excluded from the English version). The 'double grasp' has indeed mutated, if not been abolished, and if we think back to the impasse of the window/countryside, it might even have been resolved.

As Michelet did with history – 'remake the lives of the dead' [refaire la vie des morts] (2002, I, 123) – bringing the thereof the past to the *now* of the historian's writing – Barthes does the same for Japan 'over there'. In other words, the isomorphism Michelet/History with Barthes/Japan – the past, as we say after all, is a foreign country – suggests a distance that must be addressed by a 'double grasp'. But we are also living in a post-May 1968 world, and 1969 is often cited as a hellish realization of the failure of May 1968 to overthrow the system. 'to live amid the unhabitable' (1985a, 87) in 1970 might not entail for Barthes a search for nihilism – or if it does, it is a productive, pleasurable nihilism. Indeed, the poet Georges Perros, on finishing reading *Empire of Signs*, wanted Barthes to 'japanise the whole world' (1973, 295).

In *Empire of Signs*, it is ultimately the 'Western' dialectic that Barthes deconstructs, so as to found a new one – explicitly in the section 'Millions of Bodies' onwards – but this dialectic is one which is, or, leads to the void, or rather which leads only to the void. This is a 'two-term dialectic' – truncated, amputated, 'open', but thereby modernized, globalized and intensified: a hyper-dialectic. And finally, the 'new dialectic' is that which lives a double life, that is, within writing itself; in writing, it is the dialectic of the abyss, the deployment of the peremptory/provisional (as opposed to its negative-dialectical counterpart), but a writing of jolt that is alternated – just as in Nietzsche – with a writing of flow. The 'new dialectic' is the overcoming of determinisms: the outside has won out over the inside; in short, a new writing.

The 'new dialectic' – the critique of Hegelian dialectics – that we have seen in Barthes's 'double grasp' leads to a provisional if predictable suggestion: that the Haiku is the 'new dialectic'. But in what way could the paradoxical, the suspension or the dialectic, the forestalling of synthesis be deeply linked to the Haiku? We can certainly see an 'antithetical', if not paradoxical, form in Barthesian writing. Consider the way one Japanese critic, Seki Osuga Otsuji, describes the Haiku and its 'grasp':

> If one does not grasp something – something which does not merely touch us through our senses but contacts the life within and has the dynamic form of nature – no matter how cunningly we form our words, they will give only a hollow sound. Those who compose haiku without grasping anything are merely exercising their ingenuity. The ingenious become only selectors of words and cannot create new experiences from themselves. (cited in Yasuda 1957, 29)

In the Haiku, in the 'new dialectic', 'there is nothing to *grasp* [Il n'y a rien à *saisir*]' (1982b, 110). In a move that foresees the 'Neutral', Barthes questions 'grasp' fundamentally, developing what he later calls the NVS (NWG). Indeed, the 'Neutral' is specifically linked to the Japanese notion of *ma* or *between-ness* which, unlike Blanchot's definition of the Neutral, 'resists being passive and submissive by its very existence' (Innami 2011, 114). This is not only a reversal in respect of Michelet's 'double grasp'; it may also be the effect of the essay in critical mode, a creative criticism, even an essayistic poetry – what Barthes calls a 'disalienation' (2002, III, 654).

It is in this period that, following the fascination for Japanese grammar, Barthes is acutely aware of the obverse of Japanese grammar:

> we can speculate whether the sentence, as a practically dosed syntactic structure, is not itself, already, a weapon, an operator of intimidation: every complete sentence, by its assertive structure, has something imperative, something comminatory about it. [...] And conversely, there is a mastery of the sentence which is very close to power: to be strong is first of all to finish one's sentences. Does not grammar itself describe the sentence in terms of power, of hierarchy: subject, subordinate, complement, etc.? (1986, 109)

There is then a political battle over language, or rather over the very structure of language. Could a diary of his visit to China in 1974 resolve this in any way, find a way forward?

Travels in China: **Writing A Diary of Dissidence within Dissidence?**

Barthes glimpses a way out for writing, as we saw above in Morin's 'dialectical writing' (2015a, 57–60), especially in its use of an 'open' (that is, non-synthesized) dialectic. It is precisely this aspect of dialectical writing that we investigate in Barthes's diary-writing during his trip to China in 1974. We will also see a deeply 'political Barthes' in the seminar he gives to his students on his return, heavily qualifying Hiddleston's view (2010) that the 'postcolonial' Barthes pays 'little attention to history or politics': it is true that his writings tend to sublimate political facts into elliptical and essayistic analyses; but it is always dangerous to discount or marginalize the political subtext, to relegate Barthesian dissidence to an aesthetics of *écriture*, as the travel diaries in China show.

Barthes's visit to Maoist China in 1974, as part of a delegation led by his colleagues from the radical French journal *Tel Quel*, is an obvious opportunity for him to try out his writing. Japan, during his trips there between 1966 and 1970, acts as an oriental(ist?) critique of Western decline in the happier account of his visit to Tokyo and elsewhere; Japan also offers a Zen culture in which neither contradiction nor dialectic exists. Maoist China in 1974, by contrast, presents, albeit in a similar oriental distance as Japan from the 'West', a totally different set of inverse relations with Europe. Coste (2001, 352) shows how the much-touted visit of the radical *Tel Quel* group – Maoist theorists in France since 1971 – becomes a terrible agony for the Barthes in tow, but that he uses his article in *Le Monde*, on his return in May 1974, to demarcate himself from the pro-China camp. Indeed, the very title of Barthes's essay in *Le Monde* – 'So, How was China?' (2015b, 94–104) – uses the voiced question from French polity to point to the self-irony of the intellectual being quizzed. He reflects further on the question's oppressive nature in *The Neutral*:

> there is always a terrorism of the question; a power is implied in every question. [...] every question can be read as a situation of question, of power, of inquisition (the State, the bureaucracy: very questioning characters). [...] The multiplication of interviews, the

arrogance, the intimidation of the demand: index of the current ascension of journalism as power (2005, 107)

The 'not to reply' is not, however, a solution; rather, one could 'seem to answer (there is plenty of signifier) but without message. To evade not the reply but the nonreply' (2005, 205). Indeed, there is 'a real Neutral, which baffles the Yes/No, without withdrawing' (112).

As well as 'So, How was China?', we have two other sources of Barthes's strategically reticent views on his trip. First, that given to the postgraduate students in his seminar at the École Pratique des Hautes Études (EPHE) in Paris in May 1974 (2010a, 227–45). As part of the research for his experimental and humorous narrative of himself, *Roland Barthes by Roland Barthes*, he is leading a project in this seminar during 1973 and 1974, called *Le Lexique de l'Auteur* (The Lexis of the Author), which takes an author (himself, but in the third person); and, in front of his students, while re-reading all his own work over thirty years of publishing, he tries out a startling experiment: what does it look like to look at oneself through the eyes of others, of society? Barthes is certainly not the first person to do this: without his knowing, the project resembles the 'double consciousness' of African-American philosophy in W. E. B. Du Bois's *Souls of Black Folk* (1999). The visit to China was to become, therefore, an exemplary element in this experiment.

The other source – and published posthumously in 2009, at almost the same time as the 1973–74 seminar *Le Lexique de l'Auteur* – is Barthes's notebooks, or 'writer's diaries' that he keeps during the three-week visit to China (2012). Here he mentions, on a number of occasions (151, 154, 157–58, 176), meeting up with the China correspondent for *Le Monde*, Alain Bouc; this is doubtless the occasion for Barthes (and François Wahl, Barthes's editor at Les Editions du Seuil) to be invited to write for the French daily on their return from China.

Barthes never gave permission to publish these diaries and therefore this 'semi-text' – or 'avant-texte' (or fore-text) to give its critical-genetic name – is not really a 'text' in the same way as we might describe 'So, How was China?'. These diaries do not have the author's *imprimatur*; nor do they stand as part of a seminar paper destined for the ears (and no doubt, pens) of his select postgraduate students at the EPHE. Indeed, as a member of the *Tel Quel* delegation to China, Wahl considers it a complete betrayal (by Barthes's half-brother Michel Salzedo) to authorize the publication of both the *Mourning Diary* (2010b) and the *Travels in China* diaries. Wahl maintains that, if the publication of the former would have 'disgusted' Barthes due to its 'violation' of his personal life, then the latter's publication would have been 'taboo' because it was 'not written' and infringed his 'absolute respect of writing and its own logic'. However, as Éric Marty points out, Wahl, soon after Barthes's death, authorizes the publication of Barthes's personal diaries, *Paris Evenings*, that are much more personal (Birnbaum 2009a). Furthermore, parts of Barthes's China diaries are published, in facsimile, in the catalogue for the 2002-2003 exhibition at the Centre Pompidou (Alphant and Léger 2002, 208–25). It is with these textual caveats in mind, coupled with the stipulation of dialectical research sketched out above, that we will consider Barthes's writing in these diaries.

'Abyssal' Writing

There is one other possible influence on Barthes's writing in this early 1970s period. Although not Nietzschean – 'I am not Nietzschean, it is simply that I read Nietzsche', he declared in his seminar in 1974 – he was clearly working with the German philosopher's aphoristic way of writing (2007a, 462). Discussing with Raymond Bellour, in an interview in 1970, his aim to find a 'discontinuous discourse' against a 'dissertational discourse', he welcomes, on the one hand, a Lévi-Strauss who was trying to get past the 'monodic' nature of the dissertation in favour of a 'polyphonic composition'; and, on the other, Lacan whose writing resists 'secular censorship' in which the 'spark' or abrupt formulation is excised from writing (1985a, 72): 'there has been no equivalent of Nietzsche in France', someone who 'dares to discourse from spark to spark, abyss to abyss' (on Nietzsche's style, Nehamas 1985, 13–41).

Interestingly, it is precisely this word 'abyssal' that the renowned sceptical sinologist Simon Leys (the penname of the Belgian Pierre Rykmans) uses to criticize Barthes's article in *Le Monde*, accusing him of embarrassed 'jesuitism' (Leys 1979, 88). But, as Coste hints (2001, 352), this is a 'solution' that Barthes adopts in the published article, deeply aware of the friends and colleagues, especially the coterie at *Tel Quel* (Philippe Sollers, Julia Kristeva, and the poet Marcelin Pleynet who all travel with him in April 1974) who are pro-China. However, keen to show how Barthes feels constrained from different and contradictory directions to say the right thing about China, Coste does not underline that, between 1970 and the trip to China in 1974, Barthes makes a number of asides that suggest a sympathy with *Tel Quel*'s pro-Maoist views in this period. On various occasions in interviews and published articles, as we mentioned in the foreword, Barthes suggests that China is somehow different, both from the West and totalitarian Soviet Union, and is, since the Cultural Revolution of 1966, more advanced even; and though not involved in the political cheerleading of a Antonietta Macciocchi in her 1971 book *De la Chine* (and who initiates the *Tel Quel* visit to China), Barthes is clearly curious about the claims made for the progressive nature of Maoism and the China which results from it. Indeed, what is touching in the *Travels in China* diary, according to one critic, is precisely the 'growing disillusionment of a group of friends' who were once 'ready to believe the true left has risen in the East' (Wood 2009, 12).

Though Kristeva and Sollers will both later claim that their revolutionary Sinophilia between 1971 and 1976 was, above all, a way of distancing themselves from the betrayals of the French Communist Party in the wake of May 1968. However it is difficult to ignore the obsessive way in which they lead *Tel Quel*, through resignation after resignation from its editorial board, into its Maoist fervour, illustrated by the numerous *dazibaos* – Chinese revolutionary slogans as posters that Barthes describes in *Travels in China* – that adorn the walls of the Paris office of *Tel Quel* (Marx-Scouras 1996, 166–174).

At the same time, Barthes could not but be aware of the political critique at the time of Mao's China. In Maurice Nadeau's journal *La Quinzaine littéraire* for example, there are anonymous but highly critical remarks in a review of Jean Pasqualini's *Prisonnier de Mao* (anon. 1975, 22–23). Also, Barthes is a member of the editorial committee of the New-Left journal *Arguments* when, in 1961, it publishes a special number (no. 23, third term) on China, 'China without myths', which includes critical analyses by Trotskyists Pierre Naville and David Rousset, as well as an extract from the travel diary of R. H. S. Crossman.

It is to Barthes's credit then that he goes to China in good faith, on a fact-finding mission, partly also out of solidarity with Sollers and Kristeva. Therefore, given the speed with which Barthes tires of Sollers's behaviour in Maoist mode and the subsequent dispute between Sollers and Wahl over China, not to mention the enthusiasm of Kristeva for the progressive nature of women's politics in China (1986b), the whole visit is a politically and personally sensitive one. In their work on the *Tel Quel* visit to China, Forest (1995, 475–85) and ffrench (1995, 183–89) set out the debate and then rupture between Wahl (and to a certain extent Barthes) on the one hand, and Sollers and Kristeva on the other; in response to Wahl's reticent and mildly critical series of articles in *Le Monde* that follow on from Barthes's – 'China without utopia' (15–19 June 1974) – the subsequent numbers of *Tel Quel* (59, 60 and 61), following Sollers's criticism of Wahl's article (Sollers 1974) are largely given over to the journal's ongoing Sinophilia; only for the inevitable recanting, following Mao's death in September 1976, to be expressed by Sollers in *Le Monde* (1976). It is this tension between a 'scientific' mission and a personal investment in an anti-Western project with *Tel Quel* that defines the diaries that Barthes keeps during the three-week visit.

It is important to stress that Barthes is particularly sensitive at the time of his visit to China to issues of self-presentation in the diary. As part of the *Lexique de l'auteur* project that he is leading in the EPHE seminar with his students in 1974, he is acutely aware of the self, especially as it appears in Gide's *Journal* and Proust's fictional account of how to start writing *A La Recherche du Temps Perdu*, and also in the historicized ways in which Barthes himself had considered both of these texts at earlier stages of his own writing career (in 1942 and 1966 respectively) (2010a, 97, 324, 349). Barthes might have held ambivalent views on the writer's diary (1986, 359–73); but he certainly thinks carefully about the self that emerges from them.

Indeed, the 1973–74 seminar investigates not only 'life as text' – clearly a gesture towards the diary form – but also the 'doubled' figure of the writer. Barthes hints at this 'split' in 1964 (1972, xiii). Now, in 1973 – and following his splitting of the writer Pierre Loti into two characters (1990c, 107) – he proposes 'RB I' (the writer who has written) and 'RB II' (the writer who will write), indicative of the 'infinite duplicity' of a writer (2010a, 324–25). Though it should not be suggested that Barthes's diaries are simply his seminar in preparation, it is no coincidence that he 'performs' his visit to China in his seminar once back in Paris. Indeed – as Anne Herschberg Pierrot points out in a footnote at the start of the 'Sur la Chine populaire' seminar that Barthes gives on 8 May 1974 (that is, only four days after his return) – he uses the three *carnets* that make up his China travel-diary, as well as the fourth book which systematizes these three *carnets*, to write an analysis for his students (2010a, 229n1).

The diaries written in China figure then the tension between political project and the social expectations of the writing self, to which the 'abyssal' mode of writing will contribute. Birnbaum (2009b, 1) maintains that much of Barthes's writing in the diaries revolves around the 'war' between, on the one hand, language as 'breath of fresh air [bouffée]' – a positive form of free human-speech acts – and, on the other, language as 'brick' [an ideologically-fixed 'lump' of stereotyped language]. We will see how the 'abyss' is not just a way to address this 'war', but also to add another determinant (including, but going beyond, the societal and personal need to respond to friends' and colleagues' demands for a 'response' to China) that of the dialectic as a search for facts, subjectively interpreted, but not (purely) impressionistic nor superficial.

Birnbaum argues that the *Travels in China* diaries (2012) and the *Mourning Diary* (2010b) of three years later have one thing in common: they show that writing can emerge from the stereotype, the 'bricks' of State ideology in China and the 'pathos' following his mother's demise. Birnbaum's view is important because these two very different diaries figure Barthes belief that both phenomena – a propaganda trip to China and deep sorrow at his maternal loss – stymie writing. Unlike his experience of Japan, the experience of China seems to offer to Barthes no writerly opportunities:

> All these notes will probably attest to the failure, in this country, of my writing (in comparison with Japan). In fact, I can't find anything to note down, to enumerate, to classify. (2012, 57).

Yet he transforms this 'failure' into writing, for *Le Monde* (and for his seminar), just as his mourning at his mother's demise will lead to his treatise on Photography, *Camera Lucida*. But also it would seem that both diaries have scientific pretensions, what Macé (2009) calls 'a form of writing at the level of living'. Macé sees something 'elliptical' and 'minimal' in Barthes's diaries as part of the 'grand art' of the 'notation' written without any 'overhang [surplomb]' – and this 'overhang' will come into play in the published pieces 'So, How was China?' (2015b, 94–104) and *Camera Lucida* (1984) respectively. For Macé, the *Travels in China* diaries show a Barthes as a good 'school boy' taking notes, but often concentrating, in his notations, on (seemingly irrelevant) incongruities found in his surroundings – a shirt that is too long, for example (a detail that clearly prefigures a sensitivity to the *punctum* in *Camera Lucida*) – as part of a resistance to the ideological control of the organized, State-sponsored visit. It is this dialectical mix of the objective search for the realities of Maoist China and the subjective experience of being there in its daily reality that will guide our analysis of Barthes's writing in the diaries.

'No Comment'?

> 'I doubt that [Gide's] *Journal* has much interest,
> if reading the work has not awakened some
> initial curiosity as to the man.'
>
> (Barthes 1982a, 3)

In *Travels in China* (2012) we see Barthes not simply tiring of Sollers's hyper-enthusiasm for Maoist China, but also offering patient and searching questions about the true nature of China in 1974. Listening to the official accounts of the USSR's undermining of China's development following the Sino-Russian split of 1960 and the subsequent ideology launched by Mao of 'Independence and Autonomy', Barthes's critique of Stalinism

– also experienced in Romania in the late 1940s during the Communist takeover – is in evidence, if only in an 'aside' in his diaries (signalled by the square brackets that are interjected between his note-taking):

> More and more this strikes me as obvious: searchlight on the national problem (counting on one's own strength), total opacity on the social-revolutionary – which means that, at the present stage of the journey, nothing really sets China apart from a Stalinist state. (2012, 60)

In the now familiar technique of voicing the other – or *prosopopoeia* – Barthes speaks as though he were a Chinese person as they castigate the Trotskyist Left Opposition in China during the revolutionary period of 1926 and 1927, in a way that sounds like the infamous 'Third' period in Stalin's Russia in the 1930s during which Trotskyists were deemed to be 'social fascists':

> (Liu Renjing: became a Trotskyist 1927. 1929, creates Left opposition organization to Leninism. Trotskyists in China: in guise of the left, undermined the CPP, in collusion with the Kuomintang.) [...] Chen Duxiu: veered towards Trotskyism. Ultra Right = Ultra Left! [...]: on the left in appearance, on the right in essence. The end!' (2012, 36–37)

And he describes Stalin and Trotsky (184). Of course, this 'brick' of ideology against Trotskyism in China that Barthes is ironically voicing here is a complete travesty of history; as Trotsky points out in 1927 (and Mao, at the time, seemed to share a similar view), it was in fact the Chinese Communist Party, under strict instructions from Stalin and Bukharin, that united with the Kuomintang, with the disastrous consequences that ensued (Trotsky 1964).

In what we might call an example of 'dissidence within dissidence' – Maoism is highly 'dissident' in early 1970s France – Barthes is not reticent about seeing Maoist China in this period as 'Stalinist', a claim that is refuted by Sollers in his editorial for the special number of *Tel Quel* on China (Sollers 1974). Gradually in his diaries on China, we see Barthes beginning to become suspicious of the claims made in the interminable speeches of welcome and historical explanation, if only because of the gaps in the information given. In another interesting aside – again signalled by the square brackets – he breaks off from the description of 'very fine' calligraphy to suggest how China might be perceived:

> [Three levels of perception:
>
> 1) Phenomenology: what I see. Western manner.
> 2) Structural: how it works: description of the operational apparatus. Stalinist level.
> 3) Politics: socio-revolutionary struggles. For which Revolution. Struggles between lines, etc.] (2012, 62–63).

The rub for Barthes, as the diaries go on, is that the French visitors in the *Tel Quel* delegation are not being shown anything but generalities – delivered in the regular 'bricks' of official state ideology – that doing nothing but hide China's true social realities. At the end of a long list of figures and information on China's promethean expansion built on self-reliance – '[vague and banal [...], a bit like a child's game, very Fourierist]' – Barthes delivers his critical judgement: '[Never anything on the way wages work, the properly social, owners]' (2012, 88).

As well as ironically voicing the 'bricks' of ideology of the guides and the officials welcoming the *Tel Quel* group, Barthes's diaries in China also use a more dramatic technique to chip away at the dis- and mis-information that is being meted out. On a number of occasions the diaries break off to describe how Sollers and others try to get the main guide, Zhao, to hand over the translators' list of the various 'bricks' of ideology that they need in order to help with French communication. This 'absolute semiotic document', as Barthes calls it (2012, 75), is, according to Marcelin Pleynet's diary of the visit (cited in Barthes 2012, 205 n1), never forthcoming, with Zhao refusing to hand it over to the *Tel Quel* group. Nevertheless, Barthes's reaction to this is a will to systematize these 'bricks': '[Make a list of the X stereotypes (bricks) that I have gathered]' (2012, 98). It would seem that from this point on, the diaries begin, slowly but inexorably, to show someone losing heart in finding out about the 'real' China. Remembering the State verdict on Michelangelo Antonioni's disparaging documentary on China, *Chung Kuo China* (1972) – the film that made him want to visit China (1997, 66) –, as '[... "Contemptible method and treacherous intent"]', Barthes writes in his diary that, presented with a visit to the Ming tomb, he has lost interest: 'I stay in the car while the others get out, take photos. Can't be bothered' (2012, 79). Later, he begins to tire of the endless and unending addresses: '[The longwinded speeches continue. School, Family, Society, etc. but my thoughts drift.]' (85).

It is here perhaps that the real tension in Barthes's diary emerges. Keen to find out about contemporary China – as the lengthy and dutiful notes taken in the diary attest – but mindful, at the same time, of the ideological control that the presentation of Chinese society under Mao entails, Barthes is also sensitive to the need to present the Chinese people accurately. It is here that the 'abyssal' way of writing the diary that Barthes adopts – be it directly Nietzschean, 'from spark to spark' as he put it, or 'dialectical' in the way that Morin's writing is able to show a 'broadening of meaning' (2015a, 59) – is at its most intense, if not its most fruitful.

Barthes's fascination with the 'minute' detail of Japanese culture in *Empire of Signs* is now redirected to the vastly different situation of Maoist China. Indeed, following a throwaway line (from Zhao, presumably, who has just been described as hoping to see to every wish of the *Tel Quel* visitors, be it peonies in the hotel room or a spicy dish in Luoyang), 'Mao likes red chilli; he powders his dish with it', Barthes hints at not only a future text on China but at the very writing of these diaries:

> One possibility for a text on China would be to *sweep* across it, from the most serious, the most structured (the burning political issues) to the subtlest, most futile things (chilli, peonies). (2012, 95)

This 'text' is never published in Barthes's lifetime. There are hints of it in 'So, How was China?', but this article in *Le Monde* is concerned with his return to Paris and moreover with the expectations of him, on all sides of the political divide. It possibly exists as a 'text', however, in the seminar that he gives four days after his return, but which is published only posthumously (and, again, without Barthes's *imprimatur*).

In the seminar, Barthes is categorical about the status of what he is about to deliver to the students: 'I warn from the start. This rough and ready talk plays on the over-turning of appearances, a dialectic of illusions, no paragraph of which therefore is true in itself, the over-turning must be awaited each time: impossibility of *quoting* what I say' (2010a, 230). But before this stage of the journey, indeed whilst waiting at Orly airport at the very start of the first diary, Barthes sets the stylistic tone for the rest of the diaries. Following the slightly humorous opening of *Travels in China* – '11 April. Departure, washed from head to toe. Forgot to wash my ears' (2012, 5) – Barthes moves straight to one of the key issues surrounding his (and *Tel Quel*'s) views on China, namely what is expected of them on their return and what might actually get reported to French society:

> Echo in *Le Quotidien de Paris*. They're expecting a *Return from China* and *Afterthoughts on China*. But what if they really got: *Afterthoughts on My Return to France*? (2012, 5)

Barthes is far too aware of the episode in André Gide's life when, in the mid-1930s, he made a similar visit to the Soviet Union and wrote *Back from the USSR* with the subtitle that Barthes has in mind, *And Afterthoughts on My Return* (Gide 1939), for Barthes to actually carry out his threat – though it would be wrong to say that *Travels in China* does not contain occasional elements of this type of reflection on France. Barthes returns to this idea a little later in the first diary in China, as he (inadvertently, it would seem) prefigures the title of his essay in *Le Monde* that he will go on to write on his return: 'So, what needs to be written isn't *So, what about China?* but *so, what about France?*' (2012, 8). Interestingly, he supplies part of the answer to this when he describes the first evening and the questioning of the *Tel Quel* delegation by 'the Writer' from China in relation to philosophical journals in France, their 'Object of Research', the influence of Soviet philosophy and its revisionism, and records their very revealing views on these questions (2012, 46–48). There is also the moment at the Xinhua Printing Works in Beijing, on the second day of the visit (Sunday 14 April 1974), described ecstatically by Barthes, but ironically qualified in the comment that followed: 'Everywhere banners saying "Welcome to *Tel Quel*". If only we could see French factories like this! *Tel Quel* in France? Every workshop: applause. [...] "But is it really rightfully yours, M. Barthes, this applause addressed to you by workers?"' (2012, 17–18). See also, in Notebook 2, where he feels uncomfortable visiting workers hard at work: '[A bit shameful to be strolling around as tourists among these alienated workers at their labour]' (2012, 107).

Barthes's gut sense of political affiliation is also in evidence. He is perspicacious in dismissing Alain Peyrefitte's book (1973) as part of 'bourgeois democracy': the book is dedicated to (amongst others) one Maurice Papon, who, in 1981, is discovered to have participated, as the *préfet* in Bordeaux during the Nazi Occupation, in the transportation to the concentration camps of over a thousand Jewish-French children, and convicted in 1998 of complicity in crimes against humanity; this is not to mention Papon's suppression of Algerian nationalists in Constantine during the 1950s nor his role as the Paris *préfet de police* when, in October 1961, up to 200 Algerians were murdered by the French police.

More important than Peyrefitte's bankrupt politics however is the desire to get to know China, Chinese people and the Chinese way of life. In order to record his impressions, Barthes adopts, from the very start of the diaries, an elliptical form of notation, in which, first (and as we have seen above), voices and voicing are detached and abstracted from the body speaking. Other examples of the 'voicing' of Chinese people's views are evident; the following opinion is not presented between inverted commas for example: 'All this well-being has been accumulated by us ourselves. [...] Our own efforts, no need to request state investment' (2012, 11). Second, the frames of reference of the notation are swiftly overturned by a change of subject or a change in perception. For example, in the following Barthes's mind seems to be flitting, butterfly-like, between very different topics:

> Go back over the echo in the *Quotidien de Paris*, show the lousy ethics it's based on.
>
> How boring! To have the downsides of fame (the echo of a private trip) and none of the (financial) advantages.
>
> If I were to be executed, I'd ask people not to bank on my courage. I'd like to be able to get slightly drunk beforehand (on Champagne and food).
>
> They're huddled at the back of the plane, their eyes closed like – might I say this affectionately – little pigs, plump little animals; they're penned in too, in a sense.
>
> I'd like to say, to J. L., to R., cynically (but they'd understand): become, in writing, *someone*. (2012, 6)

Rather than a pure stream of consciousness, this writing shows a mind in dialectical, abysmal turbulence, churning over current impressions, potential 'images' of himself that might emerge after his return and thoughts about those people in France that are close to him at this time – presumably, Jean-Louis Bouttes and Roland Havas, both of whom are students in Barthes's EPHE seminar in 1974 and, possibly, (at different times) lovers of his.

Though it is not easy to fill in the ellipses between these very varied topics, the reader of Barthes's *Travels in China* learns very quickly that the ellipsis – the writing from 'spark to spark', from 'abyss to abyss', beloved of Nietzsche – will be the dominant mode of notation for the rest of the diaries. More importantly perhaps is that, following this opening, the elliptical notation style shifts to brief interjections, usually between square brackets, in which Barthes breaks off from the speedy note-taking in which he is involved to record the seemingly insignificant daily phenomenon. However, whereas, at the very start of the trip, he describes in minute detail the people he sees around him in Tiananmen Square (2012, 8–9), by the time the mini-lectures by Chinese officials have started, his observations are no longer the main prose of the diaries, but interjected in square brackets between the recording of salient facts about Chinese production:

- Vegetables: last year, 230 million pounds + apples, pears, grape, rice, maize, wheat; 22,000 pigs + ducks.

[Long table covered with light-green waxed cloth. People on both sides. Clean. At the far end, five huge painted thermoses (their samovar)]
   Stages: Mutual aid group [...]. (2012, 10)

However, as the trip goes on, these elliptical interjections in square brackets begin to concentrate on a number of themes: the taste of different teas, the weather, countryside, sexual mores and social customs, Chinese clothes, faces and overall morphology of the Chinese body. It is as if these ellipses are moments of looking up in which Barthes can turn away from, refuse even, the 'bricks' of Chinese state ideology with which he is being bombarded; but which are also notations of an ethnographic character, sometimes graphically reproduced by Barthes in his occasional, amusing sketches. It is the descriptions of the flavours of the various regional teas that remain in this reader's mind, served from the ubiquitous thermos flask. For example: '[Shanghai tea is much less nice than Beijing tea, which was golden and perfumed]', but the former is better when '[more golden, with jasmine]'; and the green tea in Shanghai is '[insipid and lukewarm]'. Though keen to analyse the 'Tea system', Barthes is finding, by the end of the first week, that all of the tea is becoming 'insipid' (2012, 23, 32, 42 and 51). The semiological analysis of tea is well-known since the publication of *Empire of Signs*, the ritual of which is placed (in a positive manner) within Japan's codes of empty but significant social gestures. Here in China four years later by contrast, Barthes considers tea as one of the ideological phenomena that glue Chinese society together, as he describes it in his seminar once back in Paris (2010a, 235–37). Indeed, the culture of tea-drinking that he experiences in China becomes part of the ethnographic 'blocking [verrouillage]' of Chinese society for the Western visitor mindful of China's claims to be a 'progressive' and even 'advanced' society. He describes the function of tea in the seminar, alongside the other themes mentioned above – sexuality, countryside, social behaviour and lack of religion – as what he calls the 'insignificant non-political' (2010a, 236). He mentions this 'blocking' in the diaries, considering it 'successful': '[Any book on China cannot help but be exoscopic. A selective, kaleidoscopic display.]' (2012, 165). This impenetrability of Chinese society for Barthes – 'This impossibility to reply' – then becomes the 'blandness [fadeur] of China, its *'peaceful'* experience of 'meanings [...] exempted '(2015b, 98–99) when he writes the controversial essay in *Le Monde*, 'So, How was China?' and takes up his 'unfathomable' stance of 'suspending' his judgement about China for his French readers.

However, there is one missing link in the genesis of this 'no comment' stance that Barthes finally and publicly adopts in *Le Monde* with respect to (his trip to) China, that is the theme of politics, what he calls in his seminar on China 'The Political Text' (2010a, 239–45).

Politics versus Politicization

   The whole trip: behind the double-glazed
   window of language and the Agency.

(Barthes 2012, 150)

As the trip goes on, Barthes's diaries are increasingly sceptical as to the accurate picture of life for Chinese people that is emerging:

> [For this country, two sorts of pertinence: 1) Gaze of bourgeois democracy: Peyrefitte, admiration for the state, Efficiency, condemnation of indoctrination; this point of view can be adopted and maintained *before* coming here. Coming here doesn't change anything; 2) Gaze from within socialism; debates: bureaucracy, Stalinism, power, class relations, etc. The opacity remains.] (2012, 111–12)

By the end of the visit, on the day before the return to Paris, Barthes seems to have come to some kind of solution for this 'opacity'. Describing one French person's attempts to see China from the inside, and 'at the other end of the spectrum' those Westerners who 'continue to see China *from the point of view* of the West', Barthes decides that both 'gazes are, for me wrong. The right gaze is *a sideways gaze*' (2012, 177). Then, on the last day, he pursues his thoughts on the 'sideways gaze', in his quest to account for what he has seen, experienced and understood of Maoist China: '[It will be necessary to distinguish what I have learned *on the first level* and *on the second level* [...].]' (2012, 185). And after a brief aside on the 'excellent' ham and pork sandwiches and then on how it is impossible to get the Chinese 'to admit to the least anti-Stalinism', he explains what he means by the two levels as part of a 'sideways gaze'. The formulation is striking for its classically dialectical form:

> [We would have:
>
> I   Level of the Signifier
> II Level of the Signified (discourses produced)
> III Level of the Text making and unmaking itself (real politics, struggle between different lines, etc.)] (Barthes 2012, 186)

This is precisely the approach that is taken in the EPHE seminar on China that he gives four days after his return.

Here Barthes strikes me as perfectly Orwellian: 'politics' in China in 1974 is the opposite of the politicization that Barthes wants to enact in *Mythologies* (against the de-politicization operated by bourgeois and petty-bourgeois ideology via myth). Here Barthes's diary looks very different from that written by Simon Leys during the first years of the Cultural Revolution between 1967 and 1969 (Leys 1977, 55–210). Though, in his diary, he becomes gradually more sceptical, Leys never engages in any politicized ethnography of China; whereas Barthes's diaries try to combine reportage (witnessing) and description of daily Chinese life and social realities, with a political distance that implies scepticism, and all in order for him to be expected to say the right things on his (eagerly awaited) return to France. No wonder that Barthes suffered heavily from migraines during his visit!

Must we then think of these travel diaries as some kind of writing failure? Certainly, these notes in the form of a diary are, probably, not meant by Barthes to be published. He even underlines in the 1974 seminar that China not being a country of the *Haiku* like Japan means that there is a 'poverty of my notes, of my own writing in this respect' (2010a, 238). Nevertheless, at the end of *Travels in China*, reading through his 'notes to make an index', he writes that 'if [he] were to publish them as they are, it would be exactly a piece of Antonioni' (2012, 195). He would begin the text, '(if I write one)', with the contrast between the French and Chinese meals in the aeroplane; and he then ends notebook 3 with the following plan:

> Summary: three admirations, two resistances, one question.
> I 1. Satisfaction of needs
>   2. Intermixing of layers
>   3. Style, Ethics
> II 1. Stereotypes
>   2. Morality
> III Place of Power (2012, 196)

It would take a further analysis of the seminar on China at the EPHE to establish the extent to which this dialectical formulation is implemented in his analysis. But one provisional suggestion is that Barthes, on his return to Paris, feels unable to achieve this. Indeed, the locking-away of Chinese life behind the uninterpretable practices of life such as tea-drinking, or the absence of sexualized interaction, seems to have led Barthes to see China as a society that is (for him) impossible to comment upon.

But what Barthes has, possibly inadvertently, given us in his *Travels in China*, is the outline of a critique of totalitarianism and its ideological functions. The diaries also present a fascinating impression of China under Mao that deploys the 'voice-off', the ironic technique of *prosopopoeia* used. Indeed, the ironically-voiced injunction 'we *must* be dialectical' (written between inverted commas) says so much about how Barthes thought *and* wrote in relation to the views and expectations that others might have of him. And even though China offers little or none of the charm he encounters in Japan – 'No trace of an incident, a fold, no trace of a *haiku*' (2012, 75) – and in a 'country where there's nothing Political that's Text', in this 'radicalism' and 'fanatical monologism' of 'monomaniac discourse', a '*fabric* [or] text without a gap' that 'sharpens one's wits politically and infantilize[s] the rest', in which he could not imagine living (2012, 173, 192), Barthes's attention to minute details, his distractions from the scientific task in hand and his elliptical writing style in his diaries in China, afford us a glimpse of what this 'fold' – intensely political – might be.

Chapter Eight

'OPACITY'

In the final two chapters of this book, we turn our attention to what might be called a 'Politics of self'. The self becomes a key site of dialectical interplay between the apersonal and what Barthes calls the 'for-me' of Nietzscheanism. The apersonal is not, however, to be taken as a complete erasure of the subject (Lordon 2013). Rather than 'dropping the subject' (Goh 2015, 1–23), Barthes proceeds to radically relativize its position, using various strategies of decentring, re-ordering and exempting, in particular in the notion of the *Neutral*. This search for a non-determinism of self, a suspension of stereotypes of the person's image, is naturally dependent on the rising fame in the final decade of his life:

> Do laudatory adjectives appease me at least? How does the Neutral man behave when faced with 'compliments'? The compliment pleases, it doesn't appease, it doesn't bring rest […] in the received compliment, there is for sure a moment of narcissistic tingle; but (quickly) past this first instant, the compliment, without wounding (let's not exaggerate!), makes one uneasy: the compliment puts me in apposition to something, it adds the worst complement to me: an image (compliment = complement). For there is no peace in images. (Barthes 2005, 56–57)

Furthermore, as we saw with the 'double grasp' in Michelet's writing of history and then its development in the writing on Japan into the 'no wish-to-grasp (*aucun vouloir-saisir*)', *saisir*, a synonym in French for both 'understand' and 'record', is slowly but surely deconstructed: it is the search for 'peace', away from the 'images' that the Other and society in general attach to the self, that leads Barthes to opacity.

No Wish to 'Understand' nor 'Grasp'

> 'Transparence needs to be combatted everywhere.'
>
> *(Glissant 1981, 356)*

> '"Understanding", isn't it a modern virus?'
>
> *(Barthes 2007a, 119)*

Reminiscing, towards the end of his life, about his friendship with Barthes, the Moroccan sociologist Abdelkébir Khatibi (1997, 25) describes an intriguing, regular exchange: 'Barthes would say to me privately, in response to a reproach frequently made to him: "When someone tells me to *be clear*, what they really mean is *be like me*"'. Revealing not so much a tetchy theorist of semiotics as an astute commentator on interpersonal relations, the retort from Barthes summarizes two decades of critical — and often complex — research on language. From the 1950s to the 1970s, he works extensively to account for how communication between humans operated, in all its forms and media, by locating semiology within political, ideological and social realities. However, by the mid-1970s, at the height of his career, Barthes begins to theorize the self within this language nexus. The demand for his work to have 'clarity' in the very language that he uses to describe how language operates hides a more troubling phenomenon: how linguistic exchange seems to *force* the self into the straitjacket held by the Other. The interpersonal skills of communication in modern life thus become an illness – a virus (to reinforce our own experience of pandemics in the twenty-first century) — that make 'understanding' into what Jameson calls 'the prison-house of language'.

It is the critique of 'clarity' that brings Barthes's work into a parallel with the Martinican poet and novelist, Édouard Glissant. Though Britton (1999, 202n18) identifies Barthes as the 'relation' overlap in post-colonial theory, little evidence has emerged (as of yet) to suggest that Glissant and Barthes knew each other well. They did, however, cross paths, in the early years of their career, on the editorial board of the radical-Left literary journal, *Les Lettres Nouvelles*; and in many of the two dozen numbers of the journal where Barthes's 'monthly mythologies' first appeared, Glissant also intervened on variety of literary topics. Furthermore, the developments in Glissant's writing, especially in the 1990s, belie a distinctly Barthesian influence. The decentering of self, the complex dialectic of writing/orality, the privileging of 'partage' [sharing] evident in Glissant's work (1994, 112–16) are all *loci* in Barthes's work of the 1970s, especially in *How to Live Together*.

Glissant and Barthes also share a critique of science that mobilizes Nietzsche, Glissant (1994, 129) underlining the importance of Nietzsche in the 'rupture of the speech of "comprehension"', just as Barthes, quoting Nietzsche, regrets that science, 'blinded by the desire to know all, at any cost', lacks the 'délicatesse' to stand back: 'we are scientific', concludes Barthes, 'through a lack of subtlety' (2007a, 389). Indeed, if the 'desire to know' is a form of violence (Lyotard 1971, 218), both Glissant and Barthes deploy opacity as a strategy against 'knowing' the Other, against the oppression that accompanies knowledge. For Glissant, opacity is, as we shall see, a political demand for cultural sovereignty of decolonized peoples; whereas, for Barthes, opacity is a form of Ethics — how to behave with the Other, whether people or other cultures — that sees language both as a site of oppression *and*, dialectically, the potential route towards forms of disalienation. For Barthes, opacity also becomes a place, a space in which the *acratic* can escape the *encratic* of society's *doxa*, a strategy developed most keenly in his seminars of the early 1970s (Amigo Pino 2022, ch. 5).

Both Glissant's strategy of opacity and Barthes's refusal of 'clarity' have an antecedent in the work of the African-American historian W. E. B. Du Bois. In *The Souls of Black Folk*, Du Bois identified 'double consciousness' as a tool in the continued oppression of African-Americans in the wake of the failed Reconstruction that followed the end of slavery. A 'peculiar sensation', *double consciousness* is this 'sense of always looking at oneself through the eyes of others, of measuring one's soul by the tape of a world that looks on in amused contempt and pity' (1999 [1903], 5).

We will consider how the *Neutral* not only tries to wrest control of *double consciousness* in favour of the self, but also represents a highly political move towards opacity. Indeed, De Villiers (2005; 2012, 127) describes it as an (unmarketable) political strategy, allowing the question of Barthes's own homosexuality to be sidestepped, in an act of opacity that runs counter to D. A. Miller's 'bringing out' of Barthes (1992). A critique of social relations may not be able to counter the powerful, political, psychological and ideological distortions operated by *double consciousness*; but we will see how Barthes's discussion of opacity begins to address the social dynamic beneath it.

Text: Intention and Performance

Greco (2020) relates opacity to enigma in *S/Z*, but it is also important in 'The Death of the Author'. The discussion of opacity and transparence begins early in Barthes's career. In *Writing Degree Zero* he sets out the relationship, in the seventeenth century, between Literature and language as one of aristocratic 'clarity', but one which began to break down at the end of the eighteenth:

> Classical art could have no sense of being a language, for it *was* language, in other words it was transparent, it flowed and left no deposit.... [T]owards the end of the eighteenth century this transparency becomes clouded; literary form … acquires a weight. (1967a, 9)

However, it was not so much the French Revolution of 1789 as the failed revolution of 1848 that confirms the modern appearance of literary language as a (potentially infinite) plural set of styles with which a writer signalled their relationship to the modern institution 'Literature'. Barthes challenges Jean-Paul Sartre's infamous view in *What is Literature?* (1949) that language is 'transparent': 'Since words are transparent and since the gaze looks through them, it would be absurd to slip in among them some panes of rough glass' (Sartre 1949, 25); though this comment from Sartre is qualified by Guerlac (1993). Barthes will later claim, in a 1971 interview in *Tel Quel*, that his 'degree zero' theory of 1848 is the 'turning-point' for the demise of 'clarity', thereby 'marxianizing' Sartre's view of literary language (1998, 252). We will return to this debate later in the chapter. The critique of 'clarity' becomes in *Criticism and Truth* the basis, as we saw in Chapter Five, for Barthes creative criticism; it also informs the famous quote in *Roland Barthes by Roland Barthes* whereby communication is never transparent: 'I have a disease, I see language' (1994, 161). What joins creative criticism's refusal of 'clarity' and the 'disease' of seeing the mediation operated by language, is the opacity of the text.

In the very first paragraph of 'The Death of the Author', published in French in 1968, Barthes sets out his critique of authorial intentions by using the theory of the *inorigins* of textual meanings — what we might call the text's opacity — but emphasizes also the continuity of this *inorigin* across ages and civilizations. This is not the 'inorigins' of wealth that he identifies in Balzac's *Sarrasine* (1974, 21); rather, the radical refusal to tie writing to person:

> [W]riting is the destruction of every voice, of every point of origin. Writing is that neutral space, composite, oblique space where our subject slips away, the negative where all identity is lost, starting with the very identity of the body writing.
>
> No doubt it has always been that way. (1977, 142)

Griffiths (2014, 34–35) seems to ignore this 'inorigin' in his contrast of Glissant's 1969 collection of essays *L'intention poétique* with Barthes's 'The Death of the Author'. Griffiths claims that, in sharp distinction to Glissant, Barthes's 'diachronic emphasis on the paradoxical modernity of the author function is contrasted with the premodern'; and that this division contributes to a 'relegation' of the primitive past in which, for Barthes, there was no notion of 'genius' for the narrator of stories until the author of the modern period appeared. This, Griffiths suggests, contrasts with Glissant's theory of poetic intention in which 'the shaman, story-teller, *quimboiseur*, is sustained into the present'. But Griffiths' view of a Glissant 'divergent' from Barthes's textualist radicalism is misplaced.

Though he acknowledges Barthes's Marxian point about how capitalism has tried, in textualist terms, to attach authority to author — and that 'certain writers have long since attempted to loosen it' (such as Mallarmé, Valéry and Proust) — Griffiths imparts an unproblematic Hegelian progressivism to Barthes's theory of 'inorigins' and genius. He suggests that 'it is unsurprising' that Glissant's 'assertion of a synchronic and cross-cultural approach to authorial intention … should emerge against a field in French theory' beholden to a 'diachronic emphasis' (Griffiths 2014, 35). In fact, far from Barthes historicizing the primitive against the modern, the 'death of the author' theory considers story-telling as a performance that stands in direct opposition to the author of stories:

> [I]n ethnographic societies the responsibility for a narrative is never assumed by a person but by a mediator, shaman or relator, whose 'performance'— the mastery of the narrative code – may possibly be admired but never [their] 'genius'. (Barthes 1977, 142)

Pace Griffiths, Barthes's comment clearly smacks of an intervention in favour of, a justification for, oral culture; but it is clearly the non-proprietary dimension that Barthes wants to underline in orality, a topic in Glissant's later work to which we will return. Indeed, Glissant's practice of narrative 'inorigins' in his own fictional writings, the multiple voices that narrate the Caribbean créole stories of the past, is mirrored in Barthes's creative criticism that, as we saw in Chapter Five, dramatizes the multiple voices of the text.

Furthermore, as we saw in the notion of the 'voice-off' (Carlier 2000, 388–89), there is a double nature to Barthes's *own* voice in 'The Death of the Author'. It is as if Barthes himself has to 'perform' the 'death of the author' thesis in such a way that we, paradoxically, listen to the theory but do not impart (any? too many?) intentions to the very essayist (Barthes) proposing 'the death of the author' theory. This is not so much Barthes sidestepping a performative contradiction — how can he *tell* us the death of the author (intentionally, as it were)? Rather, the 'voice-off' used in 'The Death of the Author' plays out an opacity of the self in which the skilled essayist relates to the contemporary world, not (so much) by abandoning clarity for opacity, but by the essay playing out a collection of 'voices'— of 'performances' of the essayistic code — which then provocatively undermine the author's authority over *any* text, including Barthes's ownership of his own essay.

What is more, this performance of the text in the reading act is multiple (in one reader) and infinite (in all of those readers to come): this is precisely the import of Glissantian Intention and its 'Relation'. 'Relation' — as a central concept in Glissant's theoretical work — is a non-hierarchical, non-reductive relation to the Other (Britton 1995, 315). Furthermore, Griffiths' sharp differentiation of Glissantian Intention from Barthesian 'inorigins' is not considering the opacity of the text. Surely, in Glissantian terms (to turn the tables), Barthes is proposing not only the 'inorigins' of the plurality of voices, but also an opacity of the text that relativizes intention; but by localizing intention within the act of reading (and not in the writing), he is merely strengthening it; because, as we saw in *S/Z*, creative criticism involves the highly intentional 'stereography' of reading *and* re-writing. In Glissantian terms, the 'intention' of creative criticism is global, 'deterritorialized'.

Furthermore, Glissant's deployment of opacity not only represents an 'epistemological resistance' to, a radical 'writing back' against, colonialism and neo-colonialism, but also allows the reader to be on an 'equal footing' with the poet, a 'collective poetics' and 'affirmative modality for reading, writing and interacting in the postcolonial world'; and this in turn avoids a reductive (passive) definition of opacity in favour of a globalized *'imprévisible'* (Allar 2015, 54). This is precisely the import of Barthes's 'The Death of the Author'. The parallels between Glissant and Barthes's textualism go further: 'rather than expressing anxiety about an inaccessible "deeper" meaning concealed beneath the surface of the text, Glissant emphasises the material text itself' (Allar 55). Indeed, with these parallels in Glissant and Barthes's emphases on a counter-poetics in mind, we might suggest that one link between Glissant's theory and poetry has a bearing on Barthes's own strategy of opacity in tactical, 'Neutral' silence, which is inaugurated, as we saw, on the return from China.

Indeed, discussing the opaque in Glissant's poetry, Villani (2016) uses the 1950s 'Palo Alto' work on 'Incommunication' led by Geoffrey Bateson, for whom refusing to communicate is a form of communication. In a parallel with Barthes's developing of tactical 'silence', Villani relates Bateson's 'double bind' experiments – in which a person suffering a bipolar moment, for example, cannot process two incongruent messages of which they are not allowed to discuss the incongruence and from which they cannot escape – to the strategic refusal in Glissant's multi-voiced créole poetry to communicate, to allow an act of 'comprendre (understanding)'. Glissant deftly splits this word into two syllables, com- and -prendre, with which to illustrate the post-colonial view that 'understanding' *necessarily* involves 'prendre (taking)'; and 'taking' for Glissant, as the descendant of enslaved Africans in Martinique, is part-and-parcel of Europe's anthropological attempts at achieving a scientific transparence of non-Western cultures. The anti-colonial poet's 'Incommunication' then is not a failure to transmit information, but a reasoned political strategy against Western science and its concomitant racist expropriation. Where opacity is a strategy for Glissant to defend against colonialism, for Barthes it is one of a defence of the self against the oppressive predations generated by the social relations of class society.

But before we look at Barthes's 'Neutral' strategy and its role in mobilizing opacity, we must investigate briefly Barthes's early attitude to opacity following his Marxian critique of Sartrean transparence that we discuss below. Like Glissant's use of opacity, it is concerned with language; but, in Barthes's approach, language is treated not as an immediate form of communication, but precisely as a mediated form of social relations.

Opacity as a means to 'grasp' Mediation?

Barthes is acutely aware of the need for a concept of mediation in a phenomenological understanding of perception, especially, as we saw in Chapter Two, in countering the human mind's susceptibility to the ideology function of myth and its attendant distortions. As a conclusion to the study of how myth operates under capitalist social relations, the implication is that we cannot *see* the ideology in social relations while also participating in its circulation. Barthes's (partial) solution to this — at least across the period of the 1960s known as 'High' structuralism — is to invoke semiology, as the science of signs, with which to show how communication between humans (in whatever form) operates on (at least two) different levels. In a sense, the semiological demonstration of language's susceptibility to producing second-order meanings which then superimpose themselves on the simple, first-order meaning generated by the signifier-signified association, is an attempt to expose the mediated — or connotative — manner in which we experience communication. Michelet's historiography is able to be both *in* the time of the history described (in which the future is perfectly, we might say, opaque to the actants described) and, simultaneously, viewing and describing this moment from the vantage point of much later as the historian tries to make sense of the same history (an 'intellection' that, we might then say, makes the subsequent meaning of the events 'transparent'). As we saw in previous chapters, the 'double grasp' manages then to solve (in some sense) the historian's version of the window/countryside conundrum: the 'countryside' is the moment of history (the historian 'walking' with the people in their making of history) and the 'window', the 'tableau' that the historian constructs from a time in the future and which sees the mediated historical event being described.

Though Barthes never leaves behind his work on and fascination with Michelet, there is little doubt that the dramatic social and political events of May 1968 in France play their part in heavily nuancing all notions of the 'double grasp'. Despite the 'stereographic' approach deployed in his 1970 essay *S/Z*, the creative criticism adopted by Barthes to consider how we read and re-write Balzac's story *Sarrasine* prefers to rest at the surface of meaning construction. Furthermore, as we saw in *Empire of Signs*, the essay ends with an anodyne photograph of a domestic room and the elliptical caption: 'no will-to-seize and yet no offering up'; the Japanese house is 'often deconstructed' and possession annulled: 'no site which designates the slightest propriety... the center is rejected: for there is in a Japanese house nothing to *grasp*' (1982b, 110).

Thus, between Michelet's 'double grasp' in the 1950s and the 'no-wish-to grasp' in his Japan of 1970, Barthes brackets, if not overturns, all notion of 'grasping'. This stark move from a multi-tasking comprehensiveness in historiography (and which can be seen in the politicized reading of the double level of signification operated by myth in *Mythologies*) to a tactical and strategic respect of non-grasping is a key development in Barthesian thought and critique.

The 'no-wish-to grasp' — the 'nothing to grasp' — has its echo in the absence of property in favour of 'guardianship' that Glissant valorizes in the pre-Colombian Amerindian tribes of the Popul-Vuh and the Chilam-Bilam in South America. For Glissant, guardianship is the polar opposite of Western notions and practices of ownership, of 'com-prendre' (1994, 120–21). Similarly, in 'The Death of the Author', opacity allows Barthes to question the profound intention of an author in any literary text, to reject the author's ownership over, and, in *S/Z*, to a bracketing if not a discounting of the critic's traditional aim to 'penetrate' (and, in some sense, own) a story's 'secret' meaning. Thus, in the wake of May '68, the structuralist attempts to account for the double dimension of the paradigmatic and the syntagmatic are replaced by the 'symphony' of codes that the reader hears in order to act back on the text. In ways that have encouraged many to see this post-68 Barthes as 'postmodernist', the literary critic is now a creative critic whose attention to the 'surface' of communications, to how literary meaning operates, is structured in the act of reading. Postmodernist or not, the radical questioning of 'depth' in literary and other forms of communication is certainly part of a post-structuralist critique of a science of the text. Or rather, the assertion that the 'science of the text' *is* its (re-)writing by each reader represents a collapsing of the binary opposition's art/science and literature/metalanguage and which, for our purposes, suggests an opacity of the text. It is a relatively simple move for Barthes then, in the early 1970s, to apply this opacity of the text to the self: how to stop the Other – others, society in general – 'understanding' the self, or believing that it could actually 'understand' the self. The 'inorigins' of the voices in a text in *The Death of the Author* and the 'inorigins' of wealth that *S/Z* finds structuring Balzac's *Sarrasine* begin to combine in Barthes's 1970s work on an 'inorigins' of the self, to produce an opacity that refuses to allow an oppressive social determinism of each person.

Adjectival critique

'Perhaps that is what love is – the momentary or prolonged refusal to think of another person in terms of power.'

(Phyllis Rose 2020, 14)

'I am that name you give me, but I am also something else that cannot be quite named. The relation to the unnameable is perhaps a way of maintaining a relation to the other that exceeds any and all capture. That means that something about the other can be indexed by language, but not controlled or possessed, and that freedom, conceived as infinity, is crucial to any ethical relation.'

(Judith Butler, cited by Srinivasan 2020, 39).

The common concerns in Glissant's Intentions and Barthes's textual opacity are evident in the work of another créole theorist. Barthesian opacity is concerned with a critique of the adjective, uncannily echoed in the work of Raphaël Confiant (1994, 172–75) who celebrates Martinican créole language (at least the French version, and in its 'natural', oral form) precisely because it contains no adjectives. Indeed, for Barthes, the adjective plays a treacherous role.

In his two 'monthly mythologies' in November 1955, 'Moroccan Lexis' and 'Moroccan Grammar' – which are then joined together as one essay to become 'African Grammar' in *Mythologies* (1979, 103–09) – Barthes points to the ideological function of adjectives in France's attempts to persuade the French population to back its bloody colonial wars in North Africa. The adjective's role in the language of colonial control is to 'reinvigorate' the nouns deployed to communicate the naturalness of the brutal civil war in French Algeria; but, he writes, sooner or later 'all the adjectival designs which strive to give nothingness the qualities of being are the very signature of culpability' (1979, 109). He later describes the adjective as 'the poorest of linguistic categories': 'are we condemned to the adjective?', he asks (gently parodying Sartre's existentialist belief in the inevitability of 'freedom'). It is the adjective's negative role in constructions of the self that begins to dominate, as the only way to achieve any notion of perfection in relations with others is to be able 'to abolish — in oneself, between oneself and others — adjectives'. In music, 'the most facile and trivial form, that of the epithet', by creating a musical imaginary merely tries to 'reassure', 'protect from [...] loss' the subject that is 'constituted' by listening (1977, 179). The adjective, far from adding colour, is, in short, the very opposite of life: 'a relationship which adjectivizes is on the side of the image, on the side of domination, of death; [...] by its descriptive quality alone, the adjective is funereal' (1994, 43, 68).

Furthermore, when the adjective is then turned into a noun, in an act of 'enallage' (or grammatically-incorrect use of a figure of speech), the existential killing of the Other is complete. We can now see how Barthes arrives at the 'fried' image of the subject and at the key anti-determinist notion of the *dé-classé* (the non-classifiable, without social class, that we saw in Chapter Six), of the *atopos* — without place (as opposed to *utopos*, literally 'nowhere') (1986, 350–58). The critique of adjective also completes the transition from the 'double grasp' to what he calls in *A Lover's Discourse*, in highly elliptical terms, 'Thus' [Tel]: 'the loved object [...] exonerated from any adjective' (1990a, 220); and in the *The Neutral* (2005, 52–61), the adjective is the arch enemy.

However, it is not a simple case of denying the adjective:

> Refusal, suppression, censorship of adjectives [is not] abolition, lapse, obsolescence, erasure: preparation for experiments in linguistic abolition: they are to be found in the borderline languages (and not in the endoxal language). (2005, 57)

In the *The Neutral*, there are no simple ways around the 'predication' of the adjective:

> On the one hand, the loving subject covers the other with laudatory adjectives (a polynymy well known to theology or to religious practice; for example: litanies to the Virgin); but also, or finally, unsatisfied by this rosary of adjectives, feeling the rending lack from which predication suffers, he comes to seek a linguistic way of addressing this: that the totality of imaginable predicates will never reach or exhaust the absolute specificity of the object of his desire: he moves from polynymy to anonymy - to the invention of words that are the zero degree of predication, of the adjective. The 'Adorable!' the 'je ne sais quoi', the 'it' the 'something', etc. (2005, 91)

It is not simply, as Illouz maintains (2012, 232), that verbal processing before an image *reduces* the ability to recognize the image; hence the briefest expression possible 'Thus [Tel]' that Barthes advocates in his treatises on the discourse of love (1990a, 220–21) and on photography (2016b, 101–06). It is first and foremost that the use of the adjective is an abusive predication on the Other, as well as on the self.

In this way, Barthes is questioning not just the image applied to the subject (him, as it happens — how else can we know?!), but also to the Other, especially the loved other, in his attempt to avoid what Braidotti (2002, 13) calls the temptation of the 'metaphorization of others'. Barthes's solution then is to develop the 'neutral' form: in trademark Barthesian fashion — proposing a behaviour essayistically, that is, purely utopian — he devises what he calls the 'no-wish-to-grasp' (NWG [NVS]), or 'non-will-to-possess' (NWP)' (1990a, 233). If, as Felski (2015, 97) suggests, language for the later Barthes becomes a form of 'symbolic violence' in which 'to speak is […] to subjugate', then the political, the politics of critique, has, rather than disappeared, moved onto ever more subtle, finer, more 'delicate' terrain.

Barthesian NWG = Glissantian relation?

The NWP is a crucial move that some have seen as a negative side to Barthes's sexual politics. For example, Knight (1997, Chapter Five) describes the visit to, and writing on, Morocco as 'an unhappy sexuality'. However, in line with the NWG (NVS), Saint-Amand (1996) does not see in *Incidents* any orientalism in suggesting the interchangeability of the young Moroccan boys described by Barthes, instead a vague and at worst disinterested account, at best using each individual Moroccan name for the boys as the start of a literary fantasy (see also Boulaâbi 2013, 35–52). Saint-Amand (2017) also points to Barthes's desire to get beyond, in gay sexuality and erotics, the simple (Hegelian?) binaries of active/passive, possessing/possessed and solicitor/solicited, which is then contrasted with Guy Hocquenhem's anus-oriented libidinal sexuality (636–37), to find a more sensual sexuality, a 'délicatesse' in what Barthes calls a 'transgression of transgression' (1994, 65–66). Indeed, for Saint-Amand, *Incidents*, far from an allusive treatise on sex, is in fact 'a very subtle liquidation of sex' (1996, 156n7).

The refusal of sexual 'taking' (prendre) that Saint-Amand (2017, 641) finds in Barthes's attitude to sexuality chimes with Glissant's cultural and political critique of 'prendre'. But De Villiers' point is also a question of 'tactics', pointing out (2012, ix–xi) that, if sexuality is not declared, it tends to signal, in a homophobic society, homosexuality, and that Barthes uses opacity to thwart 'confession' only for this opacity itself then, inevitably, to signify homosexuality (and, presumably, so on…).

It is not surprising then the NVS (NWG) tactic is rhetorically negative ('no-wish'); but conceptually, and even in practice, it is a positive form of action to avoid 'enallage'. For Eric Marty (2006, 333), the very abbreviation 'NVS' avoids the evil of classification and illusion that besets the Word, for the Letter, by being anterior to the Word, acts so as to neutralize its 'Terror'. The capitalization of 'Terror' here is doubtless Marty's allusion to Barthes's early interest in ancient Greek theatre, in which the word is a form of terror (Coste 2016a). The NVS invites silence, effacement, suspension and not liquidation of the imaginary nor renouncement, and involves no oblation nor lassitude: 'non' here is not negative, except that it is without adjective: the Neutral, 'neither coloured nor deep', is what Marty calls (328–29, 324–25) 'alterity without others'.

Barthes analyses oblation briefly in his seminars on the *Discours amoureux*, in relation to Goethe's fictional and Heine's poetic writings on love, deciding that oblation's ultimate end, suicide, is, psychoanalytically and in reality, a 'failed experiment' (2007a, 218–20). It suffers above all from the 'Bad night' of attachment to things, in distinction to the 'good night' of 'obscurity'. The 'will-to-grasp (*vouloir-saisir*)' must therefore end, but its opposite, the NVS (NWG), must not — unlike oblation — be seen (Marty, 323 commenting on Barthes 1990a, 232–34). Oblation then is part of the West's cartesian belief in the rational and equal nature of human social relations. The Cartesianism of the 'ego isolated' leads to Barthes's belief that the 'fascism of language' is its alienating imposition of individuality and the concomitant exclusion of complexity (O'Meara 2012, 126–27). The conflictual dualism of self-and-other can be overcome in Barthes's schema by creating the NVS (NWG), aiming, as O'Meara puts it, at a 'non-dualistic harmony' in which, dissolved in nature, the self is not beholden to binary conceptions. The NVS is an 'ethics of non-committal', involving a *délicatesse*, an 'aeration' of Haiku and morality. The 'ultimate project', announces Barthes in his 1977 Inaugural Lecture (1982a, 459), is to 'inquire into the conditions and processes by which discourse can be disengaged from all will-to-possess (*vouloir-saisir*)'.

There is no need for us to dwell on the origins of the NVS (NWG) in Taoism. But it suggests a relation of human-to-human outside of the (modern) Western ideology of 'understanding' the other. As a 'dream of a minimal sociality' (2005, 201), the NVS is, in *How to Live Together*, an 'acceptable distance' in which idiorrhythmia and the excessiveness of *délicatesse* allow for the self to flourish socially and collectively (Stan 2014). Indeed, Glissant's shattering of being, in favour of 'Relation', seems driven by the same concerns as Barthes's NVS.

The critique of property is well known as a key part of the theories of the young Karl Marx and private property is often a synonym in his work for class relations. The human being has become, writes Marx, 'the tense essence of private property' for it is inside each person not external to them; and he relates this directly to (heterosexual) marriage and to the exclusive and communal ownership of women, but which appears to man as the most '*natural* relation of human being to human being' (1975, 342, 346–47). It is against this background that we must consider the section 'Opacity and transparence' in *Roland Barthes by Roland Barthes* for the way it addresses the contradiction of social relations.

The brief fragment 'Opacity and transparence' in *Roland Barthes by Roland Barthes* (1994, 138) is actually based on a much longer version (2010a, 331–42), whose 34 fragments were originally intended to be the organizing system for *Roland Barthes by Roland Barthes*. In other words, the binary opacity/transparence — in genetic terms — is a key, if subsequently marginalized, opposition in the account of his writing career up until 1975. In the posthumously-published, much longer version, called 'Argument' (2010a, 331–42), Barthes sets out the idea that, from the start of his writing career, the Opacity and the Transparence of social relations play out in a 'simultaneity' of chronology and logic (331). The 34 fragments appear to be an intellectual's *apologie* of semiology – as Validity that critiques all 'Causes' – against Marxism as Truth and 'Alibi' (338) which, in its exclusion from language and from the freedom of 'production' is condemned to a form of oblation (336). In short, Barthes underlines the 'oscillation' in his work between seeing the opacity of social relations in the stereotypes of life, and then, ultimately (or utopically), its transparency, which is the desire for *rest* in which 'social interlocution' and its thickness can be glimpsed opening up, lightening up even disappearing into invisibility. However, this merely leaves the writer in a double bind. The greater the 'social division' the greater, paradoxically, the opacity of this social division — and here is the window/countryside conundrum we saw in *Mythologies* above — against which the 'subject' struggles as best they can; at the same time, if they are themselves 'the subject of language' their 'battle cannot have a direct political outcome' — such is the opaque nature of language that we saw in *Writing Degree Zero* above — because this would mean a return to the stereotypes of opacity. Naturally, Barthes sees this contradiction as a spiral along which his writing moves — in oscillation — to the same places but always, across time and subject, arriving further down the line, in what he calls an 'apocalyptic' battle. Nevertheless, he stresses, this battle is part of life, of living and breathing under capitalist social relations.

Using the Glissantian word 'partage', Barthes affirms that the writer 'shares excessively', breathing out heavily (exaspérait) the values of the critique of those social relations contained in the stereotype; and yet, at the same time, the writer lives 'utopically' taking in air (respire), breathing in the 'final transparency' of social relations. This is the life of breathing: pushing out combative air to clear opacity, and taking in air with which to be able to continue the combat (1994, 138); indeed 'exaspéré' (exasperated) is then used in the very next figure, 'Antithesis' (138). It leads to Barthes wanting to affirm the 'right to difference' but this allows him only to recognize a further contradiction — the critique of liberalism accompanied by a defence of 'freedom of expression' — which is resolved, partially only, by a sublimation into the 'distance' afforded by the NVS (NWG), a 'democracy of differences' which Barthes sees as redolent of Charles Fourier's utopianism (2010a, 334–35).

The NVS cannot get beyond the contradictions of social relations (how could it under Capitalism?), and Barthes's emphasis on the social relations in opacity ignores, or at least marginalizes, opacity between cultures. Nevertheless, one of Barthes's strategies for avoiding transparency of cultures is to explore the Neutral. Japan for example is presented as deliberately opaque in *Empire of Signs*, in which the Neutral, as one critic (Smith 2016, 55) has underlined, becomes a less judgemental way of travelling: the Neutral in Japan 'dodges', 'baffles' and 'outplays' the contrastive machinery of meaning-production, which is otherwise 'unshakeable' for Barthes. There is little sense of opacity being, finally, positive in Barthes's work, as Griffiths argues for it to be in Glissant's work and in its prelude to a world 'Relation'. Opacity is a fact of language and of social relations under Capitalism; and in personal relations, the only recourse, to Barthes's mind, is an NVS strategy. It is not so much that 'too much clarity obscures' (Pascal cited in Goldmann 2016, xxvi, trans. mod.), but that 'the neutral can be violent, can invest the adjective instead of the substantive' (2005, 256), suggesting that Barthes's *Neutral* is almost synonymous with opacity:

> How many times, in our lives, do we have to deal with 'frank' people (that's to say, who show off being so): in general, that precedes a small 'attack': one clears oneself (in a tactless way) of one's own tactlessness; but the worst about frankness is that in general it is an open door, and wide open, onto stupidity. To me, it seems difficult to have the proposition 'I will be frank' followed by anything else but a stupid statement. (2005, 25)

The 'So, How was China?' article on the return from the *Tel Quel* trip we considered in Chapter Seven is a type of opacity, inviting the '"Frankly, I don't know"' (2005, 24) of the *Neutral*. There is consequently, in Blanchot's words, 'opacity in transparency':

> I would transcribe the paradox in this way: the subject (who I am): like a score (large surface of staves): each part (each wave) is independent, clear, vivid, sung and heard vividly; but in me, underneath me, there is no me to read the whole, vertically, harmoniously [...] hyperconsciousness, Neutral: I am clear to myself but without truth: a very clear language (nothing hermetic, abstruse), but without referent; for everything I believe about myself is false and I am without truth nevertheless [...] my sharpness is useless. or again: there is no orchestra conductor in me who could read the score in its verticality. (2005, 100)

It is precisely the 'verticality' of language that dominates in Barthes's divergence from a Sartrean conception of language.

'Writing Degree Zero' versus Sartre?

Kristeva (2000, 200–01) rightly reminds us of the philosophical similarities of Sartrean and Barthesian conceptions of the act of writing. However, opacity is at the heart of Barthes's critique of Sartre at the Liberation and in his later claims to have 'marxianized' Sartre. This marxianization of Sartre's literary theories concentrates, first, on language and style (Roger 1986, 47); only then to propose, a materialist, class-based analysis of the development of the French language since the seventeenth century, involving a form of 'internal colonisation' (Stafford 2014) which Barthes sees taking place in the imposition of a Paris-region French across the highly varied linguistic France, in the lead-up and especially after the French Revolution (Barthes 1947; 2015a, 1–6). It is important to insist not just on a critique of Sartre in this materialist understanding of the development of modern French language but also on its anti-Stalinism (Barthes 1950, 4; Stafford 1998, 29–30).

Where Sartre's argument is significantly different from Barthes's is the transparent nature of language: 'The function of a writer is to call a spade a spade. If words are sick, it is up to us to cure them' (Sartre 1949, 284). Indeed, Barthes refers implicitly to this famous quotation from Sartre in 'Myth Today', where, in a footnote, he suggests that, 'if there is a "health" of language', it is in 'the arbitrariness of the sign which is its grounding' (Barthes 2009, 150n7).

Sartre's belief in the transparency of words, though not Stalinist itself, does lead him into some positions in the politics of literature that today seem regrettable and at times not far from the socialist realism and their Stalinist injunction; and, in his haste to draw out the nature of committed writing, Sartre falls prey to what Robin (1986) calls 'the obsession with transparence'. Though Birchall (2004, 125) rightly underlines Sartre's clear distancing from Stalinist notions of 'representation' in literature, Sartre also dismisses poetry, leading him, regrettably, to consider Surrealism as 'Trotskyising', a 'safety valve' (148, trans. mod.). Needless to say that, considering the efforts in 1948 to create a new revolutionary political organization, the *Rassemblement Démocratique Révolutionnaire* (or RDR), with Trotskyists such as David Rousset and others from the *Revue Internationale* (such as Pierre Naville and Maurice Nadeau) and non-aligned left-wing (such as Claude Bourdet and Albert Camus in the newspaper *Combat* for which Barthes is writing at the time) and for all of whom Surrealism is a crucial form of radicalism, such a view of Sartre's is pure anathema and for one recent critic 'puerile, perverse' (Surya 2004, 299–300). Sartre also appears economistic, if not inconsistent as to his view of the bourgeoisie's slow climb to power in his expression cited above of 'very calmly attaining economic pre-eminence'. This *longue durée* view seems to ignore anything but the economy, adhering to a 'stages' view of history that is at odds with Barthes's adoption of Trotsky's dialectical understanding cultural *longue durée* (Stafford 1998, 20–24). Thus, in the *Les Temps Modernes* debate with Claude Lefort (1947), Sartre sides with the 'stagist' view of historical change of the Vietnamese Communist Tran Duc Thao; and, despite his praise of Thao's book on marrying dialectical materialism with phenomenology (2015b, 17–19), Barthes is surely with Lefort on this question.

Barthes knows well Moscow and Eastern-bloc dogmatism. Several writings unpublished in his lifetime from 1946 and 1947, that is before the first article on the 'degree zero' thesis in August 1947, show his dissident Marxism developing. Both 'Sketch of a Sanatorium Society' and 'The Future of Rhetoric' (2018, 64–66, 102–13) use a logic of dialectics – in the latter, the work of George Plekhanov and Marx on poetry (113) – in order to develop a historical criticism involving 'calling into question the fundamental structure of society' (104). But it is one of the two 'Romanian texts' from 1948 and 1949 that reveals Barthes's earliest anti-Stalinism. In the first of these on contemporary popular song in Paris (115–18), there is a Micheletist attention to the 'people'; but in the second, 'Politicization of Science in Romania' (118–23), he turns his attention to the deformations of science by Stalinism.

Considering 'the invariable elements of all Stalinist writing', Barthes proceeds to analyse 'the "basic" language of communism' (121): 'clichés' whose 'incantatory power' is gradually 'to impose upon the reader's critical thinking the desired automatisms'. Using a 'nominalism [...] that is equivocal' and 'crude tautologies', 'the basic process of all Stalinist statements' is exposed (121–22). Above all, he denounces the Stalinist campaigns that use a word – such as '"cosmopolitanism"' – while Stalinist purges take place; and such words become, via 'this deliberately spectacular process', added then to the 'lexicon of orthodox communism' (122). In this sense, Barthes is operating a transparent reading of Stalinist vocabulary: against the opaque deployment of 'cosmopolitanism', he mobilizes a transparency. As Samoyault points out (2017, 157n38), Barthes uses this early writing on Stalinism 'word for word' in *Writing Degree Zero* as he hints at a 'Trotskyist writing' (Barthes 1967a, 30). He also applies Trotsky's dialectical understanding of modernity to the understanding of language.

Dialectics of language in modernity

The simplistic view that the French Revolution radically changed the French language is first dismissed. Against the classical French of the court of the seventeenth and eighteenth centuries – 'to speak like Vaugelas meant [...] to be connected to the exercise of power' – Barthes underlines the existence of a 'revolutionary mode of writing proper', but this was still within 'the great Form of classicism':

> The Revolution did not modify the norms of this writing, since its force of thinkers remained, all things considered, the same having merely passed from intellectual to political power. [...] The Revolutionaries had no reason to wish to alter classical writing; they were in no way aware of questioning the nature of man, still less his language, and an 'instrument' they had inherited from Voltaire, Rousseau or Vauvenargues could not appear to them as compromised. (Barthes 1967a, 27)

This maintenance of the very structure of language across the Revolution did not stop the revolutionaries using a language that reflected the 'Blood which had been shed'; and Barthes describes 'the theatrical amplification', the 'signs of inflation', the 'extravagant pose', in an 'exact writing' in which writing was never 'more incredible, yet [...] never less spurious': 'modelled on drama[,] it was also the awareness of it' (27–28). This explains the opening words of *Writing Degree Zero* (1967a, 7) in which Barthes cites the swear-words used by the revolutionary Hébert, during the French Revolution, in the news-sheet *Le Père Duchêne* – the weak English translation for which one critic has regretted and discussed (Rabaté 2002, 71–74). Borrowing from Michelet, Barthes suggests that the violent writing used during the Revolution 'was the entelechy of the revolutionary legend' as it struck 'fear into men's hearts and imposed upon them a citizen's sacrament of Blood' (Barthes 1967a, 28).

This idea seems to chime with Sartre's view of the rising bourgeois class before the Revolution, whereby '[c]onfronted with a ruined nobility, it was in the process of very calmly attaining economic pre-eminence' (Sartre 1949, 99). However, 10 pages later, Sartre changes tack when he underlines that 'the political triumph of the bourgeoisie which writers had so eagerly desired convulsed their condition from top to bottom and put the very essence of literature into question' (109–10). For Barthes by contrast, for whom all revolutions in literary language are 'greatly over-rated [...] storms in an inkwell' (2015a, 4), it is not the French Revolutionary period of 1789–94 that heralded a revolution in the French language but the period around 1848–51 when the writer's conscience is split and the beginning of literary modernity can be seen in the 'plural' forms of writing that emerge thereafter.

Here is Barthes's argument against Lukács (1969), for whom the death of Balzac in 1850 heralded the decline of the 'historical' novel and the beginning of literature's decadence and its loss of radical direction. In Barthes's argument, the 'essential break'

(1967a, 24) in writing is when in 1850 Europe sees 'the scission (completed by the revolution of June 1848) of French society into three mutually hostile classes, bringing the definitive ruin of liberal illusions' (1967a, 66). It is here in 1850, and not in 1789, that 'the decisive changes in mentality and consciousness' take place and it is these that contrast the 'modes of writing' of a Balzac to that of a Flaubert (24). The implication is that the dramatic events of 1848–51, described ironically described by Marx as 'the 18th Brumaire' of Louis Bonaparte's in which the nephew's seizure of power was a 'farce' in relation to the 'tragedy' of Napoleon Bonaparte's coup of 1799 (Marx and Engels 1978, 9), resulted in the political and ideological disorientation of the writer and led to the pluralization of writing forms. It is for this reason that Barthes suggests that only bourgeois writers 'can feel that bourgeois writing is compromised', since 'the disintegration of literary language was a phenomenon which owed its existence to consciousness, not to revolution' (1967a, 79). Thus, Barthes is suggesting that the revolutions around 1850, hugely different in character from 1789–94, suddenly and irreversibly prohibited the bourgeois writer from being able to identify with any social class.

Though the 'degree zero' thesis attempts to 'marxianize' Sartrean theories of language and literature, especially in the mediation that language operates on consciousness, Barthes does display a Sartrean antipathy to poetry in 1947, which, though couched in Marxist terms, is astoundingly shrill:

> Though some have found it so, there is nothing surprising about the dormancy of poetry in the eighteenth century when that era was occupied with something else, or about the awakening of that same poetry from 1940 to 1945. It is worth noting that this apparently attentive form of literature actually falls within the framework of a poetics overwhelmed with the supernatural. (Popular expressions like poetic message, testimony, poetry as spiritual exercise, visitation of the poet, etc.) Transposing Marx's remark (with its context), we could say that poetry (and in a sense all of literature) is the opium of the empowered class, suffering not from the evils that it endures but from those that it sees. (A possible definition for philosophy as well, the esotericism of philosophical language.) (Barthes 2018, 113n1)

It implies that Barthes sees the function of certain literary forms, here poetry, as politically irresponsible.

Criticism of form?

The other major influence from Trotsky, albeit less obvious in Barthes's work, is the political understanding of culture. In a strikingly non-Marxist moment, Trotsky had maintained in 1924 and 1925, against the cultural workerism of the time, that a 'work of art should, in the first place, be judged by its own law, that is, by the law of art' (Trotsky 1991, 207). One provisional suggestion is that Barthes applied this idea to his own form of criticism. As we saw in Chapter Five Barthes's creative criticism, rather than a liberal free-for-all, is a tightly-theorized 'stereography', in which the only act of judgement possible on a literary text is a writing that is 'parametric' and which 're-covers' the text in question. This 'Menippean' option consisted in creating a new text by starting with the one to be worked on.

Trotsky wrote his firm disagreement with the notion of 'proletarian culture' in 1924 just as he was mobilizing all his energy to combat the rise of Stalin; and his argument concerned not only simply literary and cultural questions but also the very conception of the socialist Revolution. It was during his intervention in the infamous 1934 congress of Soviet writers that Trotsky's nemesis, Andreï Zhdanov (1896–1948), began to apply the *Proletkult* ideas to the Soviet party-line. As general secretary of the Central Committee, both *apparatchik* and Stalin's 'cultural thug' (Eagleton 1976, 38), Zhdanov became the architect of the philistine cultural policy of Stalin's Soviet Union of 'socialist realism', the doctrinaire formula for writing literature that had inspired the French Communist Party writers Roger Garaudy and André Stil whose work is excoriated in *Writing Degree Zero* (Barthes 1967a, 76–79).

For a short period between 1947 and 1948, the French Communist Party (PCF) had resisted the Zhdanovism of Moscow's literary policy; but after 1948, in line with the Kremlin's new cultural policy, well-known French writers Raymond Queneau, Michel Leiris and others are suddenly deemed 'bourgeois' (Lavers 1982, 117–18); and it is therefore possible to put *Writing Degree Zero* in the camp not only of anti-realism, but also of anti-socialist-realism. Indeed, in 'Writing and Revolution', Barthes, explicitly if indirectly, praises (if not defends) Queneau, whose prose writing 'revert[s] to the language of social Nature', in opposition to the 'Naturalist school' which abandons 'the insistence on a verbal Nature openly foreign to the real' that 'paradoxically evolved a mechanical art which flaunted the signs of literary convention with an ostentation hitherto unknown' (Barthes 1967a, 73–74, trans. mod.). This 'writing of Realism can never be convincing' as it is 'condemned to mere description by virtue of this dualistic dogma which ordains that there shall only ever be one optimum form to "express" a reality as inert as an object' (74). This 'conventional' mode of writing is popular in 'schools where the value of a text is assessed by the obvious signs of the labour it has cost' (75), and implicitly (Moriarty 1991, 39) that the reader is getting 'value for money'. Citing Maupassant, Daudet and Zola as examples of writers 'without a style' (as distinct from the 'neutral' of the 'degree zero' writing style), Barthes describes how they – or rather their chosen ways of writing 'without a style' – justify the Institution of Literature by using 'a literary sign at last detached from its content' and showing literature to be a 'category without any relation to other languages' (75).

Sartre's essay *What is Literature?* contains an important section on the sociology of literature's reading public (1949, section 3) which will influence Barthes's various interventions in the mid-1950s into the sociology of literature around the Franco-German journal *Documents/Akzente* (2002, I, 537–39; 2015a, 7–20, 28–34). Denis (2000, 285–92; 2003, 257–59) underlines the extent to which Sartre, and then Barthes, accept that novels (including Sartre's own) have no other reading public than a bourgeois one, and that his 'virtual public' is accessible only to the militants and fellow-travellers of the French Communist Party, in other words a left-wing readership but in the 'closed society' of Moscow-dominated literary values. Following Sartre on the sociology of reading publics, Barthes sees in this ossification of writing that certain writers try to get round the social reality that suggests a growing cultural polarization between on the one hand, 'a proletariat excluded from all culture', and, on the other, 'an intelligentsia which has already begun to question Literature itself'; into this gulf steps, in Barthes's view (rather problematically, it has to be said) 'the average public produced by primary and secondary schools' which for Barthes is 'roughly speaking' the petty bourgeoisie, the intermediary stratum that produces and consumes myth in equal measure as we saw in Chapter Two and which finds in 'a good proportion of commercial novels [...] the image *par excellence* of [...] all the striking and intelligible signs of its identity' (1967a, 75–76). As well as a key argument within modernism, augmented by Sartre's assessment of the atomization of reading publics (1949, Chapter Four), Barthes's link between a petty-bourgeois writing and socialist realism, dovetails with the argument formulated by Trotsky in 1925 against 'proletkultism':

> This lower-middle-class mode of writing [écriture petite-bourgeoise] has been taken up by communist writers because, for the time being, the artistic norms of the proletariat cannot be different from those of the *petite bourgeoisie* (a fact which indeed agrees with their doctrine), and because the very dogma of socialist realism necessarily entails the adoption of a conventional mode of writing, to which is assigned the task of signifying in a conspicuous way a content which is powerless to impose itself without a form to identify it. (Barthes 1967a, 76)

Incapable of showing a global communist world in literature (and refusing to counter the daily reality of alienation with a utopian science fiction, we might add), socialist realism is obliged to 'play the game' (to cite Sartre's example of bad faith), to reproduce 'the convention of expressiveness', to 'write well' (75) as do a Maupassant or a Daudet:

> Thus is understood the paradox whereby the communist mode of writing makes multiple use of the grossest signs of Literature, and far from breaking with a form which is after all typically bourgeois – or which was such in the past, at least – goes on assuming without reservation the formal preoccupations of the *petit-bourgeois* art of writing (which is moreover accredited with the communist public, thanks to the essays done in the primary school). (Barthes 1967a, 76)

Not only does Barthes seem to be suggesting a puerile dimension to the communist doctrine of socialist realism – and suggesting its ingrainedness in the state-school system –, but he is also underlining the enormous irony in the fact that communist writing that follows Moscovite diktats – with the exception possibly of Louis Aragon whose writing is more 'eighteenth century' (mixing Laclos with his Zola) than nineteenth century (Maupassant and Daudet) – do not manage to leave behind a bourgeois mode of writing (not to say, petit-bourgeois), a literary form that even bourgeois writers treat with great suspicion:

> Perhaps there is in this well-behaved writing of revolutionaries, a feeling of powerlessness to create forthwith a free writing. [...] And certainly the fact that Stalinist ideology imposes a terror before all problematics, even and above all revolutionary: bourgeois writing is

thought to be all in all less dangerous than its being put on trial. This is why communist writers are the only ones who go on imperturbably keeping alive a bourgeois writing which bourgeois writers have themselves condemned long ago, since the day when they felt it as endangered by the impostures of their own ideology, namely, the day when Marxism was thereby justified. (Barthes 1967a, 53)

Denis (2003, 256) considers that Barthes's argument ends in the paradox whereby 'communist aesthetics' appears to be an 'art for art's sake' typical of artistic writing of the nineteenth century, involving a 'preciosity' that is the opposite of the tenets of socialist realism. Roger (1986, 303–04) suggests that Barthes's argument is more Blanchotian than Blanchot, whilst reminding that in 1971 Barthes (1998, 253) denies any acquaintance with Blanchot's work when he writes the 'degree zero' thesis in the late 1940s.

There is then perhaps a different source for Barthes's sharp rejection of Stalinism's advocating a petty-bourgeois literary form in socialist realism. It would seem that this section on Stalinist socialist realism arrives later on in the theorization in *Writing Degree Zero*. Indeed, amongst the nine articles that Barthes publishes in *Combat* between 1947 and 1951 that went on to become the 1953 essay *Writing Degree Zero*, there are no references to socialist realism. Therefore, it may be that their inclusion is partly influenced by a 1952 article that his friend and Trotskyist colleague Maurice Nadeau published in *Les Temps Modernes* following the awarding of the Stalin Prize to the communist journalist André Stil for his 1951 novel *Le Premier Choc*. Nadeau's close reading of it have doubtless both been hidden behind the fact that the same number of *Les Temps Modernes* was overshadowed by Francis Jeanson's infamous article detailing his and Sartre's definitive break with Albert Camus (Jeanson 1952).

In the article, Nadeau (1952) voices his appreciation of the Marxist aesthetic that Stil's novel tries to deploy but criticizes the literary form that it adopts. Stil's prize-winning novel – soon to become part of a trilogy called *Au Château d'eau* – tries hard to be an 'exact representation of reality, demystified by Marxism', but does not leave behind 'the frameworks of the bourgeois novel [...] and the Catholic novel [...] of good and evil' (Nadeau 1952, 2093, 2097). For Nadeau, rather than the paradoxical 'preciosity' that Denis finds in the debate around socialist realism, Stil's novel represent a philistine rejection of 'formalism', whereby 'literature can in no way be a questioning of anything at all, not even [...] of reality, the antithesis of what we call artistic creation' (2098–99). It is not surprising then that 'self-questioning' that literature should be in Nadeau's view is precisely the conclusion in Barthes and Nadeau's joint 1952 survey on 'Left-Wing literature' (Barthes 2015b, 41). Furthermore, there is little doubt that Nadeau's use of Marxism in his literary criticism affected Barthes's view of Albert Camus's *The Plague* and the ensuing debate over the lack of historical materialism in its use of analogy (2002, I, 540–45, 573–74; Stafford 1998, 63–64).

Bernard (1972, 303–30) and Lahanque (2003) have analysed socialist realism with a similar perspective; but the critique of literary form that Barthes applies to socialist realism in *Writing Degree Zero* owes much to Nadeau's literary Trotskyism. Rather than the paradox that Denis finds in a Communist aesthetic using an outmoded petty-bourgeois literary form, Barthes identifies the political irony of a party claiming to be revolutionary reusing and strongly defending a form that even bourgeois writers long since abandoned. If we add the 'closed society' of readers of literature that Sartre described, this irony is perhaps the most striking example in *Writing Degree Zero* of a 'tragic of writing', and which is more than linked to the predominance on the Left of the 'Stalin Myth' that Barthes will go on to analyse in 'Myth Today' (Barthes 2009, 174). Indeed, this 'closed society', 'triumphant' on the Left according to Barthes (1967a, 30), is of a piece with his experience in Romania in 1947–49 as the Iron Curtain falls across Eastern Europe.

All that remains in Barthes's dissident Marxism of the mid-1950s is then a radicalization of that idea of Trotsky's in which art should be judged only by the rules of art. From this moment on, Barthes will dedicate himself to a radical form of essayism, both free and autonomous, in which the committed writer must accept the double – or 'bastard type' (1972, 149) – status of a writer who writes caustically and responsibly but outside of any political 'cause'.

'Responsible' but 'For Me': From Nietzsche to Trotsky

Barthes famously describes the 'few photographs' that he is using in *Camera Lucida* to account for Photography as 'the ones I was sure existed *for me*' (1984, 8); though this too was part of a double action of valuing and evaluation that avoids subjectivism (Oxman 2010, 82). The *for me* is part of a writing strategy that emerges in the early 1970s encouraged by the reading of Nietzsche. The disengaged form of literary and cultural approach advocated by Trotsky, in which art is judged by art alone, is augmented in 1973 by Nietzschean philosophy in the description of the 'pleasure of the text':

> If I agree to judge a text according to pleasure, I cannot go on to say: this one is good, that bad. No awards, no 'critique', for this always implies a tactical aim, a social usage, and frequently an extenuating image-reservoir. I cannot apportion, imagine that the text is perfectible, ready to enter into a play of normative predicates: it is too much this, not enough that; the text (the same is true of the singing voice) can wring from me only this judgment, in no way adjectival: *that's it*! And further still: *that's it for me*! This 'for me' is neither subjective nor existential, but Nietzschean ('... basically, it is always the same question: What is it for me?...'). (1975, 13)

This apparent subjectivism is actually seen in decidedly political terms. Barthes is acutely aware that the Left will consider his view and approach, the *for me*, found, for example, in his reading of Bataille (1986, 238–49), to be a form of disengagement (though he pre-empts the criticism of subjectivism and that of being existentially 'in situation'). But his retort is that the Left risks abandoning the 'pleasure' dimension of reading to the Right. To 'judge art by the rules of art' in Trotsky's formulation seems then to inform the adoption of the Nietzschean *for me*, not only because it removes the ideologism of critique ('tactical aim, a social usage, [...] image-reservoir [couverture imaginaire]') over which he had hesitated in *Mythologies*; but also, in-between Nietzsche's and Trotsky's seemingly different injunctions, there is the requirement of a 'responsibility' of forms.

Textual pleasure – 'bliss [jouissance]' – thwarts the adjective, 'those doors of language through which the ideological and the imaginary come flowing in' (14). Indeed, far from a political disengagement, Barthes sees this 'bliss' as part of the struggle against (but from within) language:

> the text that imposes a state of loss [état de perte], the text that discomforts (perhaps to the point of a certain boredom), unsettles the reader's historical, cultural, psychological assumptions, the consistency of their tastes, values, memories, brings to a crisis their relation with language. (14, trans. mod.)

By reading for both 'pleasure' and 'bliss', 'the subject' is able to step outside of society's control via language, by 'simultaneously and contradictorily participat[ing] in the profound hedonism of all culture [....] and in the destruction of that culture', 'enjoy[ing]' the 'consistency of their selfhood [...] and seek[ing] its loss [perte]': in short, 'a subject split twice over, doubly perverse' (14, trans. mod.). Now Barthes makes his direct allusion to the radicalism of Blanqui's 1830 *Society of the Friends of the People* in his (no doubt, ironic) invocation of a *Society of the Friends of the Text*. In his discussion of the 'scriptible' and the 'lisible' in *S/Z*, Hill (2010, 115) argues that between, on the one hand, the responsibility of 'class struggle in philosophy and on the other philosophical perspectivism [...], the gap between these two interpretations is narrower than it seems': they both convey the 'event' of Barthes's own writing. Indeed, the same could be said of the 'pleasure' and 'bliss' discussed above: they are fundamentally dependent on each other, as is the case with so many (all?) of Barthes's binary oppositions (especially in the case of *punctum* and *studium* in *Camera Lucida* which critics have ritually imbalanced in favour of the former). However, Hill's contention (117) that the difference between the *lisible* and *scriptible* is 'untenable' misses the *operative* dimension of the provisional (if also, peremptory) distinction that allows Barthes to rewrite Balzac's story (in the case of *S/Z*) so as to 'crack open the Western symbolic system'; and here, in *The Pleasure of the Text*, as a way to propose a new mode of political battle that takes this 'cracking open' onto the terrain of language itself. Here the *operative* in Barthesian writing contrasts sharply with Adorno and Horkheimer's stark (and anti-dialectical?) claim that 'the truth of a theory' being 'the same as its productiveness' is 'clearly unfounded' (1979, 244).

There is little doubt that Barthes is thinking back to the literary questions around political engagement during momentous events such as the Algerian War. In a brief 1965 interview, he points out that those writers who were politically engaged in denouncing the Algerian War, carried on writing literature in the same disengaged way (2002, V, 1024). Now in 1973, in the wake of May '68, political engagement by writers needs to work with a new form of literary politics what he calls – following the dialectical formulations he had moved through since 1946 – a science of degrees, or 'bathmology' (1994, 66–67).

Bathmology represents a dialectical spirit but in spiral form. The best example is in the bitter debates recently around the writing of Renaud Camus (a friend of Barthes's in the 1970s) on the one hand, and Camus's utterly reactionary comments in 2000 (and since) that echo the white supremacy theories of Le Pen, *père* and *fille*. Against those who seek to 'defend' Camus as an inspirational writer despite his racist views - in a manner which replays many of the debates around the 'great' writer but antisemite Louis-Ferdinand Céline – Thomas Clerc (in Sarkonak 2009, 164) tries to deploy Barthes's bathomology. Clerc believes he can attack Camus's right-wing 'overstepping [débordements]' *only* whilst (by?) affirming the skill as a writer, by being 'bathmological', that is, 'ambivalent'. This 'ambivalent' attitude can indeed be seen in another short interview that Barthes gave in 1965, this time on the antisemitic but influential writer Céline (2002, V, 1024). The 'bathmology' implies then a new 'ambivalent' type of dialectic, and one which Chapter Nine will consider as part of Barthesian 'undialectics'. Before though, we must consider the dialectical in another sense, as that of the writer in a tight political relationship with their historical moment.

Writing as 'generality'?

> The commonplace belongs to everybody and
> it belongs to me; it is the presence of everybody
> in me. In its very essence it is generality: in order
> to appreciate it, an act is necessary, an act through
> which I shed my particularity in order to adhere to
> the general.
>
> *(Sartre 1965, 137)*

We saw above how Trotsky and Nietzsche combine to form the bathmology of 'for me'. The contention now is that this begins in *Writing Degree Zero* which allows for a theorization of the writer-critic both engaged politically but 'tragically' unable to commit literature via form, in what we might call perhaps Barthes's most dialectical text; only for the rest of his career to dismantle, deconstruct, this same dialectical approach. From his rejection of 'socialist realism' in *Writing Degree Zero*, to his critique of science in Soviet countries such as Romania, Barthes's political ideas after the War bear witness to the influence of Fournié. Inflected by his friendship with Maurice Nadeau, Barthes's (mildly) Trotskyist Marxism, clearly different from Sartrean thought, reflects the lamentable weakness of the 'Left Opposition' during the Cold War.

In line with this, Barthes ends his chapter on 'Political Modes of Writing' on a pessimistic if not realist note, but one which we could consider as a challenge to find a form of writing that is not alienated. Both political and intellectual modes of writing are 'in a complete blind alley, they can lead only to complicity or impotence, which means, in either case, to alienation' (1967a, 34). This then is the challenge to the essay, to the essayist, to avoid (or combine) both of these extremes of writing: how to be politically effective without being politically compromised. We will consider the politics of Barthes's essayism in the conclusion. In order to do so, we must first consider how this dialectical conception of writing relates to questions of time and space: can Barthes, while sitting at his desk, be connected to both his political moment *and* the arena of political intervention.

Barthes claustrophiliac?

It would be easy to suggest that the work on 'how to live together' that Barthes develops in the 1970s develops out of his interest in Fourier in the wake of May 1968. Indeed, both Han (2020) and Lübecker (2010) suggest that there is subtle but highly significant move in thought from Time in the early Barthes (History, Tragedy, duration) to Space (the atopic, the Neutral) in the late; and that, even though one can locate spatial concerns in the 'early' period and by the same token temporal questions in the 'late', these instances of a crossover between Time and Space across Barthes's writing career merely nuance their relative marginalization. As part of our attempt to link the *for me* of Nietzsche that he adopts with a political responsibility of the writer, we will look first at the notion of a political space of writing in the work of the 1950s, and then trace this in the final lectures at the Collège de France.

Bittner (2017) hints at the Hegelian aspects of *Writing Degree Zero*: literature is the 'consciousness of the historicity of the ideological character of the universal (bourgeoisie)'; but it is also a deeply personal essay, concerned with the political self; mainly – but not only – about writing (largely fiction with some poetry), the essay pre-empts the Nietzschean question '*for me?*'.

Using the example of the writing of the French Revolution and the writing of 'Blood' and Terror we saw above, Kristeva (2000, 203–05) dispels any notion that Barthes's views on writing are 'formalist'. She also underlines that the 1953 essay could not be further from those who tax structuralism with 'excesses [that] were anti-historical', involving rather what Nietzsche called a 'monumental history' of 'mentalities', 'mutations' in humanity's relationship to meaning; and that the 'function' of writing that Barthes describes 'should be understood as an action, dynamic, relationship, correlation, faculty, aptitude, consequence', in a word, 'freedom', in a 'crossing' that is dialectical. Kristeva also describes Barthes's designation that 'writing is a morality of form' as having a 'historial dimension' (196, trans. mod); and the historiality in Barthes's theory of the act of the writer choosing a literary form, she underlines, has nothing to do with circumscribing the 'readership' (as it is in Sartre's view of the heavily-compartmentalized reading public for literature): 'the writer is not there to make the masses literate, to educate them, to influence the redistribution of power [...]'; its '"historial" and not historical value' (197, trans. mod.) rather, she argues for Barthes's theory of writing using Heidegger's notion of 'historiality' that we saw in Chapter Four, is 'to modulate the relationship to literature', leading Barthes 'to the sources of language and to the architectonics of meaning'.

Kristeva's judicious use of historiality suggests a link to Goldmann's work. Just as *Writing Degree Zero* highlights the historical, class and social manner in which language is deployed by writers in order to signify literature, Goldmann argues that '*sociological analysis* does not exhaust a work of art and sometimes does not manage to get near it even, the essential being to find the route through which historical and social reality expresses itself *across the individual sensibility of its creator*' (1959, 62).

Indeed, in a direct link to our analysis in Chapters Two and Three of the politicized role of the chorus in both theatre and the critique of myth, Barthes quotes Kafka in his final series of lectures: '"Truth resides not in the individual but in the chorus"' (2011b,

205). At the same time, in the *Neutral* lectures, he is acutely aware of the division between the public and private. There is a '(historical) myth of two men in one subject: the exterior man, social, worldly and alienated by the constraints of worldliness (hypocrisy, etc.)' on the one hand, and the 'interior man, true and free man' on the other; in the former, it is 'the "public" that is alienated in a market society (photos, interviews, gossip, etc.): the "private" is a natural defense against the commodification of the public' involving a 'logical identification of the clandestine (or the anonymous) with the free' (2005, 141). Connected to the temporal split in the writer – the 'RB I' and 'RB II' that we saw in Chapter Seven – this also means that 'the work is socially gratuitous: you can only believe in it, devote yourself to it, by shutting yourself away in it, by creating a sort of schizophrenia, an autism within yourself[.]' (2011b, 222). Indeed, Kristeva (197) sees the Barthesian theory of *écriture* as a 'search for a mode of writing between the intimate and the social'.

Barthes theorizes the act of writing in ways which seem to respond to, and update, the 'wood-cutter' metaphor he used in *Mythologies*:

> 'To write something' […], I would take the knife (if I was metaphorically a priest) of sacrifice, or the sword, or the pen, for a Cause that is external to me, thus I was being the agent of a cause. Writing, at that time, was very much active: I was writing for a cause, in the place of someone, in order to instruct, to convince, to convert, to provoke laughter, to produce a realist novel. […] Writing as a means is to take the pen from the hands of the writer-prosecutor and to do myself the work of writing. Certainly, the object's complement (that is, the 'what') is possible, and it is of course inevitable, but it is always encompassed, embraced not by the subject who is writing as subjective personality, but in as much as the writing affects them. (2015d, 274–75)

This has its echo in *Writing Degree Zero* 25 years earlier, and which is both a spatialized and temporalized understanding of writing as 'ambiguous reality':

> [T]here is a History of Writing. But this History is double: at the very moment when general History proposes – or imposes – new problematics of the literary language, writing still remains full of the recollection of previous usage, for language is never innocent: words have a second order memory which mysteriously persists in the midst of new meanings. Writing is precisely this compromise between freedom and remembrance […]. (1967a, 22)

For Barthes, there is a fine balance to be struck between public/private, self/other, writing in solitude/connecting with the world, which has an extraordinary resonance in the world of COVID lockdowns and confinements that we have experienced globally since the outbreak in 2020:

> a subtle use of Solitude; the optimal balance would be achieved through this formula: to be alone and yet *surrounded* (with the affective nuance) by others (personally I need solitude, but I am not fanatical about it: I like it when other people are there, *around* me). (2011b, 241)

The fascination with cut-offness, with claustrophiliac autarky, is nevertheless a fantasy, a simulated and literary counterpart to the 'withness' in the writer's dialectic of private/public, and a fantasy that Barthes lives through literature, especially Gide:

> From her bed, mad, prostrate (but eating well), Mélanie revels in her room's utter lack of structure. She exercises every kind of power over her room, even that of destructuring it, and that structure (or non-structure): independent of the house-structure. Indeed, the luxury of the bedroom derives from its freedom: a structure protected from all norms, all powers; as a structure – and exorbitant paradox: it's unique. (2013, 53–54)

In contrast to Michelet who 'was able to write virtually nothing about his own time' (1984, 69), across his career Barthes stands in an oblique but engaged relationship to the moment. We saw in Chapter One how this structure plays out in notions of love, both in Barthes's experience and discussion of the sanatorium during the War and in the discussion of Goethe's Werther who, in *A Lover's Discourse*, is shown stuck in his structure. Barthes is aware of the complexity of the public/private dialectic:

> a utopia of idiorrythmic Living-Together is not a social utopia. Now, from Plato to Fourier, all written utopias have been social: an attempt to fix upon the ideal organisation of power. Personally, I have often regretted the fact that there hasn't been, I have often felt the desire to write a domestic utopia: an ideal (happy) manner of figuring, of anticipating the subject's optimum relation to affect, to the symbolic. [...] Only a written form would be capable of taking account of that – or, if you prefer, a novelistic act (if not a novel). Only writing is capable of picking out extreme subjectivity because only in writing is there a concord between the indirectness of the expression and the truth of the subject – concord that's impossible on the level of speech (and so impossible to achieve in a lecture course) because, whatever our intentions, speech is always both direct and theatrical. (2013, 130–31)

It is easy to forget that Barthes's early interest in Michelet involves a 'living together' too, even in the very historiography of the 'double grasp' that allows the historian to 'walk with' the people who are in the historical narrative being written. In the 'late' Barthes, this temporalism is conveyed in a dialectical manner: 'How to reconcile – dialecticize – the *distance* implied by the *enunciation of writing* and the *proximity*, the transportation of the present experienced as it happens?' (2011b, 17).

The late Barthes theorizes this aspect of the writer in spatial terms:

> The writer's *place*: the Margins? There are so many: there ends up being an arrogance of the Marginality – I prefer to replace it with the Image of the Interstice: the Writer = person of the Interstice. (2011b, 298)

Yet, this is also subjected to the temporality of Kairos or 'timing', what he calls the 'contingency', which is 'an exalted image of the Neutral as nonsystem, as nonlaw, or art of the nonlaw, of the nonsystem' (2005, 171). Barthes sees this living together as part, paradoxically, of a solitude:

> In Fourier, the fantasy of the Phalanstery doesn't spring from the oppression of solitude but, paradoxically, from a fondness for solitude: 'I like being alone'. The fantasy isn't a counternegation, it is not the site of a frustration experienced as its opposite: eudemonic visions coexist without contradicting each other. Fantasy: an absolutely positive scenario

that stages the positives of desire, that knows only positives. In other words, fantasy isn't dialectical (clearly!). Fantasmatically speaking, there is nothing contradictory about wanting to live alone and wanting to live together = our lecture course. (2013, 4–5)

In a 1978 interview, Barthes proposes, somewhat ironically, that it is 'scandalous' for him to searching for a 'philosophy' of the subject, outside of the 'imperatives of collectivism' (1985a, 311) that have dominated 'since Hegel'. This too is part of the Nietzschean *for me* strategy:

I belong to a generation that has suffered too much from the censorship of the subject, whether following the positivist route (the objectivity required by literary history, the triumph of philology), or the Marxist (very important – even if it no longer seems so – in my life). Better the illusions of subjectivity than the impostures of objectivity. Better the Imaginary of the Subject than its censorship. (2011b, 3)

The *For me* raises then the question of whether, and if so how, Barthes uses the dialectic.

Chapter Nine

'UNDIALECTICS'

Politics of Biography

In Chapter One, we considered the merits and appropriateness of looking at Barthes's thought and writing in a backwards, and anti-teleological, fashion. This was part of a concern to present his work in an equalized if not non-hierarchical manner that tried to disallow any privileging of the later ideas in ways that downplayed the political Barthes in favour of the aesthete. In this final chapter, we pursue the de-hierarchization of the aesthetic over the political by considering the political import of inverting History through a consideration of what we might call Barthesian dialectics: or, the 'undialectical'.

In his biography of himself (1994, 68–69), Barthes uses the figure of the spiral to account for the way in which he sees his thought returning in different forms and in different places along his career. Indeed, the spiral goes to the heart of the Barthesian conception of the dialectic, in all its guises:

> The symbolism of the spiral is the opposite of that of the circle; the circle is religious, theological; the spiral, a kind of circle distended to infinity, is dialectical: on the spiral, things recur, but *at another level*: there is a return in difference, not repetition in identity. [...] The spiral governs the dialectic of the old and the new; thanks to it, we need not believe: *everything has been said*, or: *nothing has been said*, but rather: nothing is first yet everything is new. (1985b, 218–19)

How then does the spiral – alongside the doubles, circles, returns that we have identified in Barthes's work – fit with the 'undialectical'?

Though Barthes's 'undialectical' appeared to be used in some sense negatively in relation to Sartre and Marx's inability to use language dialectically (and thereby get beyond paradox), this turns around in *Camera Lucida*. Following his mother's death, his own death suddenly appears to him 'undialectical'; for, since he has no offspring, 'the only biography is of an unproductive life', that of a 'being *pour rien*' (1994, 5, 21). In line with the Hegelian dialectic, his own death to come will produce nothing (1984, 71–72). Except that Barthes reverses chronology in the light of this non-dialectical (or anti-dialectical) situation, by considering his recently deceased mother as his daughter, as a product of his own life, and then proceeding to immortalize her by inscribing her into his essay on photography. In good essayistic fashion – that is, provisionally, provocatively, via photography, or rather via a photograph (a portrait of his mother as a young girl, the 'winter-garden' image which we never see) – this moment suggests that the final essay of his career has actually managed to inscribe his own mother into immortality, albeit in a purely writerly or intellectual manner. At the same Photography is also un-dialectical:

> [I]f dialectic is that thought which masters the corruptible and converts the negation of death into the power to work, then the photograph is undialectical: it is a denatured theater where death cannot 'be contemplated', reflected and interiorized; or again: the dead theater of Death, the foreclosure of the Tragic, excludes all purification, all *catharsis*. I may well worship an Image, a Painting, a Statue, but a photograph? (1984, 90)

It is this raising of the undialectical, the negatively undialectical of Photography (i.e., unproductive, without trace, empty in future terms), to the positive, even voluntarist, *Aufhebung* of production, that should be underlined.

As an attempt, which is finally in vain, by Barthes to turn things around, to reverse Time, and thereby overcome death, the idea of a life that is 'undialectical' is indebted to Edgar Morin and to his thesis on the history of death, first published just as they first met in 1951 and the same year as an important article by Barthes, 'Michelet, l'Histoire et la Mort' (2002, I, 109–123). The reference to Morin's work on death in the original French version (2002, V, 848) of *Camera Lucida* – but not included in the English version – also mentions the Hegelian view of the dialectics of death (Morin 1970 [1951], 287).

Shapiro (1989) points out that Hegel 'formulated the principle that the child is the death of its parents' as part of human dialectics, and hence that Barthes's own death, given his childlessness, is 'undialectical'. It is as if the idea of an undialectical being applied to himself in 1980 meant that – and lightly modifying the comment on writers 'not dialecticizing the world' but rather 'dialecticizing themselves' quoted in previous chapters – Barthes had in fact 'undialecticized' himself!

Indeed, it was Marx in *The Holy Family* who had noticed this backwards (dare we say, proto-deconstructionist?) mode in Hegel's thought: 'In Hegel's philosophy of History, as in his philosophy of nature, the son engenders the mother, the spirit nature, the Christian religion paganism, the result the beginning' (Marx 1845, chapter 8a).

In her biography (2012), Gil very persuasively places 'oscillation' as the fundamental figure and movement of Barthes's life; and, using a reverse trajectory, she highlights, as we saw in Chapter One, the paradox whereby the tragedy – the major event in Barthes's life, in her view – comes only at the very end of his life, when his mother dies only three years before he does (Gil 2012, ch. 0). Gil argues that Barthes never gets beyond 'oscillation' – might we say 'double grasp'? – until his mother dies, which opens up in philosophical terms the whole question of the 'undialectical', and the *mathesis* of the singular person that his mother represents.

Barthes pursues endlessly attempts not only to 'structuralize' phenomena – to show objects in their irreducible difference to their binary opposite(s) – but also to place them in their material and signifying relation to a social (albeit moving) totality; and this totality, at least in early Barthesian thought of the 1950s, is tightly linked to a complex conception of history and history-writing, via the nineteenth-century historian Jules Michelet, which considered how the human individual signifies, often in very different ways, across history. But crucially, Barthes wanted an eagle-eyed view of the subject acting in history, which, whilst considering the complex acts of signification that an individual can play across different epochs and places (especially once dead), also insists on a close-up link to that person in their own time of living. The idea of an eagle being able to see both the large historical landscape and a close-up of the actant in their own time is figured in Barthes's writing by a different metaphor, as we saw in Chapter Four, in that of walking 'with' a person in history and, at the same time, walking ahead of them by considering the same person from the vantage point of a later historical moment – or what E. P. Thompson called the 'enormous condescension of posterity'.

In line with this de-hierarchization, Steven Ungar argues that we should neither read Barthes 'via Proust nor Proust [...] within Barthes, but as an ongoing interplay between the two'; (1982, 8–9), and Champagne (1982) that Barthes is 'inverting' literary history with respect to Pierre Guyotat, Sade, Genet, Mallarmé and Artaud on the one hand, and La Bruyère and classical Greek rhetoricians on the other.

'Life as text'

> 'There is only one way left to escape the
> alienation of present-day society: to retreat
> ahead of it.'
>
> (Barthes 1975, 40)

Gil's psychoanalytical approach to her essayistic biography of Barthes and its attendant acts of inversion offers other deconstructive views of his life, linked to his family. Having set out the 'hole' forged by his father's tragic death in 1916 and its links to Barthes's writing (and especially to that of the fragment), she puts forward a number of family 'fictions', all of which are counter-doxal because they represent temporal inversions that are impossible in strictly historicist terms. First, Gil underlines how Barthes's mother became progressively like a girl to him, even like his own 'daughter', suggesting this as the significance of his trawl through photography to refind his recently deceased mother:

> The Greeks entered into Death backward: what they had before them was their past. In the same way I worked back through a life, not my own, but the life of someone I love. Starting from her latest image, [...] I arrived, traversing three-quarters of a century, at the image of a child. (1984, 71)

If the first half of *Camera Lucida* covers Barthes's own life and career, the second half is a 'walking back up' through his mother's. All that her death does, argues Gil in an example of Freudian *Nachträglichkeit* in which 'an effect turned out to be its own cause' (Jameson 2010, 38), is to reveal to Barthes the 'emptiness' or 'lack [manque]' across his life which writing (at least up until his mother's death) served to cover over. In other words, 'Mam'– Henriette Barthes – filled that void until 1977; and this, in Gil's 'biographical essay', is the organizing factor of Barthes's life, the 'problem' then being that this organizing principle is not revealed until three years before his own death. Gil's metaphor (25) of the (analogue) photograph and its negative coming into view as a positive image allows her to see that the death of Henriette and Barthes's subsequent death are but the beginning of 'life as text', redolent of the etymology of the word 'biography': 'life writing'.

Hence the photographic 'revelation' for Gil in *Camera Lucida* is doubly significant. Not only do we see 'Mam's' importance to Barthes; but also, 'by inversion of the chronology' – the 'undialectical' – 'the Mother makes Barthes's life into a "photograph", she reveals, by a process of inversion, the "photo" that is his life;' thus, with great historical irony, it would appear that 'Mam', finally, gives posterity to him (Gil 484–85).

Jane Gallop objects to this Mother as object and son-writer as subject, calling it 'troublingly personal, anecdotal and self-concerned' (cited in Nelson 2015, 42). But, insists Gil, this 'turning-the-tables [retournement]' of life, a 'suppression [disparition] of chronological time', is central to the final writerly (and life) strategy that Barthes devises before his own death in 1980: the 'Vita Nova'. As well as Mam's death in 1977 being the end of the first part of Barthes's life-as-text (Gil 2012, 18–19), the 'vita nova' is the moment for Barthes to look back(wards): 'I who had not procreated, I had, in her very illness, engendered my mother' (1984, 72). Barthes even sees a projection of her death, backwards as it were, on to his own (near) death between 1942 and 1946 while he was recovering in a sanatorium for tuberculosis. In his *Mourning Diary*, Barthes's deep chagrin at her death even up-ends time in his use of the quotation from the British psychoanalyst D. W. Winnicott: '*I fear a catastrophe that has already occurred*' (2010b, 203). Her demise even inverts identities: 'henceforth and forever I am my own mother' (2010b, 37). The inversion that Gil underlines (53) links up with bigger social and historical issues in Barthes's world. Due to his father's death on active service in World War I when he was one-year old, Barthes's grandparents played a significant role in his younger life – Barthes even attributes his interest in Proust to his own nostalgia for their generation (that is, the generation living at the end of the nineteenth century). Indeed, argues Gil, his maternal grandfather – Louis Binger, the explorer and reader of Jules Verne – is a part of the 'matrix figure [matricielle]', but crucially, she points out deconstructively, as far as the grandchild is concerned, grandparents come via your parents. So backwards biography might even wish to walk back further than Barthes's own life (1980>1915), and up into the nineteenth century, whereby, by osmosis, Barthes 'lived' the *belle époque* and before (around 1875), through a physical and memorial contiguity with his grandparents.

Barthes, Dialectician? In the Final Instance?

Not only a gentle allusion to the famous exhortation by Arthur Rimbaud in the final 'Adieu' section of his 1873 writings *A Season in Hell* 'One must be absolutely modern' (Rimbaud 1973, 105), the ironic injunction by Barthes 'we *must* be dialectical' (1972, 146n3) – with the 'we must' written in italics in the original French [*Il faut* être dialectique] – suggests that it is the position, the positioning, of the person analysing the outside world that counts for more than the objective nature of that outside world. Henri Meschonnic (cited in Garnier 2009, 9) maintains that Rimbaud too understood his injunction ironically. Rimbaud's modernity is intrinsically linked to his refusal of the 'modern'. Therefore, by the same token, is Barthes being dialectical in his refusal of dialectics?

Though Saussurean linguistics is based on a differential model of analysis that places the unity of opposites at the base of its method, structuralism develops this unity of opposites towards an unsynthesized, open-ended and formalist, dialectic that seems, at once, to eschew the Hegelian and Marxian one and, simultaneously, to posit a hyper-dialectical sensibility. Indeed, in a recent review article on Marxism and contradiction, Joshua Moufawad-Paul (2020) complains that the word 'dialectical' is often employed 'like a magical wand to sanctify various relational phenomena'; and that, consequently, 'dialectical and relational are taken to be synonymous [...] [and] the term "dialectical relationship" is a tautology'. Is this the case with Barthes?

Such is the regularity with which Barthes invokes dialectical thought and the inventiveness with which he designs and provisionally recommends nuances, modifications and neologisms. As well as the 'internal dialectic' which we considered in Chapter One, we have seen the 'amorous dialectic' and the 'amputated dialectic' in exposing myth, the 'two-term (or two-stroke) dialectic' in Michelet, all coined in his early career; and later, the 'new dialectic' found in Japan.

Barthes's reticence in 1960 to '*having* to be' dialectical is possibly influenced by Edgar Morin's hesitation with the dialectic (Morin 1975 [1959], 45–46), and undoubtedly connected to the publication the same year of Sartre's *magnum opus* on the dialectic. Sartre defines it antithetically, the 'anti-dialectical' being the 'intelligible moment of transcendence by materiality of individual free praxes, inasmuch as these are multiple (1991b, 456); indeed, the resultant 'practico-inert' in Sartrean thought is certainly linked to the functionalist-impersonalism we identified in *Mythologies*. Nevertheless, the alienation that anti-dialectical thought entails (Poster 1979, 37, 59) underlines that the Sartrean dialectic is synonymous with totality; and this is at odds with Barthes's growing interest in the late 1950s in the structure of the 'detail', be it in Brechtian theatre, in photography or in fashion (Barthes 2006a, 139–40). Furthermore, in the first volume, Sartre argues that though language is the 'common bond' between 'inter-individual structures' and represents an act 'which *actually* exists at every moment of History' (1991a, 99), language is nevertheless to be taken as a 'dispersal' not an act of 'totality', and which means considering humans as 'individuals [...] who are completely isolated': for Sartre, in good Hegelian fashion, the individual's 'absolute exteriority' is 'their concrete historical bond of interiority' (100). Sartre's view in 1960 of atomized individuals is likely of no use to the semiology and structuralism that Barthes is developing; and nor does it suggest that language could actually *be* dialectical.

In so doing, Barthes was gesturing towards the 'parametrism' that he would go on to praise in 1965 in his newspaper appreciation of Morin's 'dialectical writing' which we considered in Chapter Seven. The strength of this idea about language furthermore is shown by its repetition across Barthes's *œuvre*. In his 1971 piece 'Writers, Intellectuals, Teachers', for example, he underlines, once more, how language is 'undialectical': 'language [...] allows only a movement in two stages [...] (does not allow the third term other than as pure oratorical flourish, rhetorical assertion, pious hope)' (1982a, 388).

If Barthes can be considered a dialectical thinker and writer, if not an analyst of the dialectic, writing on and with the dialectic, how do we get at this dialectic in operation in his work? This is a major difficulty with his writing, with the following three options all to be avoided (at least in relation to Barthes). First, despite Marty's recent affirmations (2015, 2018) of a 'philosophical' Barthes, we must resist a simple discussion of the dialectic in philosophical terms, as this would ignore the 'suppleness' of the Barthesian dialectic. Second, and in contrast, any analysis of the dialectic that privileges the play(fullness) of writing no doubt overlooks the 'responsibility', political or intellectual, that guides Barthes; for, even in those writings not published in his lifetime such as the diaries written in China, Barthes feels the urgent need, as we saw, to write in a dialectical – rather than what Leys calls an 'abyssal' – manner. Finally, though it might be tempting to consider the Barthesian dialectic as a dialectical unity of these first two options – indeed, we will be analysing the 'responsible' nature of the 'play' of language – it may well be too tidy a way to intertwine (our) analysis and (Barthes's) writing.

The non-systematic, even down-right contradictory, way in which Barthes deploys the dialectic notwithstanding, we can affirm that, as a philosophical category and method of analysis, the dialectic in his work is both classical and modern, as devised by Hegel and then Marx, but reinvented in the structuralist and poststructuralist age (Kowalska 2015). The ambiguity in his attitude towards the dialectic, at the same time, is contained in the 'amputated' dialectic, itself considered by Barthes in dialectical fashion, and this will become, in the 1970s, a fascination for the figure of the 'spiral'. The spiral – '[t]hat dimension [temps] which is necessary for the dialectic' (2010a, 274) – goes a long way in explaining the complex and tortuous trajectory that he sees in his own work (as he looks back over it in 1973); and this is true even in the fragment 'Dialectics' in *Roland Barthes by Roland Barthes*, where he is reluctant to propose that the spiral might be, for him, the third term of the dialectic that is missing in his work, preferring to the synthesis, a '*translation* [déport]' (1994, 68–69). By an interesting parallel, Barthes and Derrida in their early careers are both impressed by the work of Tran Duc Thao in *Phénoménologie et matérialisme dialectique* (1971), which Barthes favourably reviews in *Combat* in 1951 (2015b, 17–19) and from which Derrida takes inspiration in his postgraduate studies – indeed, Jameson (2010, 103) regrets that Derrida then excises most of the work on Duc Thao's dialectical formulations from his 1954 masters' thesis on Husserl (2003).

Morin and 'parametrism'

'And even when I am
affirming, I am still asking.'

(Jacques Rigaut, cited by Barthes, 2002, I, 524)

In Chapter Seven, we looked briefly at Barthes's 1965 article praising Morin's 'dialectical writing'. The praise contains much that could be called Hegelian formalism, promoting an 'open', two-term dialectic, that is not synthesized as it would be for Marx; and Barthes uses elements of Marx's early thought to do this. 'The World as Object', in its original 1953 version, has as its epigraph a quotation from Marx (1953b, 394): 'History solves the old questions only by setting itself new ones' (and repeated in his 1965 article on Morin, 2015a, 59). Written in an unfinished 1842 article (1975b, 182–183), this quotation from Marx seems to nuance sharply Kostas Axelos' view that Marx did not only want simply to get beyond Hegelian contradictions but also 'suppress' them (Axelos 1976, 204–209).

'The World as Object' displays a highly Goldmannian analysis of class vision/outlook, which, in turn, Goldmann had borrowed from the early Lukács. Barthes here and Goldmann in *The Hidden God* point to the way in which seventeenth-century philosophers (for Goldmann) and the Dutch Masters of the same century (for Barthes) were unable to get beyond the bourgeois ideology of their masters. Barthes uses Marx's quote, in the 1953 essay on seventeenth-century Dutch painting, as part of his 'degree zero' thesis on the *longue durée*. If we remember from Chapter Eight, the *longue durée* is used to describe the slow manner in which bourgeois ideology came to ideological power not spontaneously with the Glorious Revolution of 1789–94 that handed political power to the bourgeois class, but over centuries of ideologico-cultural implantation and socio-economic ascendancy. But here, in 1965, Barthes's dialectical understanding is applied, using the same quote from Marx, to the relationship between research on the one hand, and the writing-up of this research on the other, as found in Morin's work. Barthes uses Marx's (somewhat enigmatic) quotation to illustrate the 'open' dialectic used by Morin, but without ignoring his own earlier views on the non-dialectics of language, to see whether, though research can be dialectical, writing itself tends to fail to be dialectical.

Barthes begins by describing Morin's work as triply dialectical: first, in its inspiration from Hegel and Marx (2015a, 58); second, in its understanding of the contradictory forces operating on any one phenomenon in history and which Morin is not afraid to totalize in the way that Morin includes the future as a 'natural dimension of time'; finally, and most importantly, in its 'dialectical imagination', or rather, Barthes corrects himself, in its 'imaginative' approach, in its ability to '*see* ideas, not separately or as classified culturally or tied to other ideas or phenomena, but as a kind of nomadic substance for which, from one end to the other (from Freud to Marx, and from revolution to science), books provide an enormous territory of migration' (58). While this imagination in Morin's work is 'forward-looking and syncretic', it remains critical: 'it sees with equal force what is, what should not be and what ought to be'. Barthes then cites the key phrase by Morin, and which is crucial to the dialectic at work in his research: '"The principle of synthesis in no sense extinguishes the principle of antagonism"'.

In his 1957 piece 'Brecht, Marx et l'Histoire', Barthes argues a parallel point about Brecht's use of history in relation to Marx and Engel's conception of the representation of history in theatre; unlike the views of Marx and Engels, Brecht's theatre, wrote Barthes, 'provokes History but does not divulge it, [...] poses the burning problem of History without resolving it' (2002, I, 909). Similarly, it is by following this non-synthesized dialectic that Morin's writing can take up this 'wager [which] is not easy', whereby in the modern period – as opposed to 'the time of Bonald, Fourier and Michelet' – the dialectic 'imposes infinitely more severe demands than utopia' (2015a, 59). However, 'against dialectical development', reiterates Barthes, 'language puts up a natural resistance, because language is linear and monodic'. The structure of language, in which the multiple phenomena *all at once* that is reality, can indeed be represented in language but only in series, 'one after the other'. Thus, analysis is language's domain, not synthesis nor antagonism; and, in a premonition of the *post*-structuralist insistence on *différance* – as opposed to the more static *différence* of structuralism (*différer* in French, as Derrida famously pointed out, means 'to defer' as well as 'to differ') – Barthes insists on the *temporal* aspect to meaning in a sentence as indicative of language's *in*ability to say more than one thing at once, of its failure to be dialectical (2015a, 59).

Indeed Morin, says Barthes, has unceasingly to live with this 'squaring of the circle', in which his writing (Barthes does not give any direct examples from Morin's work) is 'both direct and baroque, vigorous and *précieuse*, situated outside of literature and within rhetoric', as it attempts to impose on language that which the latter rejects the most: 'a dialectical dimension'. Barthes now cites the quote from Marx above to illustrate the dialectic in Morin's writing, how it hoists the problems encountered onto a higher, unexpected level:

> As soon as the antinomy threatens to solidify, Morin shifts it 'elsewhere', provides new terms to surround it and modify the system of which it was part [...]. In this way, he effects a real broadening of meaning. (2015a, 59)

Clearly thinking back to the Saussurean model of the sign that he had illustrated in 'Myth Today', Barthes suggests that this enlarging of meaning is not a metaphor, since a sign can have meaning only if it can be integrated into a higher order, a word being a word only because it is in a sentence. Thus, Morin's skill, says Barthes, is to take the fragmentary and heteroclite sign and to try and always imagine a 'sentence', or wider horizon, that can underpin meaning: 'This, for Morin, is what gives dialectical discourse its impetus' (60); but the movement that it entails is maintained at the level of writing. This is Morin's 'gongorism', suggests Barthes; and it is whilst describing this 'gongorism' that he now returns to his idea that writing cannot itself be dialectical. Luis de Góngora (1561–1627) was a Spanish poet known for his florid, obscure, baroque rhetoric that deploys paradoxes and puns; and in so doing, Barthes pursues the points on language and dialectics that he makes in 'Authors and Writers' (1972, 143–150).

Given that reality is *'several things at the same time'* – that is, contradictory, even dialectical –, the language of a writer is obliged to list these contradictory realities one after the other, that is, only in serial, not synthetic, fashion. Thus 'a writer', asserts Barthes, 'can declare the dialectic, but not represent it' (2015a, 59). Morin's work, however, and especially his writing in Barthes's view, seems to get around this problem. One aspect of Morin's 'being dialectical' appeared, to Barthes, to be the ability to mobilize and then manipulate facts in such a way as to show their plurality:

> a thing is never presented without its contradictory attributes, a fact is only ever defined as the – falsely symmetrical - *crossing* of a number of terms (the 'chiasmus' of old). Rhetoric here becomes a genuine dialectical instrument because in reality only form can, in the last instance, correct language's impotence to bring order to its movement, its contrariness and, generally, its *other* logic. (60)

It is, 'in the end, the expression of a serious struggle', the stakes of which are normally hidden by the 'flatness' of classical language and its desire for 'taste' and by the 'unhealthy ablutionism of the language purists'. The author [écrivain], says Barthes gesturing back to his thesis in 'Authors and Writers', 'is doomed never to produce anything concrete'; but, 'by *choosing* the way [they] speak, [the writer] can come close, through fascination, to what reality accomplishes through construction'; and this is the case for Morin: 'by setting out in a thousand ways the contrary aspects and future dimensions of phenomena, [Morin's writing] eventually drives home the need for a dialectical approach' (60). This is done, suggests Barthes, in such a way that, having read Morin, it is impossible to see things 'from just one side'; or at least, to insist on doing so is to be regretted.

There is clearly a gesture not just forwards to post-structuralism, but backwards, with the reference to rhetoric and dialectic, towards Aristotle. Writing about a parallel project that Barthes is running on Rhetoric at the same time as his 1965 essay on Morin, Barthes wonders whether Aristotle is not the key philosopher of 'so-called mass' contemporary culture and of that which underpins any critique of this culture; indeed, he argues, Aristotle's *Rhetoric* is actively beholden to the '"psychology" of the public' (1987b, 22–23). This is a dialectical understanding of culture if ever there was one; but this is not Barthes's main point. As so often with his enigmatic descriptions of others' writing, it is perhaps more of an injunction to himself on how to write (or in any other cases, how *not* to write). It will be instructive therefore to finish this consideration of language and dialectics by looking at Barthes's views on Marx and language.

Following May 1968, in the years of turmoil 1969–72, Barthes moves back, if only briefly, to Marx, having seemingly left behind his thought and writing, from 1957 onwards, for the euphoria of semiology that lasted, at least, until 1967.

'The "Capital" of Linguistic Science'

> [W]hat, *at the level of discourse*, distinguishes
> dialectics from compromise?
>
> (Barthes 1982a, 398)

It has been often suggested that since Marx defines Capital as a relation he was one of the first Structuralists (Godelier 1970). Barthes's return to Marx in 1971 (following over a decade of intensive semiological research across the 1960s) entails the outline of a new, startling project. In an interview, he expresses the desire to work on a political theory of language. What is striking about this suggestion is not so much the political nature of the project – we are, after all, in the ultra-radical period that followed the first phase of May 1968, with the Maoist turn, in particular of *Tel Quel*, now underway – but the parallel that he gives to the project: 'something like the *Capital* of linguistics' (1985a, 121). Reacting to the interviewer's assertion that language is not a 'superstructure', Barthes suggests that, whether language is a superstructure or not, 'the rapport with language is political'. He qualifies this by adding that one would not know it in a country like France which is historically and culturally '"compressed [tassée]"' and where 'the French are merely *asleep* in relation to their language, they have been chloroformed by centuries of classical authority', in contrast to those that are 'less well-off' such as Arab countries emerging from colonialism (and no doubt specifically Morocco, from where he has recently returned), where the link between language and politics is a 'burning' question. Nevertheless, drawing on his recent experience of teaching in Moroccan universities, he perceives a reactionary idea in such countries embarrassed by the old colonial language that one can separate language from literature, that one can teach the former without the latter just because the latter is considered 'bourgeois'. It is worth quoting the description of Barthes's imagined '*Capital* of linguistics' in full:

> There is no political theory of language, a methodology that would expose language's processes of *appropriation* and permit study of the 'propriety' of enunciative means[.] (1985a, 121)

One might argue that Barthes has already done this, to some extent at least, in his acts of demystification in the 1950s. Suddenly, however, Marx returns to Barthes's sights in the wake of the radical sixties, not in the tragedy-farce spiral so beloved of Marx, rather in a replay of the phosphorus metaphor that is deployed in *Writing Degree Zero* (1967a, 44): Barthes's explicit interest in Marx here in 1971, not so long before his description in 1977 of Marxism's deployment as 'stupidity' (1986, 351), seems to burn most brightly when it is close to extinguishing itself.

In his contribution to the 1971 special number of *Tel Quel* on his own *œuvre*, 'Writers, Intellectuals, Teachers', Barthes returns, in a brief section called 'The chain of discourses', to the idea that we saw above that language cannot itself be dialectical. In contrast to his view of Morin's 'dialectical writing', he now argues that Marx, despite his intense and crucial use of the dialectic, is not at all a dialectical writer. Barthes's argument – not dissimilar to the comments on the language of contradiction used by Marx in the *Communist Manifesto* that Marcuse makes (1991 [1964], 103–04) – relies on what he has said already about the linear, monadic nature of the language being not conducive to language having an ability to show the contradictory, multiple sides to reality. He uses the examples of Chomsky's theories as a rebuttal of Bloomfield's behaviourism and then semiotics' supersession of Chomsky's 'mentalism (or anthropologism)', in order to suggest that 'a new discourse can only emerge as the *paradox* which goes against (and often goes for) the surrounding or preceding *doxa*, can only see the day as difference, distinction, working loose *against* that which sticks to it' (1982a, 388). Having suggested that Marx's 'discourse is almost entirely *paradoxical*, the *doxa* being Proudhon, now someone else, and so on', he moves, with Marx, towards Vico and the two-term dialectic of the spiral:

> This twofold movement of separation and renewal results not in a circle but [...] in a spiral, and it is in this *drift* of circularity (of paradoxical form) that historical determinations are articulated. (1982a, 388)

It is precisely this (somewhat surprising) view of Marx's own 'undialectical' language that leads Barthes towards a two-term dialectic in his own writing. The 'undialectical' nature of (even) revolutionary language resembles the 'ideologism' as the only option open for the mythologist that we discussed in Chapter Two and which, in the absence of any sight of the 'Promised Land', truncates the form and outcome of its critique. Indeed, Hill supplies a good description of this unsynthesized dialectic (2010, 130–31).

White (2012, 171) argues that this discussion shows Barthes asserting that 'dialectical thinking simply does not exist'; only for White then to contradict himself somewhat, a few lines later, when he suggests that Barthes's fragment tries 'to give an alternative of [sic] dialectical thinking'. White seems to agree with Barthes that Marx's writing is 'paradoxical', not dialectical; but this is possibly a result of both Barthes's and White's arguments working with a limited set of examples, that is 'Proudhon etc'. It would seem however that Marx is, at different times, 'paradoxical' in Barthes's sense and also (classically) dialectical, depending on the context.

Though Barthes is clearly influenced by Althusserian categories in 1971 – especially the 'epistemological break' that Althusser sees Marx operating, largely, in *The German Ideology* – the above formulation does not seem Althusserian in any way (Lecercle 2008). Nevertheless, Barthes's 'structuralist' conception of language fits with Althusser's stress on relationality, what Callinicos (2014, 317) calls 'the ontological primacy of relations'. In this conception Althusser rejects the 'humanist historicism' of certain Marxists who maintain that social (including ideological and political) relations under capitalism are 'inter-human, inter-subjective'; whereas, for Althusser, humans are 'agents of the production process and the *material conditions* of the production process, in specific "combinations"' (Callinicos 2014, 317–18). Indeed, Barthes's assertion of the crucial element of the *combinatoire* in all forms of language and communication dovetails with Althusser's relationism.

Furthermore, in *'Pax culturalis'* (1986, 100–05), Barthes sets out how language is deeply class-divided, carrying this argument into the 'Writers, Intellectuals, Teachers'. Unlike in Marx's time, the modern world of mass communication facing the proletariat requires '*representatives*... in a word, *oblates* who devote themselves to the proletarian interpretation of cultural facts' (1982a, 398). But, as 'Myth Today' articulates with regard to the mythologist's exclusion from the proletariat, these 'oblates' have a 'class situation [which] is not that of the proletariat'. Furthermore, if the proletariat is '*separated*' from intellectuals by its petty-bourgeois culture and is 'mute' because it is cut off from intellectuals (and whose radical critique is the 'unconscious' of the intellectual), how, asks Barthes, do we join 'the materialist and the Freudian dialectics'? In a replay (or spiral) of his 'Promised Land' in 'Myth Today' whereby the dialectic cannot act, Barthes in 1971 is only more convinced that the language of materialist cultural critique does not speak for the masses, that it can only be 'a silk shot through with tactics [une moire de tactiques]' (398; see also 2010a, 336). By suggesting that this 'moire de tactiques' has to be mobile because different arguments over the complexity of contemporary mass culture are 'occasionally contradictory' and above all 'established on different temporalities [*temps*, in italics in French]', Barthes seems to be moving his point about language not being dialectical – but monodic and linear – onto the level of cultural critique (which is for Barthes, after all, only language).

One answer to his conundrum cited as the epigraph above, about dialectic as compromise, is that offered by *Tel Quel* in its Maoist phase of 1971 and to which Barthes alludes when he mentions those 'who finally prefer to give up the problem, to dismiss all '"culture" [...] entail[ing] the destruction of all discourse' (1982a, 398–99). But his chosen solution differs. He now vaunts the desire to write as Nietzsche does, 'from abyss to abyss' (1985a, 72). Indeed, this form of writing represents a striking continuity with his early work on Nietzsche's *The Birth of Tragedy* as discussed in his 1941 postgraduate thesis:

> In the incantations, intoxication and dialectics merge with one another; or rather, we make a mistake in dissociating them before merging them. They are but one, from the start: as witness – by dint of being harmonised before their birth – to the unique miracle that the Greeks continue to represent even to us, radiating prestige and mystery. They are spectacularly dedicated to the identification of Dionysus with Apollo, showing that we must not consider this union as a reconciliation or a later synthesis, but as a fusion by origin and nature. (1941, 138)

When Barthes suggests that the dialectic of criticism is one of tactics, it is indeed the writer who is dialecticized, and not the world. It is here that he seems supremely dialectical, in the 'compromising' sense mentioned above. The 'bastard type' (or 'third term') upon which he alights in 'Authors and Writers' in 1960 – with which to suggest that there are those writers who combine elements of Author *and* Writer – seems to summarize well his own approach to writing throughout his career.

Indeed, reviewing his own career in 1973 and 1974, Barthes feels strongly that, despite being 'bad, confused, useless', the distinction of the two types of writer in 'Authors and Writers' nevertheless remains tenable (Samoyault 2017, 419). If the formalist way in which Barthes understands and uses the dialectic resembles Merleau-Ponty's 'hyperdialectic' (1968, 91), we may be tempted also to modify slightly Barthes's enigmatic allusion to Rimbaud in '*il faut* être dialectique' to emphasize the idea differently: 'we must be *dialectical*'. Or rather: '*we must be* paradoxical'. We might add that a Frankfurt thinker such as Adorno is not a stranger to the use of paradox (Jameson 2010, 53), but Barthes differs in that he strategizes the paradox.

This 'paradoxism' – as we might call it – becomes part of a key strategy for Barthes in the wake of May '68, in which it is 'the endoxa' that is perceived as the enemy. He declares in 1971:

> [T]rue censorship, the ultimate censorship, does not consist in banning (in abridgment, in suppression, in deprivation), but in unduly fostering, in maintaining, retaining, stifling, getting bogged down in (intellectual, novelistic, erotic) stereotypes, in taking for nourishment only the received word of others, the repetitious matter of common opinion. The real instrument of censorship is not the police, it is the endoxa. Just as a language is better defined by what it obliges to be said (its obligatory rubrics) than by what it forbids to be said (its rhetorical rules), so social censorship is not found where speech is hindered, but where it is constrained to speak. (1989, 126, trans. mod.)

It is precisely this paradoxism that we now trace in relation to the dialectical, in the Hegelian notion that Barthes applied to Marx of the 'undialectical'.

'Undialectical' Marx and Hegel

> 'Mallarmé is supposed to have been
> cured by reading Hegel'
>
> *(Barthes 2011b, 254).*

It may be that one of the major characteristics – or tactics – of 'French Theory' is the deployment of 'undialectics'. From Lyotard's view of the singularity of the Holocaust (Shapiro 2004, 77n17) to Gilles Deleuze's 'what I most detested was Hegelianism and dialectics' (1995 [1973], 6), from Alain Badiou's 'politics as a nonexpressive dialectics' (2015, Chapter Three), to Derrida's work with Maurizio Ferraris (cited in Jameson 2010, 25–26) and Glissant's 'detour' (1981, 28–36), 'French Theory' has tried to modify and even overturn Hegel. Writers, thinkers, and crucially essayists in French since the 1950s, have engaged with, and then, attempted to overcome Hegelian dialectics, in what Kowalska (2015) calls 'dialectics after dialectics' and Gava (2011) 'contrariety without dialectics'. We will also suggest, tentatively, that the 'undialectical' displays affinities with Mao Tse-Tung's dialectical innovation.

Benoist (1970, 249–50) inaugurates a critical reading of Marx's language at the end of his post-May 1968 jeremiad. In Barthes's view, Marx's writing of 'the undialectical nature of language' creates a 'paradoxical writing' that could not but counter doxa (Proudhon's for example), but crucially his language was not able to operate on the world beyond anything more than a 'chain of discourse'. By raising the undialectical, the negatively undialectical (that is, unproductive, without trace, empty in future terms), to the positive, even voluntarist, *Aufhebung* of production, Barthes's 'undialectical' is not the anti- or the non-dialectical – the immobilized and ossified figure that *Mythologies* had considered as typical of, if not fundamental to, bourgeois and petty-bourgeois ideology and cultural hegemony. The 'undialectical', in other words, contains the dialectical; or rather, is not its polar opposite: acting more like a supplement, the dialectical in the 'undialectical' allows, paradoxically, for a productive, if not radical, form of critical praxis. In this sense, the 'undialectical' is to be sharply differentiated from the 'negative dialectics' of the Frankfurt School and of Western Marxism more generally. The 'undialectical', akin to Merleau-Ponty's 'hyper-dialectics', takes the dialectical to its formal and formalist extreme.

Indeed, it is a Nietzschean suspicion of Socratic dialectics that informs Barthes's approach to the dialectic. This reticence towards, or suspicion of, the written dialectic dovetails with Barthes's development of semiology and structuralist analyses.

This raises questions also about the constantly increasing importance of Hegel across Barthes's career, either as support for his ideas, more commonly though as foil. If both Bittner (2017) and Lübecker (2010) establish the Hegelian dimensions to the 'early Barthes's', both then skip to the 'late' Barthes. Bittner traces the 'absolute of literature' in the 1979 lectures on *The Preparation of the Novel*; whereas Lübecker considers Barthes's lectures on *How to Live Together*, adducing notions of community and distance that suggest an interpretation of Hegel in the 'late' Barthes at odds with Alexandre Kojève's insistence on recognition as the key element.

Indeed, Barthes's differences with Kojève's near-hegemonic imposition of his Hegel since the lectures he had given in Paris in the 1930s might have encouraged the humorous and ironic question Barthes poses: 'And if I hadn't read... ?' (1994, 100). Indeed, the idea that Barthes did not read Hegel is almost laughable, as his reading and use of Hegel is one of regularity and wide variety across his career. There is little doubt, for example, that he reads Hegel's essay on Dutch painting ([1827–30] 1964) before his visit to the Netherlands to view the painting of the Dutch masters in Delft and to write 'The World as Object' (1972, 3–12); but also that, given the Marx quote in the original epigraph, this profoundly historical-materialist reading of Dutch masters is, originally at least, Barthes's attempt to marxianize Hegel's aesthetics, just as the 'degree zero' thesis 'marxianized' Sartre's theories on literature and language.

The various iterations of dialectics in Barthes's work run alongside these 'dialectics after dialectics', but take a different route. The Barthesian dialectic – were there to be such a thing – moves towards a truly *writerly* praxis: or rather series of *essais* (experiments) in writing the dialectic, writing 'dialectically', in both signifier *and* signified. It is a sort of writing-constraint beloved of the OULIPO, but, as always with Barthes, 'responsible'. We will try to navigate the various engagements with both Hegel and Marx in Barthes's writings, without getting caught up in the lengthy debates over Marx's complex use and abandoning of Hegelian thought and method discussed recently by Callinicos (2014), Gava (2011) and Jameson (2010).

Gava's work on 'contrariety without dialectics' in Hegel and Marx gives us, however, a useful philosophical context to Barthes's suggestion that Marx's language itself is 'undialectical'. Acting more like a supplement, the dialectical in the undialectical allows, paradoxically, for a productive, if not radical, form of critical engagement. The 'undialectic' is Barthes's way to 'bend the stick' in the historical dialectic, towards a voluntarism of human agency, away from the determinism of passivity; in other words, to expose the malleability of human society in relation to its eternalist fixity.

This project in Barthes's work betrays a level of complexity because it involves a language-based investigation and theorization of Historical Materialism which will later in his career become a wider critique of the 'verisimilar' (Amossy 2002; Herschberg 2002). This does not in any way preclude a critique of Marxist language.

In 1953, Barthes describes Marxist writing as 'given to understatement [litotique]', in which 'each word is no longer anything but a narrow reference to the set of principles which tacitly underlie it' (1967a, 29). For example, by referring 'to a precise historical process', the frequently-used word 'imply' in Marxist writing eschews its neutral dictionary-definition like an 'algebraical sign representing a whole bracketed set of previous postulates': 'linked to action, Marxist writing has rapidly become a language expressing value judgments'; and this is, though 'in general explanatory', evident even in Marx's own writing. Barthes nuances his argument carefully however. Even though Stalinism builds on this 'value judgment' to create a language that is beholden to 'values' only and therefore purely 'tautological', he distinguishes Stalinized language from a true 'Marxist explanation of facts, or a revolutionary rationale of actions', in that Stalinized language describes the real merely 'in a prejudged form, [...] imposing a reading which involves immediate condemnation' (30) – what Marcuse calls (referring to Barthes's description of its 'closure') the 'self-validating enunciation' of the 'magic-authoritarian' (1991 [1964], 104).

Barthes's view that Marx's language is 'undialectical' is based on a reading of the famous 1847 critique of the anarchist maverick Pierre-Joseph Proudhon. If *The Holy Family* involved a defence of Proudhon's early critique of political economy, then *The Poverty of Philosophy*, Marx's first major critique of political economy, dismissed Proudhon's work for its use of Hegelian dialectics and for failing to rise 'above the bourgeois horizon'. Similarly, Max Raphael, whose work on ancient Greek tragedy we considered in Chapter Three, quoted Marx's view that Proudhon's petty-bourgeois mind was 'tossed back and forth' (1980, 71). For Marx, Proudhon failed to see that 'economic categories are only the theoretical expressions, the abstractions of the social relations of production'; 'holding things upside down like a true philosopher', Proudhon saw in actual relations 'nothing but the incarnation of these […] categories' (1847, Chapter Two:1, second observation).

Indeed, the very title of Marx's broadside against Proudhon illustrates Barthes's point about undialectical writing in Marx's work. The subtitle *La Misère de la philosophie* (originally written in French in 1847) – 'Une réponse à la philosophie de la misère par M. Proudhon' – was a direct inversion of the title of Proudhon's 1846 essay *Philosophie de la misère*, illustrating Marx's neatly-balanced, inverted paradox. Barthes does not mention an earlier Marx where, alongside Feuerbach's, the use of balanced and neatly chiselled paradox, or 'chiasmus', is widespread (Jameson 2010, 261); for example, in the *Introduction* to the *Critique of Hegel's Philosophy of Right* (1844) Marx famously wrote in maxim form: 'the weapon of criticism cannot replace the criticism of weapons' (1975a, 251); and on Feuerbach in 1841: 'Philosophy which begins with a thought without reality necessarily ends with a reality without thought' (Marx cited by Lucio Colletti in Marx 1975a, 24).

Unlike *The Holy Family* or *The 18th Brumaire of Louis Bonaparte*, we do not have any accurate record of Barthes's reading of *The Poverty of Philosophy* before his 1971 discussion of Marx's 'undialectical' language. Indeed, the only reference to Proudhon in the early Barthes is to the former's astoundment in 1858 at the politically-tortuous nature of Michelet's 'prodigious distance' (1987a, 202n1). However, we do find a distinctly Marxian paradox, an 'undialectic', in Barthes's 1958 critique of Voltaire that we looked at in Chapter Six.

Here Barthes writes a Marxian paradox whilst showing Voltaire's philosophical and political shortcomings: 'He has only one system and that is the hatred of system (and we know that there is nothing as fierce as the former system)' (1958, 15). In continually opposing 'intelligence' to 'intellectuality', Barthes's paradoxism argues, Voltaire had participated in a 'Manichean struggle between stupidity and intelligence' in which 'system' belonged to the former and 'all freedom of mind' to the latter (1972, 89). We will presently return to this opposition between 'stupidity' and 'intelligence'. Barthes's dialectical solution in 1958 to this paradox is to point to the liberalism that it founds, albeit a contradictory one:

> As system of the nonsystem, anti-intellectualism eludes and gains on both counts, perpetually ricocheting between bad faith and good conscience, between a pessimism of substance and a jig of form, between a proclaimed skepticism and a terrorist doubt. (89)

We saw in Chapter Six that, in opposition to Voltaire's 'incessant alibi' – 'this simplicity and this happiness [...] bought at the price of an ablation of History and of an immobilisation of the world' –, Barthes counterposes Rousseau's view of the corruption of humanity by society. However, one decade later in 1971, following his brief analysis of Marx's undialectical language and the resultant paradoxes, Barthes revisits his 1958 critique of Voltaire's lack of system. In 1966 he opposes to 'the poverty of Voltairean irony, the narcissistic product of a language with too much confidence in itself', a *'baroque'* irony that 'opens out language rather than shrinking it' (2007b, 38). Now in 1971, the baroque modifies the use of the paradox and suggests its radical potential:

> a system calling for corrections, translations, openings, and negations is more useful than an unformulated absence of system - one may then avoid the immobility of prattle and connect to the historical chain of discourses, the progress (progressus) of discursivity. (1982a, 388–389)

This is a good example of Barthes's own 'spiral'. Whereas in 1958 he resolves Voltaire's blockage of History by using the opposition of intellectual and anti-intellectual, here by contrast – faced with the same paradox – he now transcends the paradox with a forward-moving motion of the *à-coups* in Chomsky, but also of Marx's 'almost entirely' paradoxical language. For Barthes, the 'separation and renewal' involved in critiquing Proudhon, for example, does not lead to a circle but a spiral; this is thanks to the *'drift* [*déport*] of circularity (of paradoxical form)' in which the 'historical determinations' of Marx's writing could be articulated (388).

However, to get the measure of Barthes's 'undialectics' – his use of paradox – we must now consider the regular engagement with Hegel in his work.

According to Lucio Colletti (cited in Gava 2011, 245), rather than Hegel, the modern precursor of the theory of real oppositions is Kant. Nevertheless, in 1873, in the postface to the second edition of *Capital* volume 1, Marx suggested that Hegel's 'mystification' of the dialectic 'by no means prevents him from being the first to present its general forms of motion in a comprehensive and conscious manner' (1975c, 103). The battle over Hegel's dialectic thus already begun, and Barthes actively engages with both Marxian and Hegelian dialectical formulations, in particular via 'undialectics'.

Hegelian Paradox

We saw above how Barthes's very last essay, on Photography, adopts the notion of 'undialectics' to designate the (paradoxical) backwards movement of History (1984, 71–72). However, there is an equally telling deployment of Hegel at the very beginning of his career, in his 1942 article on André Gide:

> Let those who blame Gide for his contradictions (his refusal to choose among them) remember this page of Hegel: 'For common sense, an opposition between true and false is something fixed; common sense expects us to approve or to reject an existing system *en bloc*. It does not conceive the difference among philosophical systems as the gradual development of truth; for common sense diversity means only contradiction... The mind which grasps

contradiction cannot release it and keep it in its unilateralness and recognise (in the form of what seems to oppose and contradict itself) mutually necessary moments. (1982a, 6)

Quoting Hegel in 1942 from the second premise of the Preface to *The Phenomenology of Spirit* in order to defend contradiction in Gide's diaries might look like a hammer to crack a nut; but it underlines the radical spirit of contradiction, the sensitivity to dialectics, that the young Barthes is developing even before his initiation into Marxism three years later. With respect to the work on Barthes's engagement with Hegel by Bittner (2017) and Lübecker (2010), it is important not only to stretch the timescale of Hegelian thought in Barthes's work but also to consider the wider push-and-pull of Hegelianism.

Indeed, this oscillatory conception – dare we say 'two-term dialectic'? – in the early Barthes has its counterpart in the return in the 1978 lectures on *The Neutral* to Gide's 'concerned "hesitation"' around the image of themselves that the writer produces (2005, 131–133). However, he now contrasts Gide's with that adopted by his friend the novelist Philippe Sollers. Whereas Gide's tactic was one of building 'the stable image of the moving', Sollers's is that of jamming the image up as he 'prevents the image from taking':

[O]ne might feel that oscillation is some kind of tactic, a tool that the subject uses: to achieve what? Not a sublimation […] but, according to a less transcendent ethic, a 'perfect pitch' [justesse], what once upon a time one would have called [following Sartre] an 'authenticity': […] perhaps that's the point that could define a 'perfect pitch' of life […] and that would allow one to understand oscillation, alternation, as a 'desperate' tactic of the subject. (2005, 133)

This, in a sense, summarizes Barthes's regular (if minor) engagement with Hegelian thought. At times, there is a re-reading, re-ordering and even partial rejection of Hegel. For example, Hegel's philosophy of History is shown to be limited – like Michelet's – in its romanticist, organicist 'laws' of history (2015b, 4). More nuanced however is the use of Hegel by Barthes to understand the direction of meaning in clothing in relation to the body. Here, at various stages, Hegel's account of clothing, especially in the ancient Greece of his *Aesthetics*, is used in *The Fashion System* (1990b, 259) to underline the passage operated by clothing from body as 'pure sentience' to that of meaning; only then however for this passage to be subjected to Barthes's inversion of determinants: in his drawings, the illustrator Erté's silhouettes invert Hegel's schema, making 'the garment sensuous and the body into a signifier' (1985b, 107), a deconstructionist move in Barthes's analysis (Stafford, in Barthes 2006a, 153–56). There is little doubt that this inversion of determinants in Barthes's theories of clothing is linked to his suspicion of both Hegel and Marx who, in *On Racine*, are shown to have constructed systems of thought in which History and literary forms are too tightly connected and then fail to see the 'fundamental paradox': the work […] is both a sign of a history and a resistance to this history' (1992a, 155).

Importantly for Barthes then, critical practice needs to overcome the history-versus-literature dilemma:

[E]ither it is history, but then the work, literature evaporate, become a pure ideological reflection without qualification; or it is the Author, but then it is the powerful reality of the historical world that is bracketed out. (2002, I, 977)

However, this seemingly anti-determinist view is in fact a qualified, dialectical view which, as with Marx and Hegel's philosophy, insists on the double nature of reality.

Barthes's deployment of Hegelian categories raises questions as to his approach to dialectics. Bittner (2017, 4) draws on the early collaborative work of Jean-Luc Nancy and Phillipe Lacoue-Labarthe, and then on Philip Büttgen's theory, to underline the difference between *Aufhebung* and *Witz* in Hegel's writing. The latter involves a Cicero-inspired 'tollere' (elimination), in contrast to the *Aufhebung* that emphasizes the dialectic's preservation and raising. One question then is: do Barthes's various dialectical formulations partake in the *Witz*? Nancy and Lacoue-Labarthe do not see the *Witz* as anti-dialectical, rather as partaking in *Aufhebung*'s 'wish for system' [volonté du système]. In the wake of the 'Non-Vouloir-Saisir' (NVS), a resistance to volition, Barthes's final voluntarism is the 'will-to-write' (Bittner 2017, 2–3).

Barthes's most involved appreciation of Hegel however is in the relationship to Nature and reveals incipient voluntarism. We saw in Chapter Two how he nuances the cherry-tree metaphor in Marx and Engel's example of humanity's control over Nature by suggesting humanity's ability to act directly on the world, outside of the intransitivity of myth and language, characterized in the figure of the 'woodcutter'. This narrow route to a form of agency in the face of myth is also a crucial aspect of Barthes's argument that Blanchot (1957), in his otherwise thought-provoking review of *Mythologies*, inexplicably overlooks. Furthermore, 'Myth Today' involves a Marxian critique of Hegel. The dialectical structure of myth might have similarities to Hegel's 'Absolute Spirit' (Habib 2018, Chapter 8.1), but, citing Marx's critique of Hegel's definition of reality as one of 'pure essences', Habib argues that through myth Barthes presents the dialectic as a culmination of bourgeois ideology 'which reconciles, naturalizes and brings all into a harmonious totality', in a parallel with what Stedman Jones (1983, 45) describes as Lukács's view of *interiorization*.

The Marxian critique of Hegel that subtends 'Myth Today' does not however discount Hegel's writing on ancient Greece. In 1963, Barthes's 'concrete' voluntarism allows him to glimpse an unmediated world characterized in the Hegelian '*shudder* of meaning':

> According to Hegel [in *Lectures on the Philosophy of History*], the ancient Greek was amazed by the *natural* in nature; he constantly listened to it, questioned the meaning of mountains, springs, forests, storms; without knowing what all these objects were telling him by name, he perceived in the vegetal or cosmic order a tremendous *shudder* of meaning, to which he gave the name of a god: Pan. Subsequently, nature has changed, has become social: everything given to man is *already* human, down to the forest and the river which we cross when we travel. But confronted with this social nature, which is quite simply culture, structural man is no different from the ancient Greek: he too listens for the natural in culture, and constantly perceives in it not so much stable, finite, 'true' meanings as the shudder of an enormous machine which is humanity tirelessly undertaking to create meaning, without which it would no longer be human. (1972, 218–19, trans. mod.)

As Barthes's justification for 'structuralist activity', this Hegelianism does not take the law of history from Hegel (rejected, as we saw above, for its analogical lack of specificity), rather an assertion of the double nature of work, and of a work: it 'refers the exercise of the work and the work itself to a single identity' (219). This is a form of divination, a *manteia* in Hegelian thought, that has consequences for literature as a double, dialectical form – 'literature, in particular, is a mantic activity that it is both intelligible and interrogating, speaking and silent, engaged in the world by the course of the meaning which it remakes with the world, but disengaged from the contingent meanings which the world elaborates' – but also for History and revolutionary theatre in particular:

> Was it really his Marxism that was revolutionary in Brecht? Was it not rather the decision to link to Marxism, in the theater, the placing of a spotlight or the deliberate fraying of a costume? Structuralism does not withdraw history from the world: it seeks to link to history not only certain contents (this has been done a thousand times) but also certain forms, not only the material but also the intelligible, not only the ideological but also the aesthetic. (219)

Hegel's *'shudder* of meaning' was a way to describe polysemic cultures where mythic language saw meanings in everything (2015a, 92) that could also help to account for today's mass culture and the naturalization and rationalization of signs, or connotation: 'the cultural objects elaborated by our society are arbitrary (as systems of signs) and yet well-founded (as rational processes)' (1990b, 286).

This double, paradoxical aspect of culture is most clear for Barthes in how we understand photography and cultural phenomena more generally; and it was Hegel who understood this in relation to the ancient Greeks, by his placing emphasis on 'outlining the manner in which they made nature signify [rather] than by describing the totality of their "feelings and beliefs" on the subject' (1977, 30). It is the time-specific codes, rather than a simple analysis of their signifieds (which are trans-historical), that explains how, in the modern world, we commune with, for example, a press photograph. Rather than looking for the ideological content, we should, following Hegel's 'manteia' of codes of connotation, 'hope to find the forms our society uses to ensure its peace of mind and to grasp thereby the magnitude, the detours and the underlying function of that activity' (1977, 31).

This use of Hegel suggests a more active voluntarism than Julia Kristeva's 1971 account (Kristeva 1981) of Barthes's Hegelian approach to literature. Indeed, this active Hegelianism informs his analysis of Brecht's writings:

> 'Dialectic': a) Engels-Brecht: 'ownership of nature'; b) Mao-Brecht: *close* [*fine*] reading (primary/secondary) of contradictions [...]; c) finally, in the Brechtian context: instrument with an effect in sight, the potential to right [rémédiabilité] all wrongs[.] (2010a, 209–210)

The reference here to Brecht's reading of Mao on contradiction is fortuitous for our argument as it reveals an important similarity with Barthes's 'undialectics'. In 1937, Mao described contradiction thus:

> Contradictions exist everywhere, but they differ in accordance with the different nature of different things. In any given phenomenon or thing, the unity of opposites is conditional, temporary and transitory, and hence relative, whereas the struggle of opposites is absolute. (Mao 1966, 214)

The Brechtian-Maoist conception of contradiction in Barthes's 'undialectics' suggests a formalist dialectics that swings between contradictions without pausing to synthesize in any way. Bittner puts it succinctly: 'Does the either-or of the antinomy of *Witz* interrupt the both-at-once of dialectical *Aufhebung*?' (2017, 4) – though Jameson (2010, 290) reminds us that contradiction and antinomy are to be contrasted. The answer that Barthes might then give (at least with respect to Brecht) is the '*close* reading' that allows for the ability of humans to act in and on History (if only, as with Brecht, in theatrical representation), and one which 'intuits' (Jameson 291) 'the union of opposites'.

In *Roland Barthes by Roland Barthes* (1994, 97), the notion of Hegel's '*shudder* [or 'thrill'] of meaning' is then linked to the *Neutral*, which, as we shall now see, maintains a distinct, active, voluntarism, and which is prefigured by the 'new dialectic' he finds in Japan, in which, as we saw in Chapter Seven, '[i]ndividuality is simply difference, refracted, without privilege, from body to body' (1982b, 97–98).

The Neutral and NVS as Undialectics

It is perhaps the theory of the Neutral that illustrates best Barthes's 'undialectics', where he takes a seemingly passive and uncommitted figure only to insist upon its active and socially engaged dimensions, or 'radical indecision' (Hill 2010). In the search for an active definition of the Neutral, he looks for 'an avoidance of assertion' that is active, dialectical but not one-sided anti-determinist:

> I won't do more here than raise the principle of a 'file' about ways of sidestepping affirmation that occur right at the level of language (sidestepping suggests the idea that here negation – or denial – doesn't undo assertion but counters it: it is itself assertion of the no, arrogant affirmation of the negation. (2005, 44)

Crucially, this outline of a denial of negation involves, first, Hegel's characterization of ancient Greek scepticism as a 'suspension' of judgement that relies on a relation. Barthes cites Hegel's work on Plato and the Platonists: 'it is not what it is "in itself", but only in relation to an other' (Barthes 2005, 44; the translation – unfortunately and inexplicably – misses the section of the quotation from Hegel, for which see below). In this critique of 'it is' borrowed from Hegel, Barthes now returns to his youthful interest in Gide's *Journal*.

Barthes describes the following as Gide's 'systematic aspect': '"I no longer write an affirmative sentence without being tempted to add: *perhaps*"' (2005, 45). This for Barthes illustrates the 'paradox of the Neutral': 'thought and practice of the nonconflictual, it is nevertheless bound to assertion, to conflict, in order to make itself heard' (44).

However, this is purely the writer assuaging the perceived arrogance of language in its assertive mode, and Barthes's conclusion is startlingly voluntarist: 'writing is fundamentally assertive: the best remains to accept it stoically, "tragically": to speak, to write and to hold still about the wound of affirmation' (2005, 45). This represents not only a performative contradiction – a paradox: how can one affirm the affirmative nature of writing? – but also the active nature of the *Neutral*:

> Because it radically focuses on the relation of being and language, the Neutral cannot be satisfied with the modes (modalities) that officially code the attenuation of the affirmative within language. (2005, 46)

The only solution, he concludes, is 'making understood that every paradigm is badly put, which by itself would pervert the very structure of meaning' (46): this is the basis for what he calls the 'exemption' from meaning as if it were from 'military service' (2005, xv, 17), something he can only dream of (1994, 87) especially in relation to the inevitability of the Self's subjection to a social image (1986, 353). This is a formulation of 'undialectics' that, not at all devoid of volition nor active work, leads the late Barthes to make the one further undialectical formulation, the 'Non-Vouloir-Saisir' or NVS (NWG, No-wish[will]-to-grasp) that we discussed in Chapter Eight. Barthes's 'late' thoughts on diary-writing are prefigured in this 'second-wave' work on Gide, elucidating why he will go on to suggest that its sincerity is for him but 'a part of the image-repertoire albeit at a second degree' (1986, 360, trans. mod). But in terms of politics of intellectual strategies, this affirmation/denial dialectic in the Neutral underpins, or reinforces, the NVS.

As we saw, the NVS, first referenced in the 1974 seminars on the discourse of love (2007a, 245), represents a significant shift in Barthes's thought away from the 'double grasp' distilled in Michelet's historiography; but it does not at all imply any form of passivity. Within the '*Will* burns us' (1972, 77–82) of desire, of attraction, love is not negated in the NVS; otherwise why include 'wish [vouloir]'? Indeed, it is crucial for Barthes to 'underline the *intensity* of the non-will-to-possess' (Lübecker 2010, 130).

The Neutral details a number of examples of what we have called 'undialectics', including a Zen dialectic:

> (1) mountains are mountains and waters are waters ! then (2) (following a good Zen teaching): mountains are no longer mountains, waters are no longer waters ! (3) (abode of rest), once again mountains are mountains and waters waters, etc. (2005, 125).

This is the 'true movement of the Neutral', and in which 'there is a crossover from the opposite position: the first position does not return to the same place... The back-and-forth makes one pass through an experience of wising-up' (2005, 206). Similar to the 'two-term dialectic', this Zen dialectic is indicative of Barthes's perceived failure to *write* dialectically. However, there is one dialectical formulation, on 'stupidity', that allows us to see a constant in Barthesian thought, the critique of liberal tolerance – of 'liberal humanism' as Habib (2018) insists with respect to 'Myth Today' – especially in Voltaire, a Barthesian attitude that, once again, contrasts sharply with that of Adorno and Horkheimer (1979, 256–58).

Voltaire to Voluntarism

In final reference in Barthes's work to the lack of 'system' in Voltaire that builds on the paradoxism of earlier discussions, Barthes now sets out the dialectical schema thus:

1. Stupidity, tautology, narrow scientism
2. Intelligence, paranoia
3. Innocence (mystic), wisdom, 'method' (= Tao)

(2005, 125)

How does this Zen dialectic fit with the 1958 critique of Voltaire and the question of 'stupidity' we saw above? Indeed, this dialectic in *The Neutral* follows the long quotation from Voltaire's *Essai sur la tolérance* which so raised Barthes's hackles in 1958.

In *The Neutral* Barthes quotes at length from Voltaire's narration of the story of the Canton Emperor Kang-hi who adjudicates the interminable argument between the Jesuit and the Chaplain by ordering that they both be put in prison, 'until they pretend to forgive each other' (2005, 116). For Barthes, Voltaire's story, though involving 'that of escaping debate, controversy' of the Emperor's final order in ways that look like a definition of the Neutral – what he calls the 'Beside-the-point answers' (109) – Voltaire's resolution of the story's conflict is anything but indicative of the Neutral; simply because, Barthes suggests, it involves a stark and authoritarian power relation of imprisonment: 'And no Neutral is possible in the field of power' (116). Rather than the absence of a dialectic of History, Voltaire's error for the late Barthes is to have ignored the dialectic of power.

Thus the critique of power becomes part of a wider suspicion towards Hegelian logic that is evident in the late Barthes's writing. Lübecker (2010, 130–35) traces it in the 1978 interview with Jacqueline Sers on violence (1985a, 306–11) in which Barthes insists that left-wing philosophy of the 'person' is rare, defining it as part of Barthes's anti-conflictual stance but not, Lübecker suggests, a bourgeois individualism, rather an 'asocial atopia' concerned with community; though we should mention an earlier 'Leninist' perspective in a radical 1972 interview in which he accepts that, in 'precise political cases', violence can be used for 'well-defined tactical ends' but not as 'a permanent ethical attitude' (1985a, 151–152); indeed, an 'unrelenting dialectical evaluation' is needed of the 'countercultural activities' that promote '*nihilistic* action', which for Barthes must be a nihilism of language, but not 'spectacularly violent' nor 'destructive' (152).

Furthermore, Barthes's 'unrelenting dialectics' leads him to propose other forms of positive violence: 'There are in fact conditions, actions, or choices that may be violent in a positive way, or, rather, violent *and* positive: creative passions, creative radicalism!' (1985a, 309).

Following Susan Sontag's notion of silence as aesthetic, in her essay published alongside the original English version of 'The Death of the Author' in the USA (Sontag 1967), Barthes develops the 'suspension' of his views of Mao's China that we saw in Chapter Seven into a much wider politics of silence:

> The right to be quiet, the right not to listen: that rings paradoxical today. And here, a reversal: what is taking the shape of a collective, almost political-in any case, threatened by politics-demand is the right to nature's peacefulness, the right to *silere*, not the right to *tacere* [...] therefore *tacere*, as a right, still remains in the margin of the margins (which is where the true combat should be fought, infinitely). (2005, 22–23)

Lübecker considers the 'utopia of a socialism of distances' in *How to Live Together* as an antidote to hermeneutics (especially in 'So, How was China?') and to violence, which both involve an oppressive, Hegelian 'struggle for recognition' (136). The late lectures perform this utopia in a less political, more ethical, view on 'how to live together', for which literature provides the NVS. To allow literature to found what Lübecker calls 'non-collective co-existence', Barthes's teaching becomes 'deliberately *para-doxical*'. Without noticing that this is how Philippe Roger characterized Barthes's stance already in *Writing in Degree Zero* (1986, 317–18), Lübecker characterizes the politics of a sceptical Hegelian Barthes as a 'non-engaged engagement': 'where non-conflictual passion can thrive; a zone where we can enjoy sensuous life with a passion that does not divide' (138).

The voluntarism of the Neutral and the NVS is thus not total. Indeed, in *The Neutral*, Barthes is quick to critique the 'exaltation of will' (2005, 154), which he considers to be typical of the modern world (from Descartes to Hegel, though in Nietzsche it needs heavy qualification), as an arrogance of power, including a certain 'universal' which (including Marx) seems obsessively caught up in war and political history. Only Michelet's interest in the history of 'affect' allows for the Neutral and the NVS to operate, thereby returning to a dialectic from the beginning of his career where Michelet's history of sensibilities impressed the young Barthes.

However, in the *Neutral* and the NVS, it is still an 'undialectics' of the active, but without the arrogance of power. This volition extends to the very final phase of Barthes's life, to the 'will-to-write [vouloir-écrire]' of the *vita nova*, which, though 'intransitive', involves, paradoxically, an intense volition. Indeed, if it is true, as Marie Gil's biography firmly maintains, that the 'oscillation' as she calls Barthes's constant, life-long, swinging between contrary and opposing phenomena – an 'undialectics' we might say – comes to an abrupt end with the loss of his mother in 1977 inaugurating the final period of his life that Gil calls 'stasis' (2012, 466–67), then the desire to write, the voluntarism of *écriture*, seems to survive the extended mourning.

It may be that Barthes's use of the dialectic across his career has both hard and soft versions – soft as in Moufawad's complaint above, but hard as a serious attempt to understand, mobilize and relativize contradiction. Therefore, if dialectics is really about human social relations, about how humans interact via language, what about 'undialectics'? Is Barthes trying to find a language of transformation that allows human relations to flourish? If so, the theorist of (non-arrogant) transformation uses, paradoxically, an active, not passive, volition in order for power relations between humans to be suspended. There is nothing anti-dialectical or non-dialectical about 'bending the stick' towards voluntarism, to undermining and trying to outwit determinism. Perhaps the 'undialectics' in Barthes's use of Hegel and Marx, his voluntarism, should lead us to the formulation attributed to Gramsci (cited by Antonini 2019, 42n.1): 'pessimism of the intellect, optimism of the will'.

AFTERWORD: ESSAYISM AND THE POLITICS OF WRITING

> Every author has a sense in which all the contradictory passages are harmonized, otherwise that author has no sense […]. One must therefore find a sense in which all the contradictions are reconciled.
>
> *(Blaise Pascal cited in Losurdo 2020, viii)*

It seems perhaps odd, in the light of what has gone before in this book, to conclude, to close down the discussion. Perhaps then a contradiction is needed. Barthes, probably not a Barthesian (Stafford 2015a, 156–59), is very possibly a materialist moralist; that is, deeply conscious of the lived realities of alienated modern human society, which are then turned into writerly, literary essayism. Furthermore, there is no 'double' Barthes divided between aesthetics on the one hand, and the political on the other hand. Indeed, it is against the spirit of Barthesian theory and writing to divide them. Though there are clearly different Barthesian constituencies, the political and the aesthetic are not separate, merely nuances, accents and emphasis. Perhaps it is the ultimate essayistic feature – moralism – that keeps them tightly tied, at least in Barthes's world and spirit. It is necessary then finally to make some tentative suggestions as to the nature of the ethics and politics of Barthesian essayism. This will be carried out by way of a triangulation with, first, an intellectual figure whom we have regularly discussed in this book, Lucien Goldmann, and second, an essayist heavily influenced in his early career by Goldmann and Barthes, the Palestinian post-colonial critic Edward Said.

Barthes, Said, Goldmann

> The [person] interested in these disciplines [psychology, socialist moral or religion in the novel] will read essays and risk less.
>
> *(Robbe-Grillet 1965, 35, trans. mod.)*

Barthesian ethics in the 1970s have clear echoes in Edward Said's anti-imperialism, what in *Orientalism* is called the 'nonrepressive' and 'non-manipulative'. Both Said and Barthes wrote, to lesser and greater extents – and this will be the nub of this comparison – as consummate *essayists*, who, both playful and acerbic in their commentaries, were ever keen to negotiate the dichotomies of writing and reading, of modernity and classicism (in music as much as in literature), of self and other in relation to an alienated political world. However, Higgins (1981) sees Barthes escaping the Saidian dichotomy of either not speaking, or denying subjectivity, by 'writing without representing'.

We seem, in this day and age at least, to value change, inconsistency, openness and suppleness of thought, over rigid, closed, dogmatism and systematicity. And yet, both Said and Barthes are systematic thinkers: the positing of structures in order to subvert them may appear anti-systematic (and, in many ways, it is), but it is a trademark Barthes. Similarly, displacement and anti-authority may be crucial concerns throughout Said's work, but History and Politics (in its most acute form in the Middle East, down to the catastrophic *Nakba* of 1947-1948) are immutable and non-analogizable facts. Said is, of course, accused of both being Palestino-centric, and then also far too general in his work; by the same token Barthes's writing on fashion is dreary and methodical, on Balzac too elliptical and contradictory. One gets the feeling then that this is the point with Said and Barthes: their supple dialectics are themselves groundable, recuperable (usually into intellectual fads, structuralism this, post-colonialism that, etc.); and yet all we have of them is their writings, in their nudity and their pastichability.

Hence the work of Giambattista Vico, for both Said and Barthes, as an important dialectician, theorising and deploying the spiral as a figure of both change and stasis. Theirs is a Vico read through Marx (via an unmistakeable neo-Hegelianism); for Barthes, through the nineteenth-century historian Jules Michelet (a translator and scholar of Vico), and for Said, via Eric Auerbach. Of course, typically, both Michelet and Auerbach are hardly two figures of the avant-garde; yet, as we have seen, Barthes uses Michelet, especially in the 1950s, to play out important historiographical discussions – on analogy, on formalism, on sociology and ethnography – often within a Western-Marxist voluntarism; for Said, Auerbach, and Spitzer aim, and seem to be the last intellectual generation able, to blend History with Literature without the one destroying the other.

Indeed, Said certainly seemed to take on much of the originality/repetition dialectic that Barthes and other structuralists developed (Said 1984, 111–39). Said borrows Barthes's idea that, first, for a beginning in his work, one must reveal (hidden or innocent) structures, while insisting that 'there is no precursive model to follow' and that, at the same time, history 'is an order of repetition, not of spontaneous and perpetual originality' (1975, 16–17, 354). Such concerns go to the heart of Barthes's work on Racine, on fashion and clothes history, even on Balzac. Indeed, it has been argued that Barthes's radical re-reading and re-writing of *Sarrasine* in *S/Z*, is, *pace* the view of hardcore Structuralists, a deeply historical text, albeit in 'spiral'.

Other parallels between Saidian and Barthesian essayism are in evidence. Said's famous literary idea of the contrapuntal is strongly linked to the use of antithesis in Barthesian semiotics. Also common to both is a 'spirit' of literature. Just as Said insisted that TS Eliot is relevant, so Barthes re-read the French classics, across a period where Maoism was extolling 'proletarian culture' and promoting the destruction of bourgeois culture; here, Barthes (and to a lesser extent, Said) moved against the post-1968 radical flow, refusing to toe the Maoist critique of bourgeois culture that the radical journal *Tel Quel* advocated in the wake of May 1968. Indeed, Said and Barthes both worked equally on classical and modern texts, and were happy to stray outside the literary culture of their mother tongue (Said on Renan, Camus; Barthes on Loyola, Brecht and Goethe).

Thus, in their respective critical praxis, Barthes (1974, 217) and Said could both call for a radical 'suspension' of judgement.

Yet, despite the converging paths, important differences must be signalled between Barthes and Said. Their respective approaches to academia were divergent. Said favoured a humanist, tolerant method that rejected separatism in academic relations; whereas, for Barthes, the seminar was an experimental space, and in the case of the *Sarrasine* seminars (admittedly written and delivered across the dramatic events of May 1968), the seminar is treated as a space for political and ideological contestation. These are not exactly diametrical opposites but suggest an ethos (and even an epoch) that is radically different. Barthes's ethos is (ironically) politicized and Said's 'separatist' as it compartmentalizes his teaching away from his politics.

One important meeting point of Said and Barthes is around the work of Lucien Goldmann. Barthes nevertheless moved onto three distinct terrains; firstly, that of the bracketing of the author – despite, in later life, identifying with Proust the 'worker', both the 'tormented' and 'exalted' writer (1986, 278). We saw in chapter 3 how Barthes departs from Goldmann's work on tragedy and from its incipient psychologism. Whereas Goldmann in 1965 (1975, ix), in the face of criticism, partially retracts the idea that a creative act is a social rather than an individual one (part of the 'trans-individual' that accepted the importance of structures but not humans as functions of structures), the Barthes of the mid-1960s by contrast presses ahead with the idea (originating in his early work on Michelet) that the author, authority, in a text should be dissolved. Neither Goldmann nor Said was prepared to take this step.

In his review of the English translation of *The Hidden God*, Said points out (1966, 444) that Goldmann is not a 'gifted stylist', his ideas leading to a bit of a 'scrappy affair'. Here is the fundamental manner in which Barthes moves beyond Goldmann's sociology of literature, that is, in his attitude to literary form; and though Goldmann writes on form in Lukácsian ways, this approach has none of the sensitivity to the dialectics of language that Barthes slowly but surely imports into his work. Reviewing Goldmann's 1964 work on sociology of the novel, Barthes suggests that for Goldmann form is what 'others would call content' (2002, II, 248). Jacques Leenhardt, a student of Goldmann's, makes the same point, underlining Barthes's 'incentive to complete, to open up the work of analysis of texts carried out in the tradition of Lukács and Goldmann […] to find a discourse in which to speak of writing itself from a sociological perspective' (Leenhardt cited in Ungar 1983, 110).

The major difference then between Said and Goldmann on the one hand, and Barthes on the other, is the manner in which they conceive their writing. Goldmann insists (1959, 250–251) that Lukácsian essayism is distinct from philosophy in that, asking questions rather than providing answers, the essay-form in Lukács's hands needs contact, not with abstract and autonomous ideas, but with 'concrete reality': as Lukács put it: 'Every Essay puts, in golden letters, next to its title: in relation to…'. In this optic, noticed by Said (1984, 52), the essay is itself then a form 'which speaks more of the work of art than of real life' because it allows 'the big human questions (of destiny, love, duty) to be expressed in a form that has no need of the worn-out forms which works of art take'.

For Said, as for Noam Chomsky, there is a need for compartmentalization. With Barthes, there is no such compartmentalization: essayism is political critique; to write intransitively questions radically the utilitarianism that the Institution imposes upon cultural criticism. One may write in order to be 'liked', as Barthes suggests in 1969 (2015a, 85); but one writes also in order to subvert. This is perhaps one answer to the conundrum that Hill (2010, 71–91) finds in *Writing Degree Zero*, that the essay never actually tells us what this 'degree zero' is. The 'answer' to Hill's question therefore is: the essay, Barthes's essayistic *oeuvre*. Indeed, the 'amorous dialectic' that guides Barthes's essayism is precisely the intransitive nature of his writing. In today's discussions around the so-called 'post-critical' (Felski 2015), what is missing is the sensitivity in the very earliest Barthesian writings to the competing pressures on the essayist faced with ideological controls of all sorts. 'Post-critical' and 'Affective' studies are pre-empted by the one side of 'amorous dialectic' – and where, whether, when and how, one might tack towards them in the 'amorous dialectic' depends, crucially, on not abandoning the dialectical tension, on not obliterating the 'denouncing' element *also* within it; in other words, the 'post-critical' must be, simultaneously, dextrously, 'post-' *and* '-critical'. Radical essayism demands this, as a minimum.

There are indeed elements of essayistic innovation in Said, but, compared to Barthes, ultimately Said is looking for, if not hard, then certainly fixed or fixable positions. Said prefers Foucault's 'vocabulary of limits' over Barthes's 'infinite possibility of language' in what he calls Barthes's 'para-scientific treatises' (1972, 8); for Barthes, it is the search for the slippery, for the provisional.

As with Saidian concerns with exile, exilic thought is deeply essayistic, and has a central place in Barthes's writing – evident in the key Barthesian figures of 'drift', 'displacement', 'loss', 'ex-nomination', 'silence' and 'exemption of meaning'. But, for Said, in his (essayistically, brilliant) piece 'Mind of Winter: Reflections on Exile', exile is not some desired state (the Palestinians have been 'exiled by exiles'), though a 'counterpoint' is often generated by it (2001, 173, 178, 186). Said is thus far more dialectical about 'exile' than Barthes; Barthes's essayistic strategy is perhaps blind to, or too dismissive of, ideologistic critique. This may be linked to the essayistic route that Said, ultimately, refuses to take in his writing (with the exceptions mentioned).

Barthesian essayism

> In all great criticism one finds the vision
> of a New State, and yet not a brick laid towards
> directly building it.
>
> *(John Berger cited in Dyer 1986, 32)*

> '[The essay], the act of cultural, even civilisational
> survival of the highest importance.'
>
> *(Edward Said cited in Ashcroft/Ahluwalia 2001, 36–38)*

According to Hayden White (a translator of Goldmann's work furthermore), Said's attempt in his 'meditative essays' *Beginnings* to eschew both 'a logic of consecutiveness' and 'random analogy' is part of the essayist's will, and which allows him to avoid the criticism of logical inconsistency and nihilism; White insists also (1976, 364–66) that, though 'closing the gap between creative and critical literature, Said maintains a notion of the differences between metacritical and critical literature'. Though Said's 'adjacency', 'radical discontinuity', 'construction' and 'anti-dynastics' sound Barthesian in spirit, they are not applied to Said's own writing in the same way as he might apply them to literary texts. Indeed, the key to the major difference between Said's and Barthes's approaches comes in the conclusion to 'The World, the Text and the Critic' (Said 1984, 50–53).

Having suggested the complexity of 'performance' meeting the 'worldly' critic, Said then spends much of his essay discussing critical practice (in a heady mix of Ricœur, Fanon, Frye, biblical and Koranic exegesis, Marx, and Foucault, with Conrad, Hardy, Joyce, George Eliot and Wilde), only to conclude rhetorically (though this is possibly the essayist's own 'false' performance of the essay): 'But where in all this is the critic and criticism?'. Thus follows a brilliant, if brief, discussion of the essay. As close as Said gets to 'creative criticism' – though never specifically mentioning this 'tradition' beyond the perceptive comments of Lukács and Wilde – he stops short at a general analysis. In a sense, this is totally understandable: the orphic nature of the creative essay – once you look at it, define it, delimit it, you lose it, as Barthes points out in *Writing Degree Zero* (1967a, 16, 82) – may have dissuaded Said from taking the next step, that of being, himself, this 'creative critic'. The *Rubicon* that Barthes crosses, certainly from *S/Z* of the late 1960s onwards and into the 'romanesque [novelistic]' period of the 1970s, is the deliberate rewriting of academic seminar notes, of scholarly prefaces, of lecture notes, and the playful parodies and pastiches of 'regular' journalistic criticism, to make a new essayistic *œuvre*; to the extent that Han (2020) has cogently suggested that the final 'Novel' that Barthes wanted to write is, to all intents and purposes, contained in the three lecture courses at the Collège de France (2005, 2013, 2011b).

By contrast, Said's excursus on the essay describes the text as a 'system of forces institutionalized by the reigning culture', but not of the institutionalized position of the essayist that allows for the essay to escape (only temporarily, I am afraid) the institution precisely by its 'ironic' (to borrow Said's term) relationship to the intellectual and scholarly institution in which Barthes becomes a key player. Ironically then, it is here *Barthes* the worldly critic (in that he attempts to step outside the academy), and *Said*, the diligent, obedient, closed-in critic whose rigid division of university from world blocks the 'creative criticism' route. Criticism is seen by Said as an 'external' form of molestation, and yet is shown by Barthes's *S/Z* to be present in the textuality of fiction; indeed, argues Riddel (2001, 380–81), 'Said is really not concerned with documenting a history of texts that re-write other texts', citing how Said shows how mimesis revolves into parody and 'innovation to rewriting': 'Each novel recapitulates not life but other novels'; and: 'A text is in part a continuing desire to write one' (Said 1975, 152, 202). In his famous 1976 *Diacritics* interview, Said seems reluctant to allow 'avant-garde' criticism to have the creative option, merely allowing a slightly ambiguous term to emerge: 'recreative' (Said in Williams 2001, I, 4). Thus Said, (generally) unlike Barthes, runs the risk, as with so many (left) critics of literature, of 'missing' the text, of instrumentalizing literature, creative writing, of turning a text into a document.

Here then is the Trotskyan approach that Barthes adopts and then (in typical Barthesian fashion) takes to its bitter conclusion: if literature must be judged by the laws of literature alone, then Barthes will, in his literary criticism and in his writing in general, produce another literature, his own essay, as the only viable approach to a literary (or any other kind of) text. The trouble is with this argument is where does literature, the literary, literary (and by contiguity, cultural) criticism end? Do we suddenly sit up from our reading of Balzac, Jane Austen, Albert Camus and Mohammed Dib, and declare the existence of a non-literary, political world? Barthes appears aware of this in his 1969 piece on Hippies in Morocco (2006, 113). There is a sense in which, once a systematics of literary criticism is (rightfully) abandoned, literary criticism, once analyzed through the optic of the essay and through essayism, can become literature in itself: the essay is itself parametric to the deforming of literature, as it too 'deforms' (in Barthes's hands at least), in a way that Said is, perhaps, not able to accept. A scientific critique of history and society, though recognizing and using the tiny holes that seep interesting literary ideas into political critique, can then rightly be operated; this is true in spatial terms rather than in chronological order of tasks, but for which the corrosive nature of literature (including our essayistic widening of this term) can play a salutary role.

One might rightly say 'so what?' given the plight of (for example) Palestine today, – and indeed there is something deeply 'literary' about the 'late' Barthes –, but that would not be a new criticism of the literary. Indeed, Said himself is quite forthright in this direction, suggesting that it is 'quite undialectical' to make 'a literary or intellectual project immediately into a political one', quite conscious, as he is, of the individualist/collaborative nature of criticism, citing Barthes as suggesting that, ideally, semiotics should be 'cooperative and impersonal' (Said in Williams 2001, I, 17). But Barthes constantly moves on from the seminar room of collective co-operation (say, in looking at *Sarrasine*) to turn then (but usually with gestures towards his students' input) to make this work radically essayistic (for example, moving from the *Sarrasine* seminar notes to the essay *S/Z*); and that is also the point: Said, ironically for a Vicoist aware of spirals, possibly misses this in overstating how much that Barthes 'quite deliberately frees himself of [his] past attachments and habits and alliances' (cited in Williams 2001, I, 28). Barthes is on the verge of being a writer; Said, alas, is a brilliant critic.

Barthes's essayism, his political 'undialectics', seems to parallel then, if not corroborate, Trotsky's view that art is to be judged by art, whilst injecting the *for me* of Nietzschean aristocratics. Though we have shown that this Barthesian *spirit* is, paradoxically, not egotistical, where does it leave, first, the Marxist theory of art? Is radical essayism limited to a set of 'para-doxa', exposing, countering and repairing the distortions of 'doxa'? In this optic, the lengthy discussions in the 1990s around Adorno's philistinism versus his connoisseurship (Ingram 2020) seem to pass Barthes's essayism by. Second, it may be that the 'two-term' or 'amputated', dialectic is important for rebalancing – or better, holding in tight tension – all the oppositions in Barthesian theory, starting with the *punctum / studium* dyad. This is a double grasp without synthesis (privileging/negation/determinism).

Essay as literature only?

> The obsession with wanting to conclude is
> one of the most deadly and sterile manias
> belonging to humanity. Every religion and
> every philosophy claims to have God in it,
> to have looked the infinite up and down and
> to know the recipe of happiness. What arrogance
> and what emptiness! I consider, on the contrary,
> that the greatest minds and the greatest works
> have never concluded. (Flaubert 1929, 111)

Given the need for radical global change in today's world, the essay might be classed as a literary luxury, a luxury of literature. Löwy argues (in his preface to Goldmann 2016, 26) that 'there is no contradiction between a refusal of "scientism" and the desire to attain a scientific, historical and sociological knowledge of facts concerning man, a knowledge quite opposed to speculation and belletristic essay writing'. Is Barthes's essayism 'belletristic'? Is it akin to the 'speculative thought' with which Marx criticized Hegel's writing: 'It is in this dialectic […], in the grasping of opposites in their unity or of the positive in the negative, that speculative thought consists' (Marx 1847, #69)? Is the Barthesian 'illness' of 'seeing' language akin to Blaise Pascal's view that 'Those who construct antitheses by forcing the use of words are like those who put in false windows for the sake of symmetry./ Their rule is not correct speech but correct figures of speech' (Pascal 1975 [1670], series XXIII, 559)?

To answer these questions definitively would be to abandon the 'double Barthes', the 'double grasp' of Barthes, that this book has advocated. Barthes's intellectual 'strabism', evident in his view that language is a relation (fundamentally, a class relation), suggests that we need a 'double grasp' of language. If there is ONE thing that Barthes IS telling us to do, it is to double-grasp everything. But, maybe the 'stupidity [bêtise] of Barthes' (Coste 2011) is to relativize even the 'double grasp': what, then, *is* the 'single-minded' in its complexity?

Barthes's strategy in the face of the single-minded is to write the interstitial, to theorize in writing a Reticence of political commitment, a political commitment of Reticence. Like Mallarmé drawing literary inspiration from the gap between the empty page and 'Art', Barthes plays on politics and aesthetics – heavily, as we have seen in this book –, on the debate, gap and argument between the two: hesitating to commit politically, but staunchly dismissive of all and any irresponsibility of Form. This is not so much Merleau-Ponty's 'hyper-dialectics', but a *hyper-politics*; because, in this scenario – reticent politically, but engaged aesthetically – *everything* is deeply political, from food to fashion, music to maths, hair to History. But – and it is a heavy 'but' – the hyper-political is an indirect politics. The hyper-political, with its Meta-Marxism, opens up an 'ethos of the intellectual', though Barthes's 'equipollent' dialectic means that there is no guide to praxis, and therefore no 'Theory'. The three Barthesian *hyper-political* strategies of the 1950s, 1960s and 1970s – identified in this book and abbreviated (following Barthes's own abbreviation of the third of these) as Double Grasp (DG), Must Be Dialectical (MBD) and Non-Wish-to-Grasp (NWG) – are all, to the letter, indirect.

I do not know, I am afraid, what this means precisely for Politics – action – but Roland Barthes is, to my mind, part of the discussion. And, especially in these extreme times of the COVID pandemic – exasperating as they are – all I know is that Barthes allows us to breathe.

BIBLIOGRAPHY

1. Works and Writings by Roland Barthes

This bibliography includes all of Roland Barthes's posthumous publications, including journal, lecture and seminar notes not in the *Complete Works*, including those not translated into English; as well as variant versions of published articles, unpublished work and correspondence. Published translations have been used throughout, though any occasional modifications are signalled; otherwise, all other translations are my own.

A. Unpublished varia

1941. 'Evocations et incantations dans la tragédie grecque'. Dissertation for the *Diplôme d'études supérieures* (DES), Université de la Sorbonne, Paris. (Archives Roland Barthes, BNF, NAF 28630).

July 1945–May 1947. Letters to Philippe Rebeyrol not included in *Album* (Barthes 2018), held by the Bibliothèque nationale in Paris.

B. Published work, including English Translations

1947. 'Le degré zéro de l'écriture'. *Combat*, 1 August: 2.
1950. 'Triomphe et rupture de l'écriture bourgeoise'. *Combat*, 9 November: 4.
1953a. 'Pouvoirs de la tragédie antique.' *Théâtre Populaire* 2: 12–22.
1953b. 'Le monde objet'. *Les Lettres nouvelles*, June: 394–405.
1953c. 'Féminaire de Michelet'. *Les Lettres nouvelles*, November: 1085–1100.
1955. 'Les maladies du costume de théâtre'. *Théâtre Populaire* 12: 64–76.
1956. 'Bertolt Brecht à Lyon'. *France-Observateur*, 10 May: 17.
1958. 'Voltaire, le dernier des écrivains heureux?' *Actualités littéraires*, March: 13–15.
1967a. *Writing Degree Zero*. Translated by Annette Lavers and Colin Smith. London: Jonathan Cape.
1967b. *Seven Photo Models of 'Mother Courage'*. Translated by Hella Freud Bernays. *Tulane Drama Review*, 12:1 (Autumn): 44–55.
1968. *Elements of Semiology*. Translated by Annette Lavers and Colin Smith. New York: Hill and Wang.
1972. *Critical Essays*. Translated by Richard Howard. Evanston: Northwestern University Press.
1974. *S/Z: An Essay*. Translated by Richard Miller. New York: Hill and Wang.
1975. *The Pleasure of the Text*. Translated by Richard Howard. New York: Hill and Wang.
1977. *Image, Music, Text*. Translated by Stephen Heath. Glasgow: Fontana.
1979. *The Eiffel Tower and Other Mythologies*. Translated by Richard Howard. New York: Hill and Wang.
1982a. *A Barthes Reader*. Edited by Susan Sontag. New York: Hill and Wang.
1982b. *Empire of Signs*. Translated by Richard Howard. New York: Hill and Wang.
1984. *Camera Lucida, Reflections on Photography*. Translated by Richard Howard. London: Fontana.
1985a. *The Grain of the Voice: Interviews 1962–1980*. Translated by Linda Coverdale. New York: Hill and Wang.

1985b. *The Responsibility of Forms: Critical Essays on Music, Art and Representation*. Translated by Richard Howard. Oxford: Blackwell.

1985c. 'Barthes to the Third Power'. In Marshall Blonsky (ed), *On Signs*. Translated by Richard Howard. Baltimore: Johns Hopkins University Press: 189–191.

1986. *The Rustle of Language*. Translated by Richard Howard. Oxford: Blackwell.

1987a. *Michelet*. Translated by Richard Howard. Berkley/Los Angeles: University of California Press.

1987b. *The Semiotic Challenge*. Translated by Richard Howard. Oxford: Blackwell.

1987c. *Writer Sollers*. Translated by Philip Thody. Minneapolis: University of Minnesota Press.

1989. *Sade, Fourier, Loyola*. Translated by Richard Miller. Berkeley/Los Angeles: University of California Press.

1990a. *A Lover's Discourse: Fragments*. Translated by Richard Howard. London: Penguin.

1990b. *The Fashion System*. Translated by Matthew Ward and Richard Howard. Berkeley/Los Angeles: University of California Press.

1990c. *New Critical Essays*. Translated by Richard Howard. Berkeley/Los Angeles: University of California Press.

1992a. *On Racine*. Translated by Richard Howard. Berkley/Los Angeles: University of California Press.

1992b. *Incidents*. Translated by Richard Howard. Berkeley/Los Angeles: University of California Press.

1994. *Roland Barthes by Roland Barthes*. Translated by Richard Howard. Berkeley/Los Angeles: University of California Press.

1997. 'Dear Antonioni…'. In Geoffrey Nowell-Smith (ed), *L'avventura*. Translated by the Author. London: BFI: 63–68.

1998. 'Responses: Interview With Tel Quel' [1971]. Translated by Vérène Grieshaber. In Patrick ffrench and Roland-François Lack (eds), *The 'Tel Quel' Reader*. London: Routledge: 249–267.

2002. *Œuvres complètes*. Edited by Eric Marty. 5 Volumes: Vol I: 1942–1961, Vol II: 1962–1967, Vol III: 1968–1971, Vol IV: 1972–1976, Vol V: 1977–1980. Paris: Seuil.

2003. *La Préparation du roman, Cours au Collège de France 1978–1979 et 1979–1980*. Edited by Nathalie Léger. Paris: Seuil/IMEC.

2005. *The Neutral: Lecture Course at the Collège de France, 1977–1978*. Translated by Rosalind Krauss and Denis Hollier. New York: Columbia University Press.

2006a. *The Language of Fashion*. Translated by Andy Stafford. Oxford: Berg.

2006b. 'Proust Round Table'. In Gilles Deleuze (ed), *Two Regimes of Madness: Texts and Interviews 1975–1995*. Edited by David Lapoujade and Translated by Ames Hodges and Mike Taormina. New York: Semiotext(e): 29–60.

2007a. *Le Discours amoureux. Séminaire à l'École pratique des hautes études 1974–1976, suivi de 'Fragments d'un discours amoureux': inédits*. Edited by Claude Coste. Paris: Seuil.

2007b. *Criticism and Truth*. Translated by Katrine Pilcher Keuneman. London: Continuum.

2007c. *What is Sport?* Translated by Richard Howard. New Haven: Yale University Press.

2009. *Mythologies*. Translated by Annette Lavers and Sian Reynolds. London: Vintage.

2010a. *Le Lexique de l'auteur. Séminaire à l'École pratique des hautes études 1973–1974, suivi de Fragments inédits du 'Roland Barthes par Roland Barthes'*. Edited by Anne Herschberg Pierrot. Paris: Seuil.

2010b. *Mourning Diary. October 26, 1977–September 15, 1979*. Translated by Richard Howard. New York: Hill and Wang.

2010c. *Incidents*. Translated by Teresa Lavender Fagan, Photographs by Bishan Samaddar. London: Seagull.

2011a. *'Sarrasine' de Balzac. Séminaires à l'École pratique des hautes études (1967–1968 et 1968–1969)*. Edited by Claude Coste and Andy Stafford. Paris: Seuil.

2011b. *The Preparation of the Novel. Lecture Courses and Seminars at the Collège de France (1978–1979 and 1979–1980)*. Translated by Kate Briggs. New York: Columbia University Press.

2012. *Travels in China*. Translated by Andrew Brown. Cambridge: Polity.
2013. *How to Live Together*. Translated by Kate Briggs. New York: Columbia University Press.
2015a. *'A Very Fine Gift' and Other Writings on Theory (Essays and Interviews Vol. I)*. Translated by Chris Turner. London: Seagull Books.
2015b. *'The "Scandal" of Marxism' and Other Writings on Politics (Essays and Interviews Vol. II)*. Translated by Chris Turner. London: Seagull Books.
2015c. *'Simply a Particular Contemporary'. Interviews, 1970–1979 (Essays and Interviews Vol. IV)*. Translated by Chris Turner. London: Seagull Books.
2015d. *La Préparation du roman, Cours au Collège de France 1978–1979 et 1979–1980*. Edited by Nathalie Léger, Transcrip. Nathalie Lacroix, Pref. Bernard Comment. Paris: Seuil.
2016a. *'Masculine, Feminine, Neuter' and Other Writings on Literature (Essays and Interviews Vol. III)*. Translated by Chris Turner. London: Seagull Books.
2016b. *Signs and Images: Writings on Art, Cinema and Photography (Essays and Interviews Vol. V)*. Translated by Chris Turner. London: Seagull Books.
2018. *Album. Unpublished Correspondence and Texts* and Edited Eric Marty (With Claude Coste). Translated by Joel Gladding. New York: Columbia University Press.
2020. *Marcel Proust. Mélanges*. Paris: Seuil.

2. Books, Journals and Articles on Barthes Cited

Algalarrondo, H. 2006. *Les Derniers jours de Roland Barthes*. Paris: éditions Stock.
Alphant, M. and N. Léger (eds). 2002. *R/B. Roland Barthes. Catalogue de l'exposition Centre-Pompidou*. Paris: Seuil/Centre Pompidou.
Amigo Pino, C. 2022. *Apprendre et Désapprendre. Les séminaires de Roland Barthes (1962–1977)*. Louvain-la Neuve: éditions Academia.
Apel-Muller, M. 1971. 'La Nouvelle critique a lu'. *La Nouvelle Critique* 40 (January): 881–896.
Badir, S. and D. Ducard (eds). 2009. *Roland Barthes en cours (1977–1980): Un Style de vie*. Dijon: éditions Universitaires de Dijon.
Badmington, N. (ed). 2010. *Roland Barthes: Critical Evaluations in Cultural Theory*. 4 Vols. London and New York: Routledge.
———. 2016. *The Afterlives of Roland Barthes*. London: Bloomsbury.
——— (ed). 2017. *Deliberations: The Journals of Roland Barthes*. London: Routledge.
Baldwin, T. 2019. *Roland Barthes: The Proustian Variations*. Liverpool: Liverpool University Press.
Batchen, G. (ed). 2009. *Photography Degree Zero: Reflections on Roland Barthes 'Camera Lucida'*. Cambridge, MA: MIT Press.
Beckman, K. 2013 'Nothing to Say: The War on Terror and the Mad Photography of Roland Barthes'. In Karen Beckman and Liliane Weissberg (eds), *On Writing With Photography*. Minneapolis: University of Minnesota Press: 297–330.
Beer, O. 1985. 'Roland Barthes: la biographie comme un théâtre'. *Écriture* 24: 141–148.
Bertrand, J.-P. (ed). 2017. *Roland Barthes: continuités, Colloque de Cerisy en 2016*. Paris: Christian Bourgois éditeur.
Bident, C. 2012. *Le Geste théâtral de Roland Barthes*. Paris: Hermann.
Binet, L. 2017 [2015]. *The Seventh Function of Language*. Translated by Sam Taylor. New York: Farrar, Straus & Giroux.
Birnbaum, J. 2009a. 'La publication d'inédits de Barthes embrase le cercle de ses disciples'. *Le Monde*, 22 January: 20.
———. 2009b. 'Roland Barthes ose le cliché'. *Le Monde des livres*, 6 February: 1–2.
Bishop, R. and S. Manghani (eds). 2019. *Seeing Degree Zero: Barthes/Burgin and Political Aesthetics*. Edinburgh: Edinburgh University Press.
Bittner, J. 2017. 'Roland Barthes and the Literary Absolute'. *Barthes Studies* 3: 2–24.

———. 2020. *The Emergence of Literature: An Archaeology of Modern Literary Theory*. London: Bloomsbury.
Blanchot, M. 2000 (1957). 'The Great Hoax'. In Diana Knight (ed), *Critical Essays on Roland Barthes*. New York: G.K. Hall.
Boughali, M. 1986. *L'érotique du langage chez Roland Barthes*. Casablanca: Afrique-Orient.
Bougnoux, D. (ed). 2009. *Empreintes de Roland Barthes*. Nantes: éditions Cécile Defaut.
Boulaâbi, R., C. Coste and M. Lehdahda (eds). 2013. *Barthes au Maroc*. Meknes: Publications de l'université Moulay Ismaïl.
Bown, A. 2017. 'The Screen of Enamoration: Love in the Age of Google'. *Paris Review* 13 (November). https://www.theparisreview.org/blog/2017/11/13/screen-enamoration-love-age-google/ (consulted 15 April 2021).
Bremond, C. and T. Pavel. 1998. *De Barthes à Balzac. Fictions d'un critique, critiques d'une fiction*. Paris: Albin Michel.
Brown, A. 1992. *Roland Barthes: The Figures of Writing*. Oxford: Oxford University Press.
Burgelin, O. 1974. 'Le double système de la mode'. *L'Arc* 56: 8–16.
Calvet, L.-J. 1994. *Roland Barthes: 1915–1980*. Translated by Sarah Wykes. Cambridge: Polity Press.
Carlier, J.-C. 2000. 'Roland Barthes's Resurrection of the Author and Redemption of Biography'. *Cambridge Quarterly* 29:4: 386–393.
Carluccio, D. 2020. 'Barthes, Didi-Huberman et l'image pathétique'. *Irish Journal of French Studies* 20: 173–191.
Carmody, J. 1990. 'Reading Scenic Writing: Barthes, Brecht, and Theatre Photography'. *Journal of Dramatic Theory and Criticism* 1: 25–38.
Champagne, R. A. 1982. 'The Task of Clotho Re-defined: Roland Barthes' Tapestry of Literary History'. *L'Esprit créateur* 22:1: 35–44.
Clerc, T. 2010. *L'homme qui tua Roland Barthes et autres nouvelles*. Paris: Gallimard.
———. 2017. 'La chambre à moitié claire'. In Ivić and Vukušić Zorica 2017: 139–145.
Compagnon, A. (ed). 1978. *Prétexte: Roland Barthes/Colloque de Cerisy*. Paris: Christian Bourgois.
———. 1990. 'Trois vies'. *La Règle du jeu* 1 (May): 61–62.
———. 2005. *Les Antimodernes: de Joseph de Maistre à Roland Barthes*. Paris: Gallimard.
———. 2015. *L'Âge des lettres*. Paris: Gallimard.
Corbier, C. 2015. 'Nietzsche, Brecht, Claudel: Barthes face à la tragédie musicale grecque'. *Revue de littérature comparée* 353:1: 5–28.
———. 2019. '"The Material Effectiveness of Music." In Barthes's 1941 Postgraduate Dissertation "Évocations et incantations dans la tragédie grecque"'. *Barthes Studies* 5: 90–108.
Coste, C. 1998. *Roland Barthes, moraliste*. Lille: éditions Septentrion.
———. 2001. '"Alors La Chine?", Roland Barthes'. In Myriam Boucharenc and Joëlle Deluche (eds), *Littérature et reportage*. Limoges: PULIM: 339–353.
———. 2002. 'Brouillons du *Je t'aime*'. *Genesis* 19: 109–128.
———. 2009. 'Roland Barthes par Roland Barthes ou Le démon de la totalité'. *Recherches & Travaux* 75: 35–54.
———. 2011. *Bêtise de Barthes*. Paris: Klincksieck.
———. 2016a. 'Roland Barthes: Terror in Poetry'. *Barthes Studies* 2: 72–94. http://sites.cardiff.ac.uk/barthes/volumes/volume-articles/?q=volume-2 (consulted 13 May 2021).
———. 2016b. *Roland Barthes ou l'art du détour*. Paris: Hermann.
Coustille, C. 2018. *Antithèses. Mallarmé, Péguy, Paulhan, Céline, Barthes*. Paris: Gallimard, ch. IV: 183–245.
De Koven, M. 2004 [1998]. 'Modern Mass to Postmodern Popular in Barthes's *Mythologies*'. In *Gane/Gane*. Vol. II: 113–127.
De Pourcq, M. 2008. 'Roland Barthes and the Greek Desire: Tragedy, Philosophy, Writing'. Unpublished PhD Thesis, Catholic University of Leuven.
———. 2019. 'Travel, Classicism and Writing in Barthes's "En Grèce"'. *Barthes Studies* 5: 23–52.

De Villiers, N. 2005. 'A Great Pedagogy of Nuance: Roland Barthes's the Neutral'. *Theory & Event* 8: 4: np.

———. 2012. *Opacity and the Closet: Queer Tactics in Foucault, Barthes and Warhol*. Minneapolis: University of Minnesota Press.

Deguy, M. 2002. 'Le démon de l'analogie'. In *Alphant and Léger*, 2002: 86–90.

Dort, B. 1954. 'Vers une critique "totalitaire"'. *Critique* 88: 725–732.

Ehrmann, J. 1973. 'L'emprise des signes'. *Semiotica* 1: 49–76.

England, O. (ed). 2020. *Keeper of the Hearth: Picturing Roland Barthes' Unseen Photograph*. Amsterdam: Schilt.

Enthoven, R. (ed). 2010. *Barthes, dialogue avec Igor et Grichka Bogdanov, Antoine Compagnon, Éric Marty, Tiphaine Samoyault, Meiko Takizawa, Marie-Jeanne Zenetti*. Paris: Fayard/France Culture.

Fabre, G. 2001. *Pour une sociologie du procès littéraire. De Goldmann à Barthes en passant par Bakhtine*. Paris: L'Harmattan.

ffrench, P. 2019. *Roland Barthes and Cinema: Myth, Eroticism and Poetics*. London: Bloomsbury.

Fried, M. 2005. 'Barthes's *Punctum*'. *Critical Inquiry* 31:3: 539–574.

Gane, M. J. and N. Gane. 2004. *Roland Barthes*. 3 Vols. London: Sage.

Gardner, C. 2018. *Poetry and Barthes. Anglophone Responses 1970–2000*. Liverpool: Liverpool University Press.

Genesis. 2002. *Manuscrits, recherche, invention*, Number 19: 'Roland Barthes'.

Genova, P. A. 2016. 'Beyond Orientalism? Roland Barthes' Imagistic Structures of Japan'. *Romance Studies* 34:3/4: 152–162.

Gil, M. 2012. *Roland Barthes. Au lieu de la vie*. Paris: Flammarion.

Gil, M. and F. Worms (eds). 2016. *La Vita Nova. La vie comme texte, l'écriture comme vie*. Paris: Hermann.

Greco, N. P. 2020. '"The Antithesis of Inner and Outer: Abolished": Roland Barthes and the Politics of the Closet'. *Roland Barthes Studies* 6: 35–49. http://sites.cardiff.ac.uk/barthes/files/2020/11/GRECO-The-Antithesis-of-Inner-and Outer.pdf (consulted 10 January 2021).

Grossman, É. 2017. 'Le sens de la nuance (Roland Barthes)'. In *Éloge de l'hypersensible*. Paris: éditions de Minuit: 117–198.

Guittard, J. (ed). 2010. *Mythologies de Roland Barthes*. Paris: Seuil.

———. 2014. 'Hygiène du roman. Le Degré zéro de l'écriture sous influence'. *Romanesques* 6: 19–32.

Guittard, J. and N. Emeric (eds). 2019. *Barthes face à la norme: Droit, pouvoir, autorité, langage(s)*. Amiens: Mare & Martin.

Gury, C. 2012. *Les premiers jours de Roland Barthes*. Paris: Non-lieu.

Ha, M.-P. 2000. *Figuring the East: Segalen, Malraux, Duras and Barthes*. New York: SUNY Press.

Han, S. 2020. 'Le discours de Roland Barthes au Collège de France: pré-roman, trans-écriture, hyper-critique'. Unpublished PhD Thesis, université de Grenoble-Alpes.

Hanania, C. 2010. *Roland Barthes et l'étymologie*. Brussels: Peter Lang.

Hargreaves, A. 2005. 'A Neglected Precursor: Roland Barthes and the Origins of Postcolonialism'. In H. Adlai Murdoch and Anne Donadey (eds), *Postcolonial Theory and Francophone Literary Studies*. Gainesville: University Press of Florida: 55–64.

Haustein, K. 2009. 'La vie comme œuvre: Barthes with Proust'. In P. Collier (eds), *Anamnesia: Private and Public Memory in Modern French Culture*. Oxford: Peter Lang: 175–191.

Herschberg, A. 2002. 'Barthes and Doxa'. *Poetics Today* 23: 3: 427–442.

Hiddleston, J. 2010 'Displacing Barthes: Self, Other and the Theorist's Uneasy Belonging'. In *Poststructuralism and Postcoloniality: The Anxiety of Theory*. Liverpool: Liverpool University Press: 99–124.

Higgins, L. 1981. 'Barthes's Imaginary Voyages'. *Studies in Twentieth Century Literature* 5:2: 161–166.

Hill, L. 2010. *Radical Indecision: Barthes, Blanchot, Derrida, and the Future of Criticism*. Notre Dame, IN: Notre Dame University Press.

Holsinger, B. 2005. 'The Four Senses of Roland Barthes'. In B. Holsinger (ed), *The Premodern Condition: Medievalism and the Making of Theory*. Chicago: University of Chicago Press: 152–194.

Huang, H. 2013. 'Roland Barthes: Towards a New Rhetoric of *La Parole*'. In Hairong Huang (ed), *From The 'Trap' of Rhetoric to the Critique of Criticism: A Study of Western Thinking on Rhetoric From Friedrich Nietzsche to Jacques Derrida, Michel Foucault, Paul de Man and Roland Barthes*. Paris: Honoré Champion: Chapter VI.

Huppatz, D. 2011. 'Roland Barthes, *Mythologies*'. *Design and Culture* 3:1: 85–100.

Ilina, A. and Alexandru Matei. 2021. 'Committed to Writing/Writing Commitment: Roland Barthes and Jules Michelet'. *Exemplaria* 33:3, Special Number on 'Medieval Barthes' (ed). Jennifer Rushworth: 264–279.

Ivić, N. and M. Vukušić Zorica (eds). 2017. *Roland Barthes. Création, émotion, jouissance*. Paris: Classiques Garnier.

Johnson, B. 2000 [1978]. 'The Critical Difference'. In Diana Knight (ed), *Critical Essays on Roland Barthes*. New York: G.K. Hall & Co: 174–182.

Kelly, M. 2004 [2000]. 'Demystification: A Dialogue Between Lefebvre and Barthes.' In *Gane/Gane*. Vol. 1: 187–203.

Khatibi, A. 1987. 'Le Japon de Barthes'. In *Figures de l'étranger dans la littérature française*. Paris: Denoël: 57–85.

Klein, R. 1973. 'Images of the Self: New York and Paris.' *Partisan Review* 2: 295–301.

Knight, D. 1997. *Barthes and Utopia: Space, Travel, Writing*. Oxford: Oxford University Press.

——— (ed). 2000. *Critical Essays on Roland Barthes*. New York: G.K. Hall & co.

——— (ed). 2020. *Interdisciplinary Barthes*. Oxford: Oxford University Press.

Kristeva, J. 1981. 'How Does One Speak to Literature?' In *Desire in Language: A Semiotic Approach to Literature and Art*. Oxford: Blackwell: 92–123.

Langlet, I. 2002. 'Inactualité des *Mythologies*?'. In *Macé/Gefen* (eds). 2002: 127–132.

Lavers, A. 1982. *Roland Barthes: Structuralism and After*. London and Boston: Methuen.

Lecercle, J.-J. 2008. 'Barthes Without Althusser: A Different Style of Marxism'. *Paragraph* 31:1: 72–83.

Léger, N. (ed). 2002. *Roland Barthes au Collège de France*. Paris: IMEC.

Leys, S. 1979. 'Footnote to a Barthesian Opuscule'. In S. Leys (ed), *Broken Images: Essays on Chinese Culture and Politics*. Translated by Steve Cox. London: Allison and Busby: 88–89.

Lombardo, P. 1982. 'Le dernier livre'. *L'Esprit créateur* 22:1 (Spring): 79–87.

———. 1989. *The Three Paradoxes of Roland Barthes*. Athens, Georgia: University of Georgia Press.

Lübecker, N. 2010. *Community, Myth and Recognition in Twentieth-Century French Literature and Thought*. London: Continuum: Chapter 4 'Early Barthes, Late Barthes: The End of Community?'

Macdonald, A. 2003. 'Ce qui va de soi: The Agonistics of Motility in Barthes's Mythologies'. *Nottingham French Studies* 42:2: 54–66.

Macé, M. 2002. 'Barthes et l'assertion: la délicatesse en discours'. *Revue des Sciences Humaines* 268:4: 151–165.

———. 'Une écriture à même la vie'. *Le Monde des livres*, 6 February: 2.

Macé, M. and A. Gefen (eds). 2002. *Barthes au lieu du roman*. Paris: éditions Desjonquères.

Marty, E. 2006. *Roland Barthes, le métier d'écrire*. Paris: Seuil.

———. 2010. *Roland Barthes, la littérature et le droit à la mort*. Paris: Seuil.

———. 2015. 'Barthes philosophe'. *Le Monde des livres*, 23 January: 2.

———. 2018. 'Vita nova versus bios philosophikos: Roland Barthes and Michel Foucault'. In Knut Stene-Johansen, Christian Refsum, Johan Schimanski (eds), *Living Together - Roland Barthes, the Individual and the Community*. Bielefeld: Transcript Verlag: 323–333.

Mavor, C. 2007. *Reading Boyishly: Roland Barthes, J. M. Barrie, Jacques Henri Lartigue, Marcel Proust, and D. W. Winnicott*. Durham, NC: Duke University Press.

Mckeane, J. 2015. 'The Tragedy of Barthes'. *Barthes Studies* 1: 61–77.

Meagher, S. 1996. 'Reading/Writing Barthes as Woman'. *Symploke* 4:1–2: 51–60.

Michaud, G. 1989. *Lire le fragment. Transfert et théorie de la lecture chez Roland Barthes*. Ville LaSalle (Québec): éditions Hurtubise.

Miller, D. 1992. *Bringing Out Roland Barthes*. Berkeley/Los Angeles: University of California Press.

Miller, J.-A. 1978. 'Pseudo-Barthes'. In A. Compagnon, 1978: 201–211.

Moriarty, M. 1991. *Roland Barthes*. Cambridge/Oxford: Polity.

Moudileno, L. 2019. 'Barthes's Black Soldier: The Making of a Mythological Celebrity'. *The Yearbook of Comparative Literature* 62: 57–72.

Nachtergael, M. 2015. *Barthes Contemporain*. Paris: Max Milo.

———. 2017. 'Barthes à l'aune des Queer et Visual studies'. In Jean-Pierre Bertrand (ed), 2017: 417–436.

Noghrehchi, H. 2017. 'La Question du discours de l'Histoire'. In Jean-Pierre Bertrand (ed), 2017: 47–66.

Oboussier, C. 1994. 'Barthes and Femininity: A Synaesthetic Writing'. *Nottingham French Studies* 33:2: 78–93.

O'Meara, L. 2012. *Roland Barthes at the Collège de France*. Liverpool: Liverpool University Press.

———. 2020. 'Barthes and the Lessons of Ancient Philosophy'. In Knight, 2020: Chapter 9.

O'Sullivan, M. 2014. 'Roland Barthes: genèse d'un séminaire inédit'. *Genesis. Manuscrits, recherche, invention* 39. https://genesis.revues.org/1414 (consulted 23 June 2021).

Oxman, E. 2010. 'Sensing the Image: Roland Barthes and the Affect of the Visual'. *SubStance* 122, 39:2: 71–90.

Petitier, P. 2000. 'Le Michelet de Roland Barthes'. *Littérature* 119 (September): 111–124.

Philippe, G. 1996. *Bibliographie Barthes*. Rome: Memini/Paris: CNRS.

Piégay, N. and L. Zimmermann (eds). 2016. *Roland Barthes aujourd'hui*. Paris: Hermann.

Pint, K. 2010. *The Perverse Art of Reading: On the Phantasmatic Semiology in Roland Barthes' Cours au Collège de France*. Amsterdam: Rodopi.

Pommier, R. 2017. *Roland Barthes, Grotesque de notre temps. Grotesque de tous les temps*. Paris: Kimé.

Prosser, J. 2004. 'Buddha Barthes: What Barthes Saw in Photography (That He Didn't in Literature)'. *Literature and Theology* 18:2: 211–222.

Rabaté, J.-M. (ed). 1997. *Writing the Image After Roland Barthes*. Philadelphia: University of Pennsylvania Press.

Rambaud, P. and M.-A. Burnier. 1978. *Le Roland-Barthes sans peine*. Paris: éditions Balland.

Reid, M. 2001. 'S/Z Revisited'. *Yale Journal of Criticism* 14:2: 447–452.

Rice, D. and P. Schofer. 1982. '*S/Z*: Rhetoric and Open Reading'. *L'Esprit créateur* 22:1: 20–34.

Richard, J.-P. 2006. *Roland Barthes, dernier paysage*. Paris: Verdier.

Robbe-Grillet, A. 2011. *Why I Love Barthes*. Translated by Andrew Brown. Cambridge: Polity.

Roger, P. 1986. *Roland Barthes, Roman*. Paris: Fasquelle.

———. 1996. 'Barthes dans les années Marx'. *Communications* 63: 39–65.

Saint-Amand, P., Charles A. Porter and Noah Guynn. 1996. 'The Secretive Body: Roland Barthes's Gay Erotics'. *Yale French Studies* 90: 153–157.

———. 2017. 'Érotisme et euphorie'. In Jean-Pierre Bertrand (ed): 629–649.

Salazar, Ph.-J. 1993. 'Barthes et Aristote'. In C. Coquio and R. Salado (eds), *Barthes après Barthes - une actualité en questions*. Pau: Publications de l'université de Pau: 115–121.

Samoyault, T. 2017. *Roland Barthes*. Translated by Andrew Brown. Oxford: Polity.

Scheiber, A. J. 1991. 'Sign, Seme and the Psychological Character. Some Thoughts on Roland Barthes's *S/Z* and the Novel'. In Gane and Gane, 2004, II: 301–313.

Shapiro, G. 1989. '"To Philosophize Is to Learn to Die"'. In S. Ungar and B. McGraw (eds), *Signs in Culture: Roland Barthes Today*. Iowa City: University of Iowa Press: 3–31.

Shawcross, N. 1997. *Roland Barthes on Photography: The Critical Tradition in Perspective*. Gainesville: University Press of Florida.

Smith, D. 2014. 'Barthes's Xyloglossia: Structuralism and the Language of Wood'. *Nottingham French Studies* 53:3: 329–344.

Smith, P. M. 2016. 'The Neutral View: Roland Barthes' Representations of Japan and China'. *IAFOR Journal of Literature and Librarianship* 5:1 (Autumn): 53–60.
Smith, S. M. 2009. 'Race and Reproduction in Camera *Lucida*'. In J. J. Long (eds): 98–111.
Sollers, P. 2017 [1971]. 'R. B.'. Translated by Andrew Brown. In Sollers (ed), *The Friendship of Roland Barthes*. Cambridge: Polity: 33–50.
Sontag, S. 1982. 'Writing itself: On Roland Barthes'. In A. Susan (ed), *Sontag Reader*. London: Penguin: 423–446.
Stafford, A. 1998. *Roland Barthes, Phenomenon and Myth: An Intellectual Biography*. Edinburgh: Edinburgh University Press.
———. 1999. '"Mise en crise". Roland Barthes From Stage to Text'. In Victoria Best and P. Collier (eds), *Powerful Bodies: Performance in French Cultural Studies*. Berne: Peter Lang: 149–163.
———. 2015a. *Roland Barthes. 'Critical Lives' Series*. London: Reaktion Press.
———. 2015b. 'Marking a Writer's Centenary ... Backwards? The Case of Roland Barthes, 1915–1980'. *Forum for Modern Language Studies* 51:4 (October), Special Number 'The 15s' Robin Mackenzie (ed): 480–494.
Stan, C. 2014. 'A Sociality of Distances: Roland Barthes and Iris Murdoch on How to Live With Others'. *MLN* 129:5: 1170–1198.
Stewart, P. 2001. 'What Barthes Couldn't Say: On the Curious Occultation of Homoeroticism in *S/Z*. *Paragraph* 24:1 (March): 1–16.
Stivale, C. 2002. 'Mythologies Revisited: Roland Barthes and the Left'. *Cultural Studies* 16:3: 457–484.
Sun, Q. 2014. 'Roland Barthes, lecteur du XIXe siècle'. Unpublished PhD Thesis, University of Paris. http://octaviana.fr/document/182423298#?c=0&m=0&s=0&cv=0 (consulted 20 April 2021).
Tager, M. 1986. 'Myth and Politics in the Work of Sorel and Barthes'. *Journal of the History of Ideas* 47:4: 625–639.
Tel Quel. 1971 (Number 47).
Temple, W. S. 2020. '(Im)Possible Delights: Barthes's Homoerotic Travel Writing and the Photography of Bishan Samaddar'. In W. S. Temple (ed), *Redrawing the Territories of Desire and Melancholy: Le voyage homoérotique: The Travel Writings and Films of Gide, Duvert, Barthes, Genet, Taïa, Rachid O., Vallois and Bouzid*. Fasano: Schena editore: Chapter 2.
Theory, Culture, Society. 2020. 37:4, Special Number 'Neutral Life/Late Barthes', Sunil Manghani (ed).
Thody, P. 1977. *Roland Barthes: A Conservative Estimate*. London: MacVillan.
Thornhill, K. (ed). 2016. *Mystiques: A Feminist Homage to Roland Barthes*. Oxford: The Feminist E-Press.
Ungar, S. 1982. 'Barthes Via Proust: Circular Memories'. *L'Esprit créateur* 22:1: 8–19.
———. 1983. *Roland Barthes: the Professor of Desire*. London and Lincoln: University of Nebraska Press.
———. 2004. 'Saussure, Barthes and structuralism'. In Carol Sanders (ed), *The Cambridge Companion to Saussure*. Cambridge: Cambridge University Press: 157–173.
Velan, Y. 1957. 'Les *Mythologies* de Roland Barthes.' *Les Lettres nouvelles* (July–August): 113–119.
Wampole, C. 2015. 'What Would Barthes Think of His Hermes Scarf?'. *New Yorker*, 20 October. http://www.newyorker.com/books/pageturner/barthess-silken-legacy (consulted 12 July 2021).
Warner, M. 1992. 'The Song of Roland: Sex and the Single Philosopher'. *Voice Literary Supplement*, December.
Watts, P. 2016. *Roland Barthes' Cinema*. New York: Oxford University Press.
Weller, S. 2019. 'Active Philology: Barthes and Nietzsche'. *French Studies* 73:2: 217–233.
Wermer-Colan, A. 2016. 'Roland Barthes after 1968: Critical Theory in the Reactionary Era of New Media'. In *Yearbook of Comparative Literature*. : .TorontoUniversity of Toronto Press

White, E. 2012. *How to Read Barthes' Image-Music-Text*. London: Pluto.
Wilson, H. R. 2017. 'The Theatricality of the *Punctum*: Re-Viewing Roland Barthes' *Camera Lucida*'. *Performance Philosophy* 3: 266–284.
Wilson, R. J. 2000. 'A Map of Terms: The "Cultural Code" and "Ethic Psychology" in *S/Z* and "Introduction to the Structural Analysis of Narratives"'. In Gane and Gane (ed), 2004, II: 329–345.
Wiseman, M. B. 1989. *The Ecstasies of Roland Barthes*. London: Routledge.
Yacavone, K. 2012. *Benjamin, Barthes and the Singularity of Photography*. London: Bloomsbury.
Zenetti, M.-J. 2011. 'Transparence, opacité, matité dans l'œuvre de Roland Barthes, du *Degré zéro de l'écriture* à *L'Empire des signes*'. *Appareil* 7. https://journals.openedition.org/appareil/1201 (consulted 11 May 2021).
Zhuo, Y. 2011. 'The 'Political' Barthes: From Theater to Idiorrhythmy'. *French Forum* 36:1: 55–74.

3. Secondary Works Consulted

Adorno, T. 1994. *The Stars Down to Earth: And Other Essays on the Irrational in Culture*. London: Routledge.
Adorno, T. and M. Horkheimer. 1979 [1944]. *Dialectic of Enlightenment*. London: NLB.
Ahmed, S. 2014 [2004]. *The Cultural Politics of Emotion*. Edinburgh: Edinburgh University Press.
Ahnouch, F. 2004. *Abdelkébir Khatibi. La langue, la mémoire et le corps. L'articulation de la imaginaire culturel*. Paris: L'Harmattan.
Ali, T. 2015. 'It Didn't Need To Be Done'. *London Review Books*, 5 February: 11–12.
Allar, N. 2015. 'The Case for Incomprehension'. *Journal of French and Francophone Philosophy* XXIII:1: 43–58.
Almond, I. 2021. *World Literature Decentered: Beyond the 'West' Through Turkey, Mexico and Bengal*. London: Routledge.
Althusser, L. 1971a [1962]. 'The 'Piccolo Teatro': Bertolazzi and Brecht'. In For Marx (ed), Translated by Ben Brewster. London: Allen Lane Penguin Press: 129–151.
———. 1971b [1970]. 'Ideology and Ideological State Apparatuses (Notes Towards an Investigation). In *Lenin and Philosophy and Other Essays*. Translated by Ben Brewster. London: NLB: 121–173.
Amossy, R. 2002. 'Introduction to the Study of Doxa'. *Poetics Today* 23:3 (Fall): 369–394.
Anderson, P. 1979. *Considerations on Western Marxism*. London: Verso.
Anon. 1975. '[Review of Jean Pasqualini's] Prisonnier de Mao'. *La Quinzaine littéraire* 1 (15 March): 22–23.
Antonini, F. 2019. 'Pessimism of the Intellect, Optimism of the Will: Gramsci's Political Thought in the Last Miscellaneous Notebooks'. *Rethinking Marxism* 31:1: 42–57.
Ashcroft, B. and P. Ahluwalia. 2001. *Edward Said*. New York: Routledge.
Axelos, K. 1976 [1961]. *Alienation, Praxis and Techne in the Thought of Karl Marx*. Translated by Ronald Bruzina. Austin: University of Texas Press.
Badiou, A. 2012. *In Praise of Love*. Translated by Peter Bush. New York: New Press.
———. 2015. *Philosophy for Militants*. Translated by Bruno Bosteels. London: Verso.
Bakhtin, M. 1984. *Problems of Dostoevsky's Poetics*. Translated by Caryl Emerson. Minneapolis: Minnesota University Press.
Balibar, R. 1974. *Les français fictifs. Le rapport de styles littéraires au français national*. Paris: Hachette.
Balzac, H. [de]. 1964 [1831]. 'Théorie du conte'. In *La Comédie Humaine XI 'Contes drolatiques'*. Paris: NRF: 973–975.
Bannet, E. T. 1989. *Structuralism and the Logic of Dissent. Barthes, Derrida, Foucault, Lacan*. Basingstoke: Macmillan.
Bataille, G. 1970. *Œuvres complètes*. Vol. I. Paris: Gallimard.

———. 1973. *Œuvres complètes*. Vol. V. Paris: Gallimard.
Baudelaire, C. 1909 [1859]. *The Flowers of Evil*. Translated by Cyril Scott. London: Elkin Mathews.
———. 2000 [1860]. *Artificial Paradise*. Translated by Patricia Roseberry. Harrogate: Broadwater House.
Baugh, B. 2003. *French Hegel: From Surrealism to Postmodernism*. London: Routledge.
Bayard, P. 2005. *Demain est écrit*. Paris: Minuit.
———. 2009. *Le Plagiat par anticipation*. Paris: Minuit.
———. 2013. *Aurais-je été résistant ou bourreau?* Paris: Minuit.
Belsey, C. 2002. *Poststructuralism: A Very Short Introduction*. Oxford: Oxford University Press.
Ben Jelloun, T. (ed). 1976. *La Mémoire future. Anthologie de la nouvelle poésie du Maroc*. Paris: Maspero.
Benjamin, W. 1947 [1940]. 'Sur le concept d'histoire'. Translated by Pierre Missac. *Les Temps Modernes* 25 (October).
———. 1973 [1940]. 'The Theses on the Philosophy of History'. In *Illuminations*. Glasgow: Fontana: 255–266.
———. 2001. *On the Concept of History*. Translated by Dennis Redmond. http://folk.uib.no/hlils/TBLR-B/Benjamin-History.pdf (consulted 11 May 2021).
———. 2002. *The Arcades Project*. Translated by Howard Eiland and Kevin McLaughlin. Cambridge, MA: Harvard University Press.
Benoist, J.-M. 1970. *Marx est mort*. Paris: Gallimard.
———. 1975. *La révolution structurale. Althusser, Barthes, Lacan, Lévi-Strauss*. Paris: Grasset et Fasquelle.
Bensaïd, D. 2002. *Les Trotskysmes*. Paris: PUF.
Benson, S. and Clare Connors (eds). 2015. *Creative Criticism: An Anthology and Guide*. Edinburgh: Edinburgh University Press.
Berger, J. 2001. *Selected Writings*. London: Bloomsbury.
Bergson, H. 1944 [1907]. *Creative Evolution*. Translated by Arthur Mitchell. New York: Random House.
———. 1959 [1934]. *La Pensée et le mouvant*. Paris: PUF.
Bernard, J.-P. A. 1972. *Le Parti Communiste Français et la question littéraire, 1921–1939*. Grenoble: Presses Universitaires de Grenoble.
Birchall, I. 2004. *Sartre Against Stalinism*. New York/Oxford: Berghahn Books.
Bonafous-Murat, C. 2000. 'Présentation'. In Oscar Wilde (ed), *Intentions*. Translated by Philippe Neel. Paris: Librairie Générale: 7–40.
Borejsza, J. W. 2010. 'Staline et le cosmopolitisme'. *Vingtième siècle. Revue d'histoire* 108 (October–December): 113–126.
Bousfiha, N. 1992. 'Contemporary French-Language Moroccan Poetry'. *Research in African Literatures* 23:2: 113–130.
Bracht Branham, R. 2005. 'The Poetics of Genre: Bakhtin, Menippus, Peronius'. In R. Bracht Branham (ed), *The Bakhtin Circle and Ancient Narrative*. Groningen: Barkhuis Publishing: 3–31.
Braidotti, R. 2002. *Metamorphoses: Towards a Materialist Theory of Becoming*. Cambridge: Polity.
Brault, M., M. Carrière, C. Fournier and C. Jutra. 1961. 'La Lutte (Film, 28 mins)'. https://www.nfb.ca/film/la_lutte/ (consulted 17 May 2021).
Brecht, B. 1952. *Mère Courage*. Translated by G. Serreau and B. Besson, 8 Photographs by Agnès Varda. Paris: L'Arche.
———. 1960a. *Mère Courage*. Édition illustrée. Translated by G. Serreau and B. Besson, With 100 Photographs by Roger Pic, Presented and Commented by Roland Barthes. Paris: L'Arche.
———. 1960b. *Mère Courage*. Translated by G. Serreau and B. Besson, Preface by Roland Barthes With 7 Photographs by Roger Pic. Paris: L'Arche.
———. 1960c. *Grand'Peur et misère du IIIe Reich*. Translated by Maurice Regnaut and André Steiger. Paris: L'Arche.

———. 1962. *Mother Courage and Her Children*. Translated by Eric Bentley. London: Methuen.
———. 1964. *Maître Puntila et son valet Matti*. Translated by Michel Cadot, 15 Photographs By Roger Pic. Paris: L'Arche.
Britton, C. 1995. 'Opacity and Transparency: Conceptions of History and Cultural Difference in the Work of Michel Butor and Edouard Glissant'. *French Studies* 49:3 (July): 308–320.
———. 1999. *Édouard Glissant and Postcolonial Theory: Strategies of Language and Resistance*. Charlottesville: Virginia University Press.
Bull, M. 2020. 'Where is the Anti-Nietzsche?' *New Left Review* 3 (May/June): 121–145.
Bulletin de la Société Voltaire. 2015. 'Numéro 35'. 11 January. http://societe-voltaire.org/docs/bulletin/b35.html (consulted 17 May 2021).
Butler, J. 2005. *Giving an Account of Oneself*. New York: Fordham University Press.
Caillois, R. 1950. *Description du marxisme*. Paris: Gallimard.
Callinicos, A. 1995. *Theories and Narratives: Reflections on the Philosophy of History*. Cambridge: Polity.
———. 2014. *Deciphering Capital: Marx's Capital and its Destiny*. London: Bookmarks.
Carrard, P. 2017. *History as a Kind of Writing: Textual Strategies in Contemporary French Historiography*. Chicago: The University of Chicago Press.
Carver, T. and J. Farr (eds). 2015. *The Cambridge Companion to the 'Communist Manifesto'*. Cambridge: Cambridge University Press.
Caudwell, C. 1977. *Illusion and Reality: A Study of the Sources of Poetry*. London: Lawrence & Wishart.
Chambers, R. 1999. *Loiterature*. Lincoln/London: University of Nebraska Press.
Chatman, S. 1979. *Story and Discourse: Narrative Structure in Fiction*. Ithaca/London: Cornell UP.
Claudel, P. 1929. *L'oiseau noir dans le soleil levant*. Paris: Gallimard.
———. 1973 [1900]. *Connaissance de l'est*. Paris: Mercure de France.
Cohen, M. 1994. *The Wager of Lucien Goldmann*. Princeton, NJ: Princeton University Press.
Cole, T. 2015. 'Unmournable Bodies'. *The New Yorker*, 9 January. https://www.newyorker.com/culture/cultural-comment/unmournable-bodies (consulted 4 July 2021).
Coll. 1968. *Tel Quel, Théorie d'ensemble*. Paris: Seuil.
———. 2015. *Nous sommes Charlie*. Paris: Livre de poche.
Compagnon, A. 2004. *Literature, Theory and Common Sense*. Translated by Carol Cosman. Princeton: Princeton University Press.
Confiant, R. 1994. 'Questions pratiques d'écriture créole'. In Ralph Ludwig (ed), *Ecrire 'la Parole de nuit'. La nouvelle littérature antillaise*. Paris: Gallimard: 171–180.
Crary, J. 1992. *Techniques of the Observer: On Vision and Modernity in the Nineteenth Century*. Cambridge, MA/London: MIT Press.
Crehan, K. 2016. *Gramsci's Common Sense*. Durham, NC: Duke University Press.
Crowley, M. 2006. 'Dionys Mascolo: Art, Politics, Revolt'. *Forum for Modern Language Studies* 42:2 (April): 139–150.
Dahmer, H. 2021. 'Walter Benjamin and Leon Trotsky'. In F. Menezes (ed), *Trotskismos em Cuba. Retrato de um encontro*. São Paulo: Nojosa edições: 487–497.
Daix, P. 1957. *Réflexions sur la méthode de Roger Martin du Gard suivi de Lettre à Maurice Nadeau et autres essais*. Paris: Les Editeurs Français Réunis.
De Ste Croix, G. E. M. 1981. *The Class Struggle in the Ancient Greek World: From the Archaic Age to the Arab Conquests*. Ithaca: Cornell University Press.
Deleuze, G. 1996 [1973]. 'Letter to a Harsh Critic'. In *Negotiations, 1972–1990*. Translated by Martin Joughin. New York: Columbia University Press: 3–12.
Denis, B. 2000. *Littérature et engagement. De Pascal à Sartre*. Paris: Seuil.
———. 2003. 'Les écrivains engagés et le réalisme socialiste'. *Sociétés et Représentations* 1:15: 247–259.
Derrida, J. 1994. *Spectres of Marx: The State of the Debt, the Work of Mourning and the New International*. Translated by Peggy Kamuf. London: Routledge.
———. 2001. *Writing and Difference*. Translated by Alan Bass. London: Routledge.

———. 2003. *The Problem of Genesis in Husserl's Philosophy*. Translated by Marian Hobson. Chicago: University of Chicago Press.

Detweiler, R. 1978. *Story, Sign and Self: Phenomenology and Structuralism as Literary-Critical Methods*. Pennsylvania: Fortress Press.

Di Leo, J. R. (ed). 2018. *What's Wrong With Antitheory?* London: Bloomsbury.

Diderot, D. 2002. 'Ceci n'est pas un conte.' In *Les Deux Amis de Bourbonne et autres contes*. Paris: Gallimard: 51–75.

Didi-Huberman, G. 2016. *Peuples en larmes, Peuples en armes*. Paris: éditions de Minuit.

Domenach, J.-M. 1967. 'Le système et la personne'. *Esprit* 5 (May): 771–780.

Drochon, H. *Nietzsche's Great Politics*. Princeton: Princeton University Press.

Du Bois, W. E. B. 1999 [1903]. *The Souls of Black Folk: Essays and Sketches*. New York: Bartleby.com.

Dufays, J.-L. 2010. *Stéréotype et lecture. Essai sur la réception littéraire*. Brussels: Peter Lang.

Dunayevskaya, R. 1972. 'On C. L. R. James' Notes on Dialectics'. https://www.marxists.org/archive/dunayevskaya/works/1972/misc/james.htm (consulted 21 July 2021).

Durkheim, E. 1995 [1912]. *The Elementary Forms of Religious Life*. Translated by Karen E. Fields. New York: The Free Press.

Dyer, G. 1986. *Ways of Telling: The Work of John Berger*. London: Pluto.

Eagleton, T. 1976. *Marxism and Literary Theory*. London: Methuen.

———. 2021. 'The Marxist and the Messiah'. *London Review of Books*, 9 September: 27–28.

Eco, U. 1999. *Kant et l'ornithorynque*. Paris: Grasset.

Engels, F. 1884. 'Origins of the Family, Private Property and the State'. https://www.marxists.org/archive/marx/works/1884/origin-family/preface.htm (consulted 7 June 2021).

———. 1954 [1878]. *Anti-Dühring. Herr Eugen Dühring's Revolution in Science*. Moscow: Foreign Languages Publishing House.

Etiemble, R. 1961 [1952]. *Le Mythe de Rimbaud. t.2. Structure du mythe*. Paris: Gallimard.

———. 1968 [1954]. *Le Mythe de Rimbaud. t.1 Genèse du Mythe 1869–1949*. Paris: Gallimard.

Felski, R. 2015. *The Limits of Critique*. Chicago: University of Chicago Press.

ffrench, P. 1995. *The Time of Theory: A History of 'Tel Quel' (1960–1983)*. Oxford: Clarendon Press.

Fisher, M. *Capitalist Realism: Is There No Alternative?*. London: Zero Books.

Flaubert, G. 1929. 'Letter Dated 23 October 1865 to Mademoiselle Leroyer de Chantepie'. In *Correspondance*. Vol. 5. Paris: éditions Louis Conard.

Flores Khalil, A. 2003. 'A Writing in Points: Autobiography and the Poetics of the Tattoo'. *Journal of North African Studies* 8:2: 19–33.

Forsdick, C. 2005. *Travel in Twentieth-Century French and Francophone Cultures*. Oxford: Oxford University Press.

Garnier, X. 2009. 'Modernités littéraires en Afrique: injonction ou évidence?'. *Itinéraires* 3: 89–101.

Gava, J.-F. 2011. *Contrariété sans dialectique. Logique et politique hégéliennes face à la critique sociale marxienne*. Paris: L'Harmattan.

Genette, G. 1963. 'Réponse à un questionnaire'. *Tel Quel* 14: 69–70.

———. 1966. 'Structuralisme et critique littéraire'. In *Figures I*. Paris: Seuil: 145–170.

Gide, A. 1939. *Back From the USSR*. Translated by Dorothy Busy. London: Secker and Warburg.

Glissant, E. 1969. *L'intention poétique*. Paris: Editions du Seuil.

———. 1981. *Le Discours antillais*. Paris: Editions du Seuil.

———. 1994. 'Le chaos-monde, l'oral et l'écrit'. In Ralph Ludwig (ed), *Ecrire la Parole de nuit. La nouvelle littérature antillaise*. Paris: Gallimard: 111–129.

———. 1997 [1992]. *Poetics of Relation*. Translated by Betsy Wing. Ann Arbor: University of Michigan Press.

———. 2020 [1996]. *Introduction to a Poetics of Diversity*. Translated by Celia Britton. Liverpool: Liverpool University Press.

———. 2020 [1997]. *Treatise on the Whole-World*. Translated by Celia Britton. Liverpool: Liverpool University Press.

Godelier, M. 1970. 'System, Structure and Contradiction in *Das Kapital*'. In Michael Lane (ed), *Structuralism: A Reader*. London: Jonathan Cape: 340–358.

Goh, I. 2015. *The Reject: Community, Politics, and Religion After the Subject*. New York: Fordham University Press.

Goldmann, L. 1959 [1950]. *Recherches dialectiques*. Paris: Gallimard.

———. 1971. *Situation de la critique racinienne*. Paris: L'Arche.

———. 1975 [1964]. *Towards a Sociology of the Novel*. Translated by Alan Sheridan. New York: Tavistock Publications.

———. 2016 [1955]. *The Hidden God: A Study of Tragic Vision in the 'Pensées' of Pascal and the Tragedies of Racine*. Translated by Philip Thody. London: Verso.

Gontard, M. 1981. *Violence du texte. La littérature marocaine de langue française*. Paris: L'Harmattan/SMER.

Gramsci, A. 1971. *Selection From the Prison Notebooks*. London: Lawrence & Wishart.

Greimas, A.-J. 1983 [1956]. 'Pour une sociologie du langage'. In *Arguments* 1 (Facsimile, Vol. 1). Toulouse: Privat: 16–19.

———. 2000 [1956]. 'L'actualité du saussurisme.' In Greimas (ed), *La mode en 1830. Langage et société: écrits de jeunesse*. Paris: PUF: 371–382.

Greisch, J. 1997. 'La 'cohésion de la vie': la trace comme effet-signe et l'historialité'. *Noésis* 1: 4–38.

Griffiths, M. R. 2014. 'Toward Relation: Negritude, Poststructuralism, and the Specter of Intention in the Work of Édouard Glissant'. *Discourse* 36:1: 31–53.

Guerlac, S. 1993. 'Sartre and the Powers of Literature: The Myth of Prose and the Practice of Reading'. *MLN* 108:5: 805–824.

Habib, M. A. R. 2018. *Hegel and the Foundations of Literary Theory*. Cambridge: Cambridge University Press: Chapter 8 'Hegel, Language and Literary Theory'.

Halberstam, J. 2005. *A Queer Time and Place: Transgender Bodies, Subcultural Lives*. New York: New York University Press.

Hall, B. K. 1999. 'The Paradoxical Platypus'. *Bioscience* 49:3 (March): 211–218.

Hamon, P. 1977. 'Pour un statut sémiologique du personnage'. In R. Barthes, W. Kayser, W. Booth and Ph. Hamon (eds), *Poétique du récit*. Paris: Seuil: 115–180.

Harrison, O. C. and T. Villa-Ignacio (eds). 2016. *Souffles-Anfas: A Critical Anthology From the Moroccan Journal of Culture and Politics*. Stanford: Stanford University Press.

Heath, S. 1981. *Questions of Cinema*. Bloomington: Indiana University Press.

Hegel, G. W. F. 1805–1806. 'Scepticism'. In *Lectures on the History of Philosophy I*, 2, D. https://www.marxists.org/reference/archive/hegel/works/hp/hpscepticism.htm (consulted 19 August 2021).

———. 1964 [1827–1830]. 'La peinture hollandaise, ou la transfiguration de la vie quotidienne'. In *Esthétique de la peinture figurative*. Paris: Hermann: Chapter 6.

Hibbitt, R. 2011. 'Reflections on the Fruitful Error'. In Rhian Atkin (ed), *Textual Wanderings: The Theory and Practice of Narrative Digression*. Oxford: Legenda: 27–36.

Hjelmslev, L. 1968 [1943]. *Prolégomènes à une théorie du langage*. Translated by A.-M. Léonard. Paris: éditions de Minuit.

Hook, S. 1936. *Pour comprendre Marx*. Translated by Mario Rietti. Paris: Gallimard.

———. 1943. *The Hero in History: A Study in Limitation and Possibility*. New York: John Day.

Horvat, S. 2016. *The Radicality of Love*. Cambridge: Polity.

Hughes, E. J. 2011. *Proust, Class, Nation*. Oxford: Oxford University Press.

Illouz, E. 2012. *Why Love Hurts: A Sociological Explanation*. Cambridge: Polity.

Ingram, P. 2020. 'Adorno's Philistinism: The Dialectic of Art and Its Other'. *Historical Materialism* 28:3 (September): 82–112.

Innami, F. 2011. 'The Departing Body: Creation of the Neutral In-Between Sensual Bodies'. *Asian and African Studies* XV: 3: 111–130.

Jack, B. 1995. *Francophone Literatures: An Introductory Survey*. Oxford: Oxford University Press.

Jackson, R. 2020. 'Gramsci, Left Populism and Class Struggle'. *International Socialism Journal* 166: 135–158.
Jaeger, W. 2014. *Paideia. La formation de l'homme grec*. Translated by André and Simonne Devyver. Paris: Gallimard.
James, C. L. R. 1980 [1948]. *Notes on Dialectics. Hegel-Marx-Lenin*. London: Allison & Busby.
Jameson, F. 2010. *The Valences of the Dialectic*. London: Verso.
Jaurès, J. 1956 [1900–1908]. 'Critical Introduction to *The Socialist History of the French Revolution*'. In Fritz Stern (ed), *The Varieties of History: From Voltaire to the Present*. Cleveland, OH: Meridian Books: 158–169.
Jeanson, F. 1952. 'Albert Camus, ou l'âme révoltée'. *Les Temps Modernes* 79 (May): 2070–2090.
Joussain, A. 1950. *La Loi des révolutions*. Paris: Flammarion.
Jubert, R. 2005. *Graphisme, typographie, histoire*. Paris: Flammarion.
Karatani, K. 1993. *Origins of Modern Japanese Literature*. Translated and Edited by Brett de Bary. Durham: Duke University Press.
———. 1995. *Architecture as Metaphor: Language, Number, Money*. Translated by Sabu Kohso. Cambridge, MA: MIT Press.
———. 2012. *History and Repetition*. Translated by Seiji M. Lippit. New York: Columbia University Press.
———. 2020 [1974]. *Marx: Towards the Centre of Possibility*. Translated by Gavin Walker. London: Verso.
Keegan, P. 2020. 'Emily of Fire and Violence'. *London Review of Books*, 22 October: 7–9.
Khaïr-Eddine, M. 2020. *Agadir*. Translated by Pierre Joris and Jake Syersak. Monee, IL: Diálogos Books.
Khatibi, A. 1971. 'De la critique du langage à la lutte des classes'. *Le Monde*, 17 December: 17.
———. 1974. *La Blessure du nom propre*. Paris: Denoël.
———. 1997. *L'œuvre de Abdelkébir Khatibi (Préliminaire)*. Rabat: Marsam.
———. 2016 [1971]. *Tattooed Memory*. Translated by Peter Thompson. Paris: L'Harmattan.
Kierkegaard, S. 1996. *Papers and Journals: A Selection*. Translated by Alasdair Hannay. London: Penguin.
Kitto, H. D. F. 1956. 'The Greek Chorus'. *Educational Theatre Journal* 8:1: 1–8.
Knight, D. 2007. *Balzac and the Model of Painting: Artists' Stories in 'La Comédie Humaine'*. Oxford: Legenda.
Kornbluh, A. 2014. *Realizing Capital: Financial and Psychic Economies in Victorian Form*. Oxford: Oxford University Press.
Kosik, K. 1970. *La Dialectique du concret*. French Translated by Roger Dangeville. Paris: Maspero.
Kosofsky Sedgwick, E. 1994. *Tendencies*. London: Routledge.
Kowalska, M. 2015. *Dialectics Beyond Dialectics: Essay on Totality and Difference*. Oxford and Frankfurt: Peter Lang.
Kracauer, S. 1995. *The Mass Ornament: Weimar Essays*. Translated by Thomas Y. Levin. Cambridge, MA: Harvard University Press.
Kristeva, J. 1986a [1969]. 'Word, Dialogue and Novel'. In Toril Moi (ed), *The Kristeva Reader*. Oxford: Blackwell: 34–61.
———. 1986b [1974]. *About Chinese Women*. Translated by Anita Barrows. London/New York: Marion Boyars Publishers.
———. 2000. *The Sense and Non-Sense of Revolt: The Powers and Limits of Psychoanalysis*. Vol. I. Translated by Jeanine Herman. New York: Columbia University Press.
Kuhn, T., Giles, S. and Silberman, M. (eds). 2017. *Brecht on Performance: Messingkauf and Modelbooks*. London: Bloomsbury.
La Boétie, E. . 1574. 'De la servitude volontaire, ou le Contr'un'. http://www.singulier.eu/textes/reference/texte/pdf/servitude.pdf (consulted 20 May 2020).
Laâbi, A. 1970. 'Au sujet d'un certain procès de la littérature maghrébine écrite en français'. *Souffles* 18 (March–April): 62–65.
———. 2005. *Histoire de la poésie marocaine depuis l'Indépendance*. Paris: La Découverte.

———. 2012. *The Rule of Barbarism*. Translated by André Naffis-Sahelu. Brooklyn/Gorée/Maastricht: Island Position.

Lahanque, R. 2003. 'Les romans du réalisme socialiste français'. *Sociétés et Représentations* 1:15: 177–194.

Le Cour Grandmaison, O. 2020. '8 mai 1945 en France et en Algérie : mythologie nationale versus histoire coloniale.' *Médiapart*, 6 May. https://blogs.mediapart.fr/olivier-le-cour-grandmaison/blog/060520/8-mai-1945-en-france-et-en-algerie-mythologie-nationale-versus-histoire-coloniale (consulted 5 May 2021).

Lears, T. J. J. 1985. 'The Concept of Cultural Hegemony: Problems and Possibilities'. *The American Historical Review* 90:3: 567–593.

Lefebvre, H. 1971 [1966]. 'Claude Lévi-Strauss et le nouvel éléatisme'. In *L'idéologie structuraliste*. Paris: éditions Anthropos: 45–110.

———. 2003. 'Henri Lefebvre'. In Stuart Elden, Elizabeth Lebas and Eleonore Kofman (eds), *Key Writings*. London: Continuum.

Lefort, C. 1947. 'Les pays coloniaux'. *Les Temps Modernes* 18 (March): 1068–1094.

Lenin, V. I. 1981. *Collected Works 20, 38*. New York: Progress.

Lévi-Strauss, C. 1955. 'Réponse à Roger Caillois'. *La Nouvelle Nouvelle Revue Française* 5 (May): 935.

———. 1963. *Structural Anthropology*. Translated by Brooke Grundfest Schoepf. Harmondsworth: Penguin.

Leys, S. 1977. *The Chairman's New Clothes: Mao and the Cultural Revolution*. Translated by Carol Appleyard and Patrick Goode. London: Allison and Busby.

Ligouri, G. 2016. *Gramsci's Pathways*. London: Haymarket.

Long, J. J., A. Nobel and E. Welch (eds). 2009. *Photography: Theoretical Snapshots*. Oxon: Routledge.

Lordon, F. 2013. *La Société des affects. Pour un structuralisme des passions*. Paris: Seuil.

Losurdo, D. 2020. *Nietzsche, the Aristocratic Rebel: Intellectual Biography and Critical Balance-Sheet*. Translated by Gregor Benton. Chicago: Haymarket Books.

Lourau, R. 1969. *L'instituant contre l'institué*. Paris: Anthropos.

———. 1971. *L'analyse institutionnelle*. Paris: Minuit.

Lovatt, A. 2019. *Drawing Degree Zero: The Line From Minimal to Conceptual Art*. University Park, PA: Pennsylvania State University Press.

Lucken, M. 2021. 'The Limits of *Ma*: Retracing the Emergence of a 'Japanese' Concept'. *Journal of World Philosophies* 6 (Summer): 38–57.

Lukács, G. 1969. *The Historical Novel*. Translated by H. S. Mitchell. London: Penguin.

Lunn, E. 1982. *Marxism and Modernism: An Historical Reading of Lukács, Brecht, Benjamin and Adorno*. Berkley and Los Angeles: California University Press.

Lyotard, J.-F. 1954. *La Phénoménologie*. Paris: PUF.

———. 1971. *Discours, figure*. Paris: Klincksieck.

———. 1974. 'Adorno as the Devil'. Translated by Robert Hurley. *Telos* 19 (Spring): 127–137.

———. 1989. *The Lyotard Reader*. Oxford: Blackwell.

———. 1994. *Lessons on the Analytic of the Sublime*. Translated by Elizabeth Rottenberg. Stanford: Stanford University Press.

Macé, M. 2006. *Le Temps de l'essai. Histoire d'un genre en France au XXe siècle*. Paris: Belin.

———. 2011. *Façons de lire, manières d'être*. Paris: Gallimard.

Macfarlane, H. 2015. 'Manifesto of the German Communist Party (1848). First English translation (abridged) by Helen Macfarlane (1850)'. In *Carver/Farr*, 2015: 261–282.

Malabou, C. 2005. *The Future of Hegel: Plasticity, Temporality and Dialectic*. Translated by Lisabeth During. London: Routledge.

Mao Tse-tung. 1966. *Quotations From Chairman Mao Tse-tung*. Beijing: Foreign Language Press.

Marcuse, H. 1991 [1964]. *One-Dimensional Man: Studies in the Ideology of Advanced Industrial Society*. London: Routledge.

———. 2000 [1969]. *An Essay on Liberation*. Boston: Beacon Press.
Martin, J. 2015. 'The Rhetoric of the Manifesto'. In *Carver/Farr*, 2015: 50–66.
Marx, K. and F. Engels. 1845. 'The Holy Family, or Critique of Critical Criticism'. https://www.marxists.org/archive/marx/works/1845/holy-family/index.htm.
———. 1847. 'The Poverty of Philosophy: Answer to 'The Philosophy of Poverty''. https://www.marxists.org/archive/marx/works/1847/poverty-philosophy/index.htm.
———. 1965. *The Manifesto of the Communist Party*. Beijing: Foreign Languages Press.
———. 1974. *The German Ideology*. London: Lawrence & Wishart.
———. 1975a. 'Economic and Philosophical Manuscripts (1844)'. In *Early Writings*. Translated by Rodney Livingstone and Gregor Benton. London: Penguin: 279–400.
———. 1975b. *Collected Works*. Vol. I. London: Lawrence & Wishart.
———. 1975c [1867]. *Capital*. Vol. I. London: Penguin.
———. 1978 [1849]. *The 18th Brumaire of Louis Bonaparte*. Beijing: Foreign Languages Press.
Marx-Scouras, D. 1996. *The Cultural Politics of 'Tel Quel'. Literature and the Left in the Wake of Engagement*. Pennsylvania: Penn State Press.
Mascolo, D. 1953. *Le Communisme. Révolution et communication ou la dialectique des valeurs et des besoins*. Paris: Gallimard.
———. 2011 [1955]. *Sur le sens et l'usage du mot 'Gauche'*. Clamecy: Nouvelles Editions Lignes.
Matoré, G. 1953. *La méthode en lexicologie. Domaine Français*. Paris: Marcel Didier.
Mau, S. 2021. "The Mute Compulsion of Economic Relations': Towards a Marxist Theory of the Abstract and Impersonal Power'. *Historical Materialism* 29:3: 3–32.
Mepham, J. 1972. 'The Theory of Ideology in *Capital*.' *Radical Philosophy* 2: 12–19.
Merleau-Ponty, M. 1964. *Signs*. Translated by Richard McCleary. Evanston: Northwestern University Press.
———. 1968. *The Visible and the Invisible*. Translated by A. Lingis. Evanston: Northwestern University Press.
Meyer-Plantureux, C., R. Pic and B. Besson. 1995. *Bertolt Brecht et le Berliner Ensemble à Paris*. Paris: Marval.
Michaux, H. 1967. *Connaissance par les gouffres*. Paris: Gallimard.
Michelet, J. 1962 [1831]. *Introduction à l'Histoire universelle, Tableau de la France*. Paris: Armand Colin.
Miller, K. 2008. *Doubles: Studies in Literary History*. London: Faber.
Milling, J. and G. Ley. 2001. *Modern Theories of Performance*. New York: Palgrave.
Mongin, O. 1989. 'Mai 68 et les sciences sociales: un remarquable indice'. *Bulletin de l'Institut de L'Histoire du Temps Présent*, 11: 21–26.
Morin, E. 1956. *Le cinéma ou l'homme imaginaire*. Paris: Minuit.
———. 1967. *Commune en France. La métamorphose de Plozevet*. Paris: Fayard.
———. 1970 [1951]. *L'homme et la mort*. Paris: Seuil.
———. 1975 [1959]. *Autocritique*. Paris: Seuil.
Morsy, Z. 1969. *D'un soleil réticent*. Paris: Grasset.
———. 1970. 'Profils culturels et conscience critique au Maroc'. *Journal of World History* XII:4: 588–602.
———. 1976. 'Une letteratura senza avvenire: le palimpseste maghrébin'. In T. Ben Jelloun (ed.), *La Mémoire future. Anthologie de la nouvelle poésie du Maroc*. Paris: Maspero: 127–144.
Moufawad-Paul, J. 2020. 'Review of Torkil Lauesen, *The Principal Contradiction*'. In *Marx and Philosophy Review of Books*, November. https://marxandphilosophy.org.uk/reviews/18514_the-principal-contradiction-by-torkil-lauesen-reviewed-by-joshua-moufawad-paul/ (consulted 14 December 2020).
Mufti, A. 2005. 'Global Comparativism'. In H. Bhabha and W.J.T. Mitchell (eds), *Edward Said: Continuing the Conversation*. Chicago: Chicago University Press: 122–128.
Nadeau, M. 1952. 'Le prix Staline'. *Les Temps Modernes* 79 (May): 2091–2099.
Nehamas, A. 1985. *Nietzsche. Life as Literature*. Cambridge, MA/London: Harvard University Press.

BIBLIOGRAPHY

Nelson, M. 2015. *The Argonauts*. Minneapolis, MN: Graywolf Press.
Niethammer, L. 1992. *Posthistoire: Has History Come to an End?* Translated by Patrick Camiller. London: Verso.
Nietzsche, F. 1993 [1872]. *The Birth of Tragedy Out of the Spirit of Music*. Translated by Shaun Whiteside. London: Penguin.
Orwell, G. 1946. 'Why I Write'. http://orwell.ru/library/essays/wiw/english/e_wiw (consulted 27 October 2019).
Owen Rowlands, L. 2021. 'Moi Aussi'. *London Review of Books*, 22 April: 28–29.
Ozouf, M. 1989. 'Revolutionary Calendar'. In François Furet and Mona Ozouf (eds), *A Critical Dictionary of the French Revolution*. Cambridge MA: Harvard University Press: 538–547.
Panchasi, R. 2009. *Future Tense: The Culture of Anticipation in France Between the Wars*. Ithaca: Cornell University Press.
Paris, J. 1953. *Hamlet*. Paris: Seuil.
Pascal, B. 1975 [1670]. *Pensées*. Translated by A. J. Krailsheimer. London: Penguin.
Perros, G. 1973. *Papiers collés*. Vol. II. Paris: Gallimard.
Peyrefitte, A. 1973. *Quand la Chine s'éveillera .. le monde tremblera. Regards sur la voie chinoise*. Paris: Fayard.
Phillips, A. 2001. *Houdini's Box: On the Arts of Escape*. London: Faber.
Poster, M. 1979. *Sartre's Marxism*. London: Pluto.
Rabaté, J.-M. 2002. *The Future of Theory*. Oxford: Blackwell.
———. 2016. *The Pathos of Distance: Affects of the Moderns*. New York/London: Bloomsbury Academic.
Rancière, J. 2013. *Dissensus: On Aesthetics and Politics*. Translated by Steven Corcoran. London: Bloomsbury.
———. 2019. *The Future of the Image*. Translated by Gregory Elliot. London: Verso.
Raphael, M. 1938. *La théorie marxiste de la conscience*. Translated by L. Gara. Paris: Gallimard.
———. 1980. *Proudhon, Marx, Picasso. Three Studies in the Sociology of Art*. Translated by Inge Marcuse. London: Lawrence & Wishart (Original French Version, 1933. Paris: éditions Excelsior).
Rees, J. 1998. *The Algebra of Revolution: The Dialectic and the Classical Marxist Tradition*. New York/London: Routledge.
Relihan, J. C. 1993. *Ancient Menippean Satire*. Baltimore: Johns Hopkins University Press.
Revermann, M. 2013. 'Brechtian Chorality'. In Joshua Billings, Felix Budelmann and Fiona Macintosh (eds), *Choruses, Ancient and Modern*. Oxford: Oxford University Press: 151–169.
Riddel, J. 2001 [1976]. 'Scriptive Fate/Scriptive Hope'. *Diacritics* 6:3: republished in P. Williams (ed), *Edward Said*. London: Sage. Vol. III: 380–381.
Rimbaud, A. 1973 [1873]. *A Season in Hell*. Translated by Enid Rhodes Peschel. Oxford: Oxford University Press.
Robbe-Grillet, A. 1965. 'On Several Obsolete Notions'. In *For a New Novel*. New York: Grove Press: 25–48.
Robin, R. 1986. *Le Réalisme socialiste. Une esthétique impossible*. Paris: Payot.
Roche, J. 2018. 'Can Biography Benefit From a Marxist Theory of Individuality? Lucien Sève's Contribution to Biographical Theory and Practice'. *Rethinking Marxism* 30:2: 291–306.
Rockmore, T. 1981. *Marxism and Alternatives*. Dordrecht: D. Reidel Publishing.
Rose, J. 2020. 'Pointing the Finger'. *London Review of Books* 42:9 (7 May): 2–6.
Rose, P. 2020 [1983]. *Parallel Lives: Five Victorian Marriages*. London: Daunt Books.
Said, E. 1966. 'A Sociology of Mind'. *Partisan Review* 33: 444–448.
———. 1972. 'Eclecticism and Orthodoxy in Literature'. *Diacritics Spring*: 2–10.
———. 1975. *Beginnings: Intention and Method*. New York: Basic Books.
———. 1984. *The World, the Text and the Critic*. London: Faber & Faber.
———. 1985 [1978]. *Orientalism*. Harmondsworth: Penguin.
———. 2001. *Reflections on Exile: And Other Cultural and Literary Essays*. London: Granta.
Sarkonak, R. (ed). 2009. *Les spirales du sens chez Renaud Camus*. Amsterdam: Rodopi.

Sarraute, N. 1956 [1948]. *Portrait d'un inconnu*. Paris: Gallimard.
Sartre, J.-P. 1949. *What is Literature?* Translated by Bernard Frechtman. New York: Philosophical Library.
———. 1964. 'Un bilan, un prélude'. *Esprit* 32 (July): 80–85.
———. 1965. *Situations*. Translated by Benita Eisler. London: Hamish Hamilton.
———. 1991a [1960]. *Critique of Dialectical Reason, Volume I: Theory of Practical Ensembles*. Translated and Edited by Alan Sheridan-Smith and Jonathan Rée. London: Verso.
———. 1991b [1985]. *Critique of Dialectical Reason, Volume II (Unfinished): The Intelligibility of History*. Translated by Quintin Hoare and Edited by Arlette Elkaïm-Sartre. London: Verso.
Schwarz, R. 1992. *Misplaced Ideas: Essays on Brazilian Culture*. Translated and Edited by John Gledson. London: Verso.
Sève, L. 1978. *Man in Marxist Theory and the Psychology of Personality*. Translated by John McGreal. Hemel Hempstead: Harvester Press.
Shapiro, S. E. 2004. '*Ecriture judaïque*: Where Are the Jews in Western Discourse?'. In D. Robbins (ed), *Jean-François Lyotard: Sage Masters of Modern Social Thought*. Vol. I. London: Sage: 64–83.
Simon, A. 1967. 'Vers un retour du tragique' (Radio Show). *France-Culture*, 6 May.
Sollers, P. 1974. 'A propos de "La Chine sans utopie"'. *Tel Quel* 59 (Autumn).
———. 1976. Letter in *Le Monde*, 22 October: 3.
Sontag, S. 1967. 'The Aesthetics of Silence'. *Aspen Magazine* 4/5: Section 3.
———. 1983 [1977]. *Illness as Metaphor*. Harmondsworth: Penguin.
Sorel, G. 1990 [1908]. *Réflexions sur la violence*. Paris: Seuil.
Srinivasan, A. 2020. 'He, She, One, They, Ho, Hus, Hum, Ita. How Should I Refer to You?'. *London Review of Books* 42 (2 July): 13.
Stafford, A. 2014. 'La "Francophonie" chez soi ? Dialectique littéraire de la "colonisation linguistique interne"'. In Claude Coste and Daniel Lançon (eds), *Perspectives européennes des études littéraires francophones*. Paris: Éditions Honoré Champion: 77–92.
———. 2020. 'The "Souverainement Orphelin" of Abdelkébir Khatibi's Early Writings: Sociology in the *Souffles* Years'. In Jane Hiddleston and Khalid Lyamlahy (eds), *Abdelkébir Khatibi: Postcolonialism, Transnationalism and Culture in the Maghreb and Beyond*. Liverpool: Liverpool University Press: 53–76.
Stalin, J. 1973 [1950]. 'Marxism and Linguistics'. In Bruce Franklin (ed), *The Essential Stalin: Major Theoretical Writings 1905–1952*. London: Croom Helm: 407–444.
Stedman Jones, G. 1983 [1971]. 'The Marxism of the Early Lukács'. In New Left Review (ed), *Western Marxism: A Critical Reader*. Thetford: Verso: 11–60.
Steiner, G. 1961. *The Death of Tragedy*. London: Faber & Faber.
Surya, M. 2004. *La révolution rêvée. Pour une histoire des intellectuels et des œuvres révolutionnaires 1944–1956*. Paris: Fayard.
Tenkoul, A. 1983. *Littérature marocaine d'écriture française. Essais d'analyse sémiotique*. Casablanca: Afrique-Orient.
Thao, Tran Duc. 1947. 'Sur l'interprétation trotskiste des événements d'Indochine'. *Les Temps Modernes* 21 (June): 1697–1705.
———. 1971 [1951]. *Phénoménologie et matérialisme dialectique*. Paris: Gordon & Breach.
Théâtre Populaire, revue trimestrielle. 1960. Number 40.
Thomas, P. 2010. *The Gramscian Moment*. London: Haymarket.
Thomson, G. 1935. 'Mystical Allusions in the Oresteia'. *Journal of Hellenic Studies* 55:1: 20–34.
———. 1941. *Aeschylus and Athens: A Study in the Social Origins of Drama*. London: Lawrence & Wishart.
———. 1945. *Marxism and Poetry*. London: Lawrence & Wishart.
Tóibín, C. 2021. 'I Haven't Been I'. *London Review of Books*, 12 August: 23–27.
Todorov, T. 1968. 'Poétique'. In François Wahl (ed), *Qu'est-ce que le structuralisme?* Paris: Seuil: 97–166.

Trotsky, L. 1964. 'The Second Chinese Revolution, 1925–1927'. In *Trotsky: The Age of Permanent Revolution*. New York: Dell: 240–246.

———. 1991 [1925]. 'Proletarian Culture and Proletarian Art'. In *Literature and Revolution*. Translated by Rose Strunsky. London: Bookmarks: 213–242.

Tucker, R. 1961. *Philosophy and Myth in Karl Marx*. Cambridge: Cambridge University Press.

Vago, B. 1977. 'Romania'. In Martin McCauley (ed), *Communist Power in Europe 1944–1949*. London: MacMillan: 111–130.

Van Rossum-Guyon, F. 2006. 'Des nécessités d'une digression : sur un métadiscours chez Balzac'. *Revue des sciences humaines* 175 (October): 99–110.

Vernant, J.-P. 1965. *Mythe et pensée chez les Grecs. Etude de Psychologie historique*. Paris: Maspero.

Véron, L. 2019. 'Peut-on penser une stylistique goldmannienne?'. *Contextes* 25.

Versaille, A. 2015. 'Introduction'. *Magazine littéraire*, March: 38.

Villani, A. 2016. 'Le poème opaque d'Édouard Glissant'. *Chimères* 90: 191–200.

Voltaire. 2000 [1763]. *Traité sur la tolérance*. Edited by John Renwick. Oxford: Voltaire Foundation.

Weiner, S. 1999. 'Two Modernities: From 'Elle' to 'Mademoiselle'. Women's Magazines in Post-war France'. *Contemporary European History* 8:3: 395–409.

White, H. 2001 [1976]. 'Criticism as Cultural Politics'. *Diacritics* 6:3: Republished in P.

Wilde, O. 1960 [1890]. 'The Soul of Man Under Socialism'. In *Plays, Prose Writings and Poems*. London: J. M. Dent & Sons Ltd: 255–288.

———. 1960 [1891]. 'The Critic As Artist'. In *Plays, Prose Writings and Poems*. London: J. M. Dent & Sons Ltd: 1–65.

Williams, P. (ed). 2001. *Edward Said*. 4 Vols. London: Sage.

Wilson, E. 1974 [1940]. *To the Finland Station: A Study in the Acting and Writing of History*. New York: Harcourt.

Wood, M. 2009. 'Presence of Mind'. *London Review of Books*, 19 November: 11–12.

Woods, G. 1998. *A History of Gay Literature: The Male Tradition*. New Haven: Yale University Press.

Worton, M. 1998. 'Cruising (Through) Encounters'. In O. Heathcote (ed), *Gay Signatures: Gay and Lesbian Theory, Fiction and Film in France, 1945–1995*. Oxford: Berg: 29–49.

Yasuda, K. 1957. *The Japanese Haiku*. Rutland, Vermont/Tokyo: Charles E. Tuttle Company.

Zumthor, P. 1990. 'La glose créatrice'. In Gisèle Mathieu-Castellani and Michel Plaisance (eds), *Le Commentaire et la naissance de la critique littéraire*. Paris: Aux Amateurs de Livres: 11–18.

INDEX

Abbé Pierre 27
Actualité littéraire 127
Adamov, Arthur 30
Adorno, Theodor xv, 28, 84, 126, 188, 206, 215, 224
Aeschylus 45–47, 50, 51, 56, 57
Ahmed, Sara xii, 9
Ahnouch, Fatima 115
Alexandrov, Georgy F. 39
Algalarrondo, Hervé 25
Ali, Tariq 131
Allar, Neal 173
Almond, Ian 114
Althusser, Louis xi, 25–26, 34, 46, 79, 205
Amigo Pino, Claudia 170
Amossy, Ruth 208
Anderson, Perry 76
Antonini, Francesca 217
Antonioni, Michelangelo 114, 162
Apel-Muller, Michel 150
Aquin, Hubert 70
Arguments xvii, 158–59
Aristotle xix, 46, 48, 53, 73, 116, 203
Arrivé, Michel 43
Artaud, Antonin 197
Auerbach, Eric 220
Austen, Jane 224
Avedon, Richard 59
Axelos, Kostas 201

Bachofen, Johann Jakob 50, 55
Bacon, Francis 80
Badiou, Alain 9, 207
Badmington, Neil xiv, 132, 145
Bakhtin, Mikaïl 93, 100, 103–6, 109
Baldwin, Tom x
Balibar, Renée 26
Balzac, Honoré de 5, 24, 31, 74–76, 91–98, 101, 103–5, 108–11, 115, 117–19, 122–24, 139, 140, 147, 171, 174–75, 182–83, 188, 220, 224
Bannet, Eve Tavor 96–98, 102, 104, 108
Barrault, Jean-Louis 50
Barrès, Maurice 12, 15–16
Barthes, Henriette ('Mam') 1, 4–6, 133–34, 142–44, 160, 195–98, 217
Barthes, Roland: **Album** (letters to) (Canetti, Georges 13, 18, 77, 93, 98; Cayrol, Jean 25; David, Robert 11–12, 13, 15, 16; Des Forêts, Louis-René 105; Rebeyrol, Philippe 47, 75); **articles, notes and interviews**: 'Am I a Marxist?' xxi; 'Authors and Writers' xviii, xx, 92, 100, 107, 145, 148, 187, 198, 202; 'Barthes to the Third Power' 6; 'Bertolt Brecht in Lyon' 66–67; '"Blue is in Fashion This Year"' 137; 'Brecht, Marx, et l'Histoire' xiii, xv, 201; 'Brecht et le discours' 74; 'The Brechtian Revolution' 35; 'A Brief Sociology of the Contemporary French Novel' 184; 'Ce que je dois à Khatibi' 111–12; 'La chronique' 5; 'Le comédien sans paradoxe' 52; 'Commentaire (préface à Brecht, *Mère Courage)*' 45, 67–71, 73; 'Critique et autocritique' 92–94, 100; 'Culture et tragédie' 47, 49, 56–57; 'Dandyism and Fashion' 142; 'Dear Antonioni…' 114; 'The Death of the Author' 74, 96, 106–7, 171–72; 'Le degré zéro de l'écriture' 3, 127, 180–81, 186; 'Deliberation' xxi, 2, 159; 'Les deux sociologies du roman' 53, 221; 'A Dialectical Writing Practice' 149, 156, 162, 201–2; 'Diderot, Brecht, Eisenstein' 74; 'Digressions' 16, 203–4; 'The Discourse of History' 103; 'The Diseases of Costume' 60; 'Do Revolutions Follow Laws?' 82, 86–87, 136, 211; '*D'un soleil réticent*' 112, 114; 'Editorial (*Théâtre Populaire* September 1954) 200; 'Edoardo Sanguineti' 106; 'The Eiffel Tower' 74; 'Enfants-copies' 31; 'Enfants-vedettes' 59–60; 'Erté, or À la lettre' 211; 'Évocations et incantations dans la tragédie grecque' [1941 'DES' post-graduate thesis] 32, 56, 95, 206; 'The Fatality of Culture, the Limits of Counter Culture' xviii, 216; 'Féminaire de Michelet' 19, 91; 'Folies-Bergère' xxi, 60; 'From Gemstones to Jewellery' 137; 'From Science to Literature' 101; 'The Future of Rhetoric' xiii, xviii, 52, 181, 183; 'The Greatest Cryptographer of Myths talks about Love' 20; '*Hamlet*, c'est beaucoup plus qu'*Hamlet*' 54; 'The Image' 141, 143, 176, 204, 215; 'Inaugural Lecture, Collège de France' 2, 92, 136, 178; 'Interview: A Conversation with Roland Barthes' 139; 'Introduction to the Structuralist Analysis of Narrative' 120–22, 137, 139; 'Kristeva's

Semeiotike' 112; 'The Last Happy Writer' (*see* 'Voltaire…' below); 'Lesson in Writing' 146–47; 'Like That (On Some Photographs by R. Avedon)' 177; 'Linguistics and Literature' 108; 'The Linguistics of Discourse' xvii; 'La Linguistique du discours' [seminar notes] 91, 101, 103, 105–6; 'Literal Literature' 79; 'Literature and Signification' 100; 'Literature Today' 53; '*Longtemps, je me suis couché de bonne heure*' 221; '*Macbeth*' 62; 'The Masters and the Slaves' 23, 79; 'Michelet, l'Histoire et la Mort' 79–80, 85, 88, 90–91, 129, 155, 196; 'Mother Courage Blind' 68; '*Musica Practica*' 176; 'New Pathways of Literary Criticism in France' 211; 'New Problems of Realism' xiii, 184; '*Œdipe Roi* [May-June 1955]' 49–50; '*Œdipe Roi* [July-August 1955]' 50; 'Of What Use is an Intellectual?' 7; 'The Old Rhetoric: an aide-memoire' 139, 203; 'On A Metaphor. (Is Marxism a Church?)' 82, 86–87; 'On Behalf of the "New Criticism", Roland Barthes Replies to Raymond Picard' 102; 'On Gide and His Journal' 1, 6, 47, 149, 160; 'On *S/Z* and *Empire of Signs*' xiv, 111, 151, 155, 158, 206; 'On the De Gaulle Regime' xvi, xviii, 46; 'On the Subject of Violence' 193, 216; 'Outcomes of the Text' 187; '*Pax Culturalis*' xviii, 205; '*La Peste*' 75, 87, 128, 186; 'Phénomène ou mythe?' 18, 21, 23, 29–30, 58; 'Phenomenology and Dialectical Materialism' 181, 200; 'The Photographic Message' 74, 213; 'Pierre Loti: *Aziyadé*' 159; 'The Plates of the *Encyclopedia*' 139; 'Pleasure in Language' 106; '*Le plus heureux des trois*' 21; 'Politicization of Science in Romania' 26, 181; 'Popular Songs of Paris Today' 181; 'Pour une histoire de l'enfance' 98; 'Pour une théorie de la lecture' xvi, xxii, 134; 'Pouvoirs de la tragédie grecque' 22, 45–46, 56, 59; 'A Problematic of Meaning' 99, 140, 213; 'Proust and Names' 120; 'Putting on the Greeks' 50, 52; 'The Reality Effect' 139; 'Rencontre en Forêt-Noire' 184; 'Réponse à une question sur Céline' 189; 'Réponse à une question sur les artistes et la politique' 188; 'Réponse de Roland Barthes à Albert Camus' 186; 'Réquichot and His Body' 195; 'Responses' [1971 interview in *Tel Quel*] 25, 109, 134, 186; 'The "Scandal" of Marxism' 45, 82; 'Seven Photo Models of "Mother Courage"' 67–68, 70, 71; 'Should Grammar be Killed Off?' 77, 143, 180, 182; 'Sketch of a Sanatorium Society' 18, 181; 'So, How Was China?' 142, 146, 156, 160, 165, 217; '*La Sorcière*' xi, 23, 79; 'Structuralisme et sémiologie' xxii; 'The Structuralist Activity' 212–13; 'Structure of the *fait divers*' 138; 'Sur la photographie' 56; 'Sur la théorie' xviii, 94, 100; 'Sur le *Système de la mode*' 137; 'Ten Reasons to Write' 113–14, 222; 'The Third Meaning: Research Notes on Several Eisenstein Stills' 57, 117; 'Triomphe et rupture de l'écriture bourgeoise' [1950] (*see* 'Should Grammar be Killed Off?'); 'The Two Criticisms' 53; 'Un univers de signes articulés vides' 155; 'Visages et figures' 64–65; '*Vita nova*' xix, 122, 198, 217; 'Voltaire, The Last Happy Writer?' (both versions) 126–32, 209; 'The War of Languages' xvii, 156; 'What is Criticism?' 100; '*Will* burns us' 215; 'The World as Object' 135, 200–1, 208, 222; 'Writers, Intellectuals, Teachers' 145, 199, 203–6, 210–11; 'Writing Reading' x; 'Writing the Event' 108; 'Yes, There Definitely is a Left-Wing Literature' 186; **BOOKS** *Camera Lucida: Reflections on Photography* xii, xiv, xxii, 1, 6, 74, 79, 90, 93, 101, 117, 132, 143, 160, 187, 188, 192, 195–98, 210; *Complete Works* 59; *Critical Essays* 20, 60, 107, 126–27, 159; *Criticism and Truth* 55, 79, 96, 97, 101–3, 105–6, 109, 110, 132, 146, 171, 210; *Le Discours amoureux: séminaire* xi, xx, 1, 9, 11, 17, 19, 47, 112, 114, 169–70, 178, 215; *Elements of Semiology* 138, 147; *Empire of Signs* 36, 73, 99, 100, 114, 117, 127, 145–55, 162, 165, 174, 179, 214; *The Fashion System* 91, 137, 147, 211, 213; *How To Live Together: Novelistic Simulations of Some Everyday Spaces* 22, 75, 116, 126, 142, 170, 178, 190–93, 207, 217; *Incidents* xi, 2, 111–12, 114, 115, 177; *Le Lexique de l'auteur* xix, xxii, 2–8, 11, 141–43, 157, 159, 163, 165, 167, 178–79, 200, 205, 213; *A Lover's Discourse: Fragments* 7, 9–12, 16–17, 19–20, 97, 101, 112, 116–17, 134, 142, 176–78, 192; *Mère Courage. Édition illustrée* 69–72, 74; *Michelet* 6, 17, 25, 59, 76, 79–80, 88–96, 98, 146, 149; *Mourning Diary* 1, 2, 157, 160, 198; *Mythologies*, and 'Myth Today' xii, xviii–xxi, 3, 17, 18, 20, 21–44, 45, 47–48, 50–52, 55, 57, 59, 65, 77–78, 84–85, 91–95, 98, 112, 116, 125, 136, 144, 146–47, 149, 154, 166, 174, 176, 179–80, 187, 191, 199, 202, 205, 207, 212, 215; *The Neutral* xiv, 1, 17, 40, 111, 119, 122, 126, 133, 140, 142, 144, 156–57, 169, 176, 178, 180, 191–92, 211, 214–17, 223; *On Racine* 53–55, 91, 147, 211; *Paris Evenings* 157; *The Pleasure of the Text* xvi, 6, 7, 109, 113, 117, 140–41, 187–88, 197,

INDEX

220; *The Preparation of the Novel* xiv, 1, 3, 46, 117, 121–24, 126, 132, 190–93, 207, 223; *Roland Barthes by Roland Barthes* x, xiii, xv, xviii, 2, 3, 6, 10, 45, 73, 95, 98, 101, 117, 134, 141, 144, 171, 176–79, 188, 195, 200, 207–8, 214, 215; *Sade, Fourier, Loyola* xv, 5, 112, 116, 125–26, 141–42, 206; *'Sarrasine' de Balzac* 5, 94, 101, 103–4, 107–9, 117–18, 122, 140; *S/Z. An Essay* 3, 5, 74–76, 81, 91–111, 114–15, 117–24, 139–43, 146–48, 171, 173–75, 188, 220, 223–24; *Travels in China* 1, 2, 142, 145–46, 156–58, 160–67, 170; *Writer Sollers* 150; *Writing Degree Zero* xiii, xxii, 8, 25, 27–29, 43, 77, 85, 92, 101, 115, 171, 179–87, 189–91, 204, 208, 217, 222–23)
Bataille, Georges 93, 96, 99, 117, 133, 143, 187
Bateson, Geoffrey 173
Baudelaire, Charles xxi, 85, 112, 118–19, 125
Baudrillard, Jean xi
Baugh, Bruce xxi
Bayard, Pierre 3–6
Beckett, Samuel xxi, 48–49, 54
Beckman, Karen xiv
Beer, Orlando 6
Bellour, Raymond 158
Belsey, Catherine 108
Ben Jelloun, Tahar 113, 115
Benjamin, Walter xv, 53, 73–74, 76, 80–90, 125
Benoist, Jean-Marie 22, 207
Bensaïd, Daniel 84
Benson, Stephen 94, 101
Berger, John 81, 154, 222
Bergson, Henri 4, 5
Bernard, Jean-Pierre 186
Bertherat, Yves 48
Besson, Benno 69
Bibal, Robert 32
Bidar, Abdennouar 131
Binet, Laurent xi
Birchall, Ian 181
Birnbaum, Jean 157–58, 160
Bittner, Jacob xi, 190, 207, 211–12, 214
Blanchot, Maurice xi, 24, 31, 42, 155, 180, 186, 212
Blanqui, Auguste xvi, 85, 188
Bloomfield, Leonard 204
Bonafous-Murat, Carle ix
Bonald, Louis vicomte de 128, 201
Bonaparte, Louis 77, 94–95, 183, 209
Bonaparte, Napoléon 183
Bonnard, André 49–50
Bordiga, Amadeo xviii
Borges, Jorge Luis 185
Bouc, Alain 157

Boudinet, Daniel 59
Boughali, Mohammed 113
Boulaâbi, Ridha 113, 177
Bourdet, Claude 181
Bourdieu, Pierre xi
Bousfiha, Noureddine 112
Bouttes, Jean-Louis 164
Bouvard, Michel 59
Bouvier, Nicolas 59
Bown, Alfie 9, 10, 12
Bracht Branham, R. 105
Braidotti, Rosi 177
Brando, Marlon 21, 29
Brault, Michel 58
Brecht, Bertolt xiii, xv, xix, 10, 26, 35, 46–47, 57–58, 60, 62, 64–74, 78, 81, 89, 95, 99, 107, 199, 201, 213–14, 220
Bremond, Claude 92, 94, 101, 103, 108–11, 119–20, 122, 148
Britton, Celia 170, 173
Brown, Andrew 26, 30, 45, 99
Brown, Norman O. 11
Bruneau, Charles 92
Bukharin, Nikolai 161
Bull, Malcolm xx
Burgelin, Olivier 147
Burgin, Victor xxii
Butler, Judith xi, 175
Büttgen, Philip 212

Caillois, Roger 82, 86, 135–37, 144
Calas, Jean 128–30
Callinicos, Alex 85, 88, 89, 205, 208
Calvet, Louis-Jean xvi, 4, 9, 59, 83, 97, 126
Camus, Albert xii, 87, 121, 128, 181, 186, 220, 224
Camus, Renaud xviii, 188–89
Canetti, Georges 13, 18, 20, 77, 93, 98
Carlier, J.-C. 107, 172
Carluccio, Danièle 58
Carmody, Jim 70
Carpentier, Sylviane 27
Carrard, Philippe 80
Carrière, Marcel: *see* Brault, Michel
Caudwell, Christopher 51, 56
Cayrol, Jean 25, 129
Céline, Louis-Ferdinand 189
Cervantes, Miguel de 93, 105
Cézanne, Paul 6
Chambers, Ross 108
Champagne, Roland A. 197
Charlie-Hebdo 130–31
Chatman, Seymour 120
Chiquer, Abdelkrim 112
Chomsky, Noam 22, 204, 210
Churchill, Winton 4
Cicero 212

Cixous, Hélène xi
Claudel, Paul xix, 33, 46, 150, 153
Clerc, Thomas xi, xii, 40, 122, 189
Clergue, Lucien 59
Cohen, Gerald Allan 89
Cohen, Marcel 42–43
Cohen, Mitchell 100
Cole, Teju 131
Colletti, Lucio 209, 210
Combat 52, 181, 186, 200
Compagnon, Antoine 4, 94, 107
Confiant, Raphaël 175
Connors, Clare: *see* Benson, Stephen
Conrad, Joseph 223
Corbier, Christophe 47, 56, 150
Coste, Claude 17, 74, 80, 96, 112, 113, 146, 156, 158, 177, 225
Cousteau, Jacques 79
Crary, Jonathan 77
Crehan, Kate 33
Croce, Benedetto 37, 39
Crossman, R. H. S. 159
Crowley, Martin xviii

Dahmer, Helmut 87
Daix, Pierre 37
Dante 39
Daudet, Alphonse 184
David, Robert 11–13, 15, 16, 20, 59
De Koven, Marianne 31, 36
De Pourcq, Maarten 51, 54, 56, 126
De Ste Croix, Geoffrey 46
De Villiers, Nicholas x, 170–71, 177
Deguy, Michel 6
Delacroix, Eugène 114–15
Deleuze, Gilles xi, xx, 5, 207
Denis, Benoît 184, 186
Derrida, Jacques xi, xii, 24, 103, 104, 115, 200, 202, 207
Des Forêts, Louis-René 105
Descartes, René 217
Detweiler, Robert 98
Dewey, John 76
Di Leo, Jeffrey xiv
Dib, Mohammed 224
Diderot, Denis 24, 93, 96
Didi-Huberman, Georges 57–58, 73, 97
Djedidi, Tahar Labib 112, 114
Domenach, Jean-Marie 24, 48
Dorival, Justin-Marie 60
Dort, Bernard 68, 81
Dostoevsky 93, 104, 105
Drochon, Hugo 47
Du Bois, W. E. B. 157, 170
Dufays, Jean-Louis 110
Duhamel, Georges 29–30
Dunayevskaya, Raya 145

Durkheim, Émile 26–27
Duvignaud, Jean 48
Duxiu, Chen 161
Dyer, Geoff 222

Eagleton, Terry 80, 184
Eco, Umberto 135
Ehrmann, Jacques 148–49
Eisenstein, Sergei 57–58, 73–74, 97
Eliot, George 223
Eliot, T.S. 8, 220
Engel, Erich 69
Engels, Friedrich xiii, 9, 17, 23, 33, 35, 37, 39–40, 50, 51, 55, 81, 84, 94, 125, 128, 183, 202, 213
England, Odette x
Erté 211
Etiemble, René 29
L'Express xvii

Fabre, Gérard 100
Falcon, André 64
Fanon, Frantz 223
Farage, Nigel 24
Faucon, Bernard 59
Febvre, Lucien 75
Felski, Rita xiv, 177, 222
Ferraris, Maurizio 207
Feuerbach, Ludwig xiv, xix, 9–10, 23, 33, 36, 209
ffrench, Patrick 11, 64, 159
Le Figaro 27, 28
Le Figaro littéraire 102
Fisher, Mark xviii
Flaubert, Gustave 6, 31, 84, 139, 183, 225
Flores Khalil, Andrea 148
Forsdick, Charles 148
Foucault, Michel xi, 123, 222, 223
Fourier, Charles ix, xv, 84, 92, 112, 116, 125, 141, 162, 179, 190, 192–93, 201
Fournié, Georges ('Philippe') 13, 15, 125, 189
Fournier, Claude: *see* Brault, Michel
France, Peter 133
Francesca, Piero della 151
Franco, General Francisco 28
French Communist Party (PCF) 158, 184
Freud, Sigmund, and Freudianism xiv, xv, xix, xxi, 4, 28, 75, 134, 197, 201, 205
Fried, Michael xiv
Frye, Northrop 223

Gallop, Jane xii, 198
Garaudy, Roger 184
Gardner, Callie 112
Garnier, Xavier 198
Gaulle, Charles de xviii, 126, 130
Gava, Jean-François 207, 208, 210

INDEX

Genet, Jean 67, 197
Genette, Gérard 100
Genova, Pamela 148, 150
Gide, André xix, 3, 6, 11, 47, 143, 148, 159, 160, 163, 191–92, 210–11, 214, 215
Gil, Marie 4–8, 133–34, 139, 143–44, 197–98, 217
Giles, Steve: *see* Kuhn, Tom
Gischia, Léon 60
Glissant, Édouard xi, 115, 149, 169–79, 207
Godelier, Maurice 203
Goethe, Wilhelm 97, 112, 178, 192, 220
Goh, Irving 169
Goldbronn, Frédéric 19
Goldmann, Lucien xvii, xxii, 24–25, 38, 53–55, 57, 77, 100, 179, 190, 201, 219, 221, 222, 225
Góngora, Luis de 202
Gontard, Marc 113
Gramsci, Antonio 33, 37, 39, 83, 217
Greco, Nicholas x, 171
Greimas, Algirdas Julien 26, 29, 37, 42–43
Greisch, Jean 92
Griffiths, Michael 172–73, 179
Groethuysen, Bernard 139
Grotius, Hugo 80
Guattari, Félix xi
Guerlac, Suzanne 171
Guittard, Jacqueline xi, 59, 92
Gury, Christian 1
Guyotat, Pierre 197

Habib, M. A. Rafey 212, 215
Halberstam, Jack 4
Hall, Brian K. 135
Hamon, Philippe 121
Han, Seokhyeon xx, 190, 223
Hanania, Cécile 6, 108
Hara-kiri 131
Hardy, Thomas 223
Hargreaves, Alec xii
Harrison, Jane 51
Harrison, Olivia 112
Hassan II, King of Morocco 113
Haustein, Katja x
Havas, Roland 164
Heath, Stephen xvi–xvii, 41
Hébert, Jacques 182
Hegel, Georg Wilhelm Friedrich xvi, xvii, xviii–ix, xx, xxi, 9–11, 14, 15, 17, 19, 20, 29, 37, 52, 68, 82, 83, 85, 86, 88, 89, 98, 100, 110, 111, 145, 150, 152, 154, 155, 172, 177, 190, 193, 195–96, 199–201, 206–17, 220, 225
Heidegger, Martin 92, 190
Heine, Heinrich 17, 112, 178
Herder, Johann Gottfried 86

Herschberg Pierrot, Anne 159, 208
Heyndels, Ralph 114
Hibbitt, Richard 110
Hiddleston, Jane xii, 100, 156
Higgins, Lynne 219
Hill, Leslie x, 46, 101, 188, 205, 214, 222
Hitler, Adolf 82, 86
Hjelmslev, Louis 27, 43
Hobbes, Thomas 113
Hook, Sidney 76–77, 80
Horkheimer, Max xv, 84, 126, 188, 216
Horvat, Srećko 9, 16
Houdini, Harry 108, 134, 139–40
Howard, Richard 101, 111
Huang, Hairong xi
Hughes, Edward x
Hugo, Victor 93, 112
Huppatz, Daniel xi
Husserl, Edmund 200

Illouz, Eva 177
Ingram, Paul 224
Innami, Fusako 155
Ionesco, Eugène 49
Irigaray, Luce xi

Jack, Belinda 114
Jackson, Robert 37
Jaeger, Werner 52
Jakobson, Roman 98, 107
James, Cyril L. R. xix, 83–84, 145
Jameson, Fredric xii, xiv, xix, xx, 10, 25–26, 28, 30, 34, 37, 46, 47, 76, 170, 197, 200, 206–9, 214
Jaurès, Jean ix, 10, 13, 74, 76, 81
Jeanson, Francis 186
Johnson, Barbara 101
Joussain, André 82, 86, 135–37, 144
Joyce, James 105, 223
Jutre, Claude: *see* Brault, Michel

Kafka, Franz 105, 190
Kant 100, 210
Karatani, Kojin xii, 145
Keegan, Paul 8
Keller, Gottfried 90
Kelly, Michael 41
Keuneman, Katrine Pilcher 103
Khaïr-Eddine, Mohamed 113
Khatibi, Abdelkebir 111–16, 146, 148, 169
Kierkegaard, Søren xi, xviii, 1
Kilger, Heinrich 62
Klee, Paul 82, 83
Klein, Richard 30
Klein, William 59
Knight, Diana x, xii, 33, 41–42, 84, 97, 110, 112, 150, 177

Kojève, Alexandre 208
Korsch, Karl 10, 76
Kosik, Karel 147
Kosofsky Sedgwick, Eve xiii
Kowalska, Malgorzata 200, 207
Kracauer, Siegfried xv, 31
Kristeva, Julia xi, 103, 105–6, 109, 112, 158, 159, 180, 190, 191, 213
Kuhn, Tom 70

La Boétie, Étienne de 26
La Bruyère, Jean de 197
Laâbi, Abdellatif 113, 116
Lacan, Jacques xi, 9, 20, 107, 122, 134, 158
Laclos, Choderlos de 185
Lacoue-Labarthe, Philippe 212
Laertius, Diogenes 104
Lafargue, Paul 37
Lahanque, Reynald 186
Langlet, Irène 32
Lanson, Gustave xiii
Lautréamont, comte de 105
Lavers, Annette 184
Le Cour Grandmaison, Olivier 32
Le Prat, Thérèse 65
Lears, T. Jackson 33
Ledru-Rollin, Alexandre 95
Lee, Stewart xi
Leenhardt, Jacques 221
Lefebvre, Georges 75
Lefebvre, Henri xviii, 24, 31, 36, 41, 91
Lefort, Claude 181
Leiris, Michel 184
Lenin, Vladimir Ilyich xvi, xvii, xviii, 3, 10, 72, 161, 216
Lettres nouvelles 27, 29, 90, 170
Lévi-Strauss, Claude 27, 29, 31, 38, 101, 137, 158
Ley, Graham: *see* Milling, Jane
Leys, Simon 158, 166, 200
Linnæus, Carl 85, 135–36, 138, 139
Lombardo, Patrizia 142
Long, Jonathan J. xxii
Lordon, Frédéric 169
Losurdo, Dominico xx, 219
Loti, Pierre 159
Louis XV, King of France 130
Lourau, René 140
Lovatt, Anna xi
Löwy, Michael 225
Loyola, Ignatius 96, 112, 141, 220
Lübecker, Nikolaj xi, 29, 190, 207, 211, 215–17
Lucian 105
Lucken, Michael 146

Lukács, Georg xv, xvii, xxii, 18, 22, 24–25, 34, 36–39, 42, 55, 75–77, 81, 182, 201, 212, 221, 223
Lunn, Eugene 82, 85
Luther, Martin 87
Luxemburg, Rosa xviii
Lyotard, Jean-François xi, 126, 128, 207

Macciocchi, Antonietta 158
Macdonald, Amanda 28, 40–42
Macé, Marielle x, xx, 96, 99, 103, 106, 113–14, 153, 160
Macfarlane, Helen 24
Le Magazine littéraire 131
Maistre, Joseph de 128
Malabou, Catherine xvii, 52
Mallarmé, Stéphane 75, 93, 103, 107, 113, 114, 123, 172, 197, 207, 225
Mann, Thomas 2
Mao Tse-tung, and Maoism xviii, xx, 6, 115, 146, 148, 156, 158–62, 166, 167, 203, 206, 207, 213–14, 216, 220
Marat, Jean-Paul 97
Marcuse, Herbert xv, 25, 126, 130, 141, 204, 208
Marr, Nicolai Y. 37
Martin, André 59, 74
Martin, James 24
Martinet, André 149
Marty, Eric xi, 9, 20, 100, 107, 146, 157, 177–78, 200
Marx, Karl, and Marxism ix–xxii, 9–11, 13, 17, 20, 22–24, 26, 28, 31, 33–41, 43, 45–49, 51–56, 75–79, 82–86, 88, 89, 93–95, 99, 100, 102, 110, 112, 125, 129, 130, 134–36, 139, 144, 154, 158, 171–73, 178–81, 183, 186–87, 189, 193, 195, 196, 199–213, 217, 220, 223–25
Marx-Scouras, Danielle xiv, 158
Mascolo, Dionys xviii
Mathiez, Albert 75
Matoré, Georges 37, 92
Mau, Søren 27, 34
Maupassant, Guy de 184, 185
Mauron, Charles 55
Mavor, Carol x
Mazon, Paul 46, 95
Mckeane, John 50, 56
Meagher, Sharon xii
Médiapart 32
Menippus; menippeanism 93, 100, 103–9, 111, 114, 117, 184
Mepham, John 34
Merleau-Ponty, Maurice 37, 150, 206, 207, 225
Meschonnic, Henri 198
Meyer-Plantureux, Chantal 68

Michaud, Ginette 73, 142
Michaux, Henri 118
Michelet, Jules ix, xi, 5–6, 10–15, 17–20, 22, 23, 25, 32, 40, 46, 58, 59, 74–99, 121, 125, 129, 136, 146, 147, 149–51, 155, 169, 174, 181, 182, 192, 196, 199, 201, 209, 211, 215, 217, 220, 221
Miller, David A. x, 171
Miller, Jacques-Alain 4
Miller, Karl xxi
Milling, Jane 58
Le Monde 131, 142, 156–60, 162, 163, 165
Mongin, Olivier 154
Montaigne, Michel de 148
Montesquieu, Charles de Secondat 86, 127
Morgan, Lewis 51
Moriarty, Michael 184
Morin, Edgar xvi, xvii, xviii, 41, 79, 149, 156, 162, 196, 199–204
Morsy, Zaghloul 74, 111–15
Moudileno, Lydie xii, 26
Moufawad-Paul, Joshua 199, 217
Moussaid, Ilham 131
Mufti, Aamir xii
Musset, Alfred de 64

Nachtergael, Magali xi, 68, 148
Nadeau, Maurice xvii, xviii, 158, 181, 186, 189
Nancy, Jean-Luc 212
Navarre, Marguerite de 96
Naville, Pierre xviii, 159, 181
Nehamas, Alexander 2, 158
Nelson, Maggie xiii, 198
Niethammer, Lutz 82, 83, 88, 89
Nietzsche, Friedrich xv, xix, xx, 2, 7, 22, 23, 36–37, 46–48, 52, 54–57, 75, 85, 99, 100, 121, 151, 153, 155, 158, 164, 169, 170, 187, 189, 190, 193, 206, 207, 217, 224
Noghrehchi, Hessam 95
Nonotte, Abbé Claude-Adrien 127
Nouveau Parti Anticapitaliste 131
Nouveau roman 119
Les Nouvelles littéraires 29–30

Oboussier, Claire xii
Ollman, Bertell 77
Ombredane, André 79
O'Meara, Lucy xi, 178
O'Neill, John 145
Orwell, George 146, 166
Osuga Otsuji, Seki 155
O'Sullivan, Maria 103–5
OULIPO 208
Owen-Rowlands, Lili xv
Oxford Companion to French Literature 133
Oxman, Elena xx, xxii, 25, 97, 114, 187

Painlevé, Jean 79
Papon, Maurice 163–64
Paris, Jean 48, 54
Paris-Match 26, 32
Pascal, Blaise 15, 38, 54, 179, 219, 225
Pasqualini, Jean 158
Patouillet, Abbé 127
Perros, Georges 155
Pessoa, Fernando 13
Pétain, Marshal Philippe 86
Petitier, Paule 79, 92, 94, 95
Peyrefitte, Alain 163–64, 166
Philippe, Gérard 60, 64
Phillips, Adam 134
Pic, Roger xiii, 22, 35, 46, 58–60, 66–74, 78, 89, 97, 101
Picard, Raymond xv, 55, 93, 102–5, 109, 146
Planchon, Roger 66
Plantu, aka Jean Plantureux 131
Plato 49, 53, 104, 192, 214
Plekhanov, George 181
Pleynet, Marcellin 158, 162
Pommier, René 148–49, 151
Poster, Mark 199
Poujade, Pierre 24, 27, 67
Prassinos, Mario 62
Propp, Vladimir 120
Prosser, Jay 90
Proudhon, Pierre-Joseph 204, 205, 207, 209, 210
Proust, Marcel x, 2–4, 6, 19, 31, 80, 109, 113, 120, 143, 153, 159, 172, 197, 198, 221

Queneau, Raymond 101, 184
La Quinzaine littéraire 158

Rabaté, Jean-Michel 182
Rabelais, François 6, 105
Racine, Jean 19, 27, 30, 31, 49, 50, 53–54, 57, 93, 96, 103, 146, 147, 150, 211, 220
Rancière, Jacques xiv, xvi
Raphael, Max 51–54, 57, 209
Rebeyrol, Philippe 19, 47, 52, 75–77
Rees, John 24
Reid, Martine 111
Relihan, Joel C. 105
Renan, Ernest 220
Renjing, Liu 161
Révelin, Noémie 134–35
Revermann, Martin 46, 72
La Revue Internationale 181
Ricœur, Paul 46, 101, 223
Riddel, Joseph N. 223
Ridgeway, William 51
Rigaut, Jacques 200
Rilke, Rainer Maria 112
Rimbaud, Arthur 18, 29–30, 198–99, 206

INDEX

Robbe-Grillet, Alain 6, 43, 119, 123, 219
Robespierre, Maximilien 97
Robin, Régine 181
Roche, Denis 59
Roche, Julian xvii
Rockmore, Tom xvii
Roger, Philippe 10, 12, 20, 48, 83, 108, 180, 186, 217
Ronsard, Pierre 112
Rose, Jacqueline xix
Rose, Phyllis 175
Rousseau, Jean-Jacques 131, 182, 210
Roussel, Henri 131
Rousset, David 129, 159, 181
Ryckmans, Pierre: *see* Leys, Simon

Sade, D.-A.-F. de 105, 112, 141, 142, 197
Said, Edward xii, xvii, 22, 25, 100, 219–24
Saint-Amand, Pierre x, 10, 77
Saint-John Perse 113
Salazar, Philippe 57
Salzedo, Michel 157
Samaddar, Bishan xi, 111–12
Samoyault, Tiphaine ix, xi, 95, 101, 107, 111, 133, 181, 206
Samuel, Raphael 75
Sanguineti, Edoardo 106
Sappho 112
Sarduy, Severo 106
Sarkonak, Ralph xviii, 189
Sarraute, Nathalie 120, 123
Sartre, Jean-Paul xiii, xix, 11, 13, 15, 22, 24, 25, 31, 47, 67, 81, 120, 122, 150–51, 171, 174, 176, 180–87, 189, 190, 195, 208, 211
Saussure, Ferdinand de xx, 24, 42–43, 103, 104, 138, 199, 202
Scheiber, Andrew J. 120, 122
Schwarz, Roberto 130
Serreau, Geneviève 69
Sers, Jacqueline 216
Sève, Lucien xvii, xxi
Shakespeare, William 93
Shapiro, Gary 196
Shapiro, Susan 128, 207
Silberman, Marc: *see* Kuhn, Tom
Silverman, Max 129
Simon, Alfred 24, 48–49
Smith, Douglas 35
Smith, Piers M. 179
Smith, Shawn M. xii
Sollers, Philippe 6, 26, 120, 122, 153, 158–62, 211
Sombart, Werner 52
Sontag, Susan 12–13, 216
Sophocles 49–50
Sorel, Georges 35–37, 128–29, 154
Souffles 103, 112–13, 116

Spitzer, Leo 220
Srinavasan, Amia 175
Staël, Nicolas de 6
Stafford, Andy xv, xvi, xxi, 8, 9, 23, 27, 75, 112, 113, 180, 181, 186, 211, 219
Stalin, Joseph; Stalinism xviii, 26, 37–40, 43, 51, 82–84, 125, 160–61, 166, 180–82, 184–87, 208
Stan, Corinne 178
Starobinski, Jean 103
Stedman Jones, Gareth 25, 34, 36, 39, 42, 75, 212
Steiner, George 51, 128
Stewart, Philip x
Stil, André 184, 186
Stivale, Charles xvi
Sun, Qian 75
Surya, Michel 181
Swift, Jonathan 105

La Table Ronde 127
Tager, Michael 36
Tel Quel xx, 100, 113, 115, 142, 146, 148, 156–63, 171, 180, 203, 204, 206
Temple, Walter S. xii
Les Temps Modernes 81, 181, 186
Tenkoul, Abderrahman 116
Tennyson, Lord Alfred 16
Thao, Tran Duc 181, 200
Théâtre Populaire xvii, 50, 60, 69, 73
Thody, Philip 127, 140
Thomas, Peter 37, 40
Thomson, George 46–57, 77, 91
Todorov, Tzvetan 101, 103
Tóibín, Colm 12
Tomachevski, Boris 120
Trotsky, Leon, and Trotskyism xvii–xviii, 83, 86, 87, 159, 161, 181–87, 189, 224
Tucker, Robert xix, 23, 33

Ungar, Stephen 103, 197, 221

Valéry, Paul xx, 172
Varda, Agnès 65
Vaugelas, Claude Favre de 182
Vauvenargues, Luc de Clapiers, marquis de 26, 182
Veil, Jacques xviii
Velan, Yves 27, 35–36, 154
Verlaine, Paul 112
Vernant, Jean-Pierre 55, 74
Verne, Jules 113, 198
Véron, Laélia 45, 54
Versaille, André 131
Vico, Giambattista 80, 204, 220, 224
Vilar, Jean 62
Villa-Ignacio, Teresa: *see* Harrison, Olivia

Villani, Arnaud 173
Vinaver, Michel 67
Voisin, Robert 60
Voltaire xiv, 26, 93, 125–32, 136, 139, 182, 209–10, 215–16

Wagner, Richard 62
Wahl, François 157, 159
Wahl, Jean xxi
Wampole, Christy xi
Watts, Philip xi, xiv, 73
Weiner, Susan xii, 28
Welch, Edward xxii
Weller, Shane xx
Wermer-Colan, Alex xv, xvi, 40
White, Ed 205
White, Hayden 25, 205, 222–23

Wilde, Oscar ix, 24, 96, 223
Williams, Patrick 223, 224
Wilson, Edmund 79–81, 85, 97
Wilson, Harry R. xiv
Wilson, Raymond J. 122
Winnicott, Donald Woods 134, 198
Wood, Michael 158
Woods, Gregory xii

Yacavone, Kathrin xi, 81, 82
Yasuda, Kenneth 155

Zenetti, Marie-Jeanne 79
Zhdanov, Andreï 37–40, 184
Žižek, Slavoj 40
Zola, Émile 184, 185
Zumthor, Paul 96

Milton Keynes UK
Ingram Content Group UK Ltd.
UKHW011340300823
427755UK00007B/62